Print politics is the first literary study of the culture of the popular radical movement for parliamentary reform in the early decades of the nineteenth century. The period was characterized by popular agitation and repressive political measures including trials for seditious and blasphemous libel. Kevin Gilmartin explores the styles and strategies of radical opposition in the periodical press, and in the public culture of the time. He argues that writers and editors including William Cobbett, T. J. Wooler, Richard Carlile, John Wade, and Leigh Hunt committed themselves to a complex, flexible, and often contradictory project of independent political opposition. They sought to maintain a political resistance uncompromised by the influence of a corrupt "system," even while addressing and imitating its practices to further their oppositional ends.

CAMBRIDGE STUDIES IN ROMANTICISM 21

PRINT POLITICS

CAMBRIDGE STUDIES IN ROMANTICISM

General editors
Professor Marilyn Butler   Professor James Chandler
University of Oxford   University of Chicago
Editorial board
John Barrell, *University of York*   Paul Hamilton, *University of Southampton*
Mary Jacobus, *Cornell University*   Kenneth Johnston, *Indiana University*
Alan Liu, *University of California, Santa Barbara*
Jerome McGann, *University of Virginia*
David Simpson, *University of Colorado*

This series aims to foster the best new work in one of the most challenging fields within English literary studies. From the early 1780s to the early 1830s a formidable array of talented men and women took to literary composition, not just in poetry, which some of them famously transformed, but in many modes of writing. The expansion of publishing created new opportunities for writers, and the political stakes of what they wrote were raised again and again by what Wordsworth called those 'great national events' that were 'almost daily taking place': the French Revolution, the Napoleonic and American wars, urbanization, industrialization, religious revival, an expanded empire abroad and the reform movement at home. This was an enormous ambition, even when it pretended otherwise. The relations between science, philosophy, religion and literature were reworked in texts such as *Frankenstein* and *Biographica Literaria*; gender relations in *A Vindication of the Rights of Woman* and *Don Juan*; journalism by Cobbet and Hazlitt; poetic form, content and style by the Lake School and the Cockney School. Outside Shakespeare studies, probably no body of writing has produced such a wealth of response or done so much to shape the responses of modern criticism. This indeed is the period that saw the emergence of those notions of 'literature' and of literary history, especially national literary history, on which modern scholarship in English has been founded.

The categories produced by Romanticism have also been challenged by recent historicist arguments. The task of the series is to engage both with a challenging corpus of Romantic writings and with the changing field of criticism they have helped to shape. As with other literary series published by Cambridge, this one will represent the work of both younger and more established scholars, on either side of the Atlantic and elsewhere.

For a complete list of titles published see end of book

PRINT POLITICS

The press and radical opposition in
early nineteenth-century England

KEVIN GILMARTIN

California Institute of Technology

CAMBRIDGE
UNIVERSITY PRESS

Published by the Press Syndicate of the University of Cambridge
The Pitt Building, Trumpington Street, Cambridge CB2 IRP
40 West 20th Street, New York, NY 10011–4211, USA
10 Stamford Road, Oakleigh, Melbourne 3166, Australia

© Cambridge University Press 1996

First published 1996

Printed in Great Britain at the University Press, Cambridge

Typeset in Baskerville MT 11/12½

A catalogue record for this book is available from the British Library

Library of Congress cataloguing in publication data
Gilmartin, Kevin, 1963–
Print politics: the press and radical opposition in early
nineteenth-century England / Kevin Gilmartin.
p.   cm. – (Cambridge studies in Romanticism; 21)
Includes bibliographical references and index.
ISBN 0 521 49655 1
1. Press and politics–Great Britain–History–19th century.
2. Great Britain–Politics and government–1800–1837.
3. Radicalism–Great Britain–History–19th century.
4. Romanticism–Great Britain. I. Title. II. Series.
PN5117 .G55   1996
072'.09034–dc20   96–19584 CIP

ISBN 0 521 49655 1 hardback
ISBN 0 521 paperback

SOUTHAMPTON INSTITUTE
LIBRARY SERVICES LTD

SUPPLIER 21

OR

DATE 6·1·97

SE

For my parents

Contents

Illustrations

Acknowledgments

In revising this book, I have often been reminded of the distance between high romanticism and a radical underworld, even in a period of expanded canons and interdisciplinary studies. It is a distance I could not have traveled without the help and encouragement of many friends and colleagues. James Chandler has read, supported, and criticized my work from the beginning; any strengths this book may have reflect his remarkable intellectual generosity, and his friendship. W. J. T. Mitchell and Elizabeth Helsinger helped guide me through the early stages of a doctoral thesis, and have continued to offer advice and encouragement. Marilyn Butler has generously shared her unparalleled knowledge of romantic period literature and culture, and her hospitality during several periods of research in England.

Not least among the pleasures of working on this book has been my introduction to the supportive community of romanticist scholars. Among those who have read or heard portions of the manuscript, and offered criticism and guidance, I am particularly indebted to Neil Fraistat, Jon Klancher, Zachary Leader, Alan Liu, Peter Manning, Ann Mellor, Marlon Ross, Orrin Wang, and David Worrall. The California Institute of Technology has provided an ideal environment in which to complete the book, and I am grateful to my colleagues in the Division of the Humanities and Social Sciences, especially Ron Bush, Monica Cohen, Jenijoy La Belle, Mac Pigman, John Sutherland, Cindy Weinstein, and Alison Winter. I have recently been challenged and encouraged by several historians of early nineteenth-century Britain, and am particularly grateful to James Epstein, Jonathan Fulcher, Iain McCalman, and Mark Philp for the patience and generosity with which they have read my work, or responded to my inquiries.

Research for this book has been supported by a Fulbright-Hays Fellowship, a Whiting Fellowship in the Humanities, and a Fletcher Jones Fellowship from the Huntington Library. The Division of

Humanities and Social Sciences at the California Institute of Technology has been very generous in its support of my work, and I am grateful to Susan Davis, David Grether, and John Ledyard. The staff at Caltech's Millikan Library has proved tireless in helping me track down obscure references and texts, and I want to acknowledge my debt to Janet Jenks and Judy Nollar in humanities reference, and to Tess Legaspi, Ruth Sustaita, Beth Nelson, and Cindy Estrada in interlibrary loan. I am grateful too for help and guidance provided by the staffs of the British Library, the Huntington Library, the Newberry Library, the Bodleian Library, and the Nuffield College Library.

Earlier versions of parts of this book have appeared in the following articles: "'Victims of Argument, Slaves of Fact': Hunt, Hazlitt, Cobbett and the Literature of Opposition," *Wordsworth Circle* 21 (1990), 90–96; "The Press on Trial: Form and Imagination in Early Nineteenth-Century Radical Culture," *Wordsworth Circle* 24 (1993), 144–47; "Popular Radicalism and the Public Sphere," *Studies in Romanticism* 33 (1994), 540–57; "'This Is Very Material': William Cobbett and the Rhetoric of Radical Opposition," *Studies in Romanticism* 34 (1995), 81–101. I am grateful to the publishers for their kind permission in allowing me to use this material again here.

My greatest debt, and the most difficult to estimate, is to Susan Ueki. She has been with the project from the beginning, and has had the patience to support it through the end.

Abbreviations

AYM	William Cobbett, *Advice to Young Men* (New York: John Doyle, 1831)
B	*The Briton*
BB	John Wade, *The Black Book; or, Corruption Unmasked!* (London: John Fairburn, 1820)
BB, new edn	John Wade, *The Extraordinary Black Book*, New Edition (London: Effingham Wilson, 1832)
BD	*The Black Dwarf*
BM	*Blackwood's Edinburgh Magazine*
CE	William Cobbett, *Cottage Economy* (Oxford University Press, 1979)
CEP	*Cobbett's Evening Post*
CL	*The Cap of Liberty*
CPR	*Cobbett's Weekly Political Register*
CRR	William Cobbett, *Rural Rides*, ed. G. D. H. Cole and Margaret Cole, 3 vols. (London: Peter Davies, 1930)
CWH	William Hazlitt, *The Complete Works of William Hazlitt*, ed. P. P. Howe, 21 vols. (London: J. M. Dent and Sons, 1930–34)
DPR	*Dolby's Parliamentary Register*
DR	*Democratic Recorder*
E	*The Examiner*
EMP	Robert Southey, *Essays, Moral and Political*, 2 vols. (London: John Murray, 1832)
ER	*The Edinburgh Review*
G	*The Gorgon*
GEL	William Cobbett, *A Grammar of the English Language* (Oxford University Press, 1984)
HA	Leigh Hunt, *The Autobiography of Leigh Hunt* (London: Cresset Press, 1949)

xiii

HC	*The Correspondence of Leigh Hunt*, ed. Thornton Hunt, 2 vols. (London: Smith, Elder and Co., 1862)
HR	*Hone's Reformists' Register*
L	*The Liberal*
LA	*London Alfred*
LJ	*Leigh Hunt's London Journal*
M	*The Medusa*
NM	*The Newgate Monthly Magazine*
PD	*Parliamentary Debates* (London: T. C. Hansard)
PD, new series	*Parliamentary Debates*, new series (London: T. C. Hansard)
QR	*The Quarterly Review*
R	*The Republican*
RB	*Extraordinary Red Book* (London: J. Blacklock, 1816)
RB, 4th edn	*The Extraordinary Red Book*, fourth edition (London: J. Johnston, 1821)
RF	*The Reflector*
RR	*The Radical Reformer*
S	*The Statesman*
SPR	*Sherwin's Weekly Political Register*
TT	*The Three Trials of William Hone* (London: William Hone, 1818)
VR	*Verbatim Report of the Two Trials of Mr. T. J. Wooler* (London: T. J. Wooler, 1817)
WBG	*Wooler's British Gazette*
WH	*The White Hat*
YD	*The Yellow Dwarf*

Introduction: locating a plebeian counterpublic sphere

This is a study of the language and strategy of London radicalism in print over the first three decades of the nineteenth century, an account of a popular reform movement's effort to recover genuine opposition from what were felt to be the calcified and merely reflex differences of a two-party system. During the Napoleonic Wars and the post-war period of economic dislocation and popular unrest, as the established parties mapped a considerable terrain of consensus, the radical movement developed a style of political opposition that aimed to replace the distinction between whig and tory with a more ominous one between the people and corrupt government, and to make the press a forum for mobilizing this distinction on behalf of radical parliamentary reform. Such a book may appear out of place in a series titled "Studies in Romanticism," and, although Leigh Hunt and William Hazlitt do figure significantly in the pages that follow, I should state from the outset that I have not mined radical prose as a footnote to romantic poetry. On the contrary, where the canonical romantic poets do appear in the pages that follow, it is as a footnote to less familiar radical writers and editors. The radical movement has long figured as a background to romanticism, particularly in studies of Blake, Wordsworth, Coleridge, and Shelley,[1] and it seems to me appropriate now to undertake a sustained analysis of radical culture from a perspective informed by, though not wholly limited to, the methods of literary scholarship. If I have not labored the question of why romanticists should be interested in radical prose, I do so out of a conviction that the answer finally lies in the interest of the account I have produced, and not in any claim I might make about it with respect to romanticism.

Recent initiatives in romantic studies, or what we should perhaps learn to call romantic period studies,[2] have informed the development of this book. Where a first wave of romantic "new historicism" tended to emphasize the way romantic poetry repressed, displaced, or idealized

political and historical content,[3] more recent work has moved beyond
the romantic canon and attended to positive rather than negative literary engagements with history. Anne Janowitz has recently identified an
"important development within romantic literary history of what we
might call plebeian studies,"[4] and it is to this plebeian school that my
own work belongs. Janowitz makes the remark in reviewing two books by
Jon Mee and David Worrall, but the field could be extended to include
recent work on popular radical culture by Jon Klancher, Michael
Scrivener, Marcus Wood, Paul Thomas Murphy, and Leonora Nattrass,
and traced back to the formative influences of Raymond Williams and
E. P. Thompson.[5] All these critics have expanded the literary canon,
extended a new historicist challenge to literary formalism, and introduced romanticist scholarship to the broader concerns of cultural
studies. Their work is resolutely interdisciplinary, emerging in dialogue
with a group of historians who have moved language to the center of an
analysis of radical politics.[6]

For my purposes here, Mee, Nattrass, and Worrall are particularly
important because they have described specific discursive strategies
in plebeian radical culture that open it up to sophisticated literary-
historical analysis. Mee's Blake is a radical *bricoleur* who "unapologetically recombines elements from across discourse boundaries" in ways
that are "typical of popular radicalism." This "eclectic combination of a
variety of received repertoires" cannot be understood according to "any
single intellectual tradition," and requires instead "a dialectical
approach" that attends to the way meanings shifted across a number of
discursive registers.[7] Nattrass' study of "rhetorical strategy" yields a
similar sense of "the artifice and experimentation of Cobbett's radical
style," evident above all in his "pragmatic exploration of a variety of
oppositional discourses."[8] Worrall's survey of a Spencean radical underworld adds to this sense of rhetorical opportunism the imperatives of
political resistance, and the obstructive counter-agency of the state.
Under the threat of surveillance and repression, radicals "circumvented
the law or stayed one step ahead of it," and exploited "sites of the dominant discourse which had become ramshackle or poorly defined or
which could be used subversively."[9] One characteristic of any rhetorical
bricolage is its capacity to accommodate contradiction, and a central
contradiction in radical culture was the way dominant political structures to some extent determined discursive opposition. If the work of
this plebeian school falls under the broad rubric of a linguistic turn in
humanistic inquiry, and seems to converge on popular radicalism in

print, it is important to insist with Worrall and others that radical culture was a public culture with a wide array of symbolic, communicative, and organizational resources, and that it cannot be understood through a close reading of arguments, tropes, and rhetorical devices. While my own work does focus on the radical press, and is for this reason pitched towards the upper reaches of the "radical underworld" mapped by Iain McCalman, I am interested in the way print resources developed in relation to other aspects of radical culture (meetings, clubs, debating societies, petition campaigns, boycotts), and in the way that broader problems of radical organization (leadership, communication, assembly, open organization) were worked through in the press.

Looking beyond romantic studies, theories of the public sphere would seem to offer a promising framework for a study of the language, organization, and public profile of the radical movement in print. In its original formulation by Jürgen Habermas in *The Structural Transformation of the Public Sphere*, the public sphere is the social space between the private sphere and the state, in which the middle class organized itself as a public over the course of the eighteenth century, through a rational–critical debate conducted in arenas like the coffee-house and the newspaper press. Habermas immediately announces, however, that his investigation "leaves aside the *plebeian* public sphere as a variant that in a sense was suppressed in the historical process."[10] And, despite the conceptual strength of his work, he has recently been criticized for inadequately addressing problems of access that lay at the core of radical reform.[11] In the wake of Oskar Negt and Alexander Kluge's "pioneering critique" of Habermas in *Public Sphere and Experience*, revisionist strategies have started to address the many social and historical variations on Habermas' eighteenth-century bourgeois theme, and have "sought to pluralize and multiply the concept. Thus we now speak routinely of *alternative* public spheres and *counterpublics*."[12] Geoff Eley's forceful statement of the revisionist case for "*competing* publics . . . at every stage in the history of the public sphere" seems particularly appropriate since it is informed by his interest in British radicalism: "By subsuming all possibilities into his 'liberal model of the bourgeois public sphere,' Habermas misses this diversity. More to the point, he misses the extent to which the public sphere was always constituted by conflict."[13] Conflict in the public sphere, and competition for control of its resources, were crucial elements of radical strategy, and the movement can be viewed as a campaign to institutionalize what Blake called "Mental Fight."[14] Richard Carlile, Painite republican, infidel, and editor of the weekly *Republican*, set up a freewheeling *"general lecturing and discussion establishment"* in an old theater called the Rotunda, and welcomed "mental conflict and discussion": "I very much desire to bring to the Rotunda all sects, all parties, all trades. For myself and friends, I can say, that we fear no discussion of any kind."[15] A revisionist account of Habermas' original concept allows us to see the contentious public assembled in the Rotunda, and in the pages of the *Republican* and other radical periodicals, as something more than a brief historical mutation, or a regrettable falling off from the polite coffee-house discussions of the eighteenth century.

In *The Function of Criticism*, Terry Eagleton disputes Habermas' claim that a real challenge to elite dominance of public life in England had to wait for Chartism, and in doing so, offers a preliminary catalogue of the resources with which popular radicalism undermined the universal aspirations of a classical public sphere: "What is emerging in the England of the late-eighteenth and early-nineteenth centuries . . . is already nothing less than a 'counter-public sphere.' In the Corresponding Societies, the radical press, Owenism, Cobbett's *Political Register* and Paine's *Rights of Man*, feminism and the dissenting churches, a whole oppositional network of journals, clubs, pamphlets, debates and institutions invades the dominant consensus, threatening to fragment it from within."[16] A crucial feature of this "oppositional network" was its extension from vigorous print arguments about public opinion to concrete assemblies of that opinion, in meetings, debating societies, and organized petition campaigns, which were then linked back to print culture through such practices as reading aloud, and transcribing meetings in the weekly press. In this way, the reform movement assembled its component parts, and linked metropolis and province, leadership and constituency, literate and non-literate audiences. The deliberate if sometimes anxious interpenetration of print and public assembly in radical culture serves to confirm and qualify Jon Klancher's view that the deterioration of an ideal eighteenth-century audience into fractured audiences had by the 1790s reduced the public sphere to "a representation instead of a practice, and . . . an image losing much of its force."[17] Like other revisionists of Habermas, Klancher attends to mediation and fragmentation in the public sphere, and approaches the very concept of the public with some skepticism. This is perhaps nowhere more imperative than when dealing with "the heroic age of popular Radicalism," with its tempting master narratives of class struggle, state treachery, and unyielding popular resistance.[18] Yet, as Bruce Robbins has observed, a post-structuralist skepticism about the empirical status of the public has its own history. For the liberal tradition especially, "the public has *always* been somewhat ghostly," at least as far back as the appearance of "the Image, Phantom, or Representative of the Commonwealth" in Locke's *Two Treatises of Government*.[19] The early nineteenth-century reform movement was a calculated intervention in the political history of these phantoms, as radical theorists proposed electoral mechanisms and discursive practices that would replace the deceptive shadow-play of "virtual representation."[20] It was resistance to this and other dominant accounts of political representation, rather than obtuse empiricism or inadequate theorization, that led to the movement's overwhelming faith in a simple descriptive representation of public opinion.[21] Distinct individual bodies were assembled at mass meetings and political clubs, and accounted for in petition drives and subscription lists. This is not to say that radical publicity never appeared in phantom form. On the contrary, the movement delighted in producing canny and subversive emulations of the state's own potent specters. Cobbett stated a first principle of radical opposition during his American exile when he announced a plan to bring down the system of paper currency by flooding England with counterfeit bills: "They can make nothing that cannot be imitated" (*CPR* 35 [1819–20], 50). The popular radical public of the early nineteenth century was both representation and practice, elusive phantom and material body. Political protest was articulated through a rich assortment of rhetorical strategies and institutional practices.

Revisionist theorists "pluralize and multiply" as well as spectralize the concept of the public sphere, and here too some historical reflection may be in order. Notions of a counterpublic and of counterpublicity do help account for the oppositional imperative behind a reform movement that undertook to write, speak, organize, and act *against* corrupt institutions and practices. Strict polarization was among the movement's first principles. "Monarchy and priestcraft, on one side, and popular knowledge, popular industry, and consequent popular liberty, on the other," were, according to Richard Carlile, "hostile principles, between which, there cannot, by any possibility, be any future peace . . . No truce, no amnesty, no patched up peace can again take place: War! War! War! Must be the cry, until popular liberty finds no opposition!!!" (*R* 7 [1823], 779). However, the same political aversion that motivated this antagonism created an equally powerful desire for autonomy, and for some refuge from corrupt influence. In key formulas like "radical reform" and "independent opposition," the movement expressed a divided motivational structure, and attempted to constitute itself in terms that were both fundamental (radical, independent) and negative or relative (reform, opposition). William Cobbett of Botley, the blunt egotist at home, coexisted with William Cobbett of Long Island, the playful counterfeiter in exile, and when it suited his purposes the editor of the *Political Register* could identify himself as one or the other, or both.[22] Eagleton's sketch of an "oppositional network" acknowledges radical resistance, but risks limiting a counterpublic sphere to the negative role of invading and frustrating dominant circuits of communication. As it turns out, *The Function of Criticism* is less interested in how radicals expressed themselves than in where their impact was felt: the dominant bourgeois public sphere was, in Eagleton's colorful account, "fissured and warped, wracked with a fury which threaten[ed] to strip it of ideological credibility."[23] At the same time, it is possible to exaggerate radical independence, as James Epstein risks doing when he describes "the attempt to fashion an autonomous and distinctly working-class or plebeian 'public sphere.'"[24] Leaving aside for the moment the vexed problem of class, radical autonomy was qualified by a negative engagement with corruption, by a desire to "imitate," as Cobbett put it, where imitation was the highest form of opposition.

This point about the limits of radical autonomy bears upon current efforts to rethink the concept of the public sphere. The revisionist idea of multiple and overlapping spheres has been affiliated with a "radical democratic" challenge to liberal theory, according to which "a central role of the media should be defined as *assisting the equitable negotiation or arbitration of competing interests through democratic processes*."[25] For the early nineteenth-century reform movement, the arbitration of competing interests was, like a phantom public and phantom statecraft, tainted by association with orthodox whig theories of interest representation, with the irregular distribution of the franchise, and, worse still, with the name of Edmund Burke. Radicals preferred a single popular interest, counterposed to the interests of a corrupt system and its specious publics, and they advocated a reformed parliament in which every adult male found individual representation.[26] Within this polarized structure, any commitment to negotiation was crucially limited. The movement recognized its own divisions, and sometimes addressed them with the rudiments of a deliberative theory of publicity.[27] There was, however, a tendency to treat internal conflict as the consequence of error or government interference, something to be corrected rather than negotiated. Radical differences were the unfortunate prelude to some final reconciliation or union, not a permanent condition to be addressed through ongoing procedures of public arbitration.[28] "When discussion has done its office," John Hunt's *Reformists' Register* announced, "truth and *unanimity* prevail."[29] Looking beyond its own ranks, the movement confronted a rift between corruption and reform that could never be negotiated, and Carlile's battle-cry took effect: "No truce, no amnesty, no patched up peace." Every imaginable interest fell under the division between popular right and oppressive rule. Apparent diversity on either side was more deceptive shadow-play, and those foolish enough to mistake their interests would find themselves on the wrong side when the battle was finally drawn. If radical protest set out from an irremediable split in politics and the public sphere, it culminated in the promise of an absolute public reconciliation. There was a widely shared sense that the millennial aftermath of reform would not require interventionist publicity, since accurate popular representation would have been returned to the House of Commons. Carlile's political campaign for liberty terminated where it met "no opposition." In "The Topic," the Spencean poet Allen Davenport provided a compelling formulation of what I take to be the utopian structure of radical discourse. Each of the poem's four stanzas projected the end of some injustice, and the closing lines imagined the termination of political desire on a national scale: "When reason, and truth, have o'er folly prevailed, / The land of Great Britain shall wish for no more" (*SPR* 2 [1818], 106).[30] Where every "wish" was answered, there would be little need to arbitrate competing interests. This utopian attitude may seem naive in retrospect, but it should come as no surprise that one of the first organized and effective counterpublics did not fully imagine for itself an ongoing role in public debate.

The radical desire for unity in opposition, and for a historical limit to counterpublic intervention, recalls Habermas' relatively monolithic theory of the classical public sphere. We are reminded of the cogency of that theory, less as a critical or interpretive tool, than as a powerful restatement of longstanding attitudes about politics and publicity. It did not, after all, require Habermas to treat as normative an idealized version of the discursive politics of the early eighteenth-century English bourgeoisie. Leigh Hunt did this too, in his role as the middle-class conscience of a radical movement that had not yet abandoned the idea that the middle and working classes could be joined in a single popular front for reform.[31] The unexpected return of a relatively polite and unitary political ideal at the heart of a movement known for conflict suggests that the revisionist case for diversity in the public sphere needs to remain sensitive to historical variations, or risk becoming as misleading as any insistence on uniformity. If, as Geoff Eley argues, "the public sphere makes more sense as the structured setting where cultural and ideological contest or negotiation among a variety of publics takes place,"[32] it is important to remember that such contests were never entirely contained within that setting, but came to be waged over structure and setting as well. Early nineteenth-century radicals were prepared to theorize the terms of public debate, and to deploy those theories (including the idea of a single public) as political weapons. The ability to discern the horizons of the public sphere and debate its contours is not our own belated privilege.

As even casual references to a "distinctly working-class or plebeian 'public sphere'" indicate, the radical polarization of public life has often been transcribed into subsequent accounts of class struggle. This book is not an intervention in the ongoing debate among social and political historians about the class dimensions of radical reform, and I have followed others in using terms like "popular" and "plebeian" to elide the problem of class. Yet it is impossible to ignore class formation entirely, if for no other reason than that any significant immersion in radical discourse confirms that the debate is no mere historiographical artifact. Recent revisions of E. P. Thompson's famous argument, that the English working class was in the early nineteenth century "present at its own making," have been concerned to show that popular radicalism in this period was concerned less with an economic split between proletariat and bourgeoisie, or between worker and master, than with an interlocking and ultimately political set of distinctions between the represented and the unrepresented, the productive and the parasitic classes.[33] In the words of Gareth Stedman Jones, "however much radicalism extended its scope during this period, it could never be the ideology of a specific class. It was first and foremost a vocabulary of political exclusion whatever the social character of those excluded." Jones derives his argument in part from a methodological insistence that class be treated "as a discursive rather than as an ontological reality, the central effort being to explain languages of class from the nature of politics rather than the character of politics from the nature of class."[34] This reworking of Marxist categories has obvious attractions for the new historicism in literary studies, since its linguistic turn makes a range of social and cultural issues more immediately available to literary scholarship. Yet some caution is in order. The challenge Jones has posed to historians with his "non-referential conception of language" may have a very different impact in other disciplines,[35] and it would be a mistake for literary studies to conclude, in a formalist fashion, that language contains every-thing we need to know about history, and that a schism between repre-sented and unrepresented (as opposed to masters and workers) can be fully understood from literary texts. In the following pages, I have tried to explore the way tensions generated by a radical "vocabulary of political exclusion" were worked out in the social and material conditions of print, and in related arenas of radical culture, as well as in the richly tex-tured terrain of political language.

It may also be worth preserving some part of E. P. Thompson's classi-cal map of the terrain. While praising Jones and other revisionists for their "convincing alternative to crude economic interpretations," John Belchem has observed that we need not give up a sense that "radicalism acquired its working-class identity during the lengthy wars against revolutionary and Napoleonic France, the harsh economic realities of which politicized the workers and produced the mass breakthrough to radicalism which the Jacobins of the 1790s had been unable to effect."[36] "Acquired" seems to me the key term here. If working-class conscious-ness, or for that matter middle-class consciousness, was not the premise of radical politics in this period, it was often its consequence or effect. Above all, the struggle to link the laboring poor with more respectable radicals, and produce a single popular front for reform, yielded recognizable class idioms, which were then refined and sharpened as plebeian radical leaders became frustrated with the apparent complicity of the middle class in a corrupt system. Permanent hostility between the two classes only became the dominant pattern after 1832.[37] My chapter on Leigh Hunt attempts to trace the middle class falling away from radical opposition to progressive accommodation, and explores the effect this development had on critical practices. Yet, even here, the pattern is not one of a sharp break or clear teleology. Hunt expressed anxieties about the radical extreme from the outset of his career, and the liberalism he subsequently helped define had important affinities with radical reform. At the same time, the elitism and progressivism that might be taken to distinguish his later work can also be found in the mixed idiom of more plebeian radicals like Richard Carlile and John Wade.

Hunt's final break with radical reform was marked above all by the retreat from a language of protest and inflexible resistance, suggesting that the essence of radicalism may have inhered, paradoxically, in a rela-tionship of political opposition. The tendency to divide society into two "hostile principles," and to cry "War!" across the fissure this opened, may be the best test for orthodoxy in a frankly heterogeneous movement. The negative and reformist (rather than revolutionary) character of the radical movement has often been treated as its great weakness, but I hope to suggest in the following pages that there were virtues to this limitation. The idea of reform guaranteed an immediate engagement with existing conditions. "The world is our lesson," Carlile insisted, "our country our text book" (*R* 9 [1824], 34). With respect to the public sphere, it was the reformist element in radicalism that focused attention upon the precise institutions and practices that would allow a popular voice silenced by corruption to speak again. The treatment of parliamentary reform as a political panacea may have been the illusion of the age, but it was in some respects a saving illusion, since it linked radical aspirations to some (radically reformed) version of existing conditions, and provided the movement with a claim upon power that even its enemies had implicitly to acknowledge. Immediate engagement infused radical argument with an energy and intensity that remains compelling to this day.

CHAPTER ONE

A rhetoric of radical opposition

PARTY, CORRUPTION, AND POLITICAL OPPOSITION

Early nineteenth-century radicalism can be defined as a protest against the dominance of two political parties.[1] The first step towards an appropriate division of the political public sphere between corrupt power and popular right was to clear away deceptive and outmoded distinctions between whig and tory. To write as a radical was to refashion the party structures that linked the authority of the state with the authority of political discourse. In an impressive account of Restoration and eighteenth-century political culture, Steven N. Zwicker has shown how "rhetorical legitimacy" was shaped by a set of debates over how and even whether the political realm should be divided: despite "strenuous efforts to deny faction and dissent," a "Jacobean ideal of unitary politics" gave way first to "the political pluralism of the Restoration" and then to relatively coherent party divisions that "hardened into system" over the course of the eighteenth century.[2] By the early nineteenth century, this binary system continued to calcify as the impact of the French Revolution reinforced its consensual character. A whole range of reformist positions came to be labeled dangerous, foreign, and disloyal – in a word, "Jacobin." Whig and tory disputes continued, but they increasingly mapped what Pierre Bourdieu has termed "the *unanimity* of doxa," a "*universe of possible discourse*" that includes both orthodoxy and heterodoxy (in this case, tory and whig positions) by excluding a "universe of the undiscussed."[3] It was to bring the undiscussed into view that the radical movement rejected tory and whig as the "Ins" and "Outs" of a single political system that simply reshuffled the wages of corruption, and, in an era of whig weakness, rarely managed even that. This rejection of party was a founding moment for radical argument. John Wade, a journeyman wool sorter become plebeian Benthamite, launched his *Gorgon* with a bold stroke that severed both parties from the people they claimed to represent: "The two parties, Whig and Tory, are . . . confederated to plunder and delude the public; their quarrels and animosities arise merely from the division of the spoil" (*G*, no. 1 [1818], 4).[4] This sweeping gesture created economic difficulties I will consider later, since it cut off the flow of party patronage that supported the English political press well into the nineteenth century.[5] It also restored Zwicker's problem of rhetorical legitimacy, by bringing into view again the ideal of a unitary politics that party had overthrown. Interestingly, political unity entered radical discourse as both stifling contemporary fact and utopian possibility: it was the narrow common ground of whig and tory consensus, and the broad popular agreement that would generate reform and prevail in its aftermath.

The radical movement responded with characteristic flexibility to the question of whether party divisions should be redrawn or rejected entirely. In the aftermath of the Peterloo Massacre, Richard Carlile launched his *Republican* with a series of provocative essays under the Painite title, "The Crisis." Though bitterly critical of "a MOCK PARLIA-MENT," Carlile seemed willing to transvalue rather than overturn existing political structures: "We must have but two parties, those who wish an effectual change, and those who are determined with their lives to support things as they are" (*R* 1 [1819], 4). Two years later his incendiary demand for a National Convention involved a more thoroughgoing republican critique of party: "A National Convention would know nothing of parties, nor factions, nor aristocrats; it would comprise the voice of the nation – the people – in their common character of citizens" (*R* 4 [1820], 474). This ambivalence about political structure ("two parties," or one "common character") was a pervasive feature of radical discourse. It makes sense only if we see how the two positions were linked, even for a republican like Carlile, by a narrative that made radical reform a fundamental change by revisionist means. The party of "effectual change" was a feature of political "crisis"; it could not long coexist with those determined "to support things as they are," and would leave in its wake nothing but "the people – in their common character." Radical protest was remedial in its orientation. Even where the movement tentatively assumed party identification, it did not comfortably imagine for itself an ongoing role in a divided political order.[6]

This attitude contradicted Edmund Burke's influential and by this time authoritative theory of party, which allowed two competing but equally legitimate claims upon state power. Organized political opposition was in Burke's account "an opposition to defend not destroy party," and party became "a persistent and enduring feature of politics."[7] Wary

of Burke and all his works, radicals took the collapse of party difference
as a reason to return to the older, country-party theories of Bolingbroke,
whose "division of constitutionists and anti-constitutionists, or of a court
and a country-party," implied that one of the two positions was illegitimate and should not remain a permanent feature of the state.[8] Even
without the French republican turn it acquired in Carlile's hands, the
radical movement's strenuous, even catastrophic understanding of political opposition was perceived as a threat in established quarters. An 1818
Edinburgh Review article by the whig lawyer and MP Henry Brougham
discerned an ominous nostalgia in the radical search for unity. The
"heated imaginations" that demanded "immediate, sweeping, radical,
unsparing" reform also rejected the compromising spirit of an established opposition, and accepted "no terms short of entire submission":
"Of course, the patrons of this very practical scheme of government,
abhorred the idea of a *regular party*: – in their Utopia it could find no
place" (*ER* 30 [1818], 200–01).[9]

The radical deconstruction of party difference was motivated in part
by the overwhelming pressure for ideological consensus that accompanied the wars against revolutionary and Napoleonic France. As "the long
counter-revolution" in Britain unfolded,[10] the whig and tory parties
developed a set of shared reactionary commitments, and used "a cry
about Jacobinism" (*CPR* 11 [1807], 816), as Cobbett termed it, to brand a
whole range of alternative positions foreign, illegitimate, and seditious.
Brougham's *Edinburgh Review* definition of radical reform as a revolutionary extreme – "No compromise must be endured with the faults of the
present system; the whole must be swept away" (*ER* 30 [1818], 200) – was
eagerly seconded by the tory *Blackwood's Edinburgh Magazine*: "Radicalism
is subversion, total excision and overthrow, – the substitution, not of one
order of polity for another, but an utter destruction of the present state of
things" (*BM* 8 [1820], 329). Radical opposition had restored what Burke's
legitimating theory of party tried to eclipse: the disturbing specter of an
opposition to destroy rather than preserve party. The whig and tory
agreement that a radical position was unacceptable only reinforced the
radical view that the two parties were in fact identical. Historians have
reached no consensus about the radical case against party, but even
Frank O'Gorman's cautious account, which rejects the radical notion of
a "phony war," acknowledges that the two parties spanned "no dramatic
ideological divisions" in this period. The party system had developed "to
conserve existing institutions," and "there were large areas of common
ground between government and opposition, especially those bearing

upon social hierarchy, the protection of property and the preservation of law and order."[11] Where dramatic social and political rifts did appear, they divided the legitimate "common ground" of party from the uncompromising threat of radical protest.

The radical movement spent a good deal of time trying to analyze the structure of an oppressive partisan consensus, in order to reverse the definitional blow that went into a statement like "radicalism is subversion." Jon Klancher's perceptive remark that the *Black Dwarf* searched for a language "capable of representing – and thus containing – the old regime's apparently limitless power" can be extended to the radical movement as a whole.[12] The search for limiting definitions and representations led back again to country-party ideology, and especially to the idea of political corruption. Wade's claim that existing party differences "arise merely from the division of the spoil" reduced the bewildering complexity of party rule to a sordid struggle for profit at the taxpayer's expense. Yet there could be no simple recourse to the political languages of an earlier century. Updated for the conditions of loyalist mobilization against a revolutionary enemy, the language of corruption extended well beyond pensioners and placemen, and became a remarkably flexible and comprehensive theory of power that treated unprecedented numbers of readers as potential political agents, in part because they had become the victims of corrupt practices. As Gareth Stedman Jones has written, "the language of corruption and deceit which had developed in the early eighteenth century as a response to the new financial practices associated with parliamentary parties and the growth of public debt" was first "broadened by Paine and Cobbett into a juxtaposition between the people and 'old corruption' or the forces of 'force and fraud,'" and then "extended" from the state "into the fabric of civil society itself."[13] The new sense of old corruption still held government ministers responsible for the abuse of power, but argued that their influence now spread outward through an increasingly complex social and political structure required by the wartime mobilization of opinion and resources. The once free and independent citizen had been reduced to what one "West-Country Labourer," in a letter to *Hone's Reformist Register*, suggestively termed "the social order slave" (*HR* 2 [1817], 351).

The effect of this redefinition of corruption was not always containment, since radicals wanted to argue that a "social order" regime violated every imaginable limit and boundary. The representation of corruption was an endless task, and its verbal formulas tended to unravel in a troubling index of extension and dispersal. Early accounts of "the

Pitt system" in Cobbett's *Political Register* established the conventions of radical discourse for decades to come:

It is sown all over the country, as regularly as corn is sown in a field. Seventy millions a year are, in one way and another, spent by the government. The government employs and pays all, and it receives all. There is a chain of dependance running through the whole nation, which, though not everywhere seen, is everywhere felt. There is not one man in one thousand who does not feel the weight of this chain. Army, navy, church, the law, sinecures, pensions, tax offices, war and navy offices, Whitehall, India-house, Bank, contract, job, &c. &c. (*CPR* 14 [1808], 585–86)

The "chain of dependence" saturated time ("regularly") as well as space ("all over"); dialectical formulations closed on themselves ("pays all, and receives all"), and alternative possibilities wound up pointing in the same direction ("one way and another"); influence was "felt" even where it was not "seen," and the whole account finally trailed off in an interminable list ("&c. &c."). This kind of prose attempted and dramatically failed to analyze what W. D. Rubinstein has termed the "dreamlike or nightmarish quality" of political corruption in this period, its residual status as the pre-modern or "*irrational*" organization of the British state.[14] A "system" of corruption was grasped as a dense metaphor or sequence of metaphors (chain, net, web, knot, nest), and any prospect of termination or escape was cut off by the insistence upon categorical absolutes (all, every, never, not).

   Where closure was achieved, and Cobbett's ominous "&c. &c." avoided, it was often through a rhetoric of despair. In a remarkable 1817 essay, "Grounds for Resisting the Ministers," T. J. Wooler retreated from the satirical manner that often characterized his weekly *Black Dwarf*, and indicated the hazards of venturing upon corrupt terrain. The writer soon lost his way amidst a proliferation of corrupt figures (language, religion, the body, monstrosity, warfare, disease) that threatened to destroy both reader and writer:

The present administration . . . sit upon the treasury bench as the proper guardians of corruption. They patronize, they defend it; and in return it feeds and supports them. It is their vocabulary and their creed. They have no other prompter, instructor, or friend. But it is sufficient for them. Corruption has only one body, but it has grown into the strength of a giant, and stretches out its hundred hands like Briareus, to snatch up whatever it can reach. The *present system* is that body of corruption, and the members of the administration are the hands by which it works. They are ready adepts in the furtherance of their objects. They were *nursed up* to their trade, and there is not an individual in the three kingdoms who has not felt them tear some comfort from them. Nothing is too little for them to notice, where money is to be obtained; though it be only a farthing, they will frame an act of parliament to seize it. And if a spark of honesty is reported to have appeared in any quarter, they will bring forth an act of parliament to crush it. They hate independence, because they know the independent detest them. They hold honesty in suspicion, because they have no pretensions to it. Their system has long been a system of pillage and deception; and no sooner did the public begin to perceive and reprobate it, than they attempted to justify their past misconduct, by seizing the last out-work of freedom, and levelling it to the earth . . . They form in reality a *political plague*, which extinguishes all patriotism, all virtue; and the contagion of their pestilential influence penetrates into every recess. Their measures have already entailed a weight of misery upon the nation which she MAY never recover from; but if they are permitted still to prescribe for our maladies there is no alternative but death. Like impudent quacks they will proceed until the tomb shall have silenced their patients. Under their guidance, we can have no recourse, but to dig "ourselves dishonourable graves." (*BD* I [1817], 97–98)[15]

"MAY never recover" was an emphatic qualification, and later in the essay Wooler turned to a favorite radical reservoir of independence, the electorate of Westminster, to escape the "pestilential influence" of the ministers. But his assurance that "their *thunder-bolts* are *pop-guns*, and their anger madness" (102) seemed hollow in the wake of this overwhelming catalogue of corruption. Political despair, often associated with the analysis of corruption as a pervasive system, was an important and frequently overlooked feature of radical discourse in this period.

Yet even an irrational order had its logic, and one way to escape despair was to translate the problem into more manageable and coherent terms. This translation was possible in part because corruption operated at the level of language and mediation. Figures *for* corruption were also figures *of* corruption, the set of fraudulent codes ("vocabulary," "creed," "trade," "measures") through which power relations were exercised. Wooler's essay closed with a promising gesture of enlightenment demystification that disclosed the underlying "Grounds" of resistance: "If we drag them to the light, expose their motives, and meet them openly and boldly, the lion's skin will drop off the back of every ass, and their braying will only excite the mirth of the assembled forest" (102). The outer "skin" of a corrupt system, its bewildering array of figures and mediations, concealed a simple and even sordid motive. The irrational nightmare of corruption was also, as Rubinstein has observed, a calculated "system of achieving wealth and status, the system *par excellence* of outdoor relief for the aristocracy and its minions."[16] A rational system required rational analysis, and the radical movement achieved this in encyclopedic catalogues of corruption like *The Extraordinary Red Book* (1816) and *The Black Book; or, Corruption Unmasked!* (1820). Shunning expansive figures of corruption, these works used modern textual and statistical procedures to dissect and classify the aristocracy's system of outdoor relief. The hundred hands of Briareus were assembled and organized according to alphabetical, chronological, and categorical principles, and records were kept of the precise amount of money that changed hands. John Wade's *Black Book*, the most impressive of these radical encyclopedias,[17] supplemented the usual list of "Places, Pensions, and Sinecures" with a series of wide-ranging essays on contemporary institutions, including "Police Establishments of the Metropolis," "Charitable Foundations," "Administration of Justice," and the "Lottery System." If there was still a residue of fantasy in the very idea of a complete catalogue of social and political life, it was at least a fantasy that allowed readers and writers to master the system rather than suffer its depredations.

Whether corruption was grasped as nightmarish figure or rational system, a radical critique never lost sight of the underlying distinction between victim and profiteer. No one could "pretend to be neutral," Hazlitt argued in his *Yellow Dwarf* essay "On the Clerical Character," particularly not clergymen who were drawn into the "alliance between Church and State" by their dependence on tithes: "*Those that are not with us, are against us*, is a maxim that always holds true" (*CWH* 7: 255–56). The intended victim of this radical suppression of "neutral" territory was the whig party, and its response to the challenge was instructive. In an 1810 *Edinburgh Review* essay on the "State of Parties," Francis Jeffrey surveyed a nation "breaking rapidly into two furious and irreconcileable parties," and conjured apocalyptic expectations as harrowing as those of the radical press: "The dangers, and the corruptions, and the prodigies of the times, have very nearly put an end to all neutrality and moderation in politics; and the great body of the nation appears to be divided into two violent and most pernicious factions; – the courtiers, who are almost for arbitrary power, – and the democrats, who are almost for revolution and republicanism." The "narrow isthmus" of "neutrality" that Hazlitt rejected became for Jeffrey the only solid ground, occupied by "the diminishing mass of the calm and the neutral" known as "the old constitutional Whigs of England" (*ER* 15 [1810], 504–06). This tactical effort to deny the tenability of certain positions and privilege others continued across the entire political spectrum. Where radicals invoked whig collaboration to deny neutrality, and whigs invoked radical and tory extremes to recover moderation, so apologists for the government invoked the fact of radical protest to discredit even moderate opposition. An 1822 *Quarterly Review* article on "The Opposition" condensed the case for guilt by association, and innocence by dissociation, in a stunning tautology. Since the ministerial press "cannot support the ministry without supporting the constitution," the whig opposition cannot criticize the ministry without enabling sedition: "they draw the boundary for the revolutionary prints" (*QR* 28 [1822], 204–05).[18]

To suggest that an uncompromising commitment to political conflict was constitutive of the radical position in this period does not mean that the movement failed to imagine less contentious modes of public communication. Not every radical utterance was an argument or assault. The rich resources of a radical counterpublic sphere convey something of its range of motivation: there were handbills, ballads, pamphlets, and tracts; dictionaries, grammars, and collections of recipes; works on history, husbandry, political economy, and law; daily newspapers, weekly pamphlets, and magazines; published versions of trials, parliamentary debates, and petitions; and transcripts of meetings, debating societies, and lectures. In this wealth of material, the radical movement exercised the deliberative as well as the critical function of a political public sphere. At the same time, radicals were deeply suspicious of any compromise with corruption, and embraced an almost puritanical sense of truth that dictated against negotiation. Richard Carlile was perhaps the most vigorous advocate of free public debate. "If there be any talisman applicable to the question of Reform," he maintained, "it must consist in the words FREE DISCUSSION" (*R* 7 [1823], 418). Yet, even where he endorsed discussion, Carlile could not help but mark its limits. He introduced an 1822 exchange between himself and a correspondent with a spirited defense of "discussion and moral controversy," but added a telling qualification: "It is common with many persons to deprecate all controversy, and others say it has no charms. I think different, and view it as the corner stone of all useful knowledge, where one of the parties happens to take the right side of the question" (*R* 6 [1822], 321–22). Radical controversy had more in common with the reformation sense of a trial of truth than with subsequent theories of interest negotiation in a democratically structured public sphere. Suspicious of whig complicity, radical publicists set out to uncover the truths obscured by corruption, and to silence rather than persuade their antagonists.

Wooler was also an advocate of public debate, and despite his ongoing campaign for radical unity, sometimes excused divisions within the movement as symptoms of vitality and democratic organization. The second volume of the *Black Dwarf* closely tracked the selection of a radical candidate for Westminster, after the suicide of Samuel Romilly in November 1818.[19] Wooler supported Major Cartwright, but tempered his disappointment when the moderate John Cam Hobhouse prevailed, and offered his own assent as evidence that radical unity might require compromise. No praise was too great for the Westminster deliberations. "To be present at a Westminster Meeting, is to mix in an assembly that would do no discredit to the best days of Republican Greece, when the whole of her citizens were met together, in their *own name*, to transact *their own business*." "Confusion," "diversity," and "clamour" were evidence of "the genial breeze of mutual freedom," and would finally "subside into a general determination to do what to each seems best calculated to ensure the good of all" (*BD* 2 [1818], 721). Yet, like Carlile, Wooler set strict limits on public debate. The record of his participation in these meetings revealed an ambivalence about public deliberation:

Mr. Wooler then alluded to the difference of opinion which existed among the reformers. This, though detrimental to the effect which would be produced by union, was certainly proof of the *freedom*, and the honesty of the reformers. The trammelled slaves of despotism were disciplined into union; and being forbidden to entertain opinions of their own, were taught, like parrots, to echo the opinions of *their masters*. This would account for the perfect union, between a Castles and a Castlereagh, an Oliver and a Canning . . . The discussion produced by real difference of opinion amongst honest men, tended to diffuse information, and to promote enquiry . . . The object in view *is one*, although the means proposed are many. Let us steadily pursue that object – a parliamentary reform – by all the means in our power. (*BD* 2 [1818], 499–500)

To recognize internal dissent was to begin to suppress it, since a shared commitment to inquiry distinguished radicals from "the trammelled slaves of despotism." Internal "difference of opinion" remained "detrimental" to the radical cause, and "discussion" should yield to the "*one*" object that divided reform from corruption. Wooler's enthusiasm for diversity turned out to be as temporary as it was limited. The *Black Dwarf* soon turned against an increasingly exclusive Westminster organization, and renewed its attacks on Hobhouse as a moderate reformer outside the pale of radical protest.

Libertarian rhetoric facilitated a radical critique of the state's machinery for policing the public sphere (prosecution, patronage, spies), but that same repressive machinery was found to limit the effectiveness of free inquiry as an oppositional strategy. Official resistance to radical communication confirmed a sense that, while negotiation might work within the movement, beyond its limits warfare was the order of the day. Dialogic modes of exchange were put to monologic purposes. Controversial works like Hazlitt's "Reply to Z" and William Hone's *Aspersions Answered* employed extensive quotations from an antagonist in order to contain and neutralize rather than accommodate criticism. Cobbett worked the phrases and idioms of corruption into his own prose to similar effect. The dialogue form was used by radicals for satirical rather than serious purposes, as in *A Dialogue on the Approaching Trial of Mr. Carlile*, which pitted the philosopher Candid's defense of Carlile against the likes of Cantwell, Officio, and Burn-all-o.[20] As reform petitions were refused and public letters went unanswered, communication with the government came increasingly to serve as a displaced form of internal radical communication. In 1819, Thomas Dolby began supplementing his *Parliamentary Register* with selections from popular petitions to the House of Commons, on the grounds that these had become part of the counterpublic sphere: "whether *Parliament* attended . . . or not, the *Nation* would" (*DPR* 1 [1819], 334). In a letter to the editor of the *Morning Herald*, Carlile went so far as to suggest the existence of two hostile and mutually exclusive circuits of political communication: "I can speak to my friends through the medium of my own (weekly) publication; but, by your permission, I desire to convey a word to my enemies, through the columns of the Herald" (*R* 10 [1824], 13). The letter was, fittingly, returned unprinted, and reached only Carlile's "friends" in the pages of the *Republican*.

No account of the radical movement, even one that focuses on print, can overlook the meetings and debates that provided a key forum for public deliberation.[21] The early nineteenth-century radical press was saturated with vivid accounts of the proceedings of these assemblies, which ranged from tiny clubs to monster meetings, and extended from London out through provincial cities into rural villages. A commitment to public deliberation was a frequent theme at these assemblies. In a meeting held at the Crown and Anchor Tavern to consider the Peterloo Massacre, Wooler pitted government violence against radical argument: "The enemies of reform might argue, might dissuade, but they ought to abstain from shedding blood (*applause*.) Let the reformers at least have fair play, let their arguments be heard and refuted; but let them not be imprisoned in place of being answered." Deliberation of a sort was then vividly realized as Wooler's moderate injunctions were met with "*a cry from some person*" demanding "*Blood for blood!*," which was in turn refuted "by a general hiss throughout the whole room" (*BD* 3 [1819], 558–60). Rudimentary as such proceedings may have been, they were often overwhelmed by the radical desire to project a unified front. Wooler's motions were in the end "put *seriatim*" to the crowd, and "carried unanimously" (563). The pressure for agreement was particularly evident in public radical celebrations. An 1818 meeting held to raise funds for William Hone, after his acquittal on three charges of blasphemous libel, yielded a series of speeches and resolutions steeped in applause and the rhetoric of assent: "We have not met to discuss any question on which . . . there can arise a difference of opinion"; "There was no feeling of difference on this occasion"; "He would not say a word on that point, because he knew full well that their feelings would dictate to them what they ought to do"; "The resolution which he was about to move accorded entirely with his sentiments, and, he was convinced, with those of every person present."[22] The proceedings were then printed and bound with *The Three Trials of William Hone*, in order to present a sharp contrast between external conflict with the government and internal accord among reformers. The excuse provided by the Chair of the meeting for Hone's failure to attend drew attention to the underlying difference from corruption that allowed the radicals to enjoy "no feeling of difference" among themselves: "When I say that [Hone] is in one respect like myself, I mean that he would rather meet a host of adversaries in the field, than the friends assembled here to day. (Laughter and applause.)" (*TT* 231).

If it was not possible to negotiate with corrupt power, the rationale for oppositional publicity might seem obscure. The image of Hone confronting "a host of adversaries in the field" was appropriately ambiguous, linking discursive warfare and actual violence. A radical search for leverage against the system often went beyond the public sphere, and beyond appeals to the old reformation principle that truth would triumph in a fair contest. Peterloo, with its stark evidence of violent repression, was a pivotal event in encouraging radical endorsements of the right of armed resistance. "I have no idea that any thing short of down right intimidation can bring our opponents to just measures," Carlile wrote in 1820, "It is a folly to talk of the weapons of reason, when they are met by those of a conscious and malignant ridicule" (*R* 2 [1820], 470). Though not wholly empty, such threats were often vague, particularly in more "respectable" radical periodicals like the *Republican*, the *Black Dwarf*, the *Gorgon*, and the *Political Register*.[23] The possibility of physical resistance frequently led back to "the weapons of reason," as violence itself was appropriated to radical argument. The *Yellow Dwarf* responded to the prosecution of Hone with the claim that "no ruinous system of government can be checked but by argument and appeals to the people, or by the actual resistance of the multitude, occasioned by its intolerable oppression. It is evidently better for both the rulers and the subjects that it should be checked by opinion, and not by the last alternative" (*YD*, no. 3 [1818], 19).[24] Beyond this rhetorical use of "the last alternative," political violence was a hazardous enterprise, and lay beyond the sympathy of many reformers. Those ultra-radicals who pursued it were often treated in the radical press as empirical evidence of the effects of a repressive regime, or as unfortunate martyrs to the wiles of government spies.

REPRESENTING THE PEOPLE: THE PRESS AND PARLIAMENTARY REFORM

It is difficult to adopt any mode of address to the *unrepresented* part of the British public. The *misrepresented* have some designated characteristic. Whether fools, or knaves, or forced or willing slaves, they have *some* appellation. The *unrepresented* are mere expletives in the political creation; and if they were not called upon to *obey* laws in the enactment of which they have no share, they might be abandoned to the apparent insignificance to which they are told the constitution of England has consigned them. Since however they are expected to *pay* and to *obey*, since they are acknowledged in the account of *collections*, they are entitled to some notice . . . Well then, gentlemen, although you are not mocked with the title of "*worthy and independent freemen!*" – although your suffrages are not courted, and *nobility*, and *wealth*, and *respectability* disdain to take you by the hand once in seven years, yet you are *something* while you have *anything* . . . You are *something*, you are indeed; and although few dare tell you what you are, you must perceive yourselves to be "*slaves, on whose chains are inscribed the words liberty and freedom!*" SLAVES? Englishmen Slaves? You are startled, and well you may be, but it should be at your *condition*, and not at the proclamation of it. Look around you. Do, I beseech you, make use of your eyes. (Wooler, "Address to the Unrepresented Part of the Community," 1818)[25]

In substituting the division between corruption and its victims for that between the whig and tory parties, the radical press appealed beyond the crown and parliament to the people, and tried to align itself with popular opinion. Just what the claim that "the sovereignty is in the People" (*CL* 6 [1819], 88) meant for a radical writer or editor was, however, a complicated affair, as recent accounts of the strength and organization of popular loyalist sentiment in this period have demonstrated.[26] The radical press was by no means sure of popular support for reform, nor of its own relationship with the support that existed. As Victor Kiernan has written, even Cobbett, who felt "more confidence in his public than most of the popular leaders," had "misgivings, and was not always . . . hopeful."[27] Like corruption, public opinion often led radical argument to despair, or to deviations from the public sphere as an instrument of reform. The tone of Wooler's "Final Address" to his readers in the last volume of the *Black Dwarf* was particularly dark: "In ceasing his political labors, the Black Dwarf has to regret one mistake, and that a serious one. He commenced writing under the idea that there was a PUBLIC in Britain, and that public devotedly attached to the cause of parliamentary reform. This, it is but candid to admit, was an error" (*BD* 12 [1824], v). This despair was partly a function of the decline in popular unrest by the mid-1820s, but it would be a mistake to see a negative radical sense of public opinion as a terminal position, reached after "the heroic age of popular Radicalism" had come to a close. The radical press was from the outset saturated with distinctions among publics, peoples, and opinions, as it struggled with its enemies over control of these empowering terms. "When we speak of the public, we must of course be understood to exclude those who hold places under the host of corruption, and those who are waiting to fill them" (*BD* 2 [1818], 179); "When I say *people*, I mean they who are employed in useful labour. All beyond these form the scum and disease of human society and have no just claim to count as a part of the people" (*R* 12 [1825], 255). The radical belief that corruption had thoroughly infiltrated civil society meant that the press and opinion were no longer counterposed to the absolutist state, as in the classical bourgeois public sphere, but were instead divided between a corrupt state and the advocates of reform.

Historians and social theorists have recently treated the concept of the public with some skepticism. In a revisionist account of French Revolutionary ideology, François Furet has argued that the notion of "the people" was not "a datum or a concept that reflected existing society," but rather "the Revolution's claim to legitimacy," a necessary "founding principle, which it was nonetheless impossible to embody."[28] We need to be cautious about translating this claim across the channel and into the nineteenth century, in part because English radicals seem to have shared some of Furet's skepticism about the people, and about revolution. The radical reform movement was not deeply committed to an abstract concept of the popular will, and instead used the social fissures that followed from corruption as a way to account for troubling

intended as a remedy

gaps between the people as principle and as datum. Radical ideology was, furthermore, remedial rather than foundational or revolutionary, in part because the movement confronted a state that also claimed to represent public opinion, and that had at its disposal sophisticated theories with which to justify such a claim. Radical appropriations of popular authority were temporary and contingent: print representations of opinion would restore the parliamentary representation of opinion. Wooler's remarkable "Address to the Unrepresented Part of the Community," quoted at the beginning of this section, appeared during a period when the *Black Dwarf* was closely tracking parliamentary elections and encouraging public meetings. Within the "Address," the impossibility of embodying popular opinion was not a troubling (and therefore suppressed) lapse in radical democratic theory, but a historically specific condition open to ironic and polemical treatment. The writer's bold "proclamation" did try to redeem the unrepresented from their "insignificance," and make "*something*" out of "nothing." But the "unrepresented" were rhetorically transformed from an inert and objective "they" into a sentient and conscious "you" in order to demonstrate their continued insignificance in the only representational sphere that finally mattered: "The elections are just concluded! What have you been doing? Nothing. You have nothing to do" (*BD* 2 [1818] 417). In English radical hands, the French revolutionary substitution of language for power remained partial and provisional.[29] Wooler's authority was limited, and his project in the "Address" was necessarily "difficult" and ironic: he could exhort the fellow slave to self-consciousness and even significance, but the practical formation of a free citizenry required electoral mechanisms that exceeded radical argument.

Any account of the intersection of language and power in popular radical culture must begin with language in print, as technology and institution, since the movement rarely considered language in the abstract. The printing press was "perhaps the most prevalent icon of late eighteenth- and early nineteenth-century radicalism."[30] Reformers were convinced that the press necessarily promoted liberty and reform – "the *art of printing* from its *nature* bids *defiance* to tyranny" (*BD* 3 [1820], 853) – and in this sense endorsed what Michael Warner has called a "Whig-McLuhanite model of print history," which tends to convert "the political history of a technology . . . into the unfolding nature of that technology."[31] Without disputing Warner's incisive critique of the way technological determinism eclipses politics and human agency, I want to suggest that popular radicalism was a special instance of the case. The liberating role of the press was for reformers so deeply contested, and so clearly bound up in an ongoing political history, that a complacent and honorific whig (or liberal) attitude became untenable. The progressive vocation of print was denied at every turn by those who believed that "the licentiousness of the press" was "the source of every evil," and were prepared to legislate on that conviction.[32] Confidence in a free press became a frankly polemical position, directed against the government's confidence in press restrictions, and its use of print as an instrument for resisting social change.[33]

The radical movement divided its time between confident assertions of the liberating role of the press and desperate calculations as to how it had been lost. "Though the corrupt and ignorant dread the existence of a free press, they feel no hesitation in converting it into an engine to serve their own purposes," Cobbett complained, "It is even a matter of doubt, whether the art of *printing* has not become a greater *curse* than it ever was a *blessing*" (*CPR* 25 [1814], 207–08). This notion of "converting" or "perverting" was a frequent theme in radical discourse, and, while it preserved a remnant of determinism, since there was a technological essence to be distorted, it also insisted that "the unfolding nature" of the technology, to return to Warner's terms, was inseparable from an ongoing "political history." Cobbett undertook to write that political history in his 1818 essay, "On the Corruption of the English Press." His narrative distinguished "two branches: the means by *Corruption* and the means by *Persecution*" (*CPR* 33 [1818], 679), and thus anticipated recent accounts of the British government's "carrot and stick" approach to press management.[34] In this period, the repressive stick involved two principal mechanisms, trials for seditious and blasphemous libel, and taxes meant to inflate the price of political news and restrict its circulation. The misleading carrot, in Cobbett's view the more subtle and insidious "means," had long involved direct party and government subsidies of the political press; under an extended radical understanding of corruption, it came to include as well a broad array of official and quasi-official methods of securing popular consent, ranging from provided education and bible societies to loyalist festivals and anti-French propaganda. The radical experience of these "means" tended to confirm even as it undermined the liberating role of print, for it stood to reason that the government would not attack an innocent technology. Prosecution for seditious or blasphemous libel became an *imprimatur* of opposition, the official acknowledgment of a discursive challenge. Again, a radical teleology of print tended to be more strenuous than its providential whig counterpart. Ominous enough in itself, Hazlitt's historical claim that the French Revolution was "a remote but inevitable result of the invention of the art of printing" (*CWH* 13: 38) acquired a more contemporary inflection when delivered by Richard Carlile, in an essay comparing unrest in Spain with "the late massacre at Manchester": "At a moment of convulsion every person capable of wielding a pike or a gun should immediately prepare themselves, and organize their movements with their neighbours . . . The whole of Europe appears in a state that was never before witnessed. The philosopher might have contemplated such a state by the progress of the Printing Press" (*R* 2 [1820], 433–34). Far from suppressing catastrophic outcomes and more violent modes of historical agency, Carlile's account linked the teleology of print with popular organization and armed insurrection.

The recognition (and experience) of press corruption went a long way towards discouraging strictly determinist attitudes: attention shifted from the nature of the technology to the conditions under which it developed. The result was evident in the *White Hat*'s account of the unstamped weekly pamphlet, a format developed by the radical movement in order to evade newspaper taxes: "The invention of printing itself scarcely did more for the diffusion of knowledge, and the enlightening of the mind than has been effected by the cheap press of this country. Thanks to Cobbett! The commencement of his two-penny register was an era in the annals of knowledge and politics, which deserves eternal commemoration" (*WH* 1 [1819], 66). The celebratory tone of a techno-determinist account remained, but new determinants were taken into account. To equate the appearance of the unstamped weekly, which made political news regularly available to working-class readers for the first time, with "the invention of printing itself" was to give factors like legal restriction, economic organization, and methods of circulation their due weight. Interestingly, the same radical innovations that motivated this account in the *White Hat* also forced conservative observers to reject technological determinism, and to develop their own narratives of corruption and perversion. When Robert Southey wanted to argue that "the press, like all other powerful engines, is mighty for mischief as well as for good," he turned for evidence to the "inflammatory harangues" that were "sold through the manufacturing districts at a halfpenny or penny each," and to parliamentary speeches that were "reported in a condensed shape" and distributed in the street (*EMP* 1: 135).

Radical writers and editors treated the press as an institution as well as a technology, and here we might invoke the notion of a "fourth estate" as an enshrined model of institutional organization. Its potential relevance to radical practice is confirmed by the *OED*, which finds an early version of the phrase in Hazlitt's remark that Cobbett was "a kind of *fourth estate* in the politics of the country" (*CWH* 8: 50).[35] Yet, as with technological determinism, some important qualifications are in order. George Boyce has shown how the idea of the press as fourth estate emerged in the early nineteenth century as a consoling "political myth" that offered "the legitimate press" a privileged role in an ideal state: "The press would act as an indispensable link between public opinion and the governing institutions of the country." This myth lifted respectable newspaper writers and editors from the low esteem in which they were generally held, and distinguished their conciliatory role with respect to public opinion from the more aggressive mobilization of opinion by "the radical or 'pauper' press."[36] The radical movement was therefore the intended victim rather than beneficiary of a theory of the fourth estate. In addition, this legitimating myth encouraged a view of the press as an autonomous institution, a new "estate" that mediated existing constitutional terms. Radical reformers were too deeply interested in recovering the authority of the third estate to have much use for a fourth, and were too convinced of print corruption to see the press as an autonomous institution with a common professional interest. When "the London Press" failed to join his campaign against the press restrictions contained in the Six Acts, Wooler could only vent his bitter disappointment: "The EDITOR of the BLACK DWARF" had been "deprived of that co-operation and assistance which he was entitled to expect from the profession to which he belongs." Traces of corporate identity remained, for Wooler was convinced that "were the London Press but true to itself . . . all the new measures would be *derided*." However, the inherent condition of shared interest had been distorted beyond repair by editorial "cowardice, duplicity, meanness, and servility" (*BD* 3 [1819], 839). What finally emerged in radical discourse was a limited and provisional version of the fourth estate, compatible with the movement's remedial self-image: the oppositional press could provide a transitional instrument through which the people reclaimed the authority in the House of Commons denied them by corruption.

If the theory of the fourth estate was a vague and emerging myth, more palpable links between the press and the British constitutional state had developed through the long struggle over the right to publish parliamentary proceedings. Although formal prohibitions against parliamentary reporting were dropped in 1771, a full and accurate account was

still a long way off, and the contest extended well into the nineteenth
century.[37] Cobbett played a pivotal role in the later phases of this history.
His *Parliamentary History of England*, begun in 1806, is now regarded as one
of the most reliable accounts of the period before the nineteenth
century,[38] and his *Parliamentary Debates* (established in 1804 but then sold
to the printer in 1812) became *Hansard's Parliamentary Debates*, still today
the official record of parliament. Southey's anxiety about the cheap distribution of parliamentary debates "in a condensed shape" suggests how
the radical representation of parliament might play into the struggle
over reform. Again, radical intervention tended to generate ironies and
reversals that undermine any straightforward (whig) narrative of
progress in the history of parliamentary reporting. The right to publish
and read what took place in the House of Commons had by the early
nineteenth century been turned *against* the reform movement, as the
theoretical limit of democratic development. The tory press learned to
answer radical attacks on corruption with the argument that parliamentary publication was a sufficient concession to extra-parliamentary
opinion, one that more than offset any advances in ministerial patronage.[39] The whig *Edinburgh Review* also treated the publication of debates
as a "democratical" accommodation that dictated against radical
demands for universal suffrage (*ER* 31 [1818], 176). The popular radical
press answered this attempt to make parliamentary reporting the limit of
reform by exceeding the new limit. After he turned a full report of
debates over to Hansard, Cobbett launched a short-lived *Parliamentary
Register* in 1820, and claimed the advantage of editorial intervention: the
"immense mass of *informal* and *casual talk*" would be excised, and notes
would be added "in order to explain things not familiar to every one,"
and to clarify "*facts*" on which "Members of Parliament are not always
infallible" (*CPR* 36 [1820], 679). Thomas Dolby's *Parliamentary Register*
(1819) grafted a similarly abbreviated record onto the two-penny weekly
format, so as to place those "with limited pecuniary means" in a position
"to read, and to decide upon the propriety of, what is said and done by
their betters." Dolby figured his editorial labor in terms that justified
Southey's anxiety about the "condensed" publication of debates:
"When it so happens that I must either give my readers a whole sheet of
verbosity or cut my way through with a pruning knife, I certainly shall
adopt the latter alternative."[40]

Radical interventions in parliamentary representation extended well
beyond these printed reports of debates. In appealing from parliament
and the parliamentary classes to popular counter-authorities (opinion,

the people, the nation, the laboring classes), radical writers and editors developed print formats that deliberately emulated the conventions of the political establishment, thereby converting reading audiences into incipient constituencies. Cobbett filled the *Political Register* with public letters to electors that echoed the similar letters of candidates in contested elections, and then extended the challenge beyond the political nation in his celebrated Address "To the Journeymen and Labourers."[41] Wooler's insistence that legislative initiative had devolved upon the people culminated in his own parody of a candidate's address, the ominous "Address to the Unrepresented." Radical encyclopedias of corruption operated in a similar fashion, as a critical extension of the reports of parliamentary committees. Drawing its embarrassing disclosures "chiefly from PARLIAMENTARY DOCUMENTS," the *Red Book* sought "to diffuse amongst the people, that information, which has hitherto been confined to the table of the House of Commons," so that "the nation" could then pass judgment upon those who held "the reins of the government."[42] The radical catalogue of corruption became a satirical and potentially seditious distortion of parliamentary reporting. If the anti-reform press maintained that the publication of debates completed the circuit of "virtual" representation by linking the public with its representatives, the *Red Book* proved that such links had been corrupted beyond any repair short of radical reform. Parliamentary authority was undermined rather than assisted by the political discourse of the radical press. In 1818, under conventional newspaper headings like "Parliamentary Proceedings," Wooler began to allude ominously to members of the House of Commons as "our self-denominated *representatives*" (*BD* 2 [1818], 85); having made political representation a self-contained procedure, he soon found that the people could stand on their own as well, and in late 1818 and 1819 replaced parliamentary reporting in the *Black Dwarf* with the "Proceedings of the People" at radical meetings (*BD* 3 [1819], 113), while at the same time promoting a radical scheme for electing "legislational attorneys" to be sent to parliament on behalf of the unrepresented. This provocative gesture verged on sedition, and Wooler was soon indicted along with Major Cartwright and others for his involvement in a Birmingham meeting that chose to send Sir Charles Wolseley to parliament.[43]

Wooler's explosive endorsement of extra-parliamentary deliberation did not eliminate a role for himself and the *Black Dwarf*. As his participation in the Birmingham meeting suggested, he was firmly embedded in the culture of public assembly and the radical "mass platform" that dominated the years 1817 through 1819.[44] Indeed, radical weeklies like the *Black Dwarf* served the reform movement in something like the capacity that parliamentary reporting served the state, linking leadership and constituency through reports of public meetings and assemblies. In this sense, periodical forms provided a kind of "weak organization."[45] John Brewer provides a conceptual framework for understanding this organization when he traces the history of an "alternative structure of politics" in Britain. This alternative political "infrastructure" of organizational and communicative resources, extending from London to the provinces and from the "parliamentary classes" to a growing "political nation," developed gradually over the course of the late eighteenth century, and was in place for the appearance of John Wilkes and a "focused radicalism" in the 1760s. "When the Wilkes affair became the predominant issue in politics it had a ready-made political organisation and culture to fall back on. Coffee houses, taverns, debating clubs, local papers and political societies, all took up Wilkes because he presented those who used such facilities with a golden opportunity to give point to their somewhat inchoate political aspirations."[46] By the early nineteenth century, this alternative political culture had been significantly reshaped. The most important development was its extension into the ranks of the disenfranchised working class: the "campaigning political journalism" of Cobbett and Wooler required "a new social class basis,"[47] and that class basis in turn yielded innovations in the style, format, and circulation of political publications. At the same time, the eighteenth-century coffee-house gave way to the tavern, to the plebeian debating club, and to the huge outdoor meetings associated with a radical "mass platform." As the bourgeois public sphere was assimilated to the constitutional state, it tended to abandon certain forms of political sociability and retreat to the virtual space of print, until it could be epitomized for Southey by the individual reader at his "breakfast table," absorbing a newspaper "while he sips his coffee" (*EMP* i: 120). A radical counterpublic, meanwhile, remained stubbornly active and physical, never confined to the printed page. Radical weeklies were saturated with speeches and debates, and with rich evidence of collective reading practices. Finally, the eighteenth-century interplay between the London and provincial press was enhanced, and to some extent overwhelmed, by the national circulation achieved by London papers like the *Political Register*, the *Examiner*, the *Black Dwarf*, and the *Republican*.[48]

While the radical press assumed a leading role in this alternative structure of politics, its sense of its own vocation remained stubbornly provisional and remedial. Parliamentary reform was the "one thing needful,"[49] and the counterpublic sphere a means to that end; fierce extra-parliamentary determination was oriented back towards parliament. This double movement, away from and back to a representative assembly, informed a wide range of radical ironies and contradictions in this period. Contested elections and parliamentary petitions, the two means of protest that offered direct access to the House of Commons, were demeaned in the radical press as often as they were endorsed, on the grounds that corruption had reduced them to a distracting farce.[50] Cobbett ruthlessly attacked a corrupt parliament only because he so fervently believed in a reformed one, and longed for the authority that awaited him there. It may not be surprising to find a reactionary radical like Cobbett arguing, in a letter emphatically written from *"exile"* in America, that his presence in the House of Commons would have "rendered '*Cheap* Publications,' and all publications, except a publication of the *Debates of Parliament*, wholly unnecessary" (*CPR* 33 [1818], 453, 455), but similar views extended to the movement's progressive and republican wing. Carlile was keenly aware that "an honest man in the House might produce ten times the effect to what he could with his pen out of the House" (*R* 2 [1820], 131), and, when he announced his decision to suspend the *Republican* in 1821, he cautiously suggested that reform was destined to dissolve the alternative structure of politics:

Under a reformed Parliament, the best place to promulgate correct principles would be in the Senate, and it would be almost sufficient for the Press to report correctly what passed. Additional arguments, for or against a particular object, would scarcely be necessary, as every thing relative to the interests and welfare of the society would be sure to find ample discussion in the proper quarter. (*R* 4 [1820], 616–17)

Unlike their romantic contemporaries and liberal successors, the unacknowledged legislators of radical reform did not disassociate power from politics, nor did they pretend that their own exclusion or exile was a source of strength. At the same time, the movement's investment in parliament as the final horizon of print authority served to limit any radical disparagement of the political press. The anxious qualifications with which Cobbett and Carlile issued their respective visions of a reformed polity – "all publications, except a publication of the *Debates of Parliament*," "almost sufficient for the Press to report correctly" – suggested that political representation would always be incomplete without some form of press intervention.

There were further ironies about radical opposition in print. Popular radicalism was associated with the rigorous accounting procedures of a descriptive theory of representation, according to which "the best Parliament would be a detailed, proportional rendering of English society."[51] The *Edinburgh Review* dismissed the radical project as "a representation, founded on numbers only" (*ER* 31 [1818], 186), and *Blackwood's* agreed that the movement would reduce MPs to "a reflecting mirror of the people they represent" (*BM* 8 [1821], 489). Strict descriptive representation was designed to close dangerous gaps in prevailing theories of interest representation and virtual representation, yet insofar as radical publicists were opponents of the present system rather than properly elected representatives, they could not help but violate their own descriptive principles. Given the hazards associated with the selection of "legislational attorneys" and the demand for a National Convention, the radical press did not always seek a direct route to the "one thing needful," nor did it consistently apply to politics the reductive minimalism of its linguistic theories.[52] Instead, radical discourse implicitly acknowledged that, until reform was achieved, the language of protest would have to assume representational status, in ways that were as vague and potentially coercive as anything the government had to offer. Cobbett ridiculed the prevailing account of parliamentary representation as a "doctrine of invisible influence, of effects without causes, and causes without effects" (*CPR* 15 [1809], 356), but he found similarly elusive authority for his own counter-representations. Confronted with disparaging remarks about radical organization in Westminster, he asked, "WHO it is that has written 'BURDETT FOR EVER' upon every wall and paling, not only in and about this immense metropolis: but in every city, town, village, and hamlet in the kingdom" (*CPR* 17 [1810], 874). When he himself later lost an election at Coventry in 1820, he blamed corruption, and produced anecdotal evidence of popular "acclamations" in order to claim the "representative" status denied him at the polls: "the words as well as actions of the mass of the people" were "clearly expressive of ardent attachment to the cause of which I was the representative" (*CPR* 36 [1820], 89). Even this meager evidence of graffiti or applause was superfluous when the sheer force of assertion became the groundwork for radical representation: the *Cap of Liberty* simply declared that "the radicals are the most numerous and most oppressed party in the nation" (*CL* 1 [1819], 149), and Henry "Orator" Hunt announced that "the people" had "all with one voice declared for *Universal Suffrage*."[53] These reckless substitutions of language for power, to return to Furet's terms, need to be understood as an oppositional strategy rather than a final theory of political representation. Cobbett's question, "WHO it is that has written," called attention to those who were presently confined to graffiti and other unofficial modes of political expression. When Wooler challenged one parliamentary "representative, as he calls himself," to justify his emphatic claim that "WE *do not want radical reform!*," and asked in turn, "Who are WE?" (*BD* 3 [1819], 679–80), he risked having the question turned on himself, and being required to account for the derivation of his own potent radical "we." The compensation for such a gambit was that, whatever its result, the limits of existing political representation would be exposed. The very possibility of ironic or dialectical play in the name of the people indicated that public opinion had at present no sure foundation. The radical movement was willing to expose fissures and inconsistencies in its own discourse because it was convinced that every existing political contradiction led back to corruption. Print opposition remained an unstable enterprise because public opinion belonged in the House of Commons.

BEYOND CORRUPTION: INDEPENDENCE, PERSONALITY, EGOTISM

Motivated equally by a suspicion of and desire for power, radical publicists developed a set of rhetorical and professional practices meant to engage corruption while warding off its dangerous influence. Popular radical leadership in the press should be understood as a distinct intellectual formation, in pursuit of "the paradoxical synthesis of the opposites of retreat and engagement" that Pierre Bourdieu has described as characteristic of the history of intellectuals.[54] For the early nineteenth-century radical writer and editor, this unstable synthesis necessarily began at the pole of autonomy or political "independence," a keyword borrowed from the lexicon of parliamentary politics, where it had long indicated characteristics like non-partisanship, local autonomy, the refusal of ministerial favor, and the possession of economic means.[55] Declarations of independence in the radical press were, then, themselves a form of political appropriation, a claim upon, as well as a claim against, established powers. Radical autonomy contained within itself the whole anxious synthesis of autonomy and engagement.

The most disruptive implication of radical independence was its challenge to the intersection of property and power, a chief obstacle to the extension of political suffrage.[56] If the effort "to take politics out of doors – to involve 'the people' without distinction of 'property' or 'intelligence'" was "the real hinge of radicalization" in the early nineteenth century,[57] then the leading rhetorical and conceptual tools in such a campaign were a set of redefinitions of independence that severed its classical republican links with property, especially landed property, while preserving its empowering consequences for (male) political participation and public personality. Though sometimes ironic or covert, in the manner of print incursions on parliamentary privilege, these redefinitions could also involve direct interventions in the political theory of representation. In one of the Black Dwarf's letters to his imaginary Japanese correspondent, boldly titled "The superior virtue of the 'LOWER ORDERS,'" Wooler reversed the connection between independence and property, and dismantled at a stroke the existing monopoly on political rights:

Whence comes it . . . that the more independent a man is said to be in point of fortune, the more servile he becomes to any system under which he lives? It is singular that wealth, which is sought after as the means of liberty, should operate in so singular a method to promote slavery; and yet it is true, that cowardice and servility are the general characteristics of the rich. (*BD* 3 [1819], 415)

The attack on the dependence of "tradesmen" and "the middle classes" (415–16) that followed involved a fairly conventional critique of mobile property, but, rather than reverting to real property, Wooler went on to appropriate independence and "republican virtue" for the "LOWER ORDERS." The lack of property, long taken to indicate exposure to influence, became in the context of modern corruption a sign of victimization, and a spur to resentment and political virtue:

The culpable negligence of the *middle orders* has already reduced the "*lower classes,*" to the lowest state of poverty and distress. By their station in society, and their accustomed interference in public affairs, the great bulk of society left its interests in their hands. This trust has been violated. Stimulated by an extremity of distress which admits of no argument, and convinced that no voice but their own would be raised in their favor, the mass of society now begins to speak for itself. The courage and firmness of poverty bids fair to accomplish, what education and wealth have been unable, or unwilling to perform. (416)

Poverty replaced property as the foundation of virtue, allowing "the great bulk of society" to assume political rights and a mature political personality ("courage and firmness") by virtue of rather than despite "their station in society."

Wooler drew strength here from a widespread tendency among radicals since the late eighteenth century to revisit Locke's derivation of labor from property, and to derive political independence from the

capacity to labor.[58] Cobbett, a leading voice in this campaign, was prepared to agree with Lord Holland that "*property* was . . . the *basis* of representation," on the condition that "labour is property," and "not only
property in itself; but . . . the *sole foundation* of all that is called real property" (*CPR* 38 [1821], 173–75).[59] The effects of such interventions in the
history of political thought were typically ambiguous. The radical movement was true to a classical republican tradition, in that it tried to escape
the instability associated with mobile property (mediation, representation, exchange) by anchoring independence in the material world. Yet
the new material foundation was a process ("labour") or an experience
("poverty and distress") rather than a product ("property"). Indeed, the
return to Locke and to labor was meant to demonstrate that landed
property could not be treated as an unmediated foundation for political
personality. At the same time, radical theory often invoked the
eighteenth-century commercial revisions of a classical tradition that
tended to abstract or psychologize independence; thus Wilkite radicalism democratized political independence by making it "to some extent a
matter of choice."[60] Even Cobbett, the inveterate materialist, appreciated the tactical benefits of a more idealized approach to political rights,
and challenged readers of every class to decide for themselves whether
to submit to corrupt influence. His 1812 letter "To the Independent
Electors of Bristol" insisted that "money and land" were an insufficient
guarantee of political autonomy: "Independence is in the mind" (*CPR*
22 [1812], 193).

The classical republican tradition had derived from property not only
independence, but the very possibility of personal autonomy and a stable
identity.[61] For this reason, the radical redefinition of independence had
to rethink personality, particularly as it was a feature of public discourse.
Michael Warner has argued that the problem of political personality in
eighteenth-century America was addressed through a "negation of
persons in public discourse": individual citizens became the abstract, disembodied subjects of a universal and typically anonymous discourse.[62]
This kind of republican "negativity" made some inroads among early
nineteenth-century English reformers. Writers and editors sometimes
concealed their personal identity (Leigh Hunt's indicator sign, Wooler's
Black Dwarf), and readers signed their letters with conventional pseudo-
nyms. But radical political culture in early nineteenth-century Britain
was not by and large a culture of anonymity. The bold signature,
"William Cobbett of Botley," was more typical, and signed articles and
letters appeared regularly in *Sherwin's Political Register*, the *Black Dwarf*, the

Republican, the *Cap of Liberty*, and the *Newgate Monthly Magazine*. The title page of the first volume of the *Black Dwarf* (Figure 1) suggests that the devices of anonymity had become merely formal: the brief "Prospectus" that introduced the editor's alter ego appeared beneath the bold announcement that the periodical was conducted "BY T. J. WOOLER." British politics had long treated personality as a qualification for political leadership as well as for the franchise, and radicals were eager to join an established order of personal politics.[63] Foxites and Pittites found themselves challenged by Wilkites, Painites, Cobbettites, and Spenceans; ministerial feuds between Canning and Castlereagh were matched by radical feuds between Cobbett and Wooler, and between Carlile and Henry Hunt. Anonymity was, furthermore, associated with a secretive, conspiratorial form of resistance that most radical leaders were eager to throw off, in favor of an open and accountable reform movement that would be less vulnerable to the intervention of spies.

Even Richard Carlile, a disciple of Paine whose discursive practices sometimes approached Warner's republican negativity, launched the *Republican* with an address "To the Public" that rejected anonymity in print:

> The editor, impressed with the importance of the moment, has resolved, that no correspondence or essays be admitted into the pages of the *Republican*, unless accompanied with the real name and address of the author. In doing this, he is aware that he will exclude much talent, but the necessity of every man making a frank and candid avowal of his principles and sentiments at the present moment, far exceeds any other feelings that may be put in competition with it. He hopes that there are to be found in the country, men, not only of talent, but with sufficient property and virtue to render them men of importance and weight in society, who dare openly avow what they think necessary to be done. Most periodical publications of the day, are filled with anonymous essays, correspondence and information on various subjects, which are as many proofs of a degree of talent existing in the country, equal, or superior, to any former period; but, it cannot be denied, that those essays, &c. would produce more effect and conviction, were they signed by some individual, whose motives and moral character are unimpeachable. (*R* 1 [1819], 1–2)

Though he soon discovered the "difficulty of getting Correspondents to sign their names and addresses" under repressive conditions, and had to drop the policy, Carlile continued to prefer signed correspondence (*R* 2 [1820], 36). The letters that appeared in the *Republican* were distinctly mixed: some readers preferred anonymity, but others proudly identified themselves as individuals willing to endorse (and in the case of subscription lists, even finance) a project officially deemed blasphemous.[64]

THE

BLACK DWARF,

A London Weekly Publication.

BY T. J. WOOLER.

Satire's my weapon, but I'm too discreet
To run a muck and tilt at all I meet,
I only wear it in a land of Hectors,
Thieves, Supercargoes, Sharpers, and directors.
Pope.

VOL. I.—1817.

Prospectus.

It may be required of us to declare whether the Black Dwarf emanates from the celestial regions, or from the shades of evil—whether he be an European sage, or an Indian savage—whether he is subject to the vicissitudes of mortality, or a phantom of the imagination—in what shape he appears, by what authority he presumes to write—what object he has in view, and whether his designs are wicked or charitable. In answer to all these probable topics of enquiry, our simple reply is, that we are not at liberty to unfold all the secrets of his prison-house, to ears of flesh and blood. We have, besides, no wish to perplex the mind, or draw too largely upon the faith of the enquirer. Were we to state what he is, the infallibility of the pope, the miracles of Mahomet, and all the wonders that wantoo fancy ever drew, would appear probable and consistent to the story we should unfold. But these disclosures we must reserve, until better times ensure the civil treatment of so singular a stranger.

In the interim, however, the Black Dwarf will not be idle. He intends to expose every species of vice and folly, with which this virtuous age, and enlightened metropolis abounds. To political delinquency he will give no quarter, even if royalty were to sanction it by private favors and reward it with public honors. He will shew no mercy to spiritual imposition, even though decorated with lawn. Neither the throne, nor the altar, will be a sanctuary against his intrusion. Secure from his invisibility, and dangerous from his power of division, (for like the polypus,

he can divide and redivide himself, and each division remain a perfect animal) he will be engaged at the same instant, in listening for evil at the portals of the temple, under the canopy of the throne, and in the gallery of the lower house; in weighing the patriotism of our patriots; in comparing the disinterested independence of our journalists; besides the stranger occupation of seeking for honesty in the mazes of the law, and humility on the bench of bishops.

The lighter and more agreeable business of the Black Dwarf, will be a survey of the drama, and the literary world in general; to foster genius, and chastise impudence; to encourage the modest, and prune the luxuriance of the redundant fancy; in short to exhibit, unbiassed by the spirit of any party, a correct reflection of merit in the mirror of impartial criticism.

To fools, and to men of sense, the Black Dwarf hopes to be equally agreeable; the former will imagine they understand him when they do not; and the latter will be able to comprehend more than he seems to utter. To the ministry and the opposition he may be equally serviceable, by teaching the latter to begin, where they leave off, and the former how dangerous it is to oppose the progress of a deluge. A well-wisher to all, but an unsecurity friend, the Black Dwarf will readily hold up a glass, in which no honest man need be ashamed to look, and every fool and knave may readily trace his resemblance.

LONDON:

PRINTED AND PUBLISHED BY T. J. WOOLER, 58, SUN STREET.

1817.

Figure 1   Title page, *Black Dwarf*, volume one (London: T. J. Wooler, 1817)

Carlile's initial account of his editorial policy ranged widely in its search
for the theoretical underpinnings of political personality, supplementing
an anti-aristocratic idiom of "talent" with a classical republican sense of
"property and virtue." It moved beyond both property and talent when
Carlile invoked "the importance of the moment" to explain his demand
for a "real name and address." Radical identity in print was acutely situated and oppositional; precipitated by a vivid sense of "present" crisis,
personality would "dare openly avow" what was "necessary to be done,"
in order to "produce" an "effect." If independence was now a matter of
choice, the choice was made under political pressure. Carlile's rejection
of anonymity in the *Republican* was followed immediately by the first of
his "CRISIS" essays, which lost no time identifying the event behind a
present "necessity": "The massacre of the unoffending inhabitants of
Manchester, on the 16th of August, by the Yeomanry Cavalry, and
Police, at the instigation of the Magistrates, should be the daily theme of
the press" (*R* 1 [1819], 3). In the framework of a physical struggle
between popular unrest and government repression, the disembodied
personality described by Warner would have proved disabling. The
negativity of popular radical discourse was a negativity of resistance, not
abstraction.

Far from denying themselves in print, radical writers and editors
maintained that repression forced them to cut a public figure. Wooler's
article, "Danger of Public Writers. Arrest of the Editor," indicated how
prosecution for seditious libel had thrust him into prominence:

It is not often that the private concerns of any individual are of sufficient importance to justify any communication of them to the public, but there are occasions on which the principles which regulate our conduct, may render a
circumstance important, that otherwise might be passed over in silence, and
consigned to a merited oblivion. It has not been the practice of the Editor of the
Black Dwarf, to preach himself, but his country; and when the principles upon
which he has vindicated what he has deemed the interests of his country, are
attacked, he is proud to be the medium of hostility, which is not so much
directed against himself, as the cause that he has espoused. (*BD* 1 [1817], 225)

A "proud" radical publicist was the effect of a determined language of
resistance meeting an equally determined machinery for policing the
public sphere. The personality that accompanied the signature of this
article, "T. J. Wooler," was suspended between opposing forces. Yet the
caution evident in this account of self indicates that Wooler knew he was
negotiating difficult terrain. A later *Black Dwarf* article condensed the
contradictions associated with radical "egotism" or "vanity" in the form

of an oxymoron, when it referred to the "democratic celebrity" of imprisoned radical writers and leaders (*BD* 5 [1820], 288). Prosecution forced Wooler to insert "self" into a "cause" that preferred principle and democratic organization to individual ambition. His response normally included both self-effacement and qualified self-promotion: "The result of these trials will be remembered and their consequences felt when the Editor sleeps in the dust. His name is now identified with the liberty of the press; and it is not without vanity that he feels he has rendered it some service" (*BD* 1 [1817], 308). The decision to identify himself in such episodes as "Editor" rather than author was significant. Radical discourse in this period tended to construct the prominent self in print around "the practice of the Editor," printer, or publisher, a set of functions that extended outward more readily than authorship to a community of readers, and to collective institutions like "the press." Wooler the "public writer" presented himself as a "*medium*" rather than an original source of "hostility," and preferred critical intervention to authorial invention.[65]

It would be a mistake simply to resolve the contradictions associated with "democratic celebrity," or to dismiss radical egotism as the regrettable consequence of individual dispositions (Cobbett's vanity, Carlile's pride). Instead, these contradictions need to be understood as a central feature of the language and practice of a radical counterpublic sphere. Richard Carlile was less cautious than Wooler in his approach to the problem:

I am so certain, that I am advocating the very best principles that can tend to bring about free discussion, to increase the happiness of mankind, and to give them lofty ideas as to equality and individual importance, that I might have been too apt to give myself airs of importance, in associating myself with those principles; but, so enamoured am I with what I am doing with those principles, that I am fired with jealousy and indignation at the least disparagement of self, because, I feel that self and principles are as near alike as any individual can be associated with any principles . . . I am, in my own judgment at the very acme of that which is right, best, and of the most importance, in a political point of view. (*R* 11 [1825], 165)

Far from suppressing inconsistency, Carlile deliberately fused "self and principles," and allowed his expansive "I" to emerge on a field of democratic ambition. His vanity would lift individuals from their subjection to existing hierarchies, and "give them lofty ideas as to equality."[66] This levelling hubris encouraged conflict, "fired" as it was "with jealousy and indignation," and confirmed the role of personal independence in

political resistance. The boundaries of the ego became a final barrier
against invasive corruption. It was on these terms that Hazlitt refused to
submit to the post-war resurrection of divine-right government that he
called "Legitimacy":

The plague-spot has not tainted me quite; I am not leprous all over, the lie of
Legitimacy does not fix its mortal sting in my inmost soul, nor, like an ugly
spider, entangle me in its slimy folds; but is kept off from me, and broods on its
own poison. He who did this for me, and for the rest of the world, and who
alone could do it, was Buonaparte. He withstood the inroads of this new
Jaggernaut, this foul Blatant Beast, as it strode forward to its prey over the bodies
and minds of a whole people . . . He, one man, did this. (*CWH* 7: 10–11)

Hero worship merged with outrageous personal pride, as the writer
made the integrity and energy of the great man available to himself and
"the rest of the world." Where independence was in the mind, political
virtue required neither property nor inherited privilege. The energy and
decision of the radical personality were themselves sufficient to resist
corruption.

   Radical egotism was as contradictory in its rhetorical and political
effects as in its premises. David Vincent has argued that a personal voice
in the radical prose of this period "served three broad functions": it provided a "transition from oral to literate modes of forming political
opinion," a "convincing and easily recognisable" source of authority,
and a more accessible political realm.[67] Craig Calhoun agrees that personal leadership fostered a sense of radical intimacy, particularly as the
movement expanded beyond "immediate social relations" to "a national
frame of reference," but he warns that leaders risked encouraging a
"dependant attitude" among their supporters.[68] The vanity of men like
Carlile, Cobbett, Henry Hunt, and Hazlitt was not always as compatible
with democracy as they wanted to believe. The propagation of "lofty
ideas as to equality" could be obstructed by the self-involvement of a
leader who put himself "at the very acme of that which is right." E. P.
Thompson's *Making of the English Working Class* anxiously relates on
almost every page how vexed a problem radical leadership became.
Organization suffered as leading individuals clashed among themselves,
and issued conflicting directives about matters of strategy. Fulsome
praise for an "intrepid, indefatigable, and consistent leader" or a
"Heroic Champion of Liberty" became a tiresome feature of radical
discourse.[69] Some form of individual leadership was no doubt necessary
if reformers were to challenge dominant structures, and Calhoun plaus-
ibly faults popular radicalism for an *exaggerated* "concern for democratic

form."[70] Yet radical egotism narrowed the movement's political base, and exposed it to criticism from without. Tory attacks often exposed the reform movement's hierarchical structure, and then traced popular unrest "to the machinations of a comparatively small number of individuals."[71] Radical leaders learned to anticipate such critiques by linking national leadership with democratic organization. When parliament refused to accept printed petitions for reform, Wooler championed Cartwright's "New Mode of Petitioning," which provided a model "form" that individuals and groups could then transcribe and adjust to "*local* circumstances" (*BD* 1 [1817], 449–54).[72] This may have been an awkward attempt to negotiate the claims of the local and the national, of writing and print, but it reflected Wooler's keen awareness of the contradictory premises of radical organization.

Attacks on reform agitation as the work of "a comparatively small number of individuals" showed how the movement's internal tensions emerged in dialogue with the logic of repression. Legal controls on the press were, as Donald Thomas has argued, instrumental in the development of a politics of personality. "In the early years of the nineteenth century individuals showed themselves far more litigious in matters of personal defamation than they had ever been before. As if to fall in with the general trend, political criticism tended more and more to involve the denigration of an individual."[73] Lord Ellenborough established the legal principle by which power circulated around individual personality in his instructions to the jury at Cobbett's 1804 trial for a libel on the Lord-Lieutenant of Ireland: "It has been observed, that it is the right of the British subject to exhibit the folly or imbecility of the members of the government. But, gentlemen, we must confine ourselves within limits. If, in so doing, individual feelings are violated, there the line of interdiction begins, and the offence becomes the subject of penal visitation."[74] This "line of interdiction" made "individual feelings" the "limit" of political criticism, in much the same way that radicalism made personal independence a buffer against corruption. Cobbett's response was as influential in radical discourse as the edict itself was in the courts. In a series of 1808 articles on the law of libel and free expression, he reprinted Ellenborough's decision, and warned that it would submerge all political criticism in an official rhetoric of praise. His counter-definition of the freedom of the press made personality the center, not the limit, of political criticism: "The liberty of the press . . . means a legal right, in any man, freely to examine, in print, into the character, talents, and conduct of any other man (especially if that other be in a public situation), and, if

he please, to censure or ridicule such character, talents, or conduct"
(*CPR* 14 [1808], 161–62, 427). The public sphere became an arena for
epic clashes between public men and public writers, a principle that
Cobbett raised to Blakean proportions over the next several years as he
forged a linked radical martyrology and corrupt demonology.[75] The supposed immunity of public officials to criticism remained a reference
point for debates about the law of libel and the rights of the press right
up through the 1820s, in print and in the courtroom.[76] Radicals complained that Ellenborough's dictum did for the public sphere what
virtual representation did for parliament, divide political authority from
public opinion, and proposed an aggressively critical press as the only
way to break the dangerous self-involvement of those in power.

THE RADICAL PROFESSION AND THE "WHOLESALE TRADE OF SEDITION"

To exercise a negative or critical function with respect to power, the
radical press had to sustain its positive links with the people. The *Yellow
Dwarf* went so far as to make the very existence of public opinion depend
upon the criticism of individual ministers by individual writers: "Public
opinion can never exist as a power in a State, unless there exist also
persons who expose to hatred and contempt those Ministers and those
laws which they conceive to be detrimental to the interests of the community" (*YD*, no. 3 [1818], 19). To sustain political disaffection alongside
popular affiliation was a difficult task, since the independence and personal autonomy that enabled criticism also required professional self-
definitions that distinguished the writer from the community, and made
the press something more than a simple organ of existing opinion. The
courts again helped map the discursive terrain, since the same legal
machinery that protected ministers threw journalists into sharp relief:
the writer emerged as "public character" when he was subjected to
prosecution and imprisonment (*BD* 1 [1817], 315). If prison sentences
were designed to contain radical discourse, they could also be taken to
reinforce its claims on public opinion, since imprisoned writers came, in
Carlile's suggestive phrase, to serve "a sort of penal representation for
the whole" (*R* 12 [1825], 644).[77] But the term "public writer" was more
ambiguous than this representative formulation allowed, since it indicated a combative relationship with government ministers as well as an
expressive relationship with public opinion. "Public men" and "public
writers" were mutually constitutive. What the radical press gained in a

claim on the state it risked losing in a claim on the people. This was vividly demonstrated when Wooler tried to argue at his 1818 trial for seditious libel that he had done nothing more than exercise his "legitimate right" as "an independent public writer" (*VR* 37). In appropriating two key terms from the lexicon of the state, Wooler disclosed even as he denied subversive intent: the "public writer" borrowed the "legitimate" mantle of the post-Napoleonic state by claiming for himself the "independent" status of the enfranchised citizen and member of parliament. The Attorney General responded with a corrosive assault on the whole notion of public writing. "Any man, who gets a room as a printing place, or a pen and ink," could claim the position of "public writer," and the hollow authority that went with it: "I am sometimes astonished when I hear these opinions and declarations about public writers – one would suppose they were some peculiarly educated, established and authorized body of men, who had passed through some previous course of probation and examination and had a right to set themselves up as *censores morum* of public men" (*VR* 71–72).[78] This challenge was shrewdly pitched in terms of a professional credential. If Wooler responded by proving himself a member of a "peculiarly educated, established and authorized body of men," he risked sacrificing his popular affiliations. To make "public writing" a professional designation would be to disengage it from public opinion.

The professional status that might follow from independent practices became another site of radical contradiction. Professionalism appeared most often in radical discourse as an absence or a missed opportunity, as when Wooler complained that he had been "deprived of that co-operation and assistance which he was entitled to expect from the profession to which he belongs." The same corrupt practices that divided the public sphere, and undermined the collective status of the "fourth estate," also destroyed the possibility of a shared professional ethic among writers and editors. Ordinary journalists too often sacrificed their autonomy to become the willing "tools" and "puppets" of party and government. The reform movement was, furthermore, ideologically predisposed to suspect professional privilege, having long complained that the legal, clerical, and military professions were integrated into a network of dependent financial and political relationships. Radical antagonism to the older professions was summed up in the levelling rage of one popular republican toast: "Soldiers at the Plough, Parsons in the Mines, Lawyers at the Spinning Jenny, and Kings in Heaven" (*R* 7 [1823], 179).[79] Entrenched professional identity held little to attract a set of writers who saw their vocation as temporary and remedial rather than permanent and custodial. Specialization itself was an object of radical suspicion. Jon Klancher has shown how the increasingly institutionalized bourgeois public sphere of the romantic period left an older pattern of self-publication to be "taken over and reworked for a new audience" in the plebeian radical press.[80] Cobbett, Carlile, Wooler, Wade, and Hone all joined in their own persons some combination of the roles of writer, editor, printer, publisher, and bookseller. This feature of the production of radical discourse was both a utopian urge to preserve a sphere of unalienated periodical labor, and a pragmatic response to political repression. "The laws of England," Carlile complained, made it "difficult for a bold and honest man to find a bold and honest publisher," and "the only effectual way of going to work" was therefore "for every author to turn printer and publisher as well."[81]

Despite radical anti-professionalism, official challenges to the authority of the "public writer" could not be ignored, particularly when they were issued in the courtroom, which served as a theater for testing the viability of a radical politics in print. During Hone's three celebrated trials for blasphemous libel in 1817, John Hunt's *Yellow Dwarf* upheld the defendant's right to criticize the government on eminently professional grounds: "In society, a division of labour is always necessary. As every man for himself cannot undertake to collect the evidence on political questions, there must necessarily be a class of persons who undertake to collect the facts and arrange the arguments in such a shape, that others may speedily decide on them" (*YD*, no. 3 [1818], 19). This commitment to specialization, and its related distinction between public opinion and the "class of persons" who organize it, was strongest among middle-class radicals, but was by no means the exclusive province of the Hunt circle. Cobbett, Wooler, Carlile, and Wade were all eager to present themselves as experts. Radical professionalism struck its deepest roots in an anti-aristocratic language of merit and talent inherited from the dissenting tradition, and later associated with liberal professionalism, bureaucratic organization, and careers open to talent.[82] Contrary to its subsequent history in the Victorian state, early nineteenth-century radical talent was levelling, disorganized, and disruptive:

The great cause of alarm among our taskmasters, the borough-faction, last year is to be looked for in *the talent*, which appeared to rise spontaneously from the mass of society, at the magic freedom. The despots had fondly imagined they combined all the talent, as well as the power of the state; or, at least, if talent should spring up out of their ranks, it would be in such isolated instances, that they could buy it up from the public cause. The public meetings called last year convinced them to the contrary. A flood of intellect burst upon their terrified imaginations. (*BD* 2 [1818], 168)[83]

The effort to cultivate a revolutionary "flood of intellect" in the interests of parliamentary reform created awkward problems for a discourse premised on the identity of writer and reader. Periodicals like the *Black Dwarf*, the *Republican*, and the *Gorgon* were filled with the rhetoric of improvement, and some of Cobbett's most influential writing came in didactic works like *Cottage Economy* and the *Grammar of the English Language*. Without entering into the vexed problem of radical respectability, and the question of whether "improvement" necessarily involved assimilation to middle-class values at the expense of plebeian culture, I would suggest that the language of talent and improvement could remain oppositional.[84] An 1823 letter to the *Republican*, signed by "James Hall, Shoemaker, and James Glover, Journeyman Tailor," was a vivid case in point. Drawing on Cobbett's *Grammar*, these two working-class autodidacts launched a stinging attack on the prose and the intellect of the Bishop of Winchester, and then counterposed their own superior "TALENT" to the Bishop's hollow demand that men like themselves should "pay *respect to superior authority*" (*R* 8 [1823], 34–37).

Radical professionalism met another crux in the economic organization of the press. Historians have long argued that British journalism assumed its modern character as a profession in the early nineteenth century, and have focused in particular on the *Times* newspaper, which refused government subsidies and party patronage, and turned instead to advertising revenue in order to finance breakthroughs like the steam press and a wider reporting network. "The future," as one historian of the press puts it, "lay with advertising; it was by advertising alone that independence could be won."[85] Radical journalists shared the *Times'* disdain for patronage, but did not discover professional independence in the brave new world of commercial advertising; even the *Examiner*, one of the few radical organs that could have secured profitable advertisements, launched itself with the bold announcement that "NO ADVERTISEMENTS WILL BE ADMITTED" (*E*, no. 1 [January 3, 1808], 8).[86] The media historian James Curran, a leading critic of the way historians have tended to link independence with commercialization, suggests that the radical reliance on subscription revenue rather than advertising established an alternative model of political independence.[87] Radical editors positioned their enhanced critical faculties at the historical juncture between eighteenth-century patronage and nineteenth-century commerce. Though a powerful challenge to established and emergent models of the market political discourse, this third way was not entirely coherent, since it required that market forces be simultaneously displayed and suppressed. Radical editors insisted that a wide readership need not involve a sordid calculation of profits: "Our object is an extensive circulation," the *Gorgon* announced, "exclusive of all pecuniary advantage" (*G*, no. 1 [1818], 8). Yet the distinction between circulation and profit broke down as a free market in ideas became the proving ground for political principles. "The victory is mine," Carlile boasted to his nemesis John Stoddart, member of the Vice Society and editor of the ultra-tory *New Times*, "my shop will be open in Fleet Street when yours is shut" (*R* 5 [1822], 13). Radical editors like Cobbett, Hunt, Wooler, and Carlile sought and achieved a string of market successes, particularly after the introduction of the unstamped weekly in 1816. Despite the dampening effect of restrictive taxation and punitive fines for libel, radical weeklies became "pacesetters in terms of circulation for the newspaper press . . . during the first half of the nineteenth century."[88]

This commercial challenge did not go unnoticed. Market success became a point of attack for critics of reform, reinforcing the radical commitment to a limited professional ethos. At Cobbett's 1810 trial for libel, the Attorney General observed that "the publication proceeded" from the defendant, and that "whatever there arose from it of base lucre and gain accrued to him alone" (*CPR* 22 [1812], 74). The accusation haunted Cobbett, and two years later, on the occasion of his release from prison, he issued a vigorous professional apology under the title "English Liberty of the Press." This essay traced the Attorney General's accusation back to the resentment of patronized writers, "who notoriously use their pens and their pencils for pay, and who do not, like me, look for remuneration to the *sale* of their works to the public." These "vile wretches" wanted "to live by the press, but . . . did not possess the requisite talents to ensure success to their endeavours, and at the same time preserve their independence . . . Such men would naturally hate me" (*CPR* 22 [1812], 82–83). "Talent" here enabled "independence" under specific market conditions; writers and editors extricated themselves from political patronage, a debased "species of traffic" (83), by looking "to the *sale* of their works to the public." As Cobbett's apology for his own practices advanced, so too did his commitment to professional specialization. To dismiss "the fruit of . . . industry and talents" as "base lucre" was to condemn "those whose business it is to inform and instruct mankind" to "poverty," or to being regarded "as sordid and base hunters after gain" (83). Cobbett then produced an impressive pantheon of literary professionalism, including the figures of Milton, Swift, Addison, Pope, Locke, and Dr. Johnson. If he succeeded in distinguishing himself from the party hack, he risked losing an identification with his readers, who now figured as passive receptacles to be informed and instructed. Independence treated as a matter of choice may have been more inclusive than independence treated as a matter of property, but *professional* independence implied the uneven distribution of the capacity to choose. Those in the "business" of producing political discourse had more opportunity than most to display their integrity. When Cobbett did later accord his reader a choice, it was the considerably less heroic choice of the political consumer: "The article is offered to the public; those who do not choose to purchase let it alone" (85).

Thus far, Cobbett's essay was a frank defense of the free market in political ideas, a political version of what Raymond Williams has called "the professional ideology of the independent artist," who discovered freedom in the market and took "the market as a definition of his social province, his real social relations."[89] Radical professionalism risked a similar narrowing of its social relations, as those who refused corruption and undertook to "instruct mankind" allowed their "business" to divide them from less enlightened readers. Yet "English Liberty of the Press" contained important countervailing tendencies, motivated by Cobbett's general suspicion of commercial relations, and by his resistance to any narrow sense of his own social function. First in its full title ("English Liberty of the Press, As illustrated in the History of the Prosecution and Punishment of WILLIAM COBBETT of Botley"), and then in its closing subscription ("Botley, Wednesday, 15th July, 1812"), this spirited defense of freedom and mobility in the market was framed by self-presentations that securely placed the writer in a rural village, and in his other vocation as farmer and landowner. Increasingly refined professional definitions were punctuated by alternative appearances of Cobbett as father, husband, farmer, neighbor, and political leader: in one episode, he surfaced at a public meeting at the Crown and Anchor Tavern (92), in another, he was enthusiastically received by the residents of Botley after his release from prison (94). From the opening lines of the essay – "Look at the Motto! English reader, look at the Motto!" (65) – the alienating effects of a professional discourse were mitigated by the oral rhythms and direct address of Cobbett's prose. This sense of intimacy was reinforced at the end of the essay by a brief notice "To Correspondents," expressing the author's gratitude for "the numerous letters of congratulation that I have received upon my enlargement" (86–94). "Enlargement" was as much the theme of this essay as professional limitation. Radical discourse could no more be confined to the literary marketplace than to the prison.

The Attorney General's disparaging remark about "base lucre" was an early skirmish in what became a sustained assault on the economic foundations of the radical press. The enemies of reform attacked "the wholesale trade of sedition," reducing radical agitation to a sordid commercial enterprise; papers like the *Examiner* and the *Black Dwarf* were said to represent an "*under-press*, conducted by men alike bankrupt in fortune and in principle."[90] One way for the government to destroy this "*under-press*" was to close its already narrow profit margins. This was the logic of the Newspaper Stamp Duties Act of 1819, which raised the price of the unstamped weekly newspaper or pamphlet, the main periodical organ of radical reform, beyond the reach of many readers, and further required that printers and publishers surrender a bond, set at three hundred pounds for the London press. Parliamentary debates revealed that the latter provision was an attempt to extend into the public sphere the traditional property requirement for the franchise. Lord Liverpool defended the bond on behalf of the government: "It was not directed against the respectable body of booksellers and printers, but against those persons who had intruded themselves into that class, and who [had] neither property, respectability, nor responsibility" (*PD* 41 [1819–20], 1590–91). Radical editors and publishers could no longer expect to set themselves up on talent, a supportive reading audience, and a small investment in a hand-press. Speaking for the whig opposition in the House of Commons, James Mackintosh attacked the provisions of the bill, but invoked the more sophisticated terms of commercial society to reinforce its class logic. A policy of repression would effectively consign "the public journals" to men "of desperate poverty," willing to "brave all the penal statutes . . . enacted against them":

The present bill . . . was calculated to prevent any respectable tradesman from interfering with newspaper property. The emoluments derived from a successful newspaper attracted men of capital to engage in them. The possession of capital was in general a guarantee for the possession of respectability. Men of property had generally a regard to their character, and to the peace of society in which they had so deep an interest. (*PD* 41 [1819–20), 1543)

The reliable personality required for a leading role in the public sphere – "a high sense of honour, a strong feeling of personal independence, and a reliance on an unimpeached and unimpeachable character" (1543) – was in this whig analysis best secured by the implicit property requirement of a commercial marketplace, rather than the explicit one of repressive legislation.

Richard Carlile was the chief victim of the official assault on the economic foundations of the radical press, and his response to persistent legal harassment extended the debate about property in the public sphere. Convicted of blasphemous libel in 1819 for publishing *The Age of Reason* and *The Principles of Nature*, Carlile was fined £1,500 and sentenced to three years in prison, a term that was extended to six years when he could not pay the fines.[91] He continued to operate his publishing and bookselling operations from Dorchester Gaol, and the government, assisted by the Vice Society and Constitutional Association, continued to arrest a series of his shophands and publishers, including his wife and sister. In 1823, the Court of the King's Bench ordered the contents of his shop seized to cover subsequent fines, and proceeded to auction "only such Works as are not deemed libellous." The auction catalogue was an extraordinary record of the contemporary canon of radical freethought. Carlile printed it with obvious pride in the *Republican*, followed by his own "Observations on the Sale," in which he disputed the government's claim that radical reform posed a threat to property: "Who will ever again tell me that I ought to respect the property and expectations of the tithe and tax-eater, after the havoc they have made with mine?" (*R* 7 [1823], 240–48). Like Cobbett, Carlile made the attack on his work an occasion for a professional and commercial apology. With his financial accounts a matter of public record, he portrayed himself as a politically committed if commercially reckless entrepreneur, possessed of the explosive form of capital recorded in the court's auction catalogue:

It is well known, that, in [1819], my business, and consequently my receipts of money, went on increasing; but I never once thought of banking or saving money. As fast as money returned, it was due by anticipations and applied for new publications. Up to the moment of my going to trial, I had not put aside a single pound, for any contingency that might occur. I had accumulated a great stock of printed paper, which was as good to me as Bank Notes, whilst I had the shop to sell in, I may say, to the value of three thousand pounds or upwards. (*R* 7 [1823], 678)

Repeated prosecutions and the closure of his shop forced Carlile to turn for financial support from his "stock of printed paper" to the subscription funds set up to help him pay his legal fees, and by 1823 he admitted

that these subscriptions rather than the sale of his publications were his
"chief support" (*R* 7 [1823], 682). In the years that followed, he remained
a resourceful, if not an astute, entrepreneur, and developed a number of
expedients to remain solvent in the face of an ongoing campaign against
him, including a scheme to accept barter in lieu of cash (*R* 11 [1825], 53),
and a "Joint Stock Book Company" for funding cheap editions of radical
and infidel publications (*R* 12 [1825], 675–76).[92]

As Mackintosh and Carlile felt their way ahead to new markets in
political discourse, Robert Southey's 1817 essay "On the Rise and
Progress of Popular Disaffection" sought to escape the seditious commerce in letters by harkening back to a time "when literature was confined to colleges and convents." The political disaffection of many
readers could be traced to the financial dislocation of a few writers: "the
real motives of our present race of libellers" proceeded from "cupidity
or poverty acting upon minds which have long since emancipated themselves from all moral restraint." Southey found ample evidence "in the
case of one incendiary," Cobbett, whose personal involvement "in
unprofitable speculations and consequent debts" had driven him to take
"advantage of the general distress," and attempt to "bring about a
revolution":

> The general tendency of men who thus throw themselves upon the world to live
> by their wits is soon determined by the disappointment which they almost uni-
> versally experience at their outset; for disappointment brings with it discontent,
> which is the parent of disaffection; and envy, which the unsuccessful are too
> prone to entertain towards those who are more fortunate than themselves, is
> inseparable from hatred, and malice, and all uncharitableness. Thus it is that of
> mere men of letters, wherever they exist as a separate class, a large proportion
> are always enlisted in hostility, open or secret, against the established order of
> things. (*EMP* 2: 82–87)

Here a maligned literary pensioner, dismissed in the *Black Book* as a "poor
apostate" who traded "principle, consistency, and independence for a
paltry £300" (*BB* 78), issued his defense of the residual system of literary
patronage represented by "colleges and convents." The radical ethic of
autonomy could create "a separate class" of literary professionals only
by uprooting the political press from "the established order of things."
Compelled "to live by their wits" in the free market, England's "mere
men of letters," like Burke's "political men of letters" in France,[93] were
sure to descend the slippery slope from individual "disappointment" to
public "disaffection" and revolutionary desire.

In bringing the whole political history of mobility and its discontents to bear upon Cobbett's financial problems (which ended in bankruptc﹢ and the loss of his Botley farm), Southey grasped a distinctive feature of radical discontent in this period, particularly when he went on to link Cobbett's personal dislocation with his appeal to a "class" of readers similarly "removed from all . . . local and personal ties" by "the manufacturing system" (89–90).[94] Even where personal irresponsibility was evident ("I had not put aside a single pound, for any contingency"), radical writers and editors did not hesitate to trace their financial difficulties to the larger pattern of corruption and repression that divided "the people" from the government. If radical mobility sometimes anticipated the privileged detachment of the liberal intellectual (Wooler's elusive Black Dwarf, Leigh Hunt's intellectual Archimedes[95]), these writers more often derived their combative restlessness from physical deprivation (fines, imprisonment, taxation, bankruptcy), and treated their dislocation as a temporary, regrettable, and widely shared condition, rather than the permanent privilege of a social class or profession. Inspired by the speaking tours of Major Cartwright and "Orator" Hunt,[96] Cobbett made his circuitous *Rural Rides* a vivid performance of his own uprootedness, which was then reflected back to him in the countenance and condition of starving laborers, abandoned farms, and declining market towns. The aim was to restore himself and others to a fixed place in a rural social order. Cobbett's expert knowledge of the system and refusal to be a willing victim may have distinguished him from the great mass of the dispossessed, but the fundamental dynamic that generated critical perspective and oppositional interest was widely distributed. While other radicals travelled in different circles, they too derived popular affiliation from a shared sense of displacement. Hazlitt drew his Jacobin "pleasure of hating" from a sense that legitimacy had denied him and the nation a viable dissenting heritage, and Leigh Hunt dreamed of returning from politics to his true poetic vocation only after political injustice had been destroyed. By joining a wide range of injustices under the sign of "system," the radical critique of corruption encouraged writers like Cobbett, Wooler, Carlile, Hunt, and Hazlitt to identify their own oppositional interests, however anxiously and imperfectly, with those of the nation at large, and to stop just short of developing a full professional ethos. Independence, dislocation, and mobility became the foundation of all radical language and action, a precondition that allowed reformers to negotiate the vast, unstructured social space beyond the traditional political elite, and knit together a protest movement on a national scale.

)f reform met radical solidarity in opposition with a divi-
at contested the extent and the common character of
on. A "system of itinerant orators" could produce the
spread discontent, but nothing more.[97] The political
extent of protest informed the bewildering dialectic of
and containment that governed reform politics in early
nineteenth-century England: the radical movement tried to extend its
own range of expression and limit the contagious spread of corruption,
while the establishment tried to preserve its monopoly on national
organization and limit radical protest to a series of local aberrations.
The government's strategy of containment was most explicit in its
response to the "mass platform," particularly in the limits on mobility
imposed by the Seditious Meetings and Assemblies Act of 1819. A
Quarterly Review article explained the logic of restricting attendance at
public meetings to inhabitants of a given city or parish:

If it be the object of the new statute, in the first instance, to limit the number,
and provide for the decorum, of popular meetings, its next end, certainly, is to
give them a character of *locality*, by excluding from them all persons not connected with the vicinity in which they are held . . . The large meetings held
during the last year, consisted in a great measure of one and the same body of
persons, who, like a strolling company of actors, trudged from place to place,
every where repeating the same dull but mischievous farce. (*QR* 22 [1820],
539–40)[98]

This politics of "*locality*" was designed to impede the development of a
national political consciousness outside parliament, and to interfere with
the totalizing logic of a radical critique of system. Sensing the gathering
force of a reactionary assault on "itinerant" radicalism in the months
before the Six Acts, Wooler opened a Birmingham speech with a confession that he was "a stranger to the persons of the immense majority of
this assemblage," but then went on to recover the collective radical "we"
(in its most vivid, oral form) by insisting that he shared their victimization: "I hope I am not a stranger to the impulse which has called it
together – not a stranger to the spirit that pervades every man who is
now called upon to decide on one of the most important questions that
ever was agitated – the means of recovering a lost right, out of the hands
of our oppressors" (*BD* 3 [1819], 482). The successful introduction and
enforcement of the Six Acts brought with it a new political logic, which
was summed up in Cobbett's *Rural Rides*. Himself dispossessed, Cobbett
rode back and forth across the South of England in an effort to uncover
the dispersed and fragmented signs of popular dispossession, and to

organize dissent through intimate local assemblies and addresses rather than (now illegal) mass meetings.

COUNTERSYSTEM AND THE ENDS OF OPPOSITION

They who affect to head an opposition, or to make any considerable figure in it, must be equal, at least, to those whom they oppose . . . Every administration is a system of conduct: opposition, therefore, should be a system of conduct likewise; an opposite, but not a dependent system. (Bolingbroke, "On the Spirit of Patriotism," 1736)[99]

May Revolutions never cease until Tyranny is extinct. (Republican Toast, 1823)[100]

The independence of the radical press was qualified not only by a concern for popular affiliation, but also by a need to remain negatively engaged with an oppressive regime. Popular radical discourse wanted to represent the illegitimate authority of corruption as well as the legitimate authority of the people. Any synthesis of "retreat and engagement" remained, as Bourdieu has suggested, "unstable and uncertain";[101] independence implied opposition, and both were imperfectly joined in a negative discourse fraught with tension and contradiction. My earlier account of the structure of a radical counterpublic sphere emphasized a pattern of hostility and conflict. "We hate the present infernal system of corruption and injustice," John Wade announced in the first number of the *Gorgon*, "and our sole object is to effect either its reform or overthrow" (*G*, no. 1 [1818], 8). The last phrase ("reform or overthrow") elided significant political differences, and suggested how hostility itself might authorize the collective radical voice ("we hate"). Official resistance to reform helped organize the movement, and provided it with a negative route to power. "Patterns of protest are," as Victor Kiernan has observed, "always partly drawn by the weapons used against them."[102] No discourse of opposition can do without an opponent. Carlile, who dedicated successive volumes of the *Republican* to the Attorney General, the King, the Vice Society, the Constitutional Association, and the Holy Alliance, was acutely aware of the dialectical structure of political struggle. "I say, kick away," he once wrote to his enemies, "for if you are quiet, I shall dwindle for want of opposition" (*R* 3 [1820], 342). Despite the tone of satirical bravado, this was an important self-reflection, a confession on Carlile's part that he was more willing to fashion himself after corrupt power than his strict professions of independence would allow.

The point of independent opposition was to influence without being influenced, to parody corruption without being corrupted. The reform movement set out to assemble an effective and relatively autonomous countersystem, or, to borrow Bolingbroke's phrase, "an opposite, but not a dependent system." John Wade vividly laid out the economic principles behind this radical countersystem when he wrote in support of a scheme to boycott taxed commodities. Unlike traditional forms of power, modern corruption required the collaboration of its victims, and therefore could not help but position these victims for resistance:

The whole borough-mongering fabric depends upon our financial system, on the ability of Ministers to levy the taxes; when the latter fail, from whatever cause, the whole system will dry up and instantly vanish. This is the *spring* that supports it, and the people are the masters of this *spring*, and whenever they choose to interrupt the current the machine will stop for want of the principle that had maintained it in motion. The more taxes the people of any country pay, the greater is the power they possess over their Rulers. Every additional tax that is imposed, does, exactly in the same proportion render the government dependent on the will of the people. (*G*, no. 12 [1818], 92)[103]

Wade went on to describe this unwitting popular empowerment as "*virtual* controul" (93), a nice appropriation of the language of corruption that signalled his awareness of the tactical ironies he was negotiating: virtual representation authorized virtual resistance.[104] Radical opposition had to reproduce the historical shift from physical force to systematic fraud:

What folly then it is to think of violence, of plots, and conspiracies, when there remains a measure so effectual, and which has never been tried. In such a remedy too, there is nothing that can alarm the most timid and tender-hearted. There is no need of pikes, gunpowder or blunderbuss, nor any thing else of a dangerous nature . . . It is a *personal* oppression, a tyranny exercised over our property, therefore let property resist it, and the remedy will exactly correspond to the evil. To this *dernier* resort the Country must eventually come, and it is a remedy peculiarly adapted to our internal situation, and the nature of the evil we have to oppose. (94)

This argument certainly reflected Wade's anxiety about armed conflict, but it cannot be reduced to that anxiety. The effort to use the logic of "system" to discover the most promising site of political intervention, to work *through* corruption rather than around or against it, was a fundamental principle of radical resistance in the early nineteenth century.

Where opposition became a first principle, the radical movement confronted what Alan Liu, in an account of the whig party in the 1790s, has called the "dialectical or negational essence" of political opposition: "Referenced on a pure relation, Opposition was in the final analysis a will to oppose independent of settled object." While Liu's formulation is astute, his notion of a "final analysis" of "the basic negational structure of opposition" risks eliding the ironies and instabilities that were also "basic" to radical, if not to whig, opposition.[105] Essence and finality were precisely what a "dialectical or negational" attitude sought to foreclose or at least forestall. As long as "Legitimacy" remained "militant" rather than "triumphant," to borrow Hazlitt's terms, political affairs were not quite "perfectly settled," and resistance was possible (*CWH* 7: 92). If reformers had learned anything from the 1790s, it was that revealing an ideological essence (Jacobin, republican, natural rights) opened the way to repression. Wade made the dialectical claim that "the people" controlled the "*spring*" of their own oppression in order to direct his readers' attention away from terminal "plots, and conspiracies" and towards an ongoing tactical intervention. If the boycott was a "*dernier* resort," this finality inhered not in radicalism itself, as an essence, but in the relationship between system and countersystem; the "machine" would "stop" when popular resistance "adapted" itself to "the nature of the evil we have to oppose." This said, Liu has identified an important feature of radical protest, noticed also by its contemporary critics. The *Edinburgh Review* offered centrist whig "principles" as an antidote to the relativity and negativity of both political extremes: radicals were obliged "to despise existing authorities," while tories were determined "to defend, with insolence, every thing that is attacked, however obviously indefensible" (*ER* 15 [1810], 507). The *Quarterly Review* was almost willing to concede the last point, but rehabilitated the defensiveness of the ministerial press as a spur to political virtue. "They cannot support the ministry without supporting the constitution, the laws, religion, and social order . . . Hence, putting principle out of view, these papers are frequently compelled to say what they would say if they were in the highest degree honest and independent." It was almost superfluous to add that "this compulsion" was "almost wholly reversed with regard to the opposition papers," whose habits of dissent led inexorably to the "anarchical principles and perilous schemes" of radical reform (*QR* 28 [1822], 204).

Faced with these criticisms, radicals sometimes abandoned tactical irony for a politics of firm principle. Rifts opened up within the movement when countersystem seemed to stray too far into the terrain of the system. Henry Hunt's 1821 project for a Great Northern Union of radical reformers, which solicited penny subscriptions for a fund to secure parliamentary seats for radical members, became a catalyst for the debate over strategy.[106] Hunt enlisted the support of Wooler, who acknowledged that "the policy of buying boroughs may be disputed," but insisted "that *all* means are fair against those who stop at no principle themselves"; the "detestable traffic . . . would be undertaken with a view to put an end to it; and the object would justify the means" (*BD* 7 [1821], 668). Tender republican consciences were more troubled by the scheme. Rejecting the attempt "to fight them with their own weapons, as it has been cunningly called," Carlile urged Wooler to embrace the "unfettered" principles of "an independent man": "Shake off all corrupt connections, and stand alone" (*R* 6 [1822], 431, 439).[107] Carlile emerged in this period as the ideological conscience of a syncretistic reform movement. Relative formulations condemned political opposition to oblivion. Without "the principles" of republicanism, "a Reformer, is a designation that amounts to nothing" (*R* 6 [1822], 65). Pointed as these clashes were, the two positions involved (ironic complicity and principled independence) were not entirely discrete: Wooler joined in a "detestable traffic" in order finally "to put an end to it," and Carlile took a firm stand on republican principles that left room for ironic engagement. Indeed, the discourse of the *Republican* was least stable where principle was most at stake, in matters of religious faith. Carlile often undermined Christian doctrine by skeptically inverting its conventions: he called his shop the "Temple of Reason," wrote sermons, welcomed martyrdom, quoted Old Testament prophecy, announced the arrival of the Anti-Christ, expressed solidarity with the Bible Societies, and even set up a quasi-religious sect called the "Zerotarian Catholic Christians."[108]

Radical disputes over mimicry and irony have their afterlife in historiographical debates over the reform movement's constitutional idiom. Cartwright and Cobbett were the leading exponents of a constitutional analysis that traced social and economic problems to political causes, and treated reform as a recovery of ancient rights lost to corruption. There were, of course, alternative idioms of protest that offered economic solutions (Spence and Owen) or circumvented the constitution (Paine and Bentham), but these made limited and uneven inroads on the radical reform movement in the early nineteenth century. E. P. Thompson treated constitutionalism as the "illusion of the epoch," an ideological residue that had to be "broken through" if reformers were to overcome their attachment to the monarchy and the representation of property.[109] From a Marxist perspective, constitutionalism was a regrettable obstacle to class consciousness and to an economic understanding of injustice. Recent challenges to strict economic determination have yielded a revisionist view that acknowledges the conceptual limitations of constitutionalism, but insists upon its genuine political challenge. John Belchem argues that constitutional reformers "did not need to appeal to an alternative value system to legitimize insurgency," because they were able to exploit "normative ambiguities" within "the very language of the ruling class." James Epstein agrees that popular radicalism sought "both to appropriate the dominant terms of national political discourse and to parody the pretensions of loyalist regard for the glorious British constitution," without "abandoning the legitimating force" of constitutional discourse.[110] Radical constitutionalism epitomized the movement's uneasy synthesis of autonomy and engagement by providing a set of relative principles, drawn from the core of the system. Without resolving the problem raised by radical sectarians like Carlile and Hazlitt ("normative ambiguities" within the dominant value system might not provide adequate leverage for resistance), the revisionist view shifts attention to ambiguity and contradiction as a *tactic* rather than an error in judgment. Radical countersystem sought to appropriate and mock the authority of a system that was not easily transcended or superseded. A revisionist approach recognizes the limits of radical reform, but explores the way those limits were alternately violated and respected, and redeployed as weapons rather than liabilities.

The motivation for an engaged countersystem was itself engaged. The strict constitutional limits laid down in Francis Holt's quasi-official *Law of Libel* (1812) suggest why the radical movement might have preferred countersystem to firm principle:

All governments are founded, either in fact, or in a fiction, the utility of which gives it the authority of a fact, upon a compact between the people and their governors, in which the former give up all their force and will, all their power and independence, to government . . . The fact, or the fiction, on which government is founded, allows or supposes one primitive and original popular assembly and common suffrage; it allows or supposes that the government was constituted in such assembly, and that, being thus constituted, it became thereafter a fundamental rule and establishment, – that is to say, what we emphatically call a Constitution. Such, therefore, are the limits to the liberty of speech and writing as affecting the nature of the constitution.

It was "within the above limits," Holt insisted, that the law of libel circumscribed the Englishman's "right to speak, to write, and petition": "He must not endanger the fundamentals of the constitution; he must not shake what is rooted, nor bring again into discussion, with a view of disturbing, what is settled . . . he must not provoke the passions of the populace to overawe the laws, and recast the system of the State."[111] Holt took a social contract that was equally binding whether it was founded in fact or fiction (disarming a Painite critique of the unwritten English constitution), and imposed it upon a people deprived of "all their force and will, all their power and independence." The fundamental critique to which radical discourse aspired was by definition impossible, since everything "rooted" was excluded from public discussion. Hazlitt suggested the logic of a tactical response to this "legitimate" constitutional state:

While any trace of liberty is left among a people, ambitious Princes will never be easy, never at peace, never of sound mind . . . It is not enough that they have secured the whole power of the state in their hands, – that they carry every measure they please without the chance of an effectual opposition to it: but a word uttered against it is torture to their ears, – a thought that questions their wanton exercise of the royal prerogative rankles in their breasts like poison. (*CWH* 7: 264)

The weakness of a perfect hegemony was that it had to be obsessed with perfection. "It is said that robbers are afraid of every noise," the *Yellow Dwarf* observed, "Tyrants and usurpers suppress every noise" (*YD*, no. 1 [1818], 7). Where the least noise or disruption was taken as a fundamental challenge to what was settled and constituted, even "a will to oppose independent of settled object" could become a matter of principled opposition.

The clearest evidence of the tactical character of radical constitutionalism was its willingness to transgress its own limits as well as those established by the state. Cobbett was the most reactionary of radicals, and an influential advocate of the ancient constitution; but the "radical change of system" (*CPR* 35 [1819], 39) that horrified Holt was a constant refrain of the *Political Register*, and when it suited his purposes, Cobbett became a progressive idealist, arguing that "the mind of man knows nothing of retrograde motion" (*CPR* 25 [1814], 547). John Wade embraced Benthamite utilitarianism while supporting constitutional reformers like Cartwright and Burdett; Wooler made the *Black Dwarf* a leading organ for Cartwright, but drew with equal facility from Paine and Bentham; Cartwright himself claimed Bentham as an ally in the quest for universal suffrage, and even Carlile mingled ancient rights with republican ideology. While it may be true that Paine and Bentham marked epistemic breaks in the history of political discourse, popular radical argument was able to bridge such gaps with what J. G. A. Pocock has called a "mixed discourse," one that was fundamentally pragmatic, flexible, and syncretistic.[112] As James Epstein has argued, "at the level of popular politics, distinctions between arguments based on historical precedent and those based on natural rights, or between popular constitutionalism and republicanism, were rarely drawn very sharply."[113]

The festive displays of language and ritual staged by the reform movement in this period became a particularly rich site for radical syncretism. At celebratory dinners, political toasts assembled discrete fragments of oppositional ideology with little regard for organization or consistency. At local meetings held in 1823 to celebrate the anniversary of Paine's birth, strict determinations of ideological purity – "Republicanism; the whole of Republicanism; and nothing but Republicanism" – did not prevent the free exercise of radical bricolage. The "author of the 'System de la Nature'" shared honors with "Cobbett, Wooler, and Hunt"; grand abstractions like "the sovereignty of the people" and "the liberty of the press" stood alongside minute particulars like "Peel's bill, which has brought the poor a cheap loaf," and the "white-hafted penknife" with which Castlereagh committed suicide. High seriousness ("May the unextinguishable lights of Philosophy soon obtain universal ascendancy over the human mind") did not prevent comic inversion ("May the Members of the Holy Alliance hold their next Congress in the New Jerusalem"), nor did strictures against violence ("May the Clouds which now obscure the Sun of Liberty be dissolved, but not in blood") interfere with revolutionary fervor ("Success to the United Nations of Spain and Portugal, and may the first shot fired against their liberties be the signal for the general emancipation of Europe"). One such dinner culminated in an explosion of syncretistic enthusiasm, with toasts offered to Joseph Gerrald, William Tell, Cervantes, Wat Tyler, Volney, Diderot, Joel Barlow, Bolingbroke, Brutus, Cassius, Cicero, Demosthenes, Shakespeare, Milton, Goldsmith, Robert Burns, Percy Bysshe Shelley, "and others of the same spirits."[114] This bewildering assembly of ancestors was particularly ironic on a birthday honoring a figure who was often taken to stand for strict republican consistency, and who had devoted his life to freeing the living from the bonds of the dead.

Inconsistency in radical discourse was not simply a result of the pressure of events and periodical production, nor of the intellectual shortcomings of a popular movement. A dialectically engaged radical opposition was keen to trace its own contradictions to the internal contradictions of a corrupt system. Towards the end of an elaborate

"Answer To Mr. Canning's Liverpool Speech," Cobbett made the tortuous logic of the ministerial speech a pretext for his own tortuous analysis: "It only remains for me to apologize to the reader for having, as I fear, put his patience to too severe a test. But, the poison was so artfully mixed up and kneaded together, that it required time to analyse it and to furnish, as I hope I have, an appropriate antidote" (*CPR* 25 [1814], 186). The opening sentences of the *Black Dwarf* offered an ambivalent account of the English constitution that prepared the way for Wooler's own comic style and imperfect constitutionalism: "Nothing puzzles an Englishman so much as the constitution of his country. It is harder than the enigma put to Oedipus. So many things opposite in themselves, have been constitutional in their turn, that the constitution is every thing, and nothing – a blessing, and a curse – the offspring of immaculate wisdom – the produce of the weakest intellect" (*BD* 1 [1817], 1). To address this enigma, Wooler produced the protean figure of the Black Dwarf, "secure from his invisibility, and dangerous from his power of division."[115] Hazlitt preferred to seize on the enigma of the Glorious Revolution, and never tired of unveiling the revolutionary heart of a counter-revolutionary British regime: "We are nothing but rebellion all over, from the crown of the head to the sole of the foot" (*CWH* 19: 270).[116] In each case, radical countersystem was a destabilizing critique of an unstable terrain. The "appropriate antidote" could not help but reproduce the quality of the "poison."

Joined with the negative "essence" of opposition, this principle of contradiction provided the movement with a narrative of its own demise. System and countersystem would eventually collapse under the accumulated weight of their internal and reciprocal contradictions. The energy of political resistance could survive only as long as the injustice to be resisted: "May Revolutions never cease until Tyranny is extinct." The idea of a self-consuming opposition went back to country-party ideology. Unlike Burke's sustained party opposition, Bolingbroke's theory of opposition was remedial and "eschatological": "Carried to its natural conclusion, it called for the extinction of Opposition as the result of its own success."[117] The eschatology of early nineteenth-century radical discourse can be found in Cobbett's expectation that his own oppositional prose would be superseded by a representative assembly, and in John Wade's insistence that his frequently revised *Black Book* would last "as long as the abuses it exposes shall endure" (*BB*, new ed., v). Radical discourse was haunted by its own inevitable extinction, which figured by turns as an imminent curse and a painfully deferred promise.

More fully apocalyptic in tone than its country-party antecedents, radical reform supplemented a political narrative of its own demise with a materialist yet specifically pre-Marxist theory of economic crisis. Corrupt government was held to create unsustainable economic pressures as it advanced from mere political bribery to an entire system of exploitation and deception, including parasitic taxation, escalating public debt, inflationary paper currency, fraudulent elections, and commercial and imperial expansion. Apprehensions of economic catastrophe were not, of course, new, and had recently been popular among political dissidents during the discouraging early years of the war with revolutionary France. However, an "economic pessimism in liberal thought" had been widely discredited around 1800, as continued economic expansion belied "the warning of finite resources."[118] The apocalyptic economic perspective then appears to have devolved from the liberal middle class to the radical working class, and to have intensified after the war. Noel Thompson has shown how a popular radical analysis that traced economic difficulties to "exogenous" political factors still managed to develop a theory of "economic crisis," based on the perception of limited resources and "general economic depression." Evidence of cyclical repetition was dismissed, so that attention could be focused on a final crisis of corruption: "Even Cobbett and radicals of his ilk, who recognised the existence of booms in economic activity, nevertheless saw them as largely illusory phenomena, the transient products of the irresponsible expansion of paper money which contained the rapidly germinating seeds of future economic catastrophe."[119] When set against capitalist and imperialist expansion, the radical view of political economy as a zero-sum game yielded a relentless calculus of deprivation: Cobbett's "rule of subtraction," Wooler's "encreasing ratio" of impoverishment, and Hazlitt's "*reductio ad absurdum*" or "mathematical ratio" of misery and exploitation.[120] Whether or not radical opposition intervened, corrupt government, commercial enterprise, and imperial expansion were sure to end when their extravagant demands confronted and recklessly exceeded the limited productive capacities of land and labor.

A theory of economic crisis completed the strange affinity between corruption and reform by providing the radical press with the specific mechanisms of its own demise. Wade's 1818 article on the "distresses of agriculture" and the "inseparably connected . . . ruin of our manufacturers and artizans" effectively knits together the radical principles of crisis, countersystem, and self-consuming opposition. Though he began by comparing the results of a bad harvest – "farms . . . abandoned; labourers, husbandmen, and mechanics . . . without employment" – with the similar "calamities of 1818," Wade treated the outcome as terminal rather than cyclical: "Now we rejoice at these things, because they indicate that the horrid system of folly, injustice and robbery has attained its acme; that it is cracking and ready to tumble on the heads of its authors." The "authors" of "the black cloud which impends over the country" were the "Borough ruffians" who controlled parliament:

To what a pass have their stupid and infatuated measures brought themselves and the Country! When we reflect on their mad career we are as much amazed at their folly as wickedness. When we reflect that to restore the loathed, the hated Bourbons, they drained the country of its specie, and substituted in its place their detested paper. When we reflect on the Debt that has been contracted; on the immense sums that must be annually raised on the property and industry of the country to support the fundholder, the landowner, the parson, and the pauper. When we reflect that the people have been goaded to madness by the wanton insolence of their oppressors. When we reflect on all these things, we say, that such an unjust, monstrous, and unnatural system, must be on the point of dissolution. Were there no more trash to be written; were there to be no more petitioning, were there to be no more meetings; were the Reformers to abstain from all exertion, the System must inevitably fall to pieces. It contains the seeds of destruction within itself. The three interests of aristocrat, fundholder, and manufacturer, must ever now be at war with each other. They have, by their combined villainy, eat up the substance of the poor, and all that is now left to the cannibals, is to devour each other. (*G*, no. 29 [1818], 226–28)

In this heady mixture of nightmare and fantasy, Wade's negative engagement with the system became a positive celebration of its self-destructive energy ("we rejoice"). System and countersystem wound down to their inevitable demise when the tensions between corruption and reform were finally expressed as tensions within corruption ("aristocrat, fundholder, and manufacturer, must ever now be at war with each other"). As Wade confronted this final crisis, agency shifted from discursive radical intervention (two-penny "trash," "petitioning," "meetings") to concrete social and economic processes ("these things"). The use of anaphora to describe a detached mental attitude ("When we reflect . . .") ratified the claim that "all exertion" was now unnecessary. Wade's tendency to shift responsibility from print opposition to economic crisis was by no means eccentric, and the radical press demonstrated a remarkable ability to sustain and revive a sense of immediate catastrophe. Two years after Wade's article, Carlile faced a similar "crisis" with "the consoling knowledge that quite enough has been done, and that the current of events cannot now be changed either way, by writing for or against" (*R* 4 [1820], 527–28), and a year after this Wooler again argued that "ruin" was imminent whether or not the government enforced "the total suppression of all writing, printing, or thinking" (*WBG* 3 [1821], 33).

Rhetorical passivity before a self-destructive system was less a retreat from political engagement than an attempt to objectify key features of discursive opposition (argument, representation, communication). A world that was marked and scarred by corruption, and thoroughly saturated with figures of exploitation and deception, could be expected to speak for itself. "When a system has been carried so far, as to render the cultivation of the earth . . . a losing business, it has written its own condemnation in such legible characters, that the fools who cannot read it, deserve no pity for their sufferings" (*WBG* 3 [1821], 417). Here we find a clue to the linguistic minimalism that has so often frustrated literary readers of radical prose. The radical press eschewed tropes and figures not because of a naïveté about how language works, but rather because it was convinced that corruption had become the master-trope of the age. Corrupt power relied on mediations that shifted figural procedures from language to the world of daily experience. Effective political opposition might prefer a rhetoric of transparent description, but it could not avoid a riot of figures (disease, decay, parasitism, atmosphere, monstrosity) when it actually described the enemy. Political corruption was a context for radical prose that foregrounded mediations too often concealed by our current interpretive idiom of "context." Neither inert, autonomous, nor external to the mind and language, corruption was the complex set of mediations and substitutions (language, print, political parties, spies, sinecures, money, manners, administration) through which relations of dominance and subordination were negotiated.[121] If radicals aspired to a rhetoric of minimal interference in order to stabilize the dangerously fluid and hypermediated world in which they lived and wrote, their motivation for this was less a naïveté about language than an acute sense of the specific historical conditions under which complex acts of communication and exchange took place.

A crisis in corruption promised to complete the dialectic of system and countersystem, allowing radical discourse to reach beyond its own contradictory practices to more stable, unitary conditions. The precise character of a world after reform was, ironically, among the least consistent features of radical ideology. Joined together by their hatred of corruption and desire for reform, radicals agreed less often about what society and publicity might look like after corruption; that this was not an insurmountable obstacle to radical organization confirmed the movement's negative foundations. The utopian suspension of opposition bears analysis above all as it illuminates the structure of further resistance. One of my aims in focusing later chapters on the work of William Cobbett and Leigh Hunt will be to explore a fundamental break in the relationship between engaged opposition and imaginary transcendence, by mapping the faultline between a popular radical critique that did not substantially survive the reforms of 1832, and an emerging liberal critique that reached its zenith in their aftermath. Despite his profound nostalgia, Cobbett remained committed to opposition, and never imagined that the downfall of corruption was an accomplished fact. Leigh Hunt by comparison grew increasingly attached to a progressive public sphere that would create a permanent and stable role for prophetic writers like himself. By the 1820s he seemed willing to inhabit this sphere of ease, and abandoned what had all along been an uncertain commitment to radical opposition.

CHAPTER TWO

Radical print culture in periodical form

POPULAR RADICALISM IN PRINT

The *success of the cause of Reform*, and of course, the happiness and peace of the country, must now, in a great degree, depend upon the efforts of the press. (Cobbett, "To the Readers of the Register," 1816)[1]

It was unnecessary for him to go into any detail of the danger in which the country was placed; that was admitted: it was known, that a conspiracy existed for the subversion of the constitution and of the rights of property; and that it was intended to subvert the fabric of the constitution in church and state. Among the means adopted for the accomplishment of this end, it was with grief he had to state, that the press was one of the principal. It had greatly contributed to produce the danger against which their lordships had to guard. (Castlereagh, Speech in the House of Lords, 1819)[2]

The privileged role that print acquired in radical expression and organization was neither an inevitable development nor an uncontested fact. Cobbett's celebration of "the efforts of the press" involved a good deal of self-promotion at the expense of leaders who could not match his mastery of print, and even fellow editors like Wooler did not share his tendency to dismiss clubs and societies as a complementary means of political communication.[3] Speaking for the government, Castlereagh seized upon the press as a source of "danger" and "conspiracy" in order to isolate and contain reform agitation, and divide radical discourse from popular opinion. Print resistance proved more difficult to control than public meetings or conspiratorial organizations, and a series of government campaigns against the radical press only succeeded in raising its profile, and making its activities the subject of public reflection and debate. As E. P. Thompson has observed, "the rights of the press" became "the fulcrum of the Radical movement," particularly after the repressive measures of 1819.[4] Radical protest was at times indistinguishable from its expression in print. A libertarian campaign for the rights of the press allowed radical publicists to invoke ancient rights and enlist the

65

support of moderate reformers, and encouraged them to account for themselves and their practices in the widest possible terms.

For Jürgen Habermas, a related interlude of self-examination forms a transitional phase in the structural transformation of the public sphere, situated after the breakdown of the classical public sphere but before "the establishment of the bourgeois constitutional state and the legalization of a political public sphere":

A press that had evolved out of the public's use of its reason and that had merely been an extension of its debate remained thoroughly an institution of this very public: effective in the mode of transmitter and amplifier, no longer a mere vehicle for the transportation of information but not yet a medium for culture as an object of consumption. Prototypically this type of press can be observed in times of revolution, when the journals of the tiniest political groupings and associations mushroom . . . As long as the mere existence of a press that critically-rationally debates political matters remained problematic, it was compelled to engage in continuous self-thematization: before the permanent legalization of the political public sphere, the appearance of a political journal and its survival was equivalent to involvement in the struggle over the range of freedom to be granted to public opinion and over publicity as a principle.[5]

Again, repressive conditions dictate that issues specific to the press, or even particular journals, accrue broad public and political significance. As Habermas' language of extension, transmission, and amplification indicates, one key to this process was the vexed relationship between the press and opinion. Where "the *success of the cause of Reform*" depended "upon the efforts of the press," what became of the people whose disenfranchisement first authorized radical discourse? If "self-thematization" was an inevitable and to some extent empowering response to legal challenges to the "mere existence" of critical opinion, what was to prevent such a stance from degenerating into self-absorption and institutional seclusion? Radical writers and editors tended to experience their privileged position in the reform movement as a source of both authority and anxiety, confidence and despair. The press was an effective "fulcrum" only if its force extended beyond itself to incorporate a broader range of rights and complaints. The intensive politics of print that came into focus in England after about 1816 was an opportunity for radical publicists only if they sustained their negative relationship with the system, and their positive relationship with public disaffections that remained in many respects diffuse, oral, and out of doors.

The self-reflective quality of print radicalism in this period meant that terms like the press and opinion, along with a host of related binaries (leadership and people, print and speech, writer and reader), were subjected to intensive political and polemical pressure. Neither fixed nor essential, these categories mapped a historically fluid and contested field upon which the radical movement and its enemies organized their activity and self-understanding. When Thompson famously divided the work of radical reform between the journalist Cobbett and the orator Hunt, he merely transcribed for historiography a vexed contemporary distinction.[6] An 1821 *Blackwood's* article had, for example, expressed relief that "the wholesale calumniator Cobbett" was master of the "pen" alone: "If he had been also endowed with 'tongue to persuade,' his attacks would have been more dangerous" (*BM* 8 [1820–21], 491). Distinctions between the "pen" and "tongue" hardened as apologists for repression traced "disloyal and seditious principles" to "a comparatively small number of individuals," operating "partly by means of the turbulence and excitement of *public meetings*, at which the most unfounded and inflammatory speeches are delivered; and partly through the medium of a *licentious press*, which . . . inundates the nation with an unexampled profusion of slanderous, seditious, and blasphemous publications."[7] This divide and conquer analysis was then codified in the Six Acts of 1819, which included a Newspaper Stamp Duties Act and a Seditious Meetings Preventions Act.

Distinctions between print and speech became a matter of jealous contention within the radical movement, too, though here the barriers tended to collapse even as they were constructed. Richard Carlile undertook to defend himself and his trade from Henry Hunt's attack upon him as a bookseller interested in "*making money* by his politics":

You seem to treat pamphlet-vending with contempt, but let me remind you that pamphlet-vending, above all other things, has given you the name you now possess . . . Pamphlet-vendors are the most important springs in the machinery of Reform. See how they are persecuted: and yet you would denounce them as unworthy of the support of the public, and contrast with them a profligate parson! We want more pamphlet-vendors and fewer talkers in the cause of reform. There are hundreds, aye thousands, capable of writing sound moral, political, and theological truths, whose minds are paralyzed for the want of bold publishers and pamphlet-vendors. (*R* 5 [1822], 261, 279)

What makes this professional apology interesting is that Carlile did not doubt the "name" of the "Orator," but insisted that he had earned it indirectly through "pamphlet-vending." The concern for "bold publishers and pamphlet-vendors" reminds us, too, that the print side of the radical equation could never be traced back to a single authorial source.

Radical print culture was a diffuse and overlapping set of practices that extended from writing to printing, publishing, and bookselling, and to oral forms of communication as well. Even within the authorial sphere, Carlile's Miltonic vision of a nation of "hundreds, aye thousands, capable of writing sound moral, political, and theological truths" was democratic rather than exclusive.

To understand what is at stake in these contests, it is worth considering James Vernon's synthetic account of the relationship between the political cultures of print and speech in nineteenth-century Britain. (I will consider Vernon's third category, the visual, in my next chapter.) While he acknowledges that the two modes "were never discrete hermetic categories," and refuses any "linear chronology of the rise of print and the corresponding decline of oral and visual media," Vernon does argue that print tended "to reconstitute the public political sphere in an ever-more restrictive fashion, excluding groups believed to be 'irrational' like women and the illiterate poor from public political debate." This thesis sometimes entails a dubious technological determinism ("print imposed fixed, verbatim meanings"), but for the most part Vernon impressively demonstrates that a more exclusive public sphere was shaped by the way print was deployed, rather than by any of its inherent characteristics. "Slowly but deliberately," he suggests, "the public political sphere and its subjectivities were redefined in ever more restrictive ways, as the accent shifted away from the public and collective uses of print to those centred upon the private uses of individual men," and as a more "expansive and inclusive" politics of outdoor assembly was lost.[8] Part of my aim in this chapter will be to show how radical writers and editors alternately resisted and assisted this tendency towards a restriction of political life, in part because they alternately enforced and transgressed the boundaries of print. Weekly papers were read aloud at public assemblies and informal political gatherings, and speeches and meetings were in turn transcribed in the press; editors refined a combative politics of print, even as they vied with orators and sought to preserve a sense of engagement beyond the printed word. The print medium became a field of struggle that opened out on, and absorbed into itself, an impressive range of activities and issues. Where official policy sought to divide and contain radical protest, the preservation of links between print and speech became a matter of the movement's survival.

As Vernon suggests, the trend was increasingly for print to make the deepest impression. A bewildering array of literary genres and printed forms were turned to radical purposes, hawked on city streets and in rural villages, circulated in periodicals and pamphlets, recirculated and read aloud in taverns and at meetings, posted on broadsheets and plac- ards, and disputed in courtrooms and both houses of parliament. Readers were advised to post newspapers in public places in order to increase their impact, and promotional graffiti was encouraged.[9] The printing press itself became "perhaps the most prevalent icon of late eighteenth- and early nineteenth-century radicalism."[10] To the reaction- ary imagination, all this activity presented the sordid nightmare of a new political Grub Street: "Libellous caricatures adorn'd the walls; / And greasy pamphlets lay on dirty stalls."[11] Radical writers, editors, and publishers were uniquely situated to experience this unprecedented saturation of political life by print. From the time he took off the "leather apron" of a journeyman tinsmith, Carlile claimed to have made "a free press and free discussion" his "whole and sole object" (*R* 7 [1823], 683). Cobbett represented his own life as an uninterrupted stream of period- ical production: "One Register does not get out of my hand, than I long to be at another" (*CPR* 39 [1821], 128–29). Individual experience was not so much mediated by as it was absorbed in the relentless discipline of print opposition.

Michael Warner has termed the American expression of this experi- ence "a fantasy of being-in-print," epitomized by the comic epitaph in which Benjamin Franklin imagined his deceased body as a book des- tined to reappear "in a new & more perfect Edition, Corrected and amended by the Author."[12] Versions of this comic fantasy did surface in Britain, but a more telling radical counterpart to the trope of "being-in- print" can be found in the collaborative work of William Hone and George Cruikshank, whose satirical obsession with the material trap- pings of print culture (typographical convention, alphabetical ordering, newspaper advertisements) came to a head in the anthropomorphic figure of the printing press in *The Political Showman – at Home!* (Figure 2).[13] Unlike Franklin's deceased embodiment in a finished book, the posture of the Showman was active and interventionist, a material "being-in- printing" as opposed to a spiritualized "being-in-print." The Showman represented a public function (instruction and disclosure) rather than an individual experience, and his technological embodiment was deliber- ately provocative. Cruikshank elsewhere represented publicity and expo- sure through an icon that placed the printing press at the center of a human eyeball.[14] These images of a radical "being-in-printing" regis- tered the movement's keen interest in production, distribution, and reception as key elements of print culture. At the same time, the

THE PRESS, invented much about the same time with the *Reformation*, hath done more mischief to the discipline of our Church, than all the doctrine can make amends for. 'Twas an happy time, when all learning was in manuscript, and some little officer did keep the keys of the library! Now, since PRINTING came into the world, such is the mischief, that *a man cannot write a book but presently he is answered!* There have been ways found out to *fine* not the people, but even the *grounds and fields where they assembled:* but no art yet could prevent these SEDITIOUS MEETINGS OF LETTERS! Two or three brawny fellows in a corner, with meer ink and elbow-grease, do more harm than an *hundred systematic divines.* Their ugly printing *letters,* that look but like so many rotten teeth, how oft have they been pulled out by the public tooth-drawers! And yet these rascally operators of the press have got a trick to fasten them again in a few minutes, that they grow as firm a set, and as biting and talkative as ever! O PRINTING! how hast thou " *disturbed the peace!* " Lead, when moulded into bullets, is not so mortal as when founded into *letters!* There was a mistake sure in the story of Cadmus; and the *serpent's teeth* which he sowed, were nothing else but the *letters* which he invented.

Marvell's Rehearsal transprosed, 4to, 1672.

Being marked only with *four and twenty letters,—variously transposed* by the help of a PRINTING PRESS,—PAPER works miracles. The Devil dares no more come near a *Stationer's* heap, or a *Printer's Office,* than *Rats* dare put their noses into a Cheesemonger's Shop.

A Whip for the Devil, 1669. p. 92.

THE SHOWMAN.

LADIES AND GENTLEMEN,

Walk *up!* walk *up!* and see the CURIOSITIES and

Figure 2   George Cruikshank, "The Showman," *The Political Showman – at Home!*
(London: William Hone, 1821)

Showman's awkward posture and centaur-like structure, more half-human and half-press than press become human, remind us that the radical project was necessarily incomplete. Franklin's "more perfect Edition" was never achieved, and in many respects never fully imagined.

Some of the same conditions that fostered radical egotism encouraged writers and editors to treat themselves as living embodiments of press authority. The brief apology for his life that Carlile produced for the *Republican* in 1823 was a vivid record of the radical career in print. "The distress and noise made by public meetings" in 1816 triggered the editor's "first attraction to politics," spurring him first "to read the 'Examiner,' 'News,' and 'Independent Whig' newspapers," then to serve as William Sherwin's bookseller and publisher, and finally to take over *Sherwin's Political Register* and make it his own *Republican* (*R* 11 [1823], 101–04). Though he never forgot the public meetings that first inspired him, Carlile channeled his political desires into the press. He fondly recalled his attempts as a young tinsmith to break into print expression:

In the manufactories, nothing was talked of but revolution, and I soon became so far fired as to begin to build castles in the air. But my first ambition was to write something that should be printed. I tried several of the newspapers; from none except the "News" could I get a notice as a correspondent. There I felt highly honoured with a couple of notices to correspondents. "A half employed mechanic is too violent" . . . It was something to be noticed, though the pieces were rejected. "Oh, if I could but get a half sheet pamphlet of my own writing printed, it was to be a novelty in politics and my fortune assuredly made." (101)

Writing was later subordinated to publishing and bookselling, but the desire for "ultimate distinction" remained (103). In the end, prosecution and imprisonment for publishing Paine's works fulfilled Carlile's ambition: "Now, though I am a prisoner, my career has been triumphant!" (104). A political life that began in "public meetings" culminated in the "triumphant" confinement of an editor and publisher.

Like other radical publicists, Carlile struggled to make his imprisonment a personal and public opportunity. "I have always considered a prison the best place for an author, particularly for a periodical work; he there finds nothing to draw his attention from that which it is essentially necessary he should confine himself to" (*R* 2 [1820], 229). The shift in function here from publisher to author is revealing, and brings into focus one of the liabilities of a radical politics in print. Under confinement, Carlile had to "confine" his attention to writing and editing, and left his shop in the hands of a series of assistants and volunteers, including his wife and sister, many of whom were themselves subsequently prosecuted and imprisoned. Dorchester Gaol was not always "the best place" even for this more limited function. During periods of intense political interest, notably the Queen Caroline affair, he complained about his situation: "Now, I feel the disadvantage of being 120 miles from London, as the most important news may come to hand between the time of my writing and the appearance of my publication; for important news must now come of necessity!" (*R* 7 [1823], 481). The *Republican* lost a good deal of its topicality, and was relatively isolated from the larger public culture of radical assembly. Other modes of editorial seclusion created similar difficulties. Leigh Hunt established his least threatening version of political independence when he insisted that "the *Examiner* lived quite alone" (*HA* 204), and Henry Brougham only succeeded in making his client look naive when, at Hunt's 1812 trial for libel, he defended the "rational and virtuous seclusion" of a young man without "political connexions."[15] When Cobbett fled England for America after the suspension of Habeus Corpus in 1817, he insisted that newspapers would keep him sufficiently informed about English politics, and even claimed the privilege of having "the condition of both countries under my eye."[16] Wooler, the most outspoken critic of Cobbett's exile, countered with the view that periodical discourse had to be produced "*on the spot*": "We might play at chess at that distance very well, if we were not anxious about finishing the game: but political movements must be more prompt, or they will generally be useless" (*BD* 1 [1817], 584, 615). As it turned out, Cobbett's work did suffer a loss of topicality. Copy sometimes failed to reach London on schedule, resulting in missed issues and unsatisfying substitutions; an article that was written on April 9th, complaining that the editor had received "no news from England, since the 3d of February," was not published until June 20th, resulting in a gap of nearly five months (*CPR* 33 [1818], 726). It was during this period that the *Political Register* lost its pre-eminent position in the radical movement to the *Black Dwarf* and other publications still produced "*on the spot*."[17]

In a preliminary address to the jury at the first of Wooler's two trials for seditious libel in 1817, the Attorney General offered a compelling image of the liabilities and rewards of a radical career in print:

The Learned Attorney stated one curious fact, as to the mode in which the alleged libel was sent into the world: – Instead of first reducing the libellous matter to manuscript, as in ordinary cases of this description, and afterwards printing it, the defendant, who was a printer by business, had set up in letter-press the matter complained of, as it arose in his imagination, thereby evincing a facility of composition, in works of this nature, which was, perhaps, without a parallel.[18]

The prosecution did not explain why this "one curious fact" was worth noticing, but it seems clear that Wooler had played into reactionary fears of the endless dissemination of print protest from the hands of plebeian autodidacts. The term "composition" referred here to "the compositor's duty" at the printing press as well as to the role of the author (*VR* 17), and Wooler's ability to merge normally discrete functions yielded a mode of production that was difficult to analyze, let alone manage and control. As author, printer, and publisher, he was wholly at home in the press. "Imagination" led immediately and effortlessly into print expression: "Being a printer, he frequently had no need of manuscript, but printed from the dictation of his mind as he proceeded."[19] This image of automatic writing with a seditious edge played out ambiguities within radical print culture, since it joined a materialist account of textual production ("set up in letter-press," "being a printer") with a more idealist, even romantic construction of print authority ("imagination," "the dictation of his mind"). In the context of a trial meant to imprison him, Wooler was curiously suspended between autonomy and engagement. His spontaneous form of communication moved easily outward from print to a vast reading public, but he applied his mind to the press in a manner that was sufficiently obsessive and self-absorbed to justify the government's hope that imprisonment might end his influence. The "facility of composition" he displayed was no more inherently seditious than the technology he employed. The challenge that landed him in court resided above all in the content of what he produced, and in his ability to put the finished product into circulation. I will return in the next chapter to the problem of content; for now, I want to take up a key medium through which the radical press circulated its disruptive effects.

PERIODICAL FORMS IN CRISIS

The weekly newspaper or pamphlet was the most important print vehicle for early nineteenth-century radical argument and opinion. While this periodical form had significant eighteenth-century antecedents, including Wilkes' *North Briton* and the *Anti-Jacobin* of Canning and Gifford,[20] William Cobbett took the first step in its nineteenth-century development with the founding of his (not yet radical) *Political Register* in 1802; the weekly format was then taken up by John and Leigh Hunt in their 1808 *Examiner*, and reinvented by Cobbett in November 1816 when he supplemented his stamped *Register*, priced at a shilling halfpenny (four pence of that going for tax), with a cheaper unstamped

version that could legally print no news, but contained the lead essay of
the more expensive paper. This "Two-Penny Trash," as it came to be
known, appeared first on a single open sheet, then more permanently as
an octavo pamphlet, subject only to the pamphlet tax of three shillings
per edition.[21] It achieved unprecedented sales in the tens of thousands
per week (estimates run as high as 70,000, though 40,000 regularly seems
more likely), as opposed to one or two thousand for the more expensive
version. For the celebrated first number, his Address "To the
Journeymen and Labourers of England, Wales, Scotland, and Ireland,"
Cobbett claimed sales of 200,000 within two months (*CPR* 32 [1817],
551).[22] His cheap weekly format was widely imitated, with some variation
in price, form, and content. Significant instances included Wooler's *Black
Dwarf* (1817–24), Hone's *Reformists' Register* (1817), Sherwin's *Weekly Political
Register* (1817–19), Wade's *Gorgon* (1818–1819), John Hunt's *Yellow Dwarf*
(1818), Carlile's *Republican* (1819–1826), the *Medusa* (1819), the *Cap of
Liberty* (1819), and the *White Hat* (1819). The cheap weekly format was
taken up for serial production as well, notably in Wade's *Black Book* (1820)
and *Dolby's Parliamentary Register* (1819); the two modes of cheap publication were briefly joined in 1817 and 1818 when Sherwin devoted a
portion of his weekly *Political Register* to a serial reprint of Paine's *Crisis*
and *Rights of Man*.[23] The radical challenge was connected with the
regular appearance of what one loyalist poet called "the SATURDAY's
lie."[24] Robert Southey traced popular unrest directly to "the weekly epistles of the apostles of sedition": "It is the weekly paper which finds its
way to the pot-house in town, and the ale-house in the country, inflaming
the turbulent temper of the manufacturer, and disturbing the quiet
attachment of the peasant to those institutions under which he and his
fathers have dwelt in peace. He receives no account of public affairs . . .
but what comes through these polluted sources" (*EMP* 1: 120, 132–33).

   These papers were as decisive an intervention in the history of print as
in the history of politics or class consciousness. As G. A. Cranfield has
written, where the daily newspaper in this period "was primarily a commercial concern, financed by advertisements, and not as yet venturing
on extended political comment," the radical weekly "contained few or
no advertisements" and was produced by "a single individual, virtually
unassisted": "Here was a new type of journalism. The whole emphasis
was on the 'editorial' essay, with its spirited attacks on domestic affairs
and its proposed remedies for the desperate plight of the economically
oppressed. It was a type of journalism which struck home as none had
done since the days of Tom Paine."[25] Despite the pattern of individual

production and editorial voice,[26] the radical weekly was by no means the product of Cobbett's genius, nor the genius of any other radical writer or editor. Cheap publication was an intervention rather than an invention. Cobbett acknowledged the intertextual determinants of his experiment when he suggested that it was a reaction to a scheme in the *Courier* newspaper for "the *circulating of little, cheap publications* in populous towns" (*CPR* 31 [1816], 612), and when he compared his unstamped paper to "Mrs. Hannah Moore's *Village Politics*" (*CPR* 32 [1817], 353).[27] Far from exerting strict proprietary control over the unstamped *Register*, he encouraged piracy, granting printers "full liberty to republish any writings of mine at any price, or in any manner, that they please" (*CPR* 31 [1816], 523).[28] Even the nickname "Two-Penny Trash" was an epithet first applied by his enemies, which Cobbett then appropriated as a badge of honor.[29] Like most aspects of radical thought and action, the radical weekly was deeply engaged and richly overdetermined. Its formal development must be understood in relation to the linked histories of press restriction, print technology, the economics of publishing, radical rhetoric and organization, and popular reading habits.

Cranfield's allusion to Paine suggests one important approach to the form. E. P. Thompson has proposed that, after the English reaction to the French Revolution, "English Jacobin" organization and a Painite discourse of natural rights were replaced by a more "pugnacious piecemeal" reform movement:

> The term "radicalism" suggests both a breadth and an imprecision in the movement. The Jacobins of the 1790s were clearly identified by their allegiance to the *Rights of Man* and to certain forms of open organisation. "Radicalism" came to include very diverse tendencies as the 19th century advanced. In 1807 it suggests as much about the courage and tone of the movement as it does about any doctrine. It suggested intransigent opposition to the Government; contempt for the weakness of the Whigs; opposition to restrictions upon political liberties; open exposure of corruption and the "Pitt system"; and general support for parliamentary reform.[30]

The early nineteenth-century radical agenda was in this account more defensive than positive or programmatic, concerned with immediate strategy rather than republican principle. Its characteristic print form, I would suggest, was the flexible and responsive weekly periodical rather than the programmatic volume or pamphlet, epitomized for the previous generation by Paine's *Rights of Man*. Thompson may of course overplay the ideological coherence of the 1790s. Mark Philp has recently offered a more nuanced account that insists upon continuity as well as change. He agrees with Thompson that the contest between Burke and Paine "set the parameters within which the ideological confrontation between loyalism and reform was fought." Paine's endorsement of the French Revolution and its principles of "natural rights and popular sovereignty" guaranteed "that these principles and the example of the French would be firmly lodged at the centre of radical politics throughout the decade." Beyond this stable center, "reformism or radicalism in the 1790s is protean stuff," though Philp does identify several "reference points." Some, like a French Revolutionary idiom, seem period specific; others, like a contest with loyalism and an orientation towards "developing events," seem consistent with later developments.[31] For my purposes here, it may be enough to say that, with the dissolution of a Painite center, radical diversity intensified in the early nineteenth century, and the orientation towards an unfolding pattern of events moved to the center of radical discourse. For Cobbett and others, the weekly newspaper or pamphlet became a sensitive "register" of the immediate social, economic, and political conditions that were increasingly felt to determine the course of reform.

The weekly periodical did not entirely replace the book and pamphlet as a mode of radical expression, nor was its development a complete break with the past. Cobbett's *Political Register* and other radical weeklies were, as I will show in more detail later, sometimes more like weekly pamphlets than newspapers. The 1790s had, furthermore, already established the weekly periodical alongside the pamphlet as an important feature of radical expression. Yet the periodical forms of the 1790s tended to be "periodical" in their production and circulation rather than their content, and they generally lacked the consistent orientation toward events or "news" that distinguished the later radical weekly. John Thelwall's *Tribune* (1795–96) announced on its title page that it consisted "chiefly of the Political Lectures" of its author. Daniel Isaac Eaton filled his *Politics for the People* (1793–95) and *Philanthropist* (1795–96) with essays and poetry, and with extracts from radical and republican authors of the past. Thomas Spence's similarly miscellaneous *One Pennyworth of Pig's Meat* (1793–95) has been described as a "creative anthology" of earlier texts;[32] its subsequent appearance in three volumes further distinguished it from a temporally situated periodical. Two productions of the London Corresponding Society, the weekly *Politician* (1794–95) and the monthly *Moral and Political Magazine* (1796–97), have more affinity with the early nineteenth-century radical weekly: both were intimately involved with matters of political organization, and the latter contained a regular section of "Foreign and Domestic Transactions." Yet neither project was successful, and the *Magazine* became an expensive miscalculation that contributed to the decline of the LCS.[33] The link between print and political organization that interests me in the radical weekly of the early nineteenth century was more effectively realized for the LCS in the practice of publishing pamphlets and volumes of political correspondence.[34] After 1799, formal correspondence was prohibited as a means of political communication, creating the organizational vacuum that was subsequently filled by the radical weekly.[35]

Richard Carlile, "self-appointed heir to the mantle of Paine,"[36] was perhaps the most visible link between the radical weekly and the Painite center of the 1790s. Yet he too was jealous of his ideological flexibility: "I have never made [Paine's] writing my Bible or Divine Revelation . . . I have no idol; but am free to follow that line of conduct and those opinions which shall promise the greatest amount of public good" (*R* 10 [1824], 392).[37] The radical weekly was the effective print vehicle for this "free" and often eclectic "line of conduct." It provided the movement with a fit interval of production, appearing often enough to preserve the close relationship with readers and events that a popular movement required,[38] without demanding outlays in labor and capital beyond the reach of an individual. Economic and technological considerations were paramount. As Thompson suggests, the years between 1816 and 1820 "were, above all, years in which popular Radicalism took its style from the hand-press and the weekly periodical. This means of propaganda was in its fullest egalitarian phase. Steam-printing had scarcely made headway (commencing with *The Times* in 1814), and the plebeian Radical group had as easy access to the hand-press as Church or King."[39] Repressive conditions enhanced this technological minimalism. Under siege from a legal campaign led by the Society for the Suppression of Vice, Carlile reflected on the tactical advantage of a "kind of business" that "might be said to be renewed every week": "We can begin any where with half an hour's preparation, and laugh at the Vice Society . . . If one web be destroyed, a few hours' work will spin another stronger and better than before" (*R* 4 [1820], 293).[40]

The radical weekly was as versatile in its format as in its mode of production. Built around a lead "editorial" essay, often signed and invested with the personal authority of the editor, these newspapers sometimes contained little else, and therefore served in effect as a weekly political pamphlet. If it seems perverse then to treat the form as a kind of newspaper, it is important to see how it emerged as a hybrid out of legal struggles over "news" content. Modeled on stamped papers like the *Political Register* and the *Examiner*, which contained news and were (strictly speaking) "weekly newspapers," the unstamped weekly pamphlet took advantage of a legal loophole that exempted periodicals containing nothing more than commentary on the news from taxes meant to keep political information out of the hands of the poor. The legal distinction between news and commentary was obscure, and unstamped papers managed to incorporate news, in part through extracts from and critical commentary on respectable daily newspapers. An 1817 essay on poor relief in *Sherwin's Political Register* began with a typical opening move, "According to the newspapers," and went on to reprint and remark upon extracts from "the Courier of the 9th instant" (*SPR* 1 [1817], 49). The legal dialectic of repression and evasion tended to blur formal categories, and open them up to political manipulation and dispute. Carlile saw the "privilege" of free postage accorded to stamped papers as an enticement to become "a newspaper," but insisted on remaining an unstamped "pamphlet" in part out of personal loyalty to the radical boycott of taxed commodities (*R* 1 [1819], xv–xvi). Wooler treaded freely on newspaper terrain, particularly in his legal and parliamentary reporting, but, when a hawker was arrested for selling the *Black Dwarf*, the editor urged his release on the grounds that "the publication in question was not a newspaper, but a pamphlet" (*BD* 1 [1817], 193–94).

When radical weeklies did extend beyond the essay format, sometimes in more expensive stamped versions, and sometimes in formal accommodations precipitated by subsequent changes in the law, they assimilated an impressive range of heterogeneous material: foreign and domestic news, market prices, reprints from books and pamphlets, transcriptions of radical meetings or trials, reports of parliamentary debates, letters to and from correspondents (a trace of 1790s organization), commentary on other newspapers and periodicals, lists of subscribers to radical causes, domestic and agricultural instruction, poetry, reviews, satirical pieces, and so on. This heterogeneity complemented the flexible, even unstable character of a format that was constantly reacting to a concerted legal campaign against its very existence. As Cobbett put it, whenever a new legal restriction "checked" a "former channel" of radical expression, editors improvised until their work "broke out" in "a new manner" (*CPR* 39 [1821], 1003–04).[41] Over the course of the three decades of its existence, the *Political Register* appeared under a number of formats and titles; it also spawned several books, some important serial compilations (including *Cobbett's Complete Collection*

of State Trials and *Cobbett's Parliamentary Debates*), an American *Register*
designed in part for matter too dangerous for English publication, and a
short-lived daily paper called *Cobbett's Evening Post*. Wooler summed up
the protean threat of the radical weekly newspaper when he introduced
his alter ego, the alien and stunted Black Dwarf, as a figure "secure from
his invisibility, and dangerous from his power of division, (for like the
polypus, he can divide and redivide himself, and each division remain a
perfect animal)": "Neither the throne, nor the altar, will be sanctuary
against his intrusion."[42]

Radical weekly newspapers were also worldly and combative, a
formal expression of the engaged character of radical discourse. Efforts
to incorporate news content through commentary on daily newspapers
established a dialogic structure of argument. Readers were encouraged
to get involved too, by contributing letters and essays, conducting controversies of their own, and joining the improvisational networks
through which news was gathered and distributed. The appearance of a
spate of radical weeklies immediately after the Peterloo Massacre in 1819
confirmed the form's intimate relation with the course of political
events. The new papers set out from a sense of imminent crisis: "At an
epoch the most eventful that ever occurred in the annals of British
history"; "The affairs of this country have now evidently reached an
important crisis"; "The times have an awful aspect."[43] In the ringing
opening sentence of his retrospective address to the first volume of the
Republican, Richard Carlile vividly mapped the critical intersection of
history and politics in periodical form, and in the life and work of an
imprisoned writer:

At the expiration of the year, at the expiration of that shadow of liberty we have
lately possessed, and at the close of the first volume of this work, I feel an
inclination, as well as a duty, to address a few words to you out of the usual way.
This work, under its present title, was commenced at a critical period; at that
moment when the troops were ordered to draw their swords on the people. It
was at this critical period, that the Editor of this work pledged himself not to
shrink from duty, because there was danger; but where there was danger, there
to take his stand . . . He was at liberty when writing that short address; the next
week he dated the first number of this work from a prison, and now he feels no
shame in saying, that it is from a prison, and under a confinement of the strictest
nature, that it is likely to be continued. The trial of the Editor occasioned some
little embarrassment in attending to this work; his removal from London has
added to that embarrassment: some little deviations have occurred from the
proposed mode of proceeding, but the Editor hopes that a candid allowance
will be made for this; and finding himself again composed and settled, to

resume the second volume with the pristine vigour of the first, if a publisher can be found under the existing state of things . . . He is fully aware of the aspect of the times: but unless they are met by a boldness equivalent to martyrdom on the part of writers and publishers, the press will become that destructive engine in England which it has proved to be in other countries. (*R* 1 [1819], vii–viii)

From the "critical period" of its inception, the *Republican* and its editor proceeded through a series of difficult events that linked the fortunes of a periodical form with the fortunes of a political movement. A preliminary "liberty" yielded quickly to Carlile's prosecution for blasphemous libel, which forced "some little deviations" in the *Republican*; these included the movement of his bookselling operations, changes in his publisher, and his own inability to write for the paper when the courtroom demanded his full attention.[44] Now that he was "again composed and settled," Carlile could promise the rehabilitation of his work in a second volume, but his subscription to the address indicated the irony of his stable situation: "Dorchester Gaol, Dec 30, 1819." Despite the dream of returning to an original condition of liberty and "pristine vigour," there was no escaping confinement and "deviation." Like other radical weeklies, the *Republican* was from the outset a form in crisis, scarred and limited by the repressive conditions under which it was produced, and eager to propagate the sense of extremity that had penetrated its own periodical rhythms. Its career was a case study in periodical discontinuity. Carlile inherited *Sherwin's Political Register*, itself the successor of an earlier *Republican*, when Sherwin feared to proceed in the repressive climate of late 1819, and immediately restored the paper's original title; working substantially from prison, he then brought his *Republican* through a number of significant disruptions, including complete suspension for the year 1821, as dozens of his shop-hands, hawkers, and publishers were arrested and imprisoned. All the while, he supplemented his trademark journal with a number of more specialized periodical projects, including the *Deist* (1819–20), the *Moralist* (1823), and the *Newgate Monthly Magazine* (1824–26). If there was no getting beyond crisis and disruption, Carlile could at least try to insure that he and his work were not always their victims. When he insisted that "the aspect of the times" be "met by a boldness equivalent to martyrdom on the part of writers and publishers," he announced his intention to represent and intervene in a rapidly unfolding crisis – to make the *Republican*, as he elsewhere put it, "a journal worthy of the times" (*R* 5 [1822], 2). Repressive conditions demanded equally vigorous print forms and political personalities.

Political periodicals, with their strong presumption of immediate reference to the world, are by definition serially linked with an unfolding pattern of events. The radical weekly newspaper was remarkable not because it was time-bound, but rather because its temporal structure was so disrupted and discontinuous.[45] Michael Warner has written suggestively about the "normative routinization of print discourse" inscribed in such early projects of the bourgeois public sphere as *The Spectator* and *Cato's Letters*, which "incorporate their ongoing – even routine – appearance in print as an assumption about political legitimacy. For Addison and Steele, and even more for Trenchard and Gordon, political publication is far from being a deviation from social order produced by crisis." By the early nineteenth century, regular periodical expectations were fully established among middle-class readers, and the division of the political press between the two parties completed its integration into the stable political life of the nation. This routine was challenged by a radical reform movement that belittled the difference between the two parties, and cultivated an ominous new class of political readers. Persistent legal harassment combined with a sense of political extremity to deprive the early nineteenth-century radical weekly of what Warner calls "continuous, normal, normative publication."[46] These periodicals can be defined as an ongoing but never routine or reassuring set of deviations motivated by crisis; they preferred to display rather than conceal their disruption, and became forms in crisis, a visible and legible sign of political upheaval. Where political periodicals had long structured time by breaking it into "predictable segments," which were then recuperated in "the comforting framework of journalistic stereotypes,"[47] the radical press sought to discomfort and challenge its readers by exposing the frightening instability of events in the latter days of a corrupt system. (For poor and working-class readers, interruptions in production were likely to be reinforced by the uneven patterns of reception associated with shared subscriptions, reading rooms, and political clubs.) The forgotten hubris of the first *Spectator*'s advertisement, "To be Continued every Day,"[48] was suddenly recollected by a set of periodicals that faced imminent suppression, and made their very appearance a defiant political gesture. Quotidian periodical conventions were a useful counterpoint to the more strenuous rhythms of radical print culture. Annual prefaces became a lively forum in which to reflect back on a journal's survival through repression and political unrest: "The *Examiner* closes its third volume under circumstances precisely similar to those at the conclusion of the two preceding years, – an increase of readers and a Prosecution by the ATTORNEY GENERAL."[49] Cobbett launched the ninth volume of the *Political Register* with a stunning Jeremiad, under the tedious newspaper heading, "Summary of Politics": "Will nothing, oh, people of England, short of destruction itself, convince you that you are on the road to destruction?" (*CPR* 9 [1806], 1). Elaborate narratives of the trial or imprisonment of an editor followed missed or late articles or numbers; changes in title and format were accompanied by detailed accounts of new laws and new strategies of evasion, under such ominous headings as "Future Publication of the Black Dwarf" (*BD* 3 [1819], 853). The survival of a paper through constant mutation became in every sense its plot. Even where this plot assumed a certain continuity, as in Wooler's linked series "Prosecution of the Editor," "Trial of the Editor," and "Liberation of the Editor" (*BD* 1 [1817], 261, 305, 353), narrative suspense hinged on a threat to the very capacity to narrate. These and countless other editorial markers of discontinuity reinforced an atmosphere of crisis, and helped the radical movement challenge both traditionalist and progressive conceptions of historical experience. History became a field of combat, strewn with gaps and obstructions, and liable to rupture at any moment under the accumulated pressure of political corruption and economic injustice.

Never simply a consequence of government harassment, periodical interruption entered the dialectical framework of system and countersystem. Radical editors alternately sought and avoided continuous production, and the state by turns enforced and prevented it. Wholly regular periodicals were from a radical perspective an imperfect vehicle with which to track a political sphere that was alternately dense and diffuse, lurching towards catastrophe, but somehow always pulling back from the brink. The radical weekly spanned the entire era of protest that extended from the Luddite riots of 1811 to the Queen Caroline affair and beyond, but episodes of acute unrest witnessed a proliferation of papers, and were punctuated too by spates of occasional pamphleteering.[50] Shortly before he suspended the *Republican* in 1821, Carlile expressed his resistance to periodical routine: "I do not expect to publish at regular periods, I shall write only when I feel an inclination, and have a subject to proceed upon. Above all things I dislike writing by measure" (*R* 4 [1820], 621–22). Occasional pamphlets consumed his energies during the year in which the *Republican* did not appear.[51] Regular appearance could also be experienced as an oppressive discipline, imposed by a government that made periodical order a prerequisite to control. As Castlereagh argued in a House of Commons debate over the Newspaper Stamp Duties Bill, "it might be necessary that the periods of publication should be required to be uniform" if "the channels of mischief" were to be stopped (*PD* 41 [1819–20], 1176). The law that was soon adopted did monitor periodical forms in part by defining their period of appearance.

Distasteful as Castlereagh's "uniform" regimen might seem to a versatile editor like Carlile, "writing by measure" was the only way to sustain a regular audience, an important consideration for a movement that relied on the press for matters of political organization.[52] Consistent appearance also challenged a political elite that had learned to fear the habit of radical reading. Conservative argument often figured the radical threat in terms of regular consumption and ingestion. An 1818 *Blackwood's* article expressed horror at the ease with which "Jacobinical journalists" managed "to hit the taste of the vulgar" through "the daily, the weekly, [and] the monthly press":

The lie that we read with a shudder to-day, is repeated to-morrow and to-morrow, for weeks, for months, and for years, till the eye and the mind learn to glance over it with unconcern. Newspapers are not studied, they are simply read. Their contents are swallowed by us when our bodies and our minds are in a state of listlessness and inaction . . . Men give themselves up gradually to their incessant and irritating influence, because they cannot always resist. (*BM* 4 [1818–19], 354–56)

Effective distribution networks extended this periodical saturation through space as well as time, until "the public mind" was "saturated with the odious poison": "In the manufacturing districts they had been circulated by every possible contrivance; every town was overflowed by them; in every village they were almost innumerable, and scarcely a cottage had escaped the perseverance of the agents of mischief" (*PD* 35 [1817], 554).[53] The conservative nightmare of periodical hegemony helps explain the sometimes erratic logic of repression in this period. Even where prison terms, fines, and confiscations did not succeed in destroying a paper, they might interrupt what Ellenborough called the "continual stream of falsehood and malignity" (*PD* 41 [1819–20], 1591), and prevent the radical attitude from becoming habitual.[54]

Print capitalism eventually found a less coercive solution to the radical challenge, and turned cheap publication to its own purposes. The year 1832 witnessed periodical reform alongside parliamentary reform, as "cheap but wholesome literature for the masses" appeared in three new magazines, *Chamber's Edinburgh Journal, The Penny Magazine of the Society for the Diffusion of Useful Knowledge,* and *The Saturday Magazine of the Society for Propagating Christian Knowledge.*[55] An 1833 *Edinburgh Review* article by the whig lawyer Henry Brougham situated these new works in relation to the

riodicals of the preceding years. Brougham wrote with a
⎯at Britain was just emerging from an extended crisis, in
⎯al authority had passed from established institutions to a
⎯le press: "The old Parliament had lost the confidence of the
⎯try; and the sense of the people having no legitimate organ, the
Newspapers, especially those of the metropolis, had usurped that office"
(*ER* 57 [1833], 247). The new popular magazines would help the nation
negotiate this unstable period of transition by transforming the tory
nightmare of mass radical reading as eating into a "delightful" whig
fantasy in which "hundreds of thousands crowd round the sources
whence the streams of pure and useful knowledge flow":

At the present crisis, we hold all these indications of popular improvement
extremely important. They afford the most solid hopes of information and
regular habits becoming so prevalent as to give the bulk of the people – even the
poorest – a perceptible influence upon the conduct of public affairs; and their
admission to a more direct share in the operations of representative government, cannot fail to follow in the course of a short time, not only with safety, but
with benefit, to the security of all our institutions. (241–42)

"Respectable" control of the press would secure regular periodicals and
"regular habits," allowing political "crisis" to come and go without
undermining public "safety" and progressive "improvement." Unwilling
to be seen to support the crudest forms of indoctrination, Brougham
argued that projects like the *Penny Magazine* were temporary conduits to
full public empowerment. Mass feedings at "the streams of pure and
useful knowledge" would teach the people "to think for themselves,"
eventually freeing them from the degrading but necessary present stage
of "dictation by the press" (242, 246). Historical progress, public
manners, and periodical forms were woven here in a providential narrative of mutual discipline and improvement.

If "Jacobinical journalists" dominated the weekly press, daily newspapers remained the print incarnation of the status quo. Daniel Lovell's
Statesman (1806–24) was the only enduring radical daily produced in
London in this period, and as a stamped paper, it was too expensive (7 d.
in 1819) to have the broad impact of the cheap radical weeklies. In parliamentary debates over the Six Acts, government and opposition
members alike singled out the "reputable" and "respectable" daily
papers as "defenders of social order" and "efficient allies" of the state.[56]
Radical publicists were keenly aware of this discrimination, and though
they ridiculed the *imprimatur* assigned to the daily press, could not ignore
its central position.[57] The "transparency of dailinesss," as Richard

Terdiman has termed it, promised an uninterrupted pattern of expectation and reception, and sure victory in the struggle for periodical dominance.[58] The daily newspaper became an object of envious speculation among leading radical publicists. Where Wooler's decision in 1824 to scale the *Black Dwarf* back to monthly production signalled its gradual demise, radical moves towards greater frequency were grasped as the empowering periodical register of a quickening crisis. While others were busy setting up weeklies in the year 1819, Cobbett supplemented his weekly assault on the system with a new daily paper, *Cobbett's Evening Post*. His Prospectus treated the project as a strategic intervention in the politics of periodicity:

Another strong motive to this undertaking, is the pressing necessity of *speedily noticing what passes in Parliament*, of which I think myself able to give a little better account than is given by the lazy and selfish wretches whose stupid comments now disgrace the daily press. Never was there a time so full of events as the present. *The fate of England* will probably depend upon what the Parliament shall do, during this very Session. To wait a week, in order to be able to observe what passes in Parliament, at such a crisis, is to neglect the means of doing a great part of the good that I think myself able to do. "Sufficient unto *the day* is the evil thereof." (*CPR* 35 [1819–20], 510–11)

This notion of a "sufficient" medium suggests a formal realism for newspaper discourse, articulated along the axis of periodical frequency: times "so full of events as the present" required a swift and capacious print vehicle.[59] The *Evening Post* left Cobbett with the problem of what to do with his less nimble weekly paper. He briefly considered monthly publication, but perhaps sensing that the new project would not take, soon committed himself to the *Register*'s original weekly format, in terms that confirmed a division of periodical labor but reversed its priority. "*Speedily noticing*" events, it seemed, meant superficially affecting them: "It is on the *Register* I rely for producing *lasting conviction* and *final success*. The Register proceeds against the fortress of Corruption by regular and steady approaches: the Evening Post acts as a *skirmisher* to keep off the assassin-like assailants, who have hitherto annoyed the main body on its march" (*CEP*, no. 5 [February 3, 1820]).

As it turned out, the *Evening Post* survived less than a year, and did not play a pivotal role in reform politics. The "overwhelmingly commercial pressures" shaping the development of the daily newspaper press in this period were a major factor in its relatively peripheral role in reform politics.[60] The cost and scale of a daily grew steadily from the end of the eighteenth century through the early nineteenth century, and advertising expanded commensurately, until "by 1820 advertisements, not subscription sales, furnished the largest part of the revenue of daily papers."[61] While the *Times* led the way into this more commercially and capitally intensive era of newspaper production, the demographics of a radical reading audience consigned the unstamped weekly to the stable "egalitarian phase" of the hand press.[62] *Cobbett's Evening Post* set out promisingly with more than a page (five columns) of reasonably diverse advertising, but by the second number this commercial space was cut in half, and within a few weeks it shrunk to a single column; later numbers often contained just a few notices for radical publications, or no advertisements at all. In this same period, readers of "respectable" dailies like the *Times, Courier,* and *Morning Chronicle* were greeted by an entire first page of commercial advertising, and a final page of paid notices for auctions and places; even a more roguish, ultra-conservative daily like John Stoddart's *New Times* managed to secure a full page of commercial advertising.[63] The *Evening Post* turned out to be a costly failure. Its main promotional function was to secure subscribers to Cobbett's bid for a parliamentary seat at Coventry, confirming his restriction to a circuit of political rather than commercial interests.[64]

Radical publicists did their best to incorporate daily expression into the weekly format, through extensive commentary on the daily press, and through rhetorical devices that mimicked more frequent appearance when events seemed to require it. During the trial of Queen Caroline, Carlile perceived a sharp increase in the density of political time, similar to the shift that motivated Cobbett's *Evening Post.* "It is difficult to say much on this business," he wrote, "every day becomes an age, and the news of yesterday is lost sight of by the more important intelligence of to-day" (*R* 4 [1820], 255). The *Republican* went on to provide a more sensitive register of this uncertain world by resorting to a diary mode: "Friday morning, Oct. 13th. – The Queen's advocates have now beaten down every tittle of evidence that has been given against her" (*R* 4 [1820], 226). Or more intimately still, in a public letter to the Queen: "P.S. Dec. 13th. It was not my intention to have divided this letter, but . . . we have come to a still more important epoch in your life, and one which appears calculated to lead to some sudden and important change" (*R* 4 [1820], 545–46). At a moment when the imprisoned Carlile was increasingly frustrated by his isolation from London politics, this vivid postscript served to knit reader, writer, and Queen together in the close atmosphere of crisis.[65] Theological dispute, it is worth noting, proceeded in the *Republican* at its regular weekly pace, unaffected by the shifting density of political time. Carlile grew painfully aware that economic and political upheaval did not necessarily touch upon matters of Christian faith.[66]

The historian Jeremy Popkin has observed that reading old newspapers reminds us "that history is something that people make without knowing how it will come out."[67] This sense of contingency became in radical hands a polemical weapon. In "Napoleon's Return," a virtuoso performance that still evokes a sense of dramatic uncertainty, Cobbett provided a vivid, present-tense account of the French leader's escape from Elba in 1815. "It is now *Tuesday noon*," the article began, "The next newspapers may inform me, that Napoleon is *at Paris*, or, that he *is dead*" (*CPR* 27 [1815], 358). Using ellipses to mark subsequent interruptions in the arrival of news, Cobbett continued to track the course of events: ". . . . . . It is now *Wednesday* afternoon, and we are told, that Napoleon was at AUTUN on Thursday, in spite of all the forces in his front and in his rear"; " . . . . . . *Thursday* afternoon. The great question is decided. Napoleon has entered Paris without a single shot being fired, except in the way of rejoicing, or the least opposition shewn to his resumption of all his former power and dignity" (366). Throughout the article, he pitted his own sense of Napoleon's "triumph" against the hostile expectations of the "legitimate" English and French press. "All that is said about the loyalty of the people of France, about the zeal and fidelity of the French soldiers, about the numerous corps which surround Napoleon: these may all be true, and they may all be false as the hearts of those who publish them" (358). "Napoleon's Return" was a daring contest, staged on the field of periodical writing, between Cobbett's own contempt for a post-Napoleonic settlement in Europe, and the official view that the French people were glad to be rid of their deposed emperor.

It would be a mistake to leave the impression that periodical crisis was a wholly enabling condition. If damage was often recuperated as a visible sign of political extremity, it could also prove overwhelming. In 1819, Thomas Dolby made it "the chief business" of his life "to bring to perfection" his *Parliamentary Register*, a project that grafted the two-penny weekly format onto the longstanding radical tradition of parliamentary publication.[68] Dolby intended these abridged weekly reports to satisfy the demand for "political information" among "the 'lower orders,'" but "perfection" turned out to be an ironic goal for a project that was doomed from the outset by the quickening pace of events. The first issue appeared according to plan on January 30, but already by the second issue Dolby was forced to announce that "the importance of the questions discussed in Parliament this week" required a supplementary sheet;

though worried about the additional expense to readers, he had "to avoid the otherwise inevitable evils, viz. *curtailment* and *delay*," and planned to continue the expedient whenever necessary. By the end of February, two numbers a week became the regular plan, with a third "in cases of emergency." In late March, Dolby announced three numbers each week, but insisted that "a work of this kind should not approach nearer: It is not like a Newspaper; it must follow with the steady march of History." The *Register* was by this time a full month behind the "steady march" of parliament, and, as the gap between production and content widened, Dolby abandoned the embarrassing periodical convention of dating his paper. The "great length and importance" of debates on finance soon forced him, despite his own protests, "to publish *daily*." The project could not long survive the strenuous pace of political intensification, and collapsed before the year was out.[69]

A FORM DEFORMED

Some deviations have taken place in the pages of the Republican, not exactly consonant with the promise of the first number, but I must plead the deviations which have occurred in my situation as an apology. (Carlile, "To the Readers of the Republican," 1820)[70]

Looking back from a late twentieth-century perspective, it may be hard to associate newspapers, even in their radical manifestation, with the kind of disruptive effects I have described. In an incisive account of the French mass daily, Richard Terdiman has described the modern newspaper as the sign of a "dominant discourse self-confidently bodied forth." This dominance, which seems "to *go without saying*," can be traced to the form's relentless display of sheer, undifferentiated content: "The newspaper is built by addition of discrete, theoretically disconnected elements which juxtapose themselves only in response to the abstract requirements of 'layout' – thus of a disposition of space whose logic, ultimately, is commercial." Current skepticism about the newspaper press is mediated in part by romantic assumptions about the stupefying rather than energizing impact of mass print culture, so it is appropriate that Terdiman pits newspaper "layout" against romantic "canons of text structure and coherence": "The newspaper can be understood as the first culturally influential *anti-organicist* mode of modern discursive construction. Its form *denies form*."[71] This daunting cultural formation was just beginning to emerge in early nineteenth-century Britain. The *Times* again led the way with innovations in typography and layout that facilitated inconsecutive (and inattentive) reading of heterogeneous material, distancing newspapers from their antecedents in more continuous news books and pamphlets.[72] Radical publicists actively resisted this emerging tendency for the print news to be "organized *as disorganization*" and as "consumer commodity,"[73] without resorting to the organicist theories of their romantic contemporaries. Cobbett treated his unstamped *Registers* as "Little Books" to be bound in volumes and preserved (*CPR* 32 [1817], 364). He joined other radical editors in producing lead essays that gathered several issues under one rubric, demanded sustained attention, and served as the formal expression of a radical belief that everything was connected, that a single system of oppression extended from rotten boroughs and legitimate monarchy to paper money, bible societies, savings banks, and tea drinking. The organizational logic of radical print culture was oppositional rather than commercial. "All my designs, wishes, and thoughts," Cobbett wrote, "have this one great object in view: *the overthrow of the ruffian Boroughmongers*" (*CPR* 35 [1819–20], 8).

Cobbett's "one great object" did not generate the internal textual coherence associated with aesthetic forms, in part because an oppositional imperative extended outward from the printed text to politics and the law, and to calculations about circulation and readership. Radical discourse presented itself as having been shaped and misshaped *from without*, not organically structured from within. The frank attention paid to extrinsic circumstances and material conditions was partly a consequence of the limited scale of radical print culture. Far from idealizing itself as original creation or imaginative expression, the radical weekly reflected on everything from print technology and methods of distribution to typographical errors and the relentless pressure of periodical deadlines.[74] For political purposes, legal harassment was the chief limit on the development of the form. As Carlile's 1820 address to his readers insisted, "deviations . . . in the pages of the Republican" could be traced to the "deviations . . . in my situation," brought about by prosecution and imprisonment. If this recourse from the page to an extrinsic "situation" suggests Terdiman's "anti-organicist" impulse, it is important to insist that the radical weekly was less concerned to "deny form" than to insist that form was being denied to it. Jerome McGann provides a useful counterpoint in his account of Byron's *Don Juan*, a nearly contemporary serial improvisation in print. Like Byron, radical editors tended to "convert the whole (i.e., the human world) into a series," and to thematize formal contingency, but, unlike Byron, they struggled with strict legal regulations on form, and did not imagine that they were abdicating prevenient control in favor of "accidents, trivia, the unexpected, 'mere' possibilities." Where the character Don Juan embodied a print "experiment" in "informality," the radical weekly was a print experience of deformation, embodied in the character of the Black Dwarf.[75] Just as Wooler's protean alter ego occupied the social and political space mapped by oppression ("neither the throne, nor the altar, will be sanctuary against his intrusion"), so papers like the *Black Dwarf* exercised their subversive mobility in a print space mapped by the government. The pleasures of accident that McGann finds so appealing in Byron would have deflected attention from a painful conspiratorial design. While respectable daily newspapers of the same period tended to allow their densely printed pages to pass as an unremarked consequence of restrictive taxation,[76] the radical press reflected obsessively on its own deformation. Even trivial shifts in format, content, title, and price could be traced to changing political and economic conditions, and to the government's sustained campaign against the very existence of the unstamped weekly format.

The ability to work through repression, and especially imprisonment, became a litmus test for the viability of radical protest in print. Though atypical in the period of its appearance, the *Newgate Monthly Magazine* was in this sense paradigmatic. Edited and written from Newgate by a group of Carlile's imprisoned shop-hands, it opened with an apologetic glance at its own circumscribed conditions: "In the perusal of the following pages, the reader must not expect to find a display of literary excellence. He is requested to consider the circumstances under which the work was commenced, and to make the consequent allowances" (*NM* I [1824–25], v).[77] The inescapable sign of the title, "Newgate," hovered over the production and reception of the magazine, but its impact was not entirely negative, since prison called attention to injustices that demanded reform. The differential hermeneutic ("make the consequent allowances") required by the *Newgate Monthly* forced the reader to attend to repressive conditions: to read was to acknowledge power. An imprisoned magazine found a way to exceed its formal limitations by circulating the restricted conditions under which it was produced. In an appropriate irony, the magazine ceased production when its editorial collective was released from prison:

In judging of the work it must be remembered that but for the religious prosecutions, the individuals who have conducted it would in all probability, never have intruded themselves upon the public . . . We stop here, not only because we have effected all we desired, but to go further would be inconvenient to ourselves. Before twelve more numbers could be published we may be very widely dispersed. (*NM* 2 [1825–26], 529–30)

This was among the most striking expressions of the logic of counter-system. Men like William Campion, a Lancaster shoemaker, and Richard Hassell, a Dorset farm laborer, found an oppositional voice in the discursive spaces opened up by a legal machinery meant to silence them. Or, as Hassell himself put it, with almost painful immediacy, "the hand which describes these lines, but for persecution for opinions, might, and most probably would, have guided a plough" (*NM* 1 [1824–25], vi). While the *Newgate Monthly* was an exceptional case, most of the leading radical writers and editors at some point worked from prison, and the effort to effect resistance from within a corrupt system was among the fundamental problems of radical discourse.

Under the pressure of its own literal and figurative imprisonment, the radical weekly became a crucible of political conflict. Denied the regular patterns of production and circulation that would allow it to "go without saying," these newspapers spoke through every feature, even those normally filtered out by a reader's expectations. Periodical markers of time were a striking case in point. Benedict Anderson has identified "the date at the top of the newspaper" as its "single most important emblem," an insistent register of the modern era's "steady onward clocking of homogeneous, empty time."[78] Yet precisely because of its importance, the date can safely be ignored when a newspaper is read in its first horizon of reception; there is only today's paper. The same conditions that disrupted the flow of radical periodicity shattered the modern sense of "empty time," and restored strenuous, pre-modern rhythms of prefiguration and millennial fulfillment.[79] The radical press was saturated with apocalyptic phrasing: "times as they are," "the work of regeneration," "the age we live in," "momentous times," "the hour of regeneration," "this 'LAST BATTLE,'" "the arrival of the day of reckoning," "*this critical time*," "the time is now nearly at hand," "the time is now come," "we await the consummation," "the hour is fast approaching," "the time hastens rapidly on."[80] Once an occasion for editorial self-congratulation, the turn of the year became an opportunity to expose ominous links between periodical time and political apocalypse, as in Wooler's article, "The Close of the Year, with the Termination of the Legal Rights of England" (*BD* 3 [1819], 841). Under these conditions, the periodical calendar returned with a vengeance to the reader's attention. The "date at the top of a newspaper" was relatively immune to tampering, since it was regu-

lated by law, but Carlile took advantage of secondary appearances of the
date in articles and letters to establish an internal interference between his
own apocalyptic expectations and the state's official marker of empty
time (Figure 3).[81] In 1822, encouraged by revolutionary episodes in
Europe and South America, he began by dating articles (in French
fashion) from the Spanish Revolution, and then moved on to more outrageous formulations: "Year 3, of the Spanish Revolution, and last, or last
but one, of the Holy Alliance"; "Year 3, of the Spanish Revolution, which
the Despots at Verona cannot revolve or digest. It will choke them"; "Year
1822, of the degrading Mythology of the Christians"; "Year 500 of
Parliamentary Corruption in this Island; and, according to the Jew Books,
about the Year 5000 of Priestcraft and Kingcraft"; "Year 1823 of the last
of the Gods." Readers soon filled the *Republican* with similarly dated
letters, in an expression of republican solidarity with their imprisoned
editor: "46th Year of American Independence"; "1822, of the era of the
bungling Carpenter's Wife's Son"; "year 1822, of Christian Delusion";
"1823d year of the fabled Jehovah the younger."[82] James Epstein has
observed that this millenarian dating reflected a desire for an unmediated
and ahistorical "republican present."[83] This seems true, but there were
important countercurrents as well. Carlile and his readers mocked
received historical narratives by constructing an alternative republican
history, with its own watershed events; they remained satirically engaged
on several fronts even as they expressed a desire to transcend local circumstances. Far from hardening into a single system, the republican calendar
remained improvisational, allowing multiple and overlapping narratives:
the "Year 500 of Parliamentary Corruption" was also "the Year 5000 of
Priestcraft and Kingcraft." Above all, these infidel citizen satirists
remained negatively engaged with the Christian narrative that authorized a state-sanctioned calendar. A republican millennium invoked all the
energy and authority of Christian eschatology in order to break its
stranglehold upon history and upon human experience.

Another normally inert feature that gathered polemical force in the
radical weekly was the identification of the printer, publisher, and the
place of publication or composition. Cobbett's exile in America and
return to England were recorded in the subscription of his articles, and
Carlile's struggle with the government and Vice Society could be traced
in the movement of his publishers and bookselling operations.[84] After
dramatically announcing his own arrest – "the reign of terror has commenced, and I now write from a prison" – William Hone added "KING'S
BENCH PRISON" to the signature of his essays, until his release from

The Republican.

No. 24. Vol. 6.]   LONDON, Friday, Nov. 8, 1822.   [PRICE 6d.

TO THE REPUBLICANS OF THE ISLAND OF GREAT BRITAIN.

Dorchester Gaol, Nov. 3, Year 3, of the Spanish Revolution, and last, or last but one, of the Holy Alliance.

CITIZENS,

IT is not often that I copy any thing from the newspapers into my publication, and rare as it may be, it is not more rare that I find any thing worth copying. However, I candidly acknowledge, that the newspaper press is improving, and that in a most satisfactory manner, under all the peculiar restrictions by which it is shackled. Hundreds of sentences that fifty or even thirty years ago would have met with certain prosecution, now appear daily, and pass unnoticed or but with little skirmishing on the part of other papers. There is a Republican tone and manner now pervading many of them, the like of which never appeared before in this country. The fact is, the circumstance is unavoidable, from the bright example which a world of Republics exhibit to us throughout America, and from the deep Radical taste for Republican forms of Government prevailing almost throughout Europe; in consequence of the miseries which Kings and Priests have engendered, and further, in consequence of the better knowledge that is beginning to pervade all the European societies. In illustration of what I here offer, I copy the following letter from the Morning Chronicle, a paper whose discussions on foreign politics, and whose foreign correspondences are beginning to be completely Republican, though in its discussion of domestic politics, it retains its old smack of Whiggery, CORRUPT WHIGGERY.

WAY OF THINKING ON THE CONTINENT.

To the Editor of the Morning Chronicle.

SIR,

BEING latey returne d from a very extensive tour in Europe

Printed and Published by R. CARLILE, 55, Fleet-Street

Figure 3   The Polemical Calendar, *Republican* 6 (1822), 737

captivity allowed the triumphant notice, "From my Home, 67, Old Bailey" (*HR* 1 [1817], 481, 500, 762). As with Carlile's republican dating, these manipulations occurred in secondary identifications of place, not in the colophon required by law. Wooler was more daring, and worked the radical claim that a prison cell was a perfect school for the plebeian autodidact into the *Black Dwarf*'s official notice of publication: "Edited, Printed, and Published by T. J. Wooler, late of 81, Bishopsgate Without, and 85, Bartholemew Close; and now of Ellenborough College, Surrey." Pleased with the results, he did not let the joke rest in obscurity, and began reprinting the colophon in a more prominent place, beneath the title of the *Black Dwarf*.[85]

Wooler used the resources of newspaper parody, an increasingly popular form during the first two decades of the nineteenth century, to intensify his polemical saturation of the printed page, and to extend his critical assault from corrupt politics to corrupt publicity.[86] The *Black Dwarf* served up festive distortions of almost every element of a respectable newspaper: there were mock news items, dedications, speeches, advertisements, market prices, court and parliamentary reports, transcriptions of meetings and trials, accounts of crimes, notices of marriages and deaths, and literary and theatrical reviews. Serious content and comic inversion were often juxtaposed to heighten the critical effect: a straightforward review of Kean's performance at Drury Lane gave way to a furiously satirical account of the latest "State Theatrical," a melodrama called "Treason without Traitors"; two weeks after the *Black Dwarf* announced the death of Princess Caroline without a black-bordered page, Wooler found a use for this somber newspaper convention in a satirical piece, "Death of the Trial by Jury in Cases of Alleged Libel."[87] These abrupt swerves from the serious to the comic were important enough to Wooler's method that when he satirized advertising, which did not normally appear in the *Black Dwarf*, the effect was both more cutting and more ambiguous. Long a staple of the political press, mock advertisements gathered new significance as the nineteenth-century radical weekly contested the field with a daily newspaper that was increasingly financed and even organized by commercial advertising. Notices in the *Black Dwarf* announcing the sale of a rotten borough, the loss of "a curious *antique* called the *Spirit of Magna Charta*," or the performance of the state "*Jugglers*" in parliament, had their immediate satirical effect, but they also registered the editor's exclusion from, and disgust with, dominant markets.[88] Wooler ridiculed a commercial development that was rapidly engineering the defeat of his own cottage enterprise, motivated by political commitment and financed by reader subscriptions. If "the future lay with advertising,"[89] then the radical weekly would seem to have no future. Cobbett confirmed this in 1821 when he finally accepted advertisements in the *Register*, but soon found himself confined to printing notices for radical publications.[90] Marcus Wood seems to me to overlook the fraught status of commercial markets in radical print culture when he treats advertising as a disruptive discourse that attracted the attention of "avant-garde" radical satirists because "it had the effect of loosening and challenging established linguistic divisions and notions of social empowerment."[91] Any celebration of advertising as a medium for satire must also consider the way satire turned on the medium, particularly its inescapable profit motive. Wooler's mock advertisements certainly drew strength from a vigorous discourse of the market, but they also mocked its circumlocutions and empty promises. It was, after all, to the commercial "dealers" in *"Falsehood"* that Wooler turned when he issued a mock advertisement on behalf of a corrupt parliament (*BD* 3 [1819], 804).

Among the most revealing of the *Black Dwarf*'s formal disruptions were its "Cross Readings in a Newspaper," a politically contrived version of the old game of reading across rather than down columns of print to produce unexpected juxtapositions (Figure 4). The effect could be merely comic ("Restlessness at night effectually cured by – Lord Castlereagh's somnolent pomposities"), but "Cross Reading" often acquired a seditious edge: "A true bill for treason and conspiracy has been found against – all the Cabinet Ministers," "The Habeas Corpus Act has been again suspended – it is hoped that the perpetrators of this daring outrage will be speedily brought to justice," "The Duke of Wellington left town yesterday – with a great number of convicts for Botany-Bay."[92] This practice of deliberate misreading and misprinting realized the hermeneutic of reversal that radical editors often prescribed for readers of a corrupt daily press.[93] The editorial dash generated a reversal of fortune at the exact point in the line where a radical defeat would have been expected. "Cross Readings in a Newspaper" were important because they returned the disruptive energy of radical satire from the margins of the newspaper (price, date, advertisements, reviews) to its core, news content, at a time when the *Black Dwarf* was legally prohibited from including straight news reports. Wooler unleashed upon his enemies the same disfiguring violence he had suffered at their hands, and recovered radical significance from the fragmentary meanings that government repression left in its wake.

(That oft the cause of falsehood varnish)
Formed round the dish luxuriant garnish.
Already were my jaws in motion,
When to my visionary notion,
'Mid lightning with an awful look,
Appeared the genius of the book.
"Reptile," he cried "desist that work,
Was mine, and I *was* Edmund Burke,
Of all productions 'tis the pinnacle
Of doctrines anti-jacobinical;
Well did I lash each gallic fool,
Foe to legitimacy's rule;
Well did I praise that pompous age
When chivalry adorned life's stage,
That 'unbought grace' of man's vocation,
That wondrous " cheap defence of nation."
When rapiers, in a dancing mood,
Jumped from their sheaths to shed the blood
Of any low-bred, swinish varlet,
Who dared to think a queen a harlot;
Blest epoch! men shall see again,
The blaze of thy refulgent reign;
Already has the work begun,
Already from before the sun,
Of right divine and indefeasible,
Each fiend (though impudent as Jezebel)
Who makes democracy his bonum
Retires abashed to pandemonium;
Already, spite of Tom Paine's volumes,
Society's Corinthian columns,
By Time to reverence consecrated,
Madrid and Rome have reinstated.
Again our friends, the Bourbon race,
Reign by the bay'nets and God's grace;
While far are fled those low-born vermin,
Who wore awhile the regal ermine.
Hail, dread legitimacy, men
Shall ne'er again invade thy den,
Thou, like the dire Asphaltian poo
Shalt all within thy vortex rule;
And as the bird that tempts its steam,
Drops lifeless on the poisoned stream;
So he who dares thy fatal breath
Shall perish by a traitors death."

Nip.

CROSS READINGS IN A NEWSPAPER.

That diabolical miscreant Castles—received the honor of knighthood at a late levee.

Ministerial plots, and humbugging conspiracies—persons desirous of furnishing the above by contract, are requested to send specimens to the office of the Secretary of State, Downing-street.

A true bill for treason and conspiracy has been found against—all the Cabinet Ministers.

The Habeas Corpus Act has been again suspended—it is hoped that the perpetrators of this daring outrage will be speedily brought to justice.

The Chancellor of the Exchequer intends to propose a tax, which will doubtless be very productive on—petitions for Parliamentary Reform.

The Prince Regent shortly intends—to walk 50 miles a day for 20 successive days.

A most diabolical plot has been lately discovered by—a poor old woman who has been insane many years.

An alarming mob assembled at Manchester on Thursday last armed with—several lots of wearing apparel.

The coroner's inquest has delivered a verdict of insanity on—the Secret Committee of the House of Commons.

The ambassador appointed to represent the British Court at Madrid is we understand—Toby the sapient pig.

Signor Jacki the celebrated monkey from Paris—has been appointed a Lord of the Bedchamber.

A sermon against adultery and drunkenness was preached on Sunday last by—the Prince Regent at Carlton House.

The Prince and Princess Cobourg have used their utmost endeavours to obtain—a son and heir.

To the admirers of ice cream and syllabubs—Mr. Canning's speeches will shortly be printed.

A most important measure has engaged the attention of the Prince Regent and the Cabinet for several days, we understand the subject of their deliberation was—a new hat and feather for the Life Guards.

The Marchioness of Hertford gave a grand concert last night to—all the prisoners under sentence of death in Newgate.

Restlessness at night effectually cured by—Lord Castlereagh's somnolent pomposities.

The Duke of Wellington intends to visit Bath for the purpose of drinking—Day and Martin's real japan blacking.
    J. H. G.

LETTERS OF THE BLACK DWARF.

NEW ADVENTURES.
From the Black Dwarf out *of the King's Bench, to the Yellow Bonze at Japan.*

My troubles are suspended, and I breath the air of liberty again. Do not mistake me: I am not entirely out of the protection of law: but it has lightened the pressure of its elastic fingers, and I am a prisoner at large. In so dangerous a vocation as that of a public writer, it is hard to say whether it is more agreeable to be within or without the walls of a prison: for the value of liberty is most materially diminished in the recollection that it depends only upon the nod of an Attorney-general, or the wink of a Secretary of State. My disposition however enables me to make the most of the present—to be heedless of the future, and indifferent as to what is past. Sorrows fade from my recollection as fast as joys: and I am content to live upon the little comfort I can reach. That I may to-morrow be at the disposal of another, is no philosophical reason why I should not be my own master to-day: nor will I eat my dinner in grief, because I may go supperless to bed.

When I left the gate of my prison house, I experienced a sensation that I never felt before: for I had never before been confined. I was in the same atmosphere, but I breathed a purer air. I was in the same spot, and the same sun shot his beams directly downwards, in the same manner that but an hour before had oppressed me with an almost insufferable langour; but I was suddenly relieved from the effect, and bustled through the busy streets with an alacrity that was even to myself inconceivable. Well might a writer of this country exclaim—" disguise thyself as thou wilt, still " SLAVERY thou art a bitter draught; and though thousands " in all ages have been made to taste of thee, thou art no " less bitter upon that account." Even a short imprisonment of two months in the King's Bench, with the free ad-

Figure 4   "Cross Readings in a Newspaper," *Black Dwarf* 1 (1817), 361–62

radical protest in print: "The nation has to thank *Six-Acts* for this publication. The spirit was in motion: it was working within: and, feeling itself checked, in its former channel, by Six-Acts, it broke out in this new manner" (*CPR* 39 [1821], 568, 1003–04).

RADICAL READING AND RADICAL ORGANIZATION

Corruption has not yet encountered a more formidable and dangerous enemy, than in the circulation of cheap, weekly publications; and the malignant, but abortive attempts, that have been made to suppress these lights and guides to the poor, prove with what detestation and alarm their progress has been viewed by the tools of power . . . Before the commencement of these weekly papers, the labouring classes were, in a great measure, precluded from political information . . . But how wonderfully is the scene changed during the last eighteen months! What a glare of light has been cast into every cottage and workshop of the kingdom! (John Wade, Introductory Essay to *The Gorgon*, 1818)[102]

It was not against the respectable press that this bill was directed, but against a pauper press, which, administering to the prejudices and the passions of a mob, was converted to the basest purposes, which was an utter stranger to truth, and only sent forth a continual stream of falsehood and malignity, its virulence and mischief heightening as it proceeded. If he was asked whether he would deprive the lowest classes of society of all political information? he would say, that he saw no possible good to be derived to the country from having statesmen at the loom and politicians at the spinning jenny. (Lord Ellenborough, Speech in the House of Lords, 1820)[103]

The problems of radical print form were never merely formal. Repression and crisis made the printed page an arena for a host of social and political contests. The price of the unstamped weekly, inextricably linked with the composition and scale of its reading audience, was among the most formidable and capacious signs of radical protest in print. Cobbett brought out the cheap *Register* during the period of his conversion to universal manhood suffrage (and disaffection from middle-class reformers), and he launched the project with an Address "To the Journeymen and Labourers" that portentously traced "the real strength and all the resources of a country" to "the *labour* of its people" (*CPR* 31 [1816], 545).[104] He and his imitators systematically evaded newspaper stamp taxes that were meant to restrict the boundaries of the political public sphere, and they took advantage of recent expansions in popular literacy to serve an increasingly working-class reading audience.[105] A class of publications became a portentous sign of the aspirations of a class of readers, and the fate of the two was inextricably joined. "The working classes had no support" in the press until "the establishment of cheap publications," John Wade cautioned, and "if they suffer the weekly pamphlets to be put down, they will likewise be put down" (*G*, no. 35 [1819], 274). Price and class migrated to the center of anti-radical commentary, yielding sustained attacks on a "pauper press" and a "cheap and low press," and Ellenborough's horrified vision of "statesmen at the loom and politicians at the spinning jenny" (*PD* 41 [1819–20], 599, 1591). Similar anxieties figured in the legal calculations about seditious effect that triggered prosecutions for seditious and blasphemous libel. "There was," Castlereagh warned, "a great difference between the effect of publications circulated at a cheap rate . . . and those which were circulated at a dearer rate in a higher circle of society, and, in fact, intended but for literary classes" (*PD* 37 [1818], 750).[106]

The development of the unstamped *Register* left no doubt as to Cobbett's interest in audience and effect. Until the address "To the Journeymen and Labourers," immediate readership had not been among his primary considerations: "While the country was in a comparative state of insensibility, I was less anxious about being read. I put my statements, my arguments, and my opinions upon record, and there I left them, quite satisfied that a time would come which would do justice to them all" (*CPR* 31 [1816], 609–10). Readers who could not afford to purchase the *Register* immediately could be expected to read it or hear it read at reform meetings, clubs, and public houses. Several factors combined in 1816 to shatter this editorial complacency: agricultural and commercial depression and renewed popular unrest convinced him that the critical "time" had at last arrived, and reports that public houses were being threatened with the loss of their licenses if they received radical papers made him fear for the survival of collective reading habits.[107] The same sense of urgency that triggered shifts from weekly to daily production was expressed along the axis of distribution: "*Now* the scene is changed. *Now* events are pressing upon us so fast, that my Register, loaded with more than half its amount in *stamp* and other expences incidental to the stamp, does not move about *sufficiently swift* to do all the good that it might do. I have, therefore, resolved to make it move *swifter*" (610). Whatever its price, the paper would hardly "move" at all through existing channels of distribution, since only stamped papers were entitled to free postage. Concerns about circulation help explain why Cobbett was so careful to tell the story of the cheap *Register* as it unfolded. Readers of every kind – "Gentleman in the Country" to purchase wholesale (522–23), "little shop-keepers, or even journeymen and labourers" for the retail trade (705) – were recruited to an alternative distribution network:

I wish again to press it upon the *Friends of Reform*, that, if they think that these publications tend to advance the interest of the country, the most *effectual* way, in which *they* can promote the circulation, is, by their carrying a few of the numbers to Booksellers or any *other persons*, in the *towns* and *villages*, and *pointing out to them the way to go to work to obtain a regular supply*. With every parcel which goes out to the country in future, there will be sent a *placard* to be put up at the window of the retailer, in order to let the public know that Registers are to be had at that house. – In future, every Register, in succession, will be ready to send, in open sheets, to the country, on the *Saturday* on which it will be first published. (622–23)

As demand for the "two-penny trash" developed, and as the government threw new obstacles in Cobbett's way, this improvisational distribution network became a chief topic in the *Register*. First in informal addresses to readers, and then in regular notices "To Hawkers" and "To Newsmen and Sellers," Cobbett could be found encouraging involvement, announcing new circulation figures, adjusting wholesale prices to increase the profit to sellers, moving and expanding his own base of operations, and fighting the arrest and intimidation of his hawkers by local magistrates.[108]

Mary Poovey has observed that, "given the anti-individualizing effect of serial publication, the range of jobs involved in producing a physical book, and the various claims that could be made on its ownership, it was by no means inevitable that authorship would be conceptualized as an individualistic activity."[109] Despite its potent editorial voice, the unstamped radical weekly confirmed this sense of alternative possibility by insisting upon collective procedures of distribution. The entire "communications circuit" that went into book production – writing, printing, shipping, bookselling, reading – was brought into view, and treated as a field for political manipulation.[110] To return to Habermas' formulation, "continuous self-thematization" in the radical press was never merely introspection. As Cobbett became increasingly absorbed in the fortunes of his experiment with unstamped publication, the *Register* absorbed and figured forth the supportive labor of readers become distributors and hawkers. His methods became a powerful model for other unstamped papers, which also enlisted readers as distributors, and sometimes inserted themselves directly into the network established by the *Register*.[111]

No one had a more tenacious grasp of the connection between the unstamped "Successors to Mr. Cobbett" and the active discontents of "the poor and ignorant part of the community" (*EMP* 2: 98) than Robert Southey, an equally astute and hostile observer of radical protest. Even before the advent of the cheap weekly press, he worried about patterns of collective reception through which papers like the *Register* and *Examiner* reached the working class. His 1812 essay, "On the State of the Poor, the Principle of Mr. Malthus's Essay on Population, and the Manufacturing System," argued that "the mob" had acquired "jacobinism" through the shared phenomenology of repetition, passivity, and mobility that linked radical publicity with factory labor. The essay elaborated the legal position that radical discourse could not be judged on the basis of its content alone: "He who finds a factious newspaper upon his breakfast table, and, casting his eyes over its columns while he sips his coffee, smiles at its blunders, or at most vents a malediction . . . has but a faint conception of its effects upon the great body of its readers." To understand those "effects," one had to understand the "circumstances" that assisted its reception among aspiring working-class politicians:

There are thousands, and tens of thousands, prepared for it by the manufacturing system, as completely as soldiers by want and cold are prepared for camp contagion. It is upon men whom that system has depraved, that the diatribes of the anarchists operate with full effect . . . Where one who can read is to be found, all who have ears can hear. The weekly epistles of the apostles of sedition are read aloud in tap-rooms and pot-houses to believing auditors, listening greedily when they are told that their rulers fatten upon the gains extracted from their blood and sinews; that they are cheated, oppressed, and plundered . . . These are the topics which are received in the pot-house, and discussed over the loom and the lathe: men already profligate and unprincipled, needy because they are dissolute, and discontented because they are needy, swallow these things when they are getting drunk, and chew the cud upon them when sober. The lessons are repeated day after day, and week after week. If madder be administered to a pig only for a few days, his bones are reddened with its dye; and can we believe that the bloody colouring of such "pig's meat" as this will not find its way into the system of those who take it for their daily food? (*EMP* 1: 120–21, 126)

Here Southey infused the conservative trope of radical reading as eating with the whole contested history of Burke's "swinish multitude." There were in fact two kinds of culinary politics in this essay, and the contrast between them was telling: a voracious working-class herd rendered Cobbett's prose more dangerous by mixing it with strong ale, while a polite middle class neutralized even seditious newspapers by judiciously taking them with their morning coffee.

For all its excesses, Southey's analysis properly focused attention on popular reading habits as an element of radical publicity. His two styles of reading had a historical as well as class dimension. The historian Roger Chartier has excavated the early modern "sociability of reading" as a counterpoint to the subsequent "privatization of the act of reading, to its retreat into the intimacy of solitude. From the sixteenth to the eighteenth century, reading out loud survived in the tavern and the coach, the salon and the café, in high society and in the household."[112] David Vincent extends this kind of analysis to English popular culture, arguing that conventional distinctions between the printed and the spoken word were not borne out in the experience of the working poor: "the literate and non literate" had long formed "a complex series of conflicting and mutually enforcing relationships," so that "when the transformation in the availability and exploitation of print took place in the early nineteenth century, it was seen as an extension of indigenous working-class habits and tastes, rather than as an importation, or imposition."[113] The radical weekly entered this mixed environment of popular communication, which included important, and to Southey's mind dangerous, bridges between print and speech, public and private, individual and community. Groups of readers shared subscriptions; newspapers were immediately available in taverns, coffee houses, and reading rooms, and when new numbers arrived, old ones passed out from hand to hand through the community; the news was read aloud at political meetings and taverns, providing a non-literate public with access to the expanding culture of print, and extending the circulation of periodicals well beyond the number of copies printed.[114]

The politicization of collective reading practices informed the development of the radical weekly. Rumors that the government was preparing to revoke the licenses of public houses that staged "*Meetings for Reading the Register*" were among the many determinants of Cobbett's unstamped *Register*. "The moment I heard of that . . . I saw, at once, that my readers, or *hearers*, (or, at least, a great part of them) must either be driven out into the high-roads and waste-lands, or that they must be supplied with reading at a *cheap rate*" (*CPR* 31 [1816], 610–11).[115] As it turned out, popular practices that converted "readers" into "hearers" could not be suppressed, and they were reinforced rather than replaced by the success of the unstamped press. "Political Protestant" societies organized in the summer of 1819 arranged for a "class-leader" to purchase cheap political publications and have them read aloud at meetings, and in this way mobilized embedded popular habits on behalf of an emerging counterpublic sphere.[116] When the Newspaper Stamp Duties Act

subsequently tripled the price of the radical weekly, editors again looked
to collective reading to soften the blow, recommending "the union of
three subscribers" or "three or four families," and more ambitious col-
lectives of "half-dozens, twenties, or thirties." The *Medusa* went so far as
to instruct vendors to loan copies of the paper to those who could no
longer afford to purchase it.[117] Again, government pressure on the production of radical discourse directed attention instead to its reception,
and encouraged readers to become political agents.

Collective reception challenged the increasingly dominant middle-
class habit of private newspaper reading about public matters, which has
often been treated by historians and cultural theorists as a symptom of
modernity. Following Walter Benjamin, who complained that newspapers tend "to isolate what happens from the realm in which it could
affect the experience of the reader," Richard Terdiman has traced the
reifying effect of the mass daily to its piecemeal layout: "The form of the
newspaper . . . instructs us in the apparently irreducible fragmentation of
daily experience, and by its normalization prepares us to live in it."[118]
Benedict Anderson similarly offers the "mass ceremony" of newspaper
reading, "performed in silent privacy, in the lair of the skull," as a "vivid
figure for the secular, historically-clocked, imagined community" of the
nation state.[119] The radical pattern of collective reading about public
matters, with an eye towards political intervention, suggests at least the
rudiments of an alternative phenomenology of the newspaper, one that
is more active, communal, and synthetic. By printing the transactions of
public meetings, including speeches, debates, and ceremonies, radical
weeklies displayed the oral and collective dimension of popular culture.
Lead essays insisted upon the connection between individual experience
and broader social and political developments. Even the personal tone
and vernacular rhythms of a radical prose style can be seen as an effort to
narrow the gap between the printed word and its popular reception.[120]
While there was disagreement within the movement about how collective reading ought to be organized, the resistance to individual reading
was widespread.[121] John Wade encouraged his readers to form "small
societies" that would "give rise to habits of reflection and reasoning" (*G*,
no. 15 [1818], 116), and Wooler made the case for communal reading in
terms that contrast nicely with Anderson's "lair of the skull":

Some writers have affected to say *avoid clubs*, and *meetings*. Stay at home and read.
Opinions may be *formed* at home perhaps better than elsewhere; but they can
only be tried in society. It is only in communion with his fellows, that man rises
to the full importance of his being . . . He, who only reads in his closet, may be

very well informed, and yet very useless. A thousand and ten thousand unconnected links will not form a chain; and mere readers are only atoms in a rope of
sand, which may be well-fashioned on the beach, but is washed in pieces by
every breaking surge. To be important, men must meet each other, unite their
knowledge and their powers, compare their sentiments, weigh together the
force of opposite statements – and draw the pure gold of truth from the dross of
the inferior ore with which it is generally combined. (*BD* 3 [1819], 248)[122]

If it remained an affair of the "closet," political reading could not issue
in the collective action that reform required. Official resistance to collective reading habits suggested that the government did not share Wooler's
disdain for the "very useless" closeted reader.[123]

If the radical evasion of newspaper taxes brought collective reading
to the center of public debate, it also suggested the means by which
unruly popular reading habits were finally brought under control. The
suppression of the unstamped press by the Newspaper Stamp Duties Act
of 1819 was a temporary measure; over the long term, the market solutions that James Mackintosh had proposed in his speech against the
Newspaper Stamp Duties Bill proved more significant. An anonymous
1824 tract urged repeal of the newspaper taxes, on the grounds that a
respectable cheap press would end the danger of collective reading. The
new working-class politician was less of a threat when he read "in his
own parlour," and consumed "his foreign and *domestic* intelligence *at
home*": "There he is safe from the influence . . . of the tavern demagogue.
There he can think for himself, and judge for himself."[124] When radical
editors resurrected the unstamped format in the early 1830s, this time in
open violation of the law, opponents of the stamp duties once again
envisioned a respectable cheap press that would privatize the reading
habits of the working class. By 1836, even the Chancellor of the
Exchequer was prepared to admit that "he would rather that the poor
man should have the newspaper in his cottage than that he should be
sent to a public house to read it." Temperance was often invoked, but the
real issue, as David Vincent has argued, was collective rather than intox-
icated reading. The ambition of a mass penny press "was to place
as much distance as possible between the oral and the literate, and
between one politically conscious working man and another. The long-
established tradition . . . of multiple readers of single copies, was to
be replaced by one individual, or at least one family, per paper."[125]

If a cheap radical press was finally overwhelmed by market forces, it
was appropriate that the unstamped weeklies of the late 1810s resisted
the commodification of print. Newspapers, it has been suggested, were

among the first disposable consumer commodities.[126] Radical editors
produced instead a durable weekly pamphlet, meant to be read and read
again, passed from hand to hand, and even bound in volumes and preserved; the absence of advertising in these papers removed them further
from the cycles of commodity exchange, and prevented market forces
from governing print layout. The nickname "Two-Penny Trash"
delighted Cobbett in part because he was convinced that his work could
not be readily disposed. He ridiculed the suspension of Habeas Corpus,
an early legal initiative against the unstamped press, on the grounds that
it came "*too late*" to prevent what was already in circulation: "Though at
the bottom of a dungeon, I shall always have the consolation to reflect,
that more, *many more*, than *a million* of my Little Books are in the hands of
my countrymen" (*CPR* 32 [1817], 364). If the notion of a "Little Book"
seems incompatible with my account of the radical weekly's engagement
with passing events, it is important to remember that this was a hybrid
form. The unstamped weekly brought to a head the tension within
radical discourse between history and the moment, between global and
local analysis, but it also mediated this tension through a consistent
orientation towards crisis. Each moment entered an apocalyptic narrative. Cobbett developed the "swifter" unstamped *Register* in 1816 not
because he was ready to abandon the permanent effect of his writing,
but because he was sure that a century of corruption had at last reached
the crisis that would yield reform. If he sometimes exaggerated the
impact of the unstamped *Register*, his claims accurately reflected a contemporary perception, shared by Southey, that this was an extravagant
form with explosive consequences. Conceived in legal transgression, the
unstamped radical weekly continued to operate beyond assigned boundaries, and threatened to exceed its own limits as it was multiplied by collective reading habits: "However decreased may be the sale, the
circulation of *The Medusa* and *The Cap of Liberty* . . . shall be in a propor-
tionate ratio increased" (*M* 1 [1819], 362). Operating outside commercial
markets, these papers were not restricted by dominant conceptions of
economic value: "A single copy may be read by a hundred, and retain all
its value" (*BD* 3 [1819], 853). If the radical weekly's will to excess seems to
reproduce the expansive urges of capitalism and corruption, it is important to recall the logic of system and countersystem: the radical movement precipitated an unprecedented expansion of the print public
sphere in order to return political representation to the House of
Commons.

Collective reading habits were perceived as a threat in part because they helped integrate individuals into broader patterns of reform agitation. In the absence of effective national organization, the radical press "provided the very tissues without which the movement would have fallen apart."[127] By discussing strategy, creating popular distribution networks, and announcing and reporting on public meetings, weekly papers embodied and figured forth a plebeian political culture in which readers could actively participate. If the *Black Dwarf* was exemplary in this regard, particularly after it became the "medium of communication" for Henry Hunt's Great Northern Union, every radical weekly was to some extent involved in practical organization.[128] Even the *Republican*, which shared the idiosyncrasies and enlightenment individualism of its editor, became a kind of "corresponding society of freethinkers."[129] Readers became writers and reporters, and accounts of regional meetings sometimes appeared under the signature, "A Reporter."[130] In the early 1820s, Cobbett encouraged his readers to keep him informed about regional conditions in agriculture, so that he could report back to them on distress throughout the country.[131] As part of his campaign against the Combination Acts, Wade printed a public "Notice to Journeymen and Labourers" in the *Gorgon* requesting "information from all parties, masters as well as men, particularly respecting the weekly wages . . . at different periods since 1777, – the nature of the employment, – the hours of working, – the prevailing diseases, – the habits of the workmen, and their mortality" (*G*, no. 20 [1818], 160); the information gathered was then incorporated into the paper in a series of statistical and narrative accounts of conditions in the trades.[132] Working-class readers were in this way encouraged to understand their own experience as part of a collective historical process, and to perceive common interests among individuals widely separated in time and space.[133] Most radical weeklies also provided extensive space for letters, essays, and poetry from correspondents; letters arrived from groups as well as individuals, and discussions and controversies often unfolded with a minimum of editorial interference. Distinct spheres of audience participation often overlapped and reinforced each other, as when the *Medusa* printed a letter recommending "Political Reading Societies" (*M* 1 [1819], 239–40), or when a correspondent of the *Cap of Liberty* proposed a "Country Reformers' News Room and Eating House" (*CL* 1 [1819], 62–63).

As James Curran has argued, the "social pattern of consumption" governing plebeian radical discourse "resulted in political newspapers having a greater agitational effect than those of today."[134] The energy of reading audiences was channeled into opposition as well as solidarity.

Key reform strategies of this period (meetings, petitions, boycotts, subscription funds) were organized through the press, and enlisted the participation of active readers. Some of these strategies may in retrospect seem crudely opportunistic, as for example the marketing of Henry Hunt's "Radical Breakfast Powder," a grain beverage, in order to deny the government tax revenue from coffee and tea.[135] But where the circulation of alternative products was not controlled by radical leaders become entrepreneurs, these campaigns were impressively democratic, requiring collective experimentation and what we might now call grassroots activism. Cobbett's advice in his *Cottage Economy* that roasted wheat might be substituted for tea and coffee prompted a letter to the *Evening Post* from a grateful female reader with her own improved method for roasting (*CEP*, no. 11 [February 10, 1820]). During the height of excitement about the boycott in 1820, radical weeklies became a clearing house for information about alternative products. Wooler captured the sense of communal fervor:

The attention of many of our correspondents is turned towards this subject; and every post brings us some fresh communication of the results of individual exertion. Experiment is busy on researches after substitutes; and the success with which it is attended, would scarcely be credited . . . Our fields, our hedges, our gardens are filled, not with mere substitutes for the idle and adulterated *luxuries*, as we have been taught to *call* them, which we have imported at such an expence, as it would seem, only to *oblige* the boroughmongers! (*BD* 4 [1820], 20)

The boycott appealed to readers in part because it was based on the inherently democratic principles of a radical countersystem: because popular labor produced the wealth that those in power consumed, even those without the right to vote had some control over the fate of corruption. As one supporter of the boycott wrote in a letter to the *Black Dwarf*, "let us *not put* the *weapons* into the hands of our *oppressors*" (*BD* 4 [1820], 244). The boycott may not have succeeded in bringing down the government, but its empowering logic drew once marginal subjects into an active role in the political public sphere.

Radical organization in print had ambiguous effects, spanned, perhaps, by the difference between a female reader advising Cobbett on the best method to roast grain, and Henry Hunt cashing in on his fame with "Hunt's Economical Powder." At its best, the radical press encouraged a diffusion of authority even as it exercised political leadership; audience activity mitigated the trend towards editorial egotism, and the radical weekly newspaper became genuinely dialectical in its rhetoric and structure, engaged with supportive readers and obstructive enemies.

Even E. P. Thompson, the most trenchant critic of radical egotism, has recognized the "dialectical nature" of argument in the *Political Register*, citing as evidence an important passage from Cobbett's 1820 letter "To the Bishop of Llandaf."[136] Cobbett wanted to convey to a man raised "in schools and colleges" the "really and truly enlightened" state of "the labouring classes," and with his keen eye for local detail, he recalled a recent visit from "six Scotsmen, all weavers," whose language and judgment had impressed him. He concluded that these men represented a new type of public political agency:

In every part of this kingdom there are multitudes of men of this description; and the whole of the mass is really and truly enlightened . . . They see further into the future than the Parliament and the Ministers. – There is this advantage attending their pursuit of knowledge. – They have no particular interest to answer; and, therefore, their judgment is unclouded by prejudice and selfishness. Besides which, their communication with each other is perfectly free. The thoughts of one man produce other thoughts in another man . . . And hence the truth is speedily arrived at. A writer engaged in the instruction of such a people, is constantly upheld, not only by the applause that he receives from them, and by perceiving that his labours are attended with effect; but also, by the aid which he is continually deriving from those new thoughts which his thoughts produce in their minds. It is the flint and the steel meeting that brings forth the fire. And, for my own part, I always say that I have derived from the people, in return, ten times the light that I have communicated to them. (*CPR* 35 [1819–20], 739–41)

If modesty was not always Cobbett's manner, this acknowledgment of the contribution made by his readers was nevertheless an important insight into the method of the *Political Register*, marking the origin and the end of his own authority as a political leader and writer.

This chapter has insisted throughout on the engagement of the radical press, even in its formal structure, with the social, economic, political, and legal conditions it addressed. Close reading has necessarily opened out on a range of issues that literary scholarship does not normally consider. Returning to Terdiman's formulation, the radical weekly was an "anti-organicist" form not because it yielded its principles of construction to external (market) forces, but rather because it systematically unravelled the whole logic of inside and outside, production and reception, text and context. What would it mean to propose that the law existed "outside" the radical weekly, as a repressive limit to its development, when these newspapers were in their content and form a direct consequence of legal restrictions, and a determinant of changes in the law? How can we distinguish radical print culture from the oral culture of political meetings, when the printed word was such a pervasive

feature of popular assembly? The radical movement actively resisted the
government's attempt to manage political protest by distinguishing and
compartmentalizing its various features – print and speech, writing and
reading, leadership and constituency. To explain the unstamped press
according to some internal logic or authorial source would be to overlook the supportive role played by readers, publishers, and distributors,
and the hostile contribution of lawyers, legislators, and the conservative
press.

I want to conclude this chapter with another formal consideration,
one that seems to mark the limit or range of radical publicity. While the
political saturation of the radical weekly directs attention to specific features, these papers were also remarkably ambitious, even totalizing in
their scope. I have already suggested that radical publicists resisted
specialization by undertaking some combination of the increasingly
divided roles of writer, editor, printer, publisher, and bookseller.
Periodical forms were in this period accompanying periodical labor on
the high road to specialization, as newspapers, magazines and reviews
parcelled out politics, culture, and commerce, and sought the appropriate periodical interval for each subject. Radical editors sought instead to
join every topic and periodical mode in a single journal. From its inception, Cobbett promised that the *Political Register* would "at once embrace
every rational object of a news-paper, a magazine, and a review."[137]
Wooler had similar ambitions, and though politics soon dominated the
Black Dwarf, he promised that a "New Series" prepared in 1823 would
restore his "original intention" and "embrace every interesting topic
of general information."[138] To some degree, the limited economic
resources of radical print culture prevented any more elaborate articulation of periodical modes; more ambitious editors, notably Cobbett,
Leigh Hunt, and Carlile, risked financial ruin. The prohibition on news
in the first phase of the cheap weekly, and the extra paper required for
the six-penny format after the Six Acts, further directed these papers
towards the function of a miscellany or review. However, synthetic forms
had a critical point as well, allowing editors to comprehend the massive
form of corruption. Carlile knew that radical reform appealed to more
readers than religious free-thought, but he defended his practice of
introducing "theological subjects or disputes in an alleged political
publication" on the grounds that "the corruptions of the legislature"
were "so deeply rooted in, and so ardently supported by the Church"
(*R* 1 [1819], xiv).[139] Radical editors fused their disparate materials in the
crucible of countersystem: every issue took its appropriate place in a

hierarchy of vice and virtue that extended upward to parliamentary corruption and radical reform. This urge to assimilate everything to "system" has often been criticized, but there can be no doubt that a principal appeal of popular radicalism was its bold proposition, in the face of the increasing complexity and fragmentation of human experience, that everything was connected.

In a world suspended between modernization and residual corruption, the radical synthesis of discrete print materials and modes was a powerfully utopian project. Throughout their careers, radical editors could be found struggling to complete forms that were damaged and disfigured from the outset: Dolby attempting "to bring to perfection" his *Parliamentary Register*; Carlile promising to return the second volume of the *Republican* to "the pristine vigour of the first"; Wooler recovering the "original intention" of the *Black Dwarf*. Resistance to professional specialization extended this Blakean struggle against social and psychic fragmentation. Like Blake's Los hammering away at Golgonooza, the figure of Wooler composing sedition at the printing press was a powerful image of redemptive labor in the face of oppressive restriction and universal disintegration. This synthetic impulse was perhaps the most romantic aspect of the radical weekly, and it betrayed the reform movement's nostalgic and even reactionary (but still oppositional) premises. If the print universe with which I opened this chapter rehearsed the trope of the world as a text, we find here its equally familiar inverse, the text as world. The last vestige of Cobbett's doomed effort to attract commercial advertising in the *Political Register* was a remarkable notice for "The Cobbett-Library" that buried evidence of his isolation from wider markets under an absolute faith in the sufficiency of his work: "When I am asked what books a young man or young woman ought to read, I always answer, Let him or her read *all* the books that I have written." If this advice seemed to "*smell of the shop*," it was at least his own shop: radical, comprehensive, and self-contained. After providing an analytical catalogue of "the Library that I have *created*" (books on education, domestic management, rural affairs, national affairs, history, travel, law, politics), Cobbett concluded that this "tolerable *shelf of books*" would make "a man of great information."[140] The "Cobbett-Library" was no isolated fantasy. Carlile offered a similar account of his own work, in an intriguing comparison between himself and a poet whose "genius" he recognized and sometimes pirated:

If a young man, fairly in search of knowledge, were to sit down and read carefully through every line that Lord Byron has written, he would find that he had scarcely added any thing to his former stock of knowledge; but if that same young man, unacquainted with the works of Thomas Paine or any other Republican writer, were to read through the ten volumes of "The Republican," with all their literary defects, with all their "clod-like" sentences, with all their misprints and mistakes, he would find, that he had gained a store of the most important knowledge. (*R* 11 [1825], 164)

Here, the fantastic hubris of print sufficiency met a frank acknowledgment of the imperfect condition of any radical library. Carlile excused even as he celebrated the modest art of political editing: the "misprints and mistakes" scattered through the *Republican* did not interfere with its primary purpose, to present the reader with a capacious "stock" of radicalizing "knowledge." Where the poet of *Don Juan* was able to recuperate contrived "literary defects" as the comic register of a liberated attitude toward the world, the "clod-like" impairments of Carlile's work remained just that, an intractable sign of the repressive conditions under which the *Republican* had been produced.

The synthetic energy of radical argument and radical form was a further challenge to prevailing trends. Suspended as it was between the daily newspaper and the monthly magazine, the radical weekly seemed unusually systematic from the one perspective, and dangerously chaotic from the other.[141] Writing for the *Edinburgh Review* during the revival of the unstamped press in the 1830s, J. R. McCulloch preached a whiggish policy of combatting the radical editor's "omnivorous system" through a reduction of the newspaper taxes that brought such a system into being. The article wove a dense web of social, economic, and textual hierarchies, and seemed unembarrassed about deploying periodical forms as instruments of social control:

The unjust stigma that now attaches to low-priced papers would be removed; and men of talent and principle would find it equally advantageous to write in them, as in those sold at a higher price. Were such an alteration made, we venture to predict that the present twopenny papers, than which nothing can be conceived more utterly worthless, would very soon be superseded by others of a totally different character; so that in this way the change would be in the highest degree beneficial. It would also, we apprehend, introduce into newspaper compiling, that division of labour, or rather of subjects, which is found in every thing else. Instead of having all sorts of matters crammed into the same journal, every different topic of considerable interest would be separately treated in a low-priced journal, appropriated to it only, and conducted by persons fully conversant with its principles and details. (*ER* 53 [1831], 436–37)[142]

The same "division of labour" and "subjects" that radical editors refused became in McCulloch's view a way of regularizing periodical discourse, encouraging psychic and social discipline, and assimilating "the lowest ranks and orders of the people" into the orderly "regimen" of a new century (437). The familiar trope of reading as eating returned to clinch the case for this more selective method of "newspaper compiling": "Those who preferred an *olla podrida* to anything else, would no doubt be sure of finding an abundant supply; while those who wished for a more select regimen, – who preferred one or two separate dishes to a multitude huddled together, would be able, which at present they are not, to gratify their taste" (437). Radical editors, soon to be superseded by McCulloch's program, escaped his reified vision of expert ascendancy and audience fragmentation because they rejected its political corollary, the theory of specific interest representation. The radical press pitted a single popular interest against the interests of corruption, and served the mixed and comprehensive audience that resulted with an "omnivorous system" of periodical production. "All we desire," Carlile modestly announced during the era of repression that led up to McCulloch's market solution, "is to have our publications read by all" (*R* 9 [1824], 709).

CHAPTER THREE

The trials of radicalism: assembling the evidence of reform

The issue you have to try, under the circumstances and the question, is – whether we are to live under the dominion of libellers, or under the controul and government of the law? . . . Gentlemen [of the Jury], if you think society can stand with the allowance of this unlimited liberty of libel, say so by your verdict, and let us shift for ourselves, in that disordered state of the world, in which each individual must do what he can for himself, in the general wreck of the community . . . but, if there be any there, who, governed by the more sacred obligation of an oath, as judicial and binding that declaration, thinks it is a libel – then pronounce this publication as I feel it my duty to pronounce it, a foul, atrocious, and malignant libel.

(Lord Ellenborough, Trial of John and Leigh Hunt,
1812)

Granting then the question to have been truly stated by Lord Ellenborough, "Whether we are to live under the dominion of libellers, or under the controul and government of the law," still he left a great part of his task unperformed; but this was *not* the question as put forward and maintained by ourselves . . . The question was, "Whether the licentious example of a Court was to be overawed by the public voice, or whether, as it was out of the reach of the law, it was to remain triumphant and destroying?" The other is an evident burlesque. By the manner in which lawyers are apt to speak of the law, one might imagine that "its controul and government" were sufficient for all the purposes of the community, and that obedience to the statutes would alone render us all that was well-constituted and amiable . . . But the moral world is regulated by opinion . . . and it was for giving this opinion its only real effect upon certain vices, by giving it *a voice*, that we maintained our exemption from a civil tribunal, and that we have subsequently, and in our opinion illegally, been condemned by it.

(Leigh Hunt, "Remarks on Lord Ellenborough's
Charge," 1812)[1]

THE LAW OF LIBEL

Though eager to assume a pivotal role in the politics of reform, radical editors did not want the formal intensity of their work to degenerate into the formal limitation that their enemies intended. Sustaining the links between the printed and spoken word, between an assembly of forces in the street and on the page, became even more important as measures like the Seditious Meetings Act succeeded in limiting the movement's public profile. Ironically, trials for seditious and blasphemous libel became a key forum for radical assembly and verbal expression during the repressive campaigns that peaked in 1817 and 1819.[2] Where the Newspaper Stamp Duties Act sought to contain radical publicity at the level of form, the law of libel targeted its *content*, and raised issues of meaning and effect. Libel trials were a juridical test of the relationship between the printed word and the world, staged before radical audiences that gathered to follow the proceedings and support embattled writers and editors. As Ellenborough's coercive jury instructions and Leigh Hunt's intransigent *Examiner* response indicate, the debates triggered by libel proceedings were intensely combative and dialectical, spilling from the courtroom to the press and back again, and spiralling outward until they seemed to pit "all that was well-constituted and amiable" against "the general wreck of the community."

Libel trials raised a number of specialized issues that moved to the center of radical argument during periods of prosecution: the use of blasphemy charges where the offense was clearly political, the packing of juries with "special jurors" sympathetic to the government, and the filing of *ex-officio* information by the Attorney General, which in effect allowed for imprisonment without trial. The very definition of the law of libel became a contested issue, particularly in matters of seditious libel, which seemed to amount to anything government ministers found obnoxious, personally or politically. After tracing the law to an obscure and "accursed origin" in the Star Chamber, and questioning its mutable history in common law, the radical press tried to deny the very existence of this key mechanism of state repression: "In fact, there was no such thing as law of libel; or, if there was, the law was written upon a cloud, which suddenly passed away, and was lost in vapour"; "The fact . . . was, that he never knew a lawyer able to perform a common-sense idea upon the subject of the law of libel"; "The word *libeller* has absolutely no meaning at all"; "The fact is, there is no *statute* defining what is or what is not libel."[3] When issued in the courtroom, such claims threw the case back to the jury. After arguing in his own defense that the law "was in fact, a shadow – it was undefinable," William Hone produced a counter-definition more favorable to his own ends: "That only could be called a libel which twelve men, sworn well and truly to try the cause, declared to be one" (*TT* 55). Calling the existence of the law into question also sharpened the contrast between the clear meanings of a radical counterpublic sphere and the obscure instruments with which it was policed and contaminated by the state. Sir Francis Burdett drew this unflattering comparison at a London meeting to raise money for Hone's defense:

There never was such a despotism as this Law of Libel, as it was called, had reared. It was a thousand times worse than the plan adopted by the tyrant Caligula, who posted up his laws, but in places so high and in letters so small that, though it was impossible to read them, it was death to commit an infraction upon their provisions. A different plan was, indeed, practised in the early times of England. The statutes were then really promulgated – they were posted in the market places and read in all the churches. (*TT* 216–17)

In public meetings like the one at which Burdett spoke, and in press debates about libel trials that opened out, as Hunt insisted, from "a civil tribunal" to the "opinion" of "the community," the radical movement attempted to force upon the government juridical procedures that were, in effect, "posted in the market." The publicity of the law became an antidote to laws against publicity.

It was no accident that the solid term "fact" introduced so many radical attacks on the law of libel as a hollow fiction ("the fact . . . was," "in fact," "the fact is"). Imprecision and insubstantiality were treated as key features of the corrupt English version of a reign of terror. When statutes were posted out of view, their exact stipulations hardly mattered. The "Terror issuing from the Darkness of the Doctrines" was, according to Bentham, sufficient intimidation: "*Fear* makes *law*."[4] The English tradition of not supervising the press until after publication, normally celebrated as a precious freedom, generated anxieties that Cobbett found more onerous than direct censorship:

I would rather give the preference to a Licenser of the press, than I would leave the definition and the punishment of libel to the dictum of any judge. In the one case, every writer is certain of impunity for what he may write and submit to the censors . . . In the other, he is constantly under the influence of fear, which not only destroys the beauty and force of his writing, but frequently renders him incapable of judging aright as to the import of a libel . . . If there were *boundaries*; if there were land-marks . . . the writer would then know what he was about; and he would, as far as the law permitted him to go, be *free* to write. But while there is no boundary; while all is left to the opinions and the taste of others, can any man be said to be *free* to write? (*CPR* 26 [1814], 196–98)

If this absence of fixed limits made corrupt power difficult to detect, it also promoted the intense dialectical struggle preferred by a radical countersystem: definitions and counter-definitions were issued, "boundaries" contested and debated, and "land-marks" endlessly mapped and remapped. Cobbett himself often conceded that, when he was finally left "*free* to write" in a reformed polity, he would have nothing to write. Among other things, the law of libel was a law of irony, endlessly productive of repression and subversion alike. Hunt reduced Ellenborough's stark choice, between "the dominion of libellers" and the "government of the law," to an "evident burlesque" not by answering the Lord Chief Justice's question, but by countering it with a second, equally polarizing question that destabilized the first, and discovered a legal transgression ("illegally . . . condemned") in the very exercise of the law.

Conservative apologists for the law of libel sometimes extended this dialogue in similar terms. In his 1812 treatise on the *Law of Libel*, dedicated to Lord Ellenborough, Francis Holt insisted that the law was "necessarily" vague because it was "left as uncircumscribed as . . . the natural possibility of the injury. In plain words, it is limited as sedition is limited, as blasphemy is limited, as gross immorality is limited; not in this or that shape, not in these or those words, but in every shape, and in every term, in which it can offend God or man."[5] This was a frank acknowledgment of the mutually constitutive character of transgression and repression: the law could only be defined as a limit exceeding the crime it contained. Yet, as Holt himself demonstrated when he later appealed to "the fundamentals of the constitution," and insisted that the exercise of free speech "must not shake what is rooted,"[6] official definitions of libel could also seek to terminate an unstable political dialogue by imposing fundamental terms. In this argument, the law was brought into being not by the endless possibility of transgression ("in every shape, and in every term"), but by the inexorable fact of state power ("what is rooted"). During parliamentary debates over the Blasphemous Libel Bill in late 1819, Ellenborough "rose chiefly to state what had occurred to him as a definition of seditious libel": "It was, he would suggest, one calculated to bring his majesty's person, or the government and constitution, or either House of Parliament, into hatred or contempt, or calculated to excite his majesty's subjects to attempt any alteration of any matter in church or state as by law established, otherwise than by lawful means" (*PD* 41 [1819–20], 966). The Constitutional Association offered a definition similarly predicated on state power:

The interests of the Community at large – or, in other words, the State, in which all the interests of all are combined, demand protection. Whatever, therefore, has a tendency to ridicule the doctrines and institutions of Religion – to relax the obligations of morality – to violate public decency – to vilify the person and dignity of the SOVEREIGN – to defame the constituted Authorities of the Empire, and the reputation of public men – or to disturb the quiet and repose of private life, in whatever manner expressed, is libellous, and ought to be suppressed.[7]

The defenders of social order recast as solid and essential the very comprehensiveness ("any alteration," "any matter," "all the interests," "whatever manner") that radicals found dangerously obscure. Far from lacking definition, the law of libel rested on the constitutional conditions of definition. It seemed to exceed every boundary only because it was the active articulation of the principle of the boundary.

For all its nightmarish scope, the law of libel had at least the advantage of providing an official test of the political impact of print discourse. Like the radical press, English criminal law approached texts through a "sociolegal calculation of the effects of publication" rather than through "hermeneutic interpretation."[8] To be prosecuted for seditious libel was to be recognized as a disturber of "what is settled." An 1822 *Quarterly Review* article did not have to look far to account for the harrowing litany of unrest that extended from Spa Fields and Peterloo to Cato Street and the Queen's trial: "That LIBELLOUS PUBLICATIONS have been the *instruments* . . . is now so generally admitted that it would be idle to offer proofs of it" (*QR* 28 [1822], 200). In practice, the role of the libel trial as a test of print agency was mitigated by the tactical ironies that linked radical protest with government repression. When writers and editors became courtroom defendants, they sometimes shed their claim upon public opinion, and instead invoked the principle of systematic self-destruction as a way of shifting responsibility from oppositional discourse to government policy. Wooler's response to prosecution in 1817 was typical of this legal strategy of displacement:

He was accused of exciting discontent against the King: he denied it. The ministers, those who trampled on the rights of the people, who kept them slaves and mocked their misery, by telling them they were free, excited discontent: it was not this paragraph or that paragraph that could so operate; but a measure hateful in itself, and destructive of ancient and indubitable rights, did indeed excite discontent and stir up to rebellion.[9]

The disruptive effect of "a measure hateful in itself" made the intervention of radical "paragraphs" irrelevant. The law assisted these evasions and ambiguities by defining libel in terms of subversive "tendency." Criminal intention on the part of the author, printer, or publisher, and criminal consequences in the world, were deemed unnecessary.[10] This principle, which entered the law as early as the landmark 1606 Star Chamber case *De famosis libellis* and was reinscribed in the Blasphemous and Seditious Libels Act of 1819, became a crux for radical attacks on the law of libel: "Only think of the extent of this word *tendency*! Only think of the boundless extent of such a word" (*CPR* 32 [1817], 360). The search for tendency, rather than effect *per se*, threatened to reduce libel to a formal game, in which texts themselves contained the whole complex dynamic of political unrest. This had advantages from the government's perspective: tendency was easier to prove than effect, and the textual focus accorded with an official policy that traced popular discontent "to the machinations of a comparatively small number of individuals."[11] But a formal definition of libel entailed risks as well, since the extraordinary repressive powers that ministers wanted could only be authorized by evidence of actual unrest. Under the tense conditions of the late 1810s and early 1820s, formal containment through the doctrine of "tendency" was not feasible, and libel remained a "sociolegal calculation." Lord Liverpool argued in the House of Lords what political trials confirmed, that patterns of effect extended beyond the printed page:

They must look not only to the nature of the libel which the libeller wrote, but they must also consider the effect it had, or was likely to have, on those to whom it was addressed. Of late years, circumstances which tended to raise the country to the height of prosperity and glory had occurred; but those circumstances, though highly beneficial, had also brought certain evils with them. (*PD* 41 [1819–20], 739)

Tendency, or the effect a piece of writing "was likely to have," included surrounding "circumstances," and considerations about "those to whom it was addressed." That radical discourse tried to incorporate what might normally be treated as circumstance (or context) further ensured that prosecution would spill beyond the formal limits of the text. The price of a publication was, for example, a feature of the text and of its impact. Once a jury was "satisfied that the libel had the tendency charged," they could assume that "its form and cheapness were calculated to accelerate its circulation, and more widely to disseminate its baneful effects" (*TT* 67).

Criminal trials influenced the construction of radical authorship as well as radical textuality. In an incisive critique of the way literary studies of censorship have tended to collapse "the writer's legal and aesthetic personalities," assimilating both to the romantic figure of "the transgressive subject," David Saunders and Ian Hunter remind us that criminal liability was attached "not to the activity of *writing* but to that of *publication*."[12] The law of libel seized upon the printed text as a set of potential effects, achieved through publication, distribution, and reception as well as composition. The campaign against Carlile's entire publishing and bookselling operation (the "war of the shopmen") demonstrated that no one involved in producing and distributing radical discourse was immune from prosecution.[13] At the same time, it is interesting to see how the law itself came to endorse the notion of transgressive authorship that Saunders and Hunter critique. As the term "author" came, under romantic auspices, to identify the unique, identifiable origin of a discursive effect, it named precisely what the government wanted to discover in its dealings with popular unrest: "the machinations of a comparatively small number of individuals." Publication and circulation were drawn under this culturally potent but (perhaps) manageable sign. At Daniel Isaac Eaton's 1812 trial for publishing Paine's *Age of Reason*, the prosecution admitted that the defendant was "not the author of the book in question," but insisted that he came to "participate in the guilt of the author" when he "published it to the world."[14] At Hone's first trial, the Attorney General insisted that Hone was "the fittest object for prosecution" because "he was at least the original publisher, if not the author," but then went on, curiously, to collapse the first role into the second: "If Mr. Hone had not actually written it with his own hand, he had been the means of its first and most extensive circulation; if not the author of the tract, he was the author of its publication; the form and price at which it was given out" (*TT* 63). Under the strain of political crisis and legal repression, radical authorship was as contradictory and richly overdetermined as radical form. Where the law pursued everyone involved in a publishing and bookselling operation, it tended to disseminate discursive responsibility through the entire "communications circuit," yielding the "war of the shopmen" and collective editorial projects like the *Newgate Monthly Magazine*. But where the law instead fixed upon an author or editor as unique source, it encouraged heroic courtroom confessions of personal responsibility: "In publishing the paper in question, he had done nothing of which he ought to be ashamed; and so far from shrinking in the avowal of his being the author of it, he gloried in this opportunity of declaring that he still maintained the sentiments which were charged against him as libelous."[15] Forced to straddle individual responsibility and collective action, radical discourse wound up reproducing the Attorney General's ambiguous notion of the "author of . . . publication." When Richard Carlile looked back on his own emergence "as a public character" in collaboration with Sherwin, he presented himself as the author of *Sherwin's Political Register*, and of an entire phase in English political history: "I may look back upon myself as the author of all his bold writing; for, it was the work of my responsibility . . . Indeed, I may, without vanity, look at myself as the author of all the excitement of 1819." Incredible as this exercise in radical egotism may seem, it was predicated on a mundane sense of what authorship entailed, for Carlile referred here to a period in which it was his "responsibility" first "to carry the publications round to the shops for sale," and then to serve as Sherwin's publisher and bookseller. "Fearless responsibility" in the face of "Castlereagh, Eldon, and Sidmouth," rather than "writing scraps of my own" or indulging in "literary finery," secured Carlile the vaunted name of author (*R* 11 [1825], 102–05).

THE COURTROOM DEFENSE AS PUBLIC OFFENSE

At the core of all these controversies over the law of libel, the trial itself became an important forum for political controversy, "a kind of gladiatorial contest between the uncompromising conservatism of Castlereagh and the unyielding demands of the radical reformers."[16] Writers and editors often conducted their own defense, and were given an opportunity to confront leading agents of the government before a sympathetic and verbally supportive audience. "Uncompromising" though the two sides may have been, their courtroom encounters became an oral performance of the shifting logic of system and counter-system, marked by the same ironies and tactical maneuvers found in print discourse. Presiding judges colluded openly with the prosecution, and defendants responded in kind, calling the authority of the court and the very legitimacy of the law into question. Lord Ellenborough's spirited intervention in Eaton's prepared defense during his 1812 trial for blasphemous libel indicated how, in an atmosphere of intense personal and political animosity, the legal framework of a trial could be fractured and contested:

[MR. EATON] I found the Bible so full of contradictions, and so full of wonderful
     things, that it induced me to examine this said Bible itself –

LORD ELLENBOROUGH – Defendant, I must inform you that this is not to be made
    use of as an opportunity for you to revile the Christian religion; and, if
    you persist in aspersing it, I will not only silence you, but I will animadvert
    on your conduct as an offence, of the grossest kind, against the dignity of
    the Court.
MR. EATON – My Lord, I have no intention whatever of giving offence.
LORD ELLENBOROUGH – If there is any thing in that paper which will serve you,
    read it; but I will not suffer the Christian religion to be reviled, while I sit
    in this court, and possess the power of preventing it.
MR. EATON – I believe there is nothing in what follows that can offend any
    person.

Eaton was allowed to continue reading his defense after he assured the
court that he was not going to continue pursuing the strategy of offense,
but he did not get far before he was interrupted again:

LORD ELLENBOROUGH observed – I will not give much time, for that paper is not
    drawn up like a defence; it is framed as an insult to the Court. Lay down
    your paper, which does not bear any semblance to a defence, and address
    the Court, if you please.
MR EATON – I conceive every part of this paper as my defence.
LORD ELLENBOROUGH – It forms part of your *offence* against the public; but I see
    nothing in it like a *defence*.[17]

A forum for "*defence*" became an "opportunity" for "*offence*," and a presiding judge was forced to test his "power of preventing" against a defendant's determination to repeat and extend his original provocation.[18]
Like the treason trials of the 1790s, the libel trials of the early nineteenth
century became what Alan Liu has called "contestatory inquiries into
the literary act," through which the state and its enemies articulated "an
entire systematics – and countersystematics – of the verbal act."[19]
Dialectical combat was not, of course, a local rift in the structure of
political conflict, so these contests spilled easily back and forth between
the courtroom and the press, as defendants found other means to express
what the law managed to silence.

    The ability to transform prosecution from an experience of defeat
into an opportunity for expression generated frank acknowledgments of
the negative structure of radical reform. "The waters of adversity, we
trust, have strengthened while they ran over us," Leigh Hunt claimed,
"and if we emerge only to be assailed with the sharpness of new winds,
the warm spirit within us, thank HEAVEN, performs its duty, and we glow,
healthfully and afresh, against the encounter" (*E*, no. 259 [December 13,
1812], 787).[20] It was possible to overestimate the pleasures of adversity;
prison terms, confiscations, and punitive fines guaranteed that radical

writers and editors did suffer at the hands of the law. But prosecution had material advantages, not the least of which was free publicity on a national scale. As the Scottish publisher of Wooler's trial wryly observed, "the defendant is under great obligations to Ministers for directing the prosecutions. The Black Dwarf, of the existence of which we were ourselves wholly ignorant, has been thereby happily advertised."[21] When Carlile was prosecuted for publishing Paine's *Age of Reason*, he was able to sell off all remaining copies of the offensive work, and circulation of the *Republican* increased in the same period by one half, to reach 15,000 copies.[22] Writers and editors who managed to continue working through their trial and imprisonment emerged with an enhanced status in the reform movement.[23] The government was acutely aware of this difficulty. In advocating stiffer penalties in the House of Lords, Ellenborough pointed out "that the prosecution and conviction of libellers under the existing law produced frequently the effect which the libeller himself had chiefly in view – that of extending the sale of his work, and thereby putting lucre in his pocket" (*PD* 41 [1819–20], 717).[24] The Blasphemous and Seditious Libels Act of 1819 stipulated banishment for a second offense, but even this was not enough to make the law an effective instrument of political control. Prosecutions dropped off substantially by the mid-1820s, under a growing perception that they were counter-productive.[25]

Given the popular radical inclination towards ritual and theater, it should come as no surprise that the movement was eager to exploit the "intensely dramatic situation" of the courtroom.[26] In printed accounts of these trials, especially those brought out by radical publishers, colorful stage directions called attention to the anger, frustration, or exhaustion of the combatants. Prominent notice was paid to heightened emotion and extraordinary incident: Cobbett's supposed arrival in court at the head of a band of supporters, the judge's refusal to hear Mary-Anne Carlile's aggressive prepared defense, and Hone's melodramatic account of his destitute poverty, in the midst of which a member of the audience fainted.[27] Jurors were a favorite target of dramatic effects. Judges pressured them with inflammatory instructions that identified the text under indictment as "a foul, atrocious, and malignant libel," or "a most impious and profane libel," and defendants challenged them to ignore the court's authority and follow their own conscience: "I leave the case entirely in your hands, as judges, not only of the fact but of the law; for I still contend that the jury are the only proper and competent judges in cases like these."[28] Jurors were drawn into the political theater of the trial when they quarrelled among themselves, or disputed the authority of the presiding judge.[29] The proceedings spilled further beyond their appointed bounds through the intervention of partisan crowds assembled in the gallery and in the streets.[30] Printed versions of these trials often opened with some notice of "the extraordinary sensation these trials occasioned throughout the metropolis,"[31] and then faithfully transcribed the applause, murmering, hissing, stamping of feet, coughing, and laughter that punctuated the proceedings. Judges responded by threatening to clear the courtroom, while defendants encouraged public demonstrations of support.[32] Wooler went so far as to enlist the audience in evidence, arguing that laughter from the gallery proved that the libel in question was a piece of entertainment rather than sedition: "It cannot be read without laughter, and every man in the Court will bear witness to the fact" (*VR* 104). Where a defendant managed to secure an acquittal, the public framework of the trial came full circle as popular intervention spilled out of the courtroom and back into the streets:

The loudest acclamations were instantly heard in all parts of the Court; *Long live the honest jury*, and *an honest jury for ever*, were exclaimed by many voices: the waving of hats, handkerchiefs, and applauses continued for several minutes. When order had been somewhat restored, Mr. Justice ABBOTT interposed, and desired that those who felt inclined to rejoice at the decision, would reserve the expressions of their satisfaction for a fitter place and opportunity. The people accordingly left the Court, and as they proceeded along the streets, the language of joy was most loudly and unequivocally expressed; every one with whom they met, and to whom they communicated the event, being forward to swell the peal. (*TT* 70)

The utopian dimensions of this communal denouement remind us that printed versions of these trials were narrative constructions, typically brought out by radical publishers to achieve a political effect. It may be tempting to read the circularity of the narrative, with its close framework of popular support, as a form of aesthetic containment.[33] In such a view, the closing fantasy of spontaneous communication and collective feeling becomes symptomatic of a radical desire to transcend real conditions of conflict, repression, and fragmentation. But it is worth insisting that the construction of a public framework for these trials was an engaged rather than an escapist gesture, a final repudiation of the government's campaign to fracture and contain radical protest. As long as word of a trial got out, in spoken and printed versions, even a guilty verdict would not be the last word.

Political trials provided a critical intersection of speech and writing, of oral and print culture, within the broad outlines of a radical counter-public sphere. Wooler's 1817 trial was a vivid case in point. I suggested earlier that the Attorney General's opening statement, which drew attention to the defendant's "curious" habit of composing at the printing press, seemed to suspend Wooler between personal isolation and public engagement. As the trial unfolded, with frequent interruptions from the audience, it became clear that Wooler and his supporters were staging a series of direct encounters meant to prevent his isolation and recover some collective identity. The counterplot of radical reconciliation culmi-nated at the end of Wooler's longest speech in his own defense:

> The Defendant . . . addressed the Jury in a speech of two hours in length, characterised by great natural powers of eloquence, and distinguished in some parts by such irresistible touches as to call forth the spontaneous plaudits of the auditory, who, notwithstanding the repeated threats of commitment by the Court for disorder, could not be restrained from expressing their coincidence in the sentiments expressed by the Defendant.[34]

The political theater of the trial converted writing into speech, reader into orator, and reading public into embodied audience. Wooler's "natural powers of eloquence" produced a seamless "coincidence" of feeling between himself and "the auditory," closing troubling rifts within a reform movement fractured by repression and internal dissension. A figure who had emerged from the informal underworld of radical as-sembly to become the editor of a celebrated radical weekly paper, but who then found himself confined to prison and to print, was able to return through the spoken word to an unmediated culture of radical sociability.[35] The circular narrative structure of the trial extended this crucial figure of reconciliation, and completed the ritual reconstruction of a stigmatized community in opposition.

Yet the very deliberateness of these communion rituals and framing devices called attention to some awkward problems of representation. To begin with, the supportive audience in the courtroom was, despite its "universal" outbursts, an imperfect synecdoche, not the entire public that the radical movement would seem to require. The defendant's "natural powers of eloquence" were, furthermore, exercised for the great bulk of the public through a secondary representation in print. Much of what I have already described in these trials invites similar sus-picion. Printed versions were typically brought out by radical publishers, and the weekly press contained ample evidence of the contrivance that went into a "spontaneous" public response. The effort to recover com-munity through "spontaneous" and "natural . . . eloquence" presents a

on of what Mary Jacobus has called the "oral fallacy of
eories of language."[36] If this seems odd in a movement so
ified with print, it is important to see how the radical ideal-
peech and unmediated intercourse was precipitated by a
campaign against public assembly. In a "Warning to the
reopie issued as the Six Acts were being debated in parliament, Wooler
cautioned that rights of free assembly were both more crucial and more
fragile than the rights of a free press:

> It is only the *union of numbers*, and the *concentration of opinion*, which has any weight
> in checking the mischievous views of a wicked administration. It is only in
> public meetings that the real voice of the people is ever heard . . . The assembled
> multitude loses sight of all private interest, and every heart beats only for the
> general good. The spark of patriotism runs with electric swiftness from pulse to
> pulse, until the whole mass vibrates in unison. Then, despots, tremble, for the
> hour of retribution is at hand! (*BD* 3 [1819], 695)

The privilege that was implicitly accorded sentiment and speech in the
courtroom was theorized here as a political program: the "heart" and
the "voice" were an avenue from "private interest" to "the general
good." Again, it might be tempting to discover in this passage evidence
of the way radical protest was contained as its energies were dissipated in
a politics of sentiment. But, for all their obvious idealization, Wooler's
account of public assembly and his courtroom experience of "coincidence" aimed to preserve, rather than evade or transcend, a radical
commitment to resistance across the entire expressive register. The
spoken word, direct contact, and collective feeling were not simply fictions projected by the radical imagination onto the past, to compensate
for the alienating effects of social and economic modernization. On the
contrary, they were actual elements of popular life, increasingly organized in this period as a form of political experience. "From the beginning of the nineteenth century through Luddism and the parliamentary
reform agitation of the 1810s," Craig Calhoun has argued, "personal
bonds among kin, neighbors, friends and co-workers provided the
primary basis for mobilization."[37] Radical editors tried to structure and
sustain these embedded relations (by advertising meetings and encouraging collective reading), and, while it is possible to fault much of what
they did, the task itself was not a fantasy. At the same time, the "natural
powers of eloquence" displayed by Wooler in court did not mitigate his
artificial powers in print. He found himself under indictment because
the *Black Dwarf* was widely circulated, and its circulation only increased
as a result of his trial. The radical effort to transform the courtroom into

a political theater, and to mobilize that theater against restrictions on print and public assembly, was motivated not by a nostalgic desire to retreat into a community of the spoken word, but rather by a desire to protect the complex interactions of political speech and print from the divisive effects of state repression.

If Cobbett tended more than most radical editors to privilege oral communication, he too provided rich evidence of the way speech and print interacted in a radical counterpublic sphere. Imprisoned for seditious libel from 1810 to 1812, Cobbett grew increasingly frustrated with his separation from his family, from his Botley farm, and from the political events that normally sustained his writing. Upon his release from Newgate, he staged a ritual return to a community free of the interference of print and repression:

The inhabitants of the village gathered round me; the young men and the boys and their fathers and mothers, listening to my account of the CAUSE of my absence . . . hearing me calling upon fathers and mothers to reflect on what I said, and on their sons to bear it in mind to the last hour of their lives. – In short, the thing ended precisely as it ought to end, in a plain appeal to the understanding of the inhabitants of a village; to young countrymen and boys, and their fathers and mothers. (*CPR* 22 [1812], 94)

Fitting though it may have been, this pastoral reconciliation was (like Wooler's courtroom epiphany) not the "end" of the affair, but a point of departure for further print engagements with the system of legal and political injustice. A "plain appeal to . . . the inhabitants of a village" took effect in the *Political Register* as a printed text that circulated among thousands of readers, in widely scattered towns and cities. In the very next issue of the *Register*, Cobbett announced his practice of reprinting an abbreviated account of his prosecution (including his return to Botley) on the last page of the paper, "so that it may, if people choose, be cut off, and pasted upon walls or other places" (*CPR* 22 [1812], 110). His desire to recover a utopian version of rural life did not stop him from enlisting the residents of Botley in print, and threatening to realize the tory nightmare of a world covered over with print protest. Again, the figure of return implied circulation rather than circularity, repetition and extension rather than closure.

RADICAL ASSEMBLY IN PRINT

Public assembly was indispensable to radical expression in print because it allowed the movement to assemble its constituent parts and challenge the government's monopoly on public authority. Abstract print claims about public opinion were suddenly and dramatically converted into (sometimes vast) outdoor assemblies of individual bodies, in a manner that integrated the politics of the street and the politics of the printed page. Yet the contradictory structure of radical representation remained, even in meetings that seemed to present an irrefutable embodiment of popular opinion. Whether it took the form of a spontaneous village gathering or a monster urban meeting, radical assembly tended to be conceived as a provisional gathering of reformers in opposition. The epiphanies of Wooler and Cobbett certainly glimpsed more than this, anticipating utopian modes of sociability, but they were immediately enlisted in support of a further oppositional engagement in print. The radical crowd was a remedial representation, designed to repair rather than reconstitute public authority. The radical movement was acutely aware that it could not on its own authority constitute the simple, descriptive representation that it prescribed for reform. Like other elements of radical discourse and action, public assembly shared the imperfection and instability of a corrupt economy of representation.

In order to explore the complex structure of radical assembly, particularly as it was transcribed in print, I want to focus on one of the period's most celebrated and widely reported crowd events, Henry Hunt's return to London from Manchester on September 13, 1819, on his way to being prosecuted for his role in the Manchester meeting that had turned into the Peterloo Massacre. An anonymous three-penny pamphlet brought out by Thomas Dolby, *The Triumphal Entry of Henry Hunt, Esq. into London*, proceeded from a polemical introduction to a fairly straightforward narrative of the event. Strict attention was paid to the organization of the event in time and space: "So early as eleven o'clock in the morning Islington was the centre of the utmost bustle"; "The principal managers of the procession assembled at an early hour at Islington"; "From Highgate, about half-past two o'clock, the crowds came pouring down."[38] Yet, as the numbers mounted, and the entire urban landscape came to be "literally covered with people" (7), a sequential narrative deteriorated. The text then resorted to a more impressionistic style, in order to capture the "politics of sight" that was among the chief attractions of crowd events: [39]

The roads were lined with hackney-coaches and taxed carts – in short, every thing that could be hired – donkey, horse, mule, waggon, or coach, were all in requisition, wherever the eye ranged. Solid masses of people covered the roads;

handkerchiefs and red ribbands floated as if out of the windows; cheers and acclamations preceded and followed, and were heard at every side of the immense cavalcade that formed the procession. The simple fasces preceded, and blessings and applauses followed, to grace the triumph. In truth, we want words to give full effect to all that presented itself to our view. We could not calculate upon any thing bordering upon the enthusiasm which was every where displayed. Streets crowded – shops shut up in all the streets through which the procession passed – no fear apparent, no dismay lurking on the countenance, and thousands entreating to know – "When will he reach this? – Have we a chance of seeing him?" – "Success to Hunt." – "They would not have sabred the people at Manchester if they expected this." (6)

As the receptive "eye" of the anonymous narrator "ranged" over an increasingly dense sequence of arresting images, active principles of textual construction gave way to the crowd's "most imposing aspect" (7). Sentence structure itself deteriorated into a rudimentary sequence of semicolons and dashes. Even the hero of the event could not resist the pressure of the spectacle, and soon "found it in vain to alter the course of the procession" (7). Mona Ozouf's work on the French Revolutionary festival has called attention to the anxieties involved in a politics of spectacle, and specifically to the risks of popular inertia in a political theater that fails to encourage active participation.[40] Dolby's pamphlet seems to have dealt with this anxiety in part by making the crowd itself the object of admiration, allowing an attitude of passive reflection to devolve upon the narrative.

Yet the objective pretensions of an impressionistic manner only threw the political claims of the text into sharp relief. This sensorium was not without motive or method. Gathered under the direction of "the principal managers of the procession," the crowd was firmly embedded in the contemporary politics of electoral reform. The decision to honor Hunt was itself a piece of "countertheater,"[41] as John Gale Jones indicated when he explained "the motives which induced the Committee of Management" to organize "a public procession": "Other public characters . . . were received with that ceremonial" (15). The event challenged the authority of the state by drawing freely from the conventions of military triumph, royal coronation, and electioneering ritual. If Hunt's refusal to allow the crowd to unyoke his horses departed from the conventions of a successful parliamentary candidate (5), this was a deliberate signal that the radical movement could not yet chair its destined member of parliament. As Gale Jones later observed, the relevant framework for Hunt's return to London was radical resistance to political corruption, not the partisan traditions of parliamentary government:

> Mr. GALE JONES said, the spectacle which all of them had that day witnessed was of a most extraordinary kind: it was not, as in contested elections, the triumph of one candidate over another, rival candidate; it was not the triumph of one faction over another faction; but it was the triumph of an honest and a genuine Englishman over that threefold monster – a ministerial, magisterial, and military despotism. (*WBG* I [1819], 307)

Hunt's return was the ritual enactment of a radical claim that party differences had been supplanted by a more catastrophic division between the people and their oppressors. Where contemporary elections were governed by "consensus and the belief in 'fair play,'"[42] this radical triumph remained stubbornly committed to political warfare. The radical crowd as autonomous expression of public will was inevitably converted into a more relative political counterstatement. When Hunt was similarly fêted in York, Carlile claimed the event was "strikingly indicative of public feeling in this country," and then turned that "feeling" against the enemies of reform: "Let those who say that a majority of the people of the country would approve the late measures of Parliament, reflect on this scene!" (*R* 2 [1820], 325). In the absence of reliable electoral mechanisms, print reflections on the urban crowd undertook to challenge the authority of the state, in the official parliamentary language of "majority" and "minority."

Like the unstamped press, radical assembly was suffused in the semiotics of political resistance. Trivial features of the urban landscape gathered polemical significance: the "taxed cart" was a swipe at the government's voracious appetite (6), a "bandaged" boy turned out to be a survivor of Peterloo (5), and "a large terrier dog" appeared, "decorated with the badge of Universal Suffrage" and with the words "No dog tax."[43] If Hunt's return was organized *against* parliamentary corruption, it proceeded *through* the contested representational space that corruption entailed. The people gathered in the streets because they were not gathered in the House of Commons, and they engaged in modes of political expression that ran contrary to the principles of reform. The traces of collective ecstasy and electioneering ritual that were evident in this scene were often attacked in a radical press committed to rational individualism and unmediated representation.[44] The anxious implication of Hunt's triumph in corrupt modes of representation culminated in an obscure and obscuring rhetoric of the urban political sublime. Efforts to estimate the precise number of individuals gathered along the route ("many thousands," then 50,000, then 200,000) broke down as the crowd swelled, and the text lost its computational as well as its narrative faculties: "We could not calculate upon any thing bordering upon the enthusiasm which was every where displayed" (6); "The assembled multitude was . . . so immense, as to defy any thing like an accurate attempt at computation" (7). Individual bodies collapsed into indistinguishable "masses of people": "All appeared one solid mass of human beings from the pavement to the tops of the houses" (8).[45] If the irrational geography of a pre-modern city was unsuited to the open air festivals of the French Revolution,[46] it could be made to serve the ends of a London reform movement more interested in political resistance than in absolute liberation. The figure of extra-parliamentary pressure was dramatically realized in the narrow streets of London: "The confined space which [Sun-street] presented, rendered the passage of the crowd still more difficult than before, and many serious accidents were produced by the pressure" (7). As the crowd swelled, it threatened the procession – "the street for a time became impassable" – and the text itself finally joined in the general paralysis: "In truth, we want words to give full effect to all that presented itself to our view" (6).[47] This rhetoric of inexpressibility before a radicalized urban sublime seemed to fulfill and undermine the event's vocation as a political counterstatement:

The *coup d'oeil* which presented itself at the confluence of the Pentonville, Islington, and City Roads, completely sets description at defiance. The heat and the dust, and the almost overwhelming pressure of the increasing multitude, did not seem to have the least effect on those who were assembled to witness a sight at once so novel and so imposing – a sight, the recollection of which cannot be forgotten, and the results of which cannot be sufficiently estimated. (6)

In order to defy its enemies, the radical movement staged "a sight" or visual "*coup*" that defied its own political and linguistic theories of simple descriptive representation. The idea that "the results" of Hunt's return to London could not be "sufficiently estimated" was appropriately ambiguous. Radical representation on this scale could have no adequate counterpart in language or in print, and was therefore unrepresentable.[48]

Historians have recently stressed the role of this kind of political ritual in promoting unity and cohesion.[49] Hunt's triumphant return clearly aimed in this direction, but it is interesting that the radical movement showed itself more willing to probe beneath the surfaces of an unrepresentable collectivity, and discover evidence of dissent, when it met the "unprecedented mass mobilization around 'patriotic' events" in this period.[50] Cobbett traced the "carousing all over the country" that greeted the royal Jubilee in 1809 to a "malignant purpose of reviving the distinction of *Jacobins* and *Anti-jacobins* by imputing disaffection" to those who refused to participate. The discovery of this division allowed him to deconstruct the entire loyalist project: "It appears strange, that, when it is their business to make the world . . . believe that the nation is *unanimous* on their side, they should let any thing drop, which amounts to a confession, that there are people, who think differently from themselves."[51] The *Examiner* followed a different route to similar "differences" in its account of the coronation of George IV. Evidence of "scanty" attendance and "*empty benches*" turned the calculating faculties of the observer of the crowd from multiplication to division: "The booths and galleries . . . were *four-fifths* empty" (*E*, no. 707 [July 22, 1821], 451, 454). Where Henry Hunt's followers extended continuously "from the pavement to the tops of the houses," an imperfect royalist crowd exposed embarrassing rifts in the urban landscape. Illuminations for the Jubilee were "partial" rather than "general": "The Mansion-house, the Bank, Royal Exchange, Lloyd's Coffee-house, the India-house . . . and all the royal tradesmen's houses, were splendidly lighted up," but "there was scarcely one lane or alley lighted up throughout the whole metropolis." In sum, "not one street in ten was illuminated" (*E*, no. 96 [October 29, 1809], 700–01).[52]

Given the radical movement's insistence upon social and political distinctions, and its anxiety about a politics that exceeded descriptive representation, it should not be a surprise that *The Triumphal Entry* wound up resisting its own collapse into singularity and stunned silence. One of the reasons for assembling reformers on this scale was, after all, to demonstrate the movement's capacity for organization, and its commitment to certain distinctions of gender, rank, and property. The narrative impulse towards clarity and order, rather than obscurity and threatening disorder, culminated in the procession of symbols arranged by the "Committee of Management" in Hunt's honor. A text that elsewhere broke off into fragmentary description and stunned silence recovered its bearings and achieved graphic clarity as it turned from the crowd to the object of the crowd's gaze, and provided "an ample description of the banners and devices":

The procession advanced from Angel Inn, in the following order:

A Horseman, with the emblem of "Unity"; a bundle of sticks, supported by a group of Footmen and Horsemen.

A Green Silk Flag, with gold letters and Irish Harp. Inscription – "Universal, Civil, and Religious Liberty"; borne and supported by six Irishmen, and numerous other Footmen.

A Footman, bearing the Flag Mourning, bound round with Crape, and inscribed – "To the immortal memory of the Reformers killed at Manchester, August 16, 1819."

Horsemen and Footmen, with a new White Flag, on which was inscribed – "Palladium of Liberty, a Free Press."

Three Carriages, in which were some persons connected with the Press.

The Landau, in which sat Mr. Hunt, it was drawn by Six Bay Horses, which, as well as the Postillions, were decorated with Scarlet Cockades.

Horsemen and Footmen, bearing the Red Flag, inscribed – "Universal Suffrage," and the Flag inscribed "Henry Hunt, the Heroic Champion of Liberty."

Mr. Hunt's Landau was surrounded by several Friends on Horseback, and Members of the Committee with White Wands and Scarlet Cockades – Hat bands with "Hunt for ever!" &c.

Carriages filled by personal friends of Mr. Hunt, and by several Ladies dressed in white.

    A White Silk Flag. Inscription – "Trial by Jury"

      A Carriage, containing Friends.

      Groups of Footmen.

    Carriages, Horsemen, and Footmen,

      Flag, "Liberty or Death."

        Groups of Footmen,

      Flag, "England, Scotland, Ireland."

    On a Red, White, and Green ground.

The cavalcade closed with groupes of carriages, horsemen, and footmen, and an immense concourse of people, who rent the air with their shouts.

The band struck up in succession, in the course of the day, the following airs – "God save the King" – "Rule Britannia" – "See the Conquering Hero comes." (6–7)[53]

This serial display of distinction and significance, located at the center of an indistinguishable mass of bodies, cleared an ample space in which to view the single body of Henry Hunt. If the procession was presented as an autonomous unit, typographically set off from the rest of the event, it too borrowed freely from the conventions of state ritual (coronations, elections, funerals), and gathered its meanings from a wider sphere of contested representations.[54] The rendition of "God save the King," for example, became multivalent and potentially threatening in an event that emulated royal ritual, but presented the body of a reform leader rather than a king. "Unity" may have been the watchword of this symbolic procession, but conflict and ambiguity were its method, and it served to bring forward rifts within the radical movement as well as between reformers and the state.[55]

Contention extended to the very idea of symbolic display. Parades like this may seem trivial in retrospect, but they were viewed with genuine alarm by the government, particularly when they incorporated slogans like "Liberty or Death." In parliamentary debates over Peterloo, ministers complained that the flags and banners raised at the meeting had been "totally destructive of good order and of loyalty," and the Seditious Meetings Prevention Act of 1819 specifically prohibited meetings "with any flag, banner, or ensign."[56] Radicals debated symbolic expression among themselves, though their worry was corruption rather than disorder. Resistance to ritual was strongest among avowed republicans, but it extended throughout the reform movement, driven in part by a sense that the politics of spectacle was subsidized by the poor. John Wade's attack on the monarchy in the *Black Book* was typical:

Royalty, after all, is an expensive government! What is a king without an aristocracy and a priesthood? and what are any of these, unless supported in splendour and magnificence? It is a system in which men are sought to be governed by the *senses*, rather than the *understanding*, and is more adapted to a barbarous than a civilized state. Pageantry and show, the parade of crowns and coronets, of gold keys, sticks, white wands, and black rods; of ermine and lawn, and maces and wigs; – these are the chief attributes of monarchy. They are ridiculous when men become enlightened. (*BB* 110)[57]

Though submerged in the narrative of Hunt's return, such attitudes had generated substantial controversy during the organization of the event:

One party wished to make his introduction as splendid, and as public as possible. He had achieved a great victory, and merited a triumphal entry, and a civic crown. This was not opposed by the other party, out of any denial of his merits, but it was contended that less ostentation would be more adapted to the display of conscious worth and real dignity. (*BD* 3 [1819], 598)

The fête of "the Heroic Champion of Liberty" was a compromise, impressive enough to honor the returning hero and warrant the admiring gaze of the crowd, conventional enough to include challenging echoes of state ritual, yet muted enough to satisfy tender republican consciences. Out of Wade's original catalogue of "the parade of crowns and coronets, of gold keys, sticks, white wands, and black rods; of ermine and lawn, and maces and wigs," only the simple white wands remained. Hunt was, furthermore, not as elaborately distanced and hierarchically framed by attendants as a king would be in a similar ceremony. The text reinforced this impression by eschewing the elaborate borders and typographical decorations that went along with print representations of crown ritual.[58]

A radical politics of spectacle also exposed gender differences within the movement. Men appeared in this procession as autonomous and empowered agents, mounted on horseback and bearing symbolic flags and wands, while women were relegated to carriages and all but effaced by the white drapery that announced their difference from the prostitutes and crones of tory caricature.[59] Distinctions were marked even in the crowd, where individual bodies tended to collapse into "one solid mass." As viewers, women were set apart from the procession by an additional set of framing devices: "The windows and balconies were filled with elegantly attired females" (8).[60] Leonore Davidoff and Catherine Hall have shown that this marginal position was characteristic of "women's place in the public world" of the nineteenth century, across the entire political spectrum.[61] The effect was particularly striking in a radical movement that was busy compensating for its own marginal role in public life. *The Triumphal Entry* raised an attitude of mere observation into something approaching political intervention: simply to be present here was to be counted among a reform constituency. As this feminine political attitude was tentatively empowered, it was denied to women. Taken off the street and away from the front rank of spectators, female reformers were absorbed into the setting: "Every window was thronged with spectators, and from several of them were exhibited red flags; the ladies in the windows were likewise distinguished by red favours" (7). The women as window-dressing became a sign of something else: wealth, virtue, respectability, and perhaps too the sense of local purchase denied Henry Hunt when he was accused of running a wandering minstrel show. The banners that passed through the streets did not of course extend their promise of "universal" suffrage to "the ladies in the windows."

Against these sharp gender distinctions, the triumphal procession did try to unite the reform movement, if only through the crude syntax of a list of constituent parts: London shared the stage with provincial cities like Manchester; England, Scotland, and Ireland were represented, as were humble "footmen" and carriaged elite, orators like Hunt and "persons connected with the Press." If radicals distrusted the hegemonic social unity they associated with state ritual, they were eager to promote solidarity, or unity in opposition.[62] The "simple fasces" was an appropriate leading symbol in the procession because its meanings extended beyond unity to resistance: as the embodiment of a Roman magistrate's power, the fasces suggested republican ideology, and a readiness to appropriate civil authority. The semiotic richness of the event helped to join all those assembled in a single expression of protest: a sharp distinction between spectator and spectacle was to some extent mitigated as the flags and banners surrounding Hunt radiated outward through a similar network of cockades, ribbons, and hatbands in the crowd.[63] The adornments of the crowd tended, however, to point back to the "Heroic Champion" and to the event's orchestrated symbolic core. Any coherent expression of radical unity here remained symbolic rather than descriptive, issuing *from* the procession and *for*, rather than *of*, the crowd.[64] Where the crowd became a spectacle in its own right, its meanings were inexpressibly sublime.

The most vexing problem of representation in *The Triumphal Entry* was the relationship between the mass of bodies in the crowd and the single body of their leader. Flags bearing the slogan "Hunt and Liberty" indicated that, like Wilkes before him, Henry Hunt had become the embodiment of reform sentiment.[65] In articulating this representative status through a subversion of crown ceremony, the celebration of his return to London set up the awkward problem of an exalted position within a democratic movement. Compensatory gestures, indicating that "Mr. Hunt bore his blushing honours meekly" (6), could not conceal the fact that the "Heroic Champion" had attained "the very pinnacle of popularity" (10). Hunt's entire career unfolded along the faultline between heroic leadership and mass democracy, and his presence here brought out important tensions within radical representation. Craig Calhoun has argued that populist leaders like Hunt "were less oriented toward representative politics than toward the sort of direct democracy of mass meetings," and "sought to go 'beyond democracy to consensus.'"[66] While there is certainly evidence for this trajectory, I would suggest that tactical necessity dictated a more permanent tension between the two modes of political organization: the "direct democracy of mass meetings" was a provisional means of articulating the "consensus" that would secure "representative politics." Convinced that they were excluded from parliament by corruption, radicals did what they had to do to make themselves seen and heard. The celebration of Hunt's return drew freely from a wide range of incompatible traditions of political representation and deliberation: parliamentary elections, the right to petition, the king's representative body, the oppositional press, universal suffrage. The aim of all these modes of resistance was to correct parliamentary representation. As Hunt moved through the streets of London, he traced an inexorable route towards his election to the House of Commons as Member for Preston in 1830. Until that time, the precise mechanisms that linked him with his supporters had to remain improvised and uncertain.

Hunt's climactic speech to his supporters confirmed the ambiguity of remedial representation. His preliminary demand for silence reiterated the trope of narrative paralysis, though here the crowd joined the text in giving way to the overwhelming voice of the hero:

Mr. Hunt then amid the loudest acclamations, mounted the box of the landau, and addressed the immense multitude who had accompanied him thus far throughout the greater part of the day. He said, Fellow Countrymen – I only ask of you to allow me to say a few words. Let none of the multitude cry "Silence," for that in itself is a preventive of order; the sound in such a tremendous assembly being always calculated to create mistake and confusion (in a few moments the most breathless attention was manifested). (8)

Hunt became articulate through the "silence" of his supporters, but that very silence, coming as it did after "*thunders of applause*" (8), was supposed to demonstrate a surprising popular capacity for collective action at his command. Hunt's pleas to the crowd were met with "Cries of 'We will! we will!'" (8), a revealing blend of popular assertion and submission. If the "Heroic Champion" was a provisional substitute for the parliamentary representative Hunt would one day become, the crowd was similarly imperfect. However large it became, it could never encompass the whole of "public feeling," and therefore spoke a synecdoche: "The conduct and patriotism you have evinced this day is not altogether your own. It is but a part of that glorious feeling which runs through every breast, and animates the mass of the population of those districts from which I came (*shouts of bravo*)" (8).[67] Satisfying as this claim may have been, *The Triumphal Entry* could not end with an expansive gesture towards an abstract public. The scope of the event finally contracted as Hunt and "300 or 400 persons" (9) retired to the Crown and Anchor Tavern, and to an organized political meeting whose structure was more complex than the simple relationship between hero and adoring crowd.[68]

Sheer consensus gave way to representation and deliberation. Yet even the enclosed and structured environment of a political meeting preserved traces of the radical dream that popular feeling could achieve uniform and undivided expression. The *"Cheers"* and *"Tumults of applause"* (15) in the tavern seemed no less loud and long than those in the streets, and a toast in support of Hunt still met with "a universal shout of applause" (11).

The tortuous dialectic of order and disorder, clarity and obscurity, in this text can be better understood in light of the difficult transition that Hunt was negotiating, for himself and for the reform movement, as he returned to London. John Belchem has shown how the strategy of the "mass platform," which culminated in Peterloo, linked a peaceable "politics of order" with a potentially violent "politics of disorder," through a tentative alliance between Henry Hunt and the elder James Watson, who secured the commitment of Spencean revolutionaries like Thistlewood and Evans to constitutional reform. Events in Manchester tested the strength of this co-operation. While most radical leaders were prepared "to rest their case on Peterloo, and revert to the 'politics of order,'" the Spencean "ultra-radicals drew a different lesson: Peterloo pointed the way to outright physical confrontation, now that the authorities had spilt the first blood." The final break in the alliance between Hunt and Watson that led to the collapse of the mass platform came during Hunt's return to London.[69] In a speech after dinner, reprinted in *The Triumphal Entry*, Hunt renounced Spencean ideology, and with it his provisional commitment to Watson and to the politics of disorder: "He had never said that there should be an equal division of property, and that there should be no poor people" (14). An event devoted to "unity" and to "an utter oblivion of the conflicts" (10) that splintered reform became an occasion for disunity. Hunt went on from here to his seat in the House of Commons, while Thistlewood and the "revolutionary party" proceeded on their course to Cato Street and the scaffold. The public unravelling of a political strategy that was inherently ambiguous about violence helps explain why physical force shadowed *The Triumphal Entry* from beginning to end, as both nightmare and fantasy, from an opening challenge to the confidence with which "the Country Gentlemen of England" held their "estate" and "rank" (2–3), to a final reflection that "in no single instance was it possible to discover any tendency to disorder" (16). The elder Watson, already prosecuted unsuccessfully for high treason over his role in the Spa Fields riots of December 1816, played a dominant role in the "Committee of

Management," and his appearance here at the head of a huge crowd was certain to inspire fear in the appropriate quarters, even if his message was one of order and discipline. Contradictory as its many signals may have been, *The Triumphal Entry* wound up issuing the same divided message as the mass platform: a popular *coup d'état* was not impossible, but for the moment the radical leadership would be content to stage a *"coup d'oeil."* The breakdown of order remained at the level of the spectacle.

"A FAIR, PLAIN, AND HONEST ACCOUNT"

While printed accounts of every form of public activity were central to the radical press in this period, trials held a special status, in part because they allowed defendants to turn the machinery of repression against itself. The law of libel required that the text or passage under indictment be read at the trial, and exempted "a fair, plain, and honest account of the proceedings of a court" from prosecution.[70] In effect, the courts licensed the reproduction of the libel. The presentation of these trials on a title page often gave prominent notice to the offensive works in question, and Hone may have indulged his satirical inclinations when, on the title page of his *Three Trials*, he referred to the three parodies in question with the abbreviation "Viz.," meaning "videlicet," or "namely," but literally, "it is permitted to see" (Figure 5). The attempt to suppress the parodies had become the authority for their further publication. Other defendants went further, and turned the trial into a forum for new provocations, which then became part of the privileged record. In a series of calculated "digressions," Wooler ridiculed the arguments of the Attorney General as "common place cant," and charged that the ministers rather than himself "deserve to be impeached" because they had "actually subverted the constitution."[71] Carlile, following the example of Spence, read into the record as much of a blasphemous work as the presiding judge would tolerate, along with corroborative evidence from other infidel and republican texts, on the grounds that the passages singled out for prosecution could not be understood out of context.[72] Most of the text of his *Mock Trials* appeared in double quotation marks, as the defendant treated the court to a reading of Paine's *Age of Reason* thinly disguised as a defense. An advertisement for the work left no doubt as to his intentions: "The sheets of the first days proceeding of Mr. Carlile's Mock Trial . . . have been reprinted, to keep on sale that very cheap edition of Paine's Age of Reason, under the form of a trial. Price

THE

THREE TRIALS

OF

WILLIAM HONE,

FOR PUBLISHING

THREE PARODIES;

VIZ.

THE LATE JOHN WILKES'S CATECHISM,

THE POLITICAL LITANY, AND

THE SINECURIST'S CREED;

ON

Three Ex=Officio Informations,

AT GUILDHALL, LONDON, DURING

THREE SUCCESSIVE DAYS,

DECEMBER 18, 19, & 20, 1817;

BEFORE

THREE SPECIAL JURIES,

AND

MR. JUSTICE ABBOTT, ON THE FIRST DAY,

AND

LORD CHIEF JUSTICE ELLENBOROUGH,

ON THE LAST TWO DAYS.

Thrice the brindled cat hath mew'd!
SHAKSPEARE.

LONDON:

PRINTED BY & FOR WILLIAM HONE, 67, OLD BAILEY

AND SOLD BY ALL BOOKSELLERS.

1818.

PRICE---WITH THE PROCEEDINGS OF THE PUBLIC MEETING---
FOUR SHILLINGS IN BOARDS.

Figure 5   Title Page, *The Three Trials of William Hone* (London: William Hone, 1818)

half a crown. It was read in the courts chiefly for that purpose" (*R* 12 [1825], 352).[73] If a judge managed to control the defense, Carlile was willing to take the next step, and republish material that had not bene- fited from the privilege of the court. When his sister, Mary-Anne Carlile, was indicted by the Vice Society as the publisher of *An Appendix to the Theological Works of Thomas Paine,* Carlile prepared an inflammatory defense on her behalf. She was silenced at the point where her defense dismissed the common law as "a common abuse," and summarily con- victed. The version of her trial brought out by Carlile, under the sensa- tional title *Suppressed Defence,* picked up her defense, literally mid-sentence, after the guilty verdict, and continued with more than thirty pages of political argument and extracts from Paine. Despite prior warning from the bench that this material was "objectionable" and liable to prosecution, Carlile was prepared to move on to the next level of response and provocation.[74]

Alan Liu has discovered a similar dialectical structure of publication and prosecution in the treason trials of the 1790s, and he suggests that it provides "a testing principle for determining the presence of active sub- version in discourse," and a clue to recent theoretical riddles about containment and transgression: "What we witness in the controversy over the sedition and treason trials is that there was no rhetorical 'action,' subversive or otherwise, that was not accompanied by a parallel action situated at the limit between the primary action and the society that contained it." This open system of "disseminatory limitation," in which "limits ceaselessly spill outwards into other limits,"[75] became if possible more intense and complex after the 1790s, as well-defined ideo- logical positions gave way to more opportunistic forms of protest, and as writers and editors made themselves increasingly astute observers of legal limitation. In debates over the suspension of Habeas Corpus and the Seditious Meetings Bill of 1817, the Attorney General argued that the law had to be refined if it was to comprehend ever more subtle pat- terns of transgression:

There were persons who engaged in practices that ought to render them liable to punishment; but who, by studying the enactments of the act in question, were enabled to keep clear of it, and defeat its object. It was therefore necessary to have a new mode of describing its operation . . . He would venture to assure gentlemen, that if a cart load of these infamous publications were to be exam- ined, any gentleman not a lawyer might say, "this is a blasphemous, and that a seditious libel"; but . . . so adroitly were the libels formed, that with the joint assistance of the best legal advice, it would be deemed scarcely possible to bring the libellers to conviction. (*PD* 35 [1817], 620–21)

Cobbett appreciated the compliment paid to his skills here, and assured his readers that he would remain "as careful as I have been, not to write any thing that even a Special Jury would pronounce to be a *libel*."[76] With every "new mode of describing" the violation of the law, the radical movement returned to "studying the enactments of the act in question," in order to discover new and more "adroitly . . . formed" modes of exceeding the description.

A framework of disseminatory limitation and transgression facilitated the dizzying reversals that characterized political conflict in this period. As the distinction between offense and defense broke down, radical defendants tried to usurp the supervening role of the court. Jurors were challenged to interpret or even ignore the law, in defiance of the presiding judge's authority to instruct them.[77] Carlile threatened to put the entire criminal justice system on trial when he opened his defense with an inquiry into the relationship between jurors and the crown.[78] A judge's power to "silence" these interventions could hamper their effectiveness in court, but, as Liu has pointed out, these contests inevitably opened out from "the official chambers of legitimation" into the press, and from there "into the 'court of public opinion.'"[79] Radical defendants used the public sphere to obtain what they called "a trial by the country" or "VERDICT of the NATION."[80] The press offered competing instructions to juries, and radical debating clubs conducted public inquiries into the propriety of specific trials, which sometimes went on until "a very large majority decided against the prosecutions."[81] While Henry Brougham represented the Hunt brothers in court in 1812, Leigh Hunt conducted a parallel and more aggressive defense in the *Examiner*. Issues excluded from the courtroom, like the role of special jurors and the question of the truth of a libellous publication, were vigorously argued, and provocative distinctions were drawn between "the Law" inside the courtroom and "Justice" outside (*E*, no. 259 [December 13, 1812], 785). In *The Prince of Wales v. The Examiner*, the version of the trial brought out by John Hunt, these "Observations by the Editor of the Examiner" were conspicuously interposed, as they had been published, *between* the jury's guilty verdict and the court's sentence of two years' imprisonment.[82] This sentence itself was not the final word, since like most radical editors Hunt continued to work from prison. The *Suppressed Defence* of Mary-Anne Carlile rebuked the judge's authority, and subverted the terminal status of the verdict, by picking up her interrupted speech after the close of the trial; radical defense shifted here from offense to final judgment. The pamphlet's title page extended these provocations, and vividly mapped the relationship of the radical press to the law (Figure 6). The sensational "SUPPRESSED DEFENCE" received first notice, while the account of the trial was diminished to an afterthought: "WITH A REPORT OF THE PROCEEDINGS." Graphically interposing between the two was a bold appeal to the "Public, as the highest Tribunal" to "JUDGE BETWEEN THE DEFENDANT, HER PROSECUTORS, AND HER JUDGE." The radical gesture of shifting initiative from the court and the prosecution to the defense required for its own completion an appeal beyond the printed page to a supportive reading public as final judge. The appearance of the *Suppressed Defence* did in fact secure significant interest in Mary-Anne Carlile's case, and even moderate reformers like Joseph Hume and David Ricardo agitated for her release.[83]

The dialectical project of generating and then violating new limits could prove endless and exhausting. The relief Cobbett felt when his trial and imprisonment "ended precisely as it ought to end," in an appeal to "the inhabitants of the village," far removed from the courtroom and the prison, can be traced to the rigors of a career spent mapping the unstable faultline between transgression and repression. There were, furthermore, clear risks to exploiting the principle of disseminatory limitation. A destabilizing challenge to the law might degenerate into the relatively empty pleasures of formulaic inversion. The mock trials brought out by several radical publishers in this period may be a case in point: cast as victims in the courtroom, radical writers tried to reverse the scenario in the imaginary space of print, in publications like Wooler's "Trial of Mr. Parliament" and Hone's *Trial of The Dog, for Biting the Noble Lord*.[84] Wooler provided vivid evidence of the frustration that could yield such a response when he complained in court that the ministers "deserve to be impeached": "Had I the means, I would endeavour to procure against them a sentence of just and general condemnation. My station in life does not enable me to do so, and I have proceeded against them in the best manner I can" (*VR* 45–46). Mock trials were a displaced "means" of reversing the charge. Yet it is worth recalling that both Wooler and Hone emerged victorious from their encounters with the law, and that the radical movement gained significant ground in the courts, particularly on the matter of special juries.[85] The government implicitly acknowledged the failure of the law of libel as an instrument of political repression when it stopped prosecuting after the middle of the 1820s. If mock trials provided writers and editors with an imaginary compensation for their own relative disempowerment, they also served to remind the government of embarrassing radical victories.

SUPPRESSED DEFENCE.

THE

DEFENCE

OF

MARY-ANNE CARLILE,

TO THE

Vice Society's Indictment,

AGAINST THE

APPENDIX

TO THE

THEOLOGICAL WORKS OF THOMAS PAINE;

WHICH

DEFENCE WAS SUPPRESSED

BY

MR. JUSTICE BEST,

ALMOST AT ITS COMMENCEMENT;

AND,

ON THE PROPRIETY OF WHICH SUPPRESSION,

THE

Public, as the highest Tribunal,

IS NOW APPEALED TO AND CALLED UPON

TO JUDGE

BETWEEN

THE DEFENDANT, HER PROSECUTORS, AND HER JUDGE:

WITH A

REPORT OF THE PROCEEDINGS

BEFORE THE

Defence was Suppressed.

LONDON:

PRINTED AND PUBLISHED BY R. CARLILE, 55, FLEET-STREET.

1821.

Price One Shilling.

Figure 6   Title Page, *Suppressed Defence. The Defence of Mary-Anne Carlile to the Vice Society's Indictment* (London: R. Carlile, 1821)

THE LANGUAGE OF FACT: APOCALYPSE WITHOUT IMAGINATION

Now it evidently makes no difference in the mischief of a libel . . . whether the subject alleged be true or false . . . This doctrine is so firmly settled, and so essentially necessary to the maintenance of the king's peace, and the good order of society, that no court of justice has at any time allowed it to be drawn into debate . . . In indictments, indeed, the word *false* is part of the formal description of the crime. We have shown it, however, in a preceding chapter, to be merely formal, and not material. It is, in fact, one of those popular adjuncts which, in the simpler times of the law, crept from common discourse into the language of pleading. It has, therefore, been retained: but, like the words, "the instigation of the devil," in an indictment for murder, it is merely surplusage. (Francis Holt, *The Law of Libel*, 1812)[86]

Censure must be founded upon truth. No man worthy of notice would venture upon falsehood, in the face of the public. Indeed, it is never *now* pretended that libels are *untrue.* They were wont to be designated *"false, scandalous,* and *malicious!"* meaning, that they were scandalous and malicious, *because* they were *false!* But when the truth was offered in evidence, it was refused; and juries are now required to find libels *scandalous,* and *malicious,* because they are *true!* The consequences have been what any politicians but ours would have expected. Libels have not only become common, but have grown in public favor. A libeller is generally considered as one who dares promulgate a dangerous truth; and both curiosity and integrity are arrayed in his favor. (Wooler, "State of the Country," 1820)[87]

So far I have explored the way prosecutions for libel measured the impact or "effect" of radical argument upon readers and the government, and provided writers with a forum in which to renegotiate their relationship with a reading audience. Libel trials were in this sense a juridical test of the "worldliness" of radical criticism.[88] Yet there was another worldly question that the law of libel refused to consider: "whether the subject alleged be true or false," that is, whether radical prose accurately reflected the disposition of things in the world. Holt's insistence that the truth of a piece of writing was no defense in cases of criminal libel drew on a common-law tradition going back to Sir Edward Coke, who had reasoned that truth or falsehood did not affect the basic problem of seditious libel, the tendency to produce a breach of the peace. It was not until the Libel Act of 1843 that defendants were given the chance to plead the truth of their work in court, and then only if they could show that publication served the public good.[89] The exclusion of truth from criminal proceedings became so firmly entrenched as to spawn the dubious legal dictum that "the greater the truth, the greater the libel," since, as one authority put it, "the greater appearance there is of truth in any malicious invective, so much the more provoking it is."[90] The radical movement responded to this prohibition with what Wooler termed "truths for courts" (*BD* 1 [1817], 140), a substantial rather than "merely formal" understanding of truth or "fact" that was tailored to the repressive conditions of the courtroom.

Holt was on firm legal ground when he claimed that truth was irrelevant, but his insistence that the courts were never "drawn into debate" on the subject was wishful thinking at best. "The question of truth," Leigh Hunt wrote ominously of his own trial, "will inevitably *force* itself into consideration" (*E*, no. 260 [December 20, 1812], 802). Radical defendants consistently challenged the court's authority to frame the debate by appealing beyond the law to the evidence of the world. Speaking in his own defense at the first of his two 1817 trials for seditious libel, Wooler claimed that the attack on the government for which he had been indicted was "an essay which I wrote as an historian, and which an historian might avow" (*VR* 62). The "grand question" obscured by the prosecution was a simple problem of reference: "Are the Ministers, or are they not, the men they have generally been described to be?" (45). A direct appeal to the jury on these grounds led the prosecuting attorney to demand that the judge intervene:

MR WOOLER – . . . It is for you Gentlemen to decide, whether I am or am not guilty; as I shall appear to have spoken *truth* or *falsehood*.

THE ATTORNEY GENERAL – I submit my Lord that the Defendant is transgressing every principle of law.

MR JUSTICE ABBOTT – You are transgressing beyond all reason and contrary to every principle of law – you must confine yourself within reasonable bounds.

MR WOOLER – I should be happy, my Lord, to confine myself to those reasonable bounds if they can be prescribed . . . (56–57)

Although the Attorney General later insisted that a criminal defendant could not "enter into a discussion whether what he has said is true or false" (76), Wooler succeeded in drawing the jury into the debate. After the presiding judge had identified the work under indictment as "a scandalous, malicious, and seditious libel," one juror demanded clarification:

ONE OF THE JURY – Are we to understand that if we find that what is stated here is true, it is still a libel.

MR JUSTICE ABBOTT – By the law of England, gentlemen, the publication of the fact, if it be injurious and calumnious to any individual, is a libel.

ONE OF THE JURY – That is, that facts are libels.

MR JUSTICE ABBOTT – the truth of the facts charged in the paper are no
justification in this proceeding . . . I could very soon refer you to many
authorities, but, without doing so, you must for the present give me credit
upon this point, for it has been laid down by many Judges. (86–87)

This first trial then ended in a disputed verdict, as the judge refused to
hear three jurors who wanted to state a special condition, specifically,
that they were "*compelled* to find the Defendant guilty" because "*truth* is
declared by the law of the land to be a libel." Wooler failed in subsequent
efforts to reverse the verdict, but he spent less than a month in jail, and
was not retried.[91] At the second trial on the following day, Wooler again
pleaded "truth," "known fact," and "historical accuracy," but the
Attorney General decided to respond in kind, looking "impartially" and
"with an equal eye of discrimination" at the defendant's claim that "the
libel contained no more than a statement of historical facts." The jury
had less difficulty under these conditions, and returned a verdict of not
guilty.[92]

Few defendants matched Wooler's success in the courtroom, but in the
press, where there was no Mr. Justice Abbott to enforce "reasonable
bounds" and discipline those found transgressing, the question of
"truth" became a rallying point for advocates of free expression. In 1816,
Henry Brougham introduced a bill in parliament to allow truth as a
defense in criminal libel cases, and supported the measure in the
Edinburgh Review with a critical review of Holt's *Law of Libel*. Brougham's
position was typically moderate, allowing defendants "to give the truth
of the statement in evidence," but also leaving room for juries, "notwithstanding of such proof, [to] find the defendant guilty" (*ER* 27 [1816],
142).[93] A popular radical position was less flexible. Cobbett claimed that
"to be punishable in any way, the thing published must be *false*" (*CPR* 18
[1810], 367); "a man should be held innocent if he were able to produce
complete proof of the TRUTH of his statements" (*CPR* 25 [1814], 808).
The radical campaign against the law of libel raised fundamental and,
Holt notwithstanding, "material" questions about political discourse.
Radical writers and editors were encouraged to map the precise conditions under which their prose would represent and transform the world.
This was a typically vexed radical project, forged in repression, and
invested with the contradictions of a legal system that politicized mere
appeals to fact by trying to expunge them from the expressive register.
Dispassionate description gathered the explosive energy of sedition and
blasphemy. The distinctive feature of radical discourse in this period was

not so much that it "aimed at moulding events rather than at recording them," as one commentator has argued, but that it sought to incorporate "moulding" in "recording."[94] Wooler's definition of the libeller as the daring advocate of a "dangerous truth" was issued under the dispassionate newspaper title, "State of the Country." Leigh Hunt's "bold" and inflexible "teller of truths" also found himself in court for having undertaken nothing more than "Explaining the True Character of His Royal Highness the Prince Regent."[95]

Although this recourse from strenuous argument to "explaining" and "historical accuracy" may have emerged in response to the law, it was not a local rift in radical discourse. In the absence of a shared ideological framework, "fact" became the common currency of early nineteenth-century radical argument. This concrete and irreducible unit of critical truth resisted the distorting medium of corruption, disarmed a post-French Revolutionary critique of utopian speculation, and was easily marshalled as evidence for popular consumption in a wide array of lists, tables, comparisons, and statistics. The motivated radical fact took its place in a long history of political discourse that extended from country-party suspicions of mediation (social, political, economic, and linguistic), through "English Jacobin" critiques of Edmund Burke's rhetorical excess, to a related Benthamite commitment to fact as an instrument with which to disassemble outmoded social and political forms and institute new ones. Jon Klancher has cogently described Paine's identification of "the surplus of power with the surplus of signs": "Against this 'metaphysics' of the sign the radical writers will cast other metaphysical weapons – principles, common sense, lived experience, empirical facts . . . The radicals' verbal truth insists upon its reference, the squaring of signs with things."[96] Radical appeals to fact intensified as post-war distress directed attention to conditions of physical deprivation. With his usual facility for historical shorthand, Hazlitt gauged the new logic of resistance that accompanied a political discourse of fact in his *Examiner* account of Southey's *Wat Tyler*: "When this poem was written, there was a rage of speculation which might be dangerous: the danger at present arises from the rage of hunger" (*CWH* 7: 191). The "rage of hunger" could only be comprehended by a political discourse that was acutely sensitive to the material facts of life under corruption.

The leading print organ for assembling fact was the radical anatomy of corruption, works like the *Red Book* (1816), *The People's Mirror* (1816), the *Black Book* (1820), *A Peep at the Peers* (1820), *A Peep at the Commons* (1820), *The*

Englishman's Mirror (1820), and *Links of the Lower House* (1821), which "gave the names of all substantial government placemen and office-holders, the annual value of their salaries, pensions and emoluments."[97] While arguably "the most important and distinctive contribution of early nineteenth-century popular radicalism," these compilations had important antecedents.[98] The title of the *Red Book* echoed P. F. M'Callum's *Le Livre Rouge; or, A New and Extraordinary Red Book* (1810), an early "List of . . . Pensions" that had little of the critical commentary of similar post-war works, but made its intentions clear in a Preface that termed pensions an "absurdity," whose advocates were "more fitted for the cells of Bedlam, than the departments of the state."[99] M'Callum's work, in turn, echoed the famous *Livre Rouge* of the French Revolution, and indicated on its title page that it was "Designed as a Companion to the Court Kalendar." This last claim is important, since it brings us to a less subversive phase in the genealogy of a factual catalogue of state. Serially published and annually revised texts like the *Court Kalendar*, *Royal Kalendar*, and *Court and City Register* began to appear in the first half of the eighteenth century, and were by no means works of resistance: they were designed to guide "Gentlemen" through the increasingly complex structure of the British state, and announced with evident pride that their information had been "corrected at the respective offices."[100] M'Callum and the post-war radicals transformed the quasi-official "Kalendar" into a polemical "Exposé" (*RB* iii) by accounting for the precise amount of money involved in each public office, and extending a critical analysis through every possible arena of corruption, from crown, parliament, and church, to the courts, the East India Company, and the Bank of England.

In these encyclopedic texts, radical discourse sought to trade the contingency of a periodical form in crisis for the permanence and security of a *"Book of Reference"* (*RB*, 4th edn, viii). A system of corruption that elsewhere generated monstrous figures and distended sentences was effectively controlled through disciplinary procedures of textual and statistical compilation: corrupt practices were classified, alphabetized, quantified, and analyzed. *Links of the Lower House*, "an Alphabetical List of the Members of the House of Commons" with their respective offices and pensions, exposed the structure of corruption through an elaborate system of cross-references that extended throughout the text, and into companion works like *A Peep at the Peers*.[101] The system became a form of knowledge, laid out before the reader as a "body of Evidence" and placed "within the reach of . . . daily reference."[102] As so often in radical discourse, this was *concrete* knowledge about *concrete* things: "Offices,

Pensions, Grants, Church-Preferment, Functions, Services" and so on were "Matters and Things," belonging to specific individuals.[103] The long and depressing history of unproductive argument about reform would end in *"solid reasons"* (*RB*, 4th edn, v) that promised to conduct the public sphere beyond commentary and dispute to the firm ground of the thing itself. "Those whose vocation it is to mislead and delude may attempt to impugn our statements," Wade announced, "but their labour will be vain, unless they can disprove our FACTS" (*BB*, new edn, 182).[104] Wooler could afford to be brief when he introduced the *Black Dwarf*'s serial publication of *A Peep at the Peers*: "Comments would be *endless*, as they are *unnecessary*. Only read the catalogue carefully, and digest its contents" (*BD* 5 [1820], 420). The metaphor was telling, a positive radical version of the government's nightmare of a culinary politics, appropriate to the "rage of hunger." Carefully assembled by editors in an analytical framework, political facts could be assimilated by readers through a hermeneutic process no more challenging than digestion.

Despite the editorial effort to clear a discursive space free of commentary and debate, it is not hard to see that facts were still rhetorical resources in a contested public sphere. "INFORMATION alone has given us that pre-eminent station which we now hold over our enemies," the editor of the *Red Book* announced, and "it becomes us to lose no opportunity of grappling with them on that ground" (*RB*, 4th edn, iv). The catalogue of corruption remained a polemical enterprise, shot through with withering satire and social criticism, and actively engaged with the official parliamentary accounts of "the Internal State of the Country" from which reformers often worked.[105] Full titles displayed a transgressive energy: *The Extraordinary Red Book*; *A Peep at the Peers*; *The Black Book; or, Corruption Unmasked!* While it is possible to discover Bentham's influence on these works, notably through Francis Place's hand in the *Gorgon* and in successive editions of the *Black Book*,[106] the notion of fact gathered a more threatening edge in the radical catalogue of corruption. Dedications and prefaces might cultivate a measured tone, but could not help succumbing in the end to a "gloomily portentous" (*RB* iv) rhetoric of crisis:

As a parting word, we would just observe, that in thus laying before the public at a cheap price, an account of the nature of virtual representation, we trust we have rendered our country an important service . . . It is true, the borough-monster, seems to be in the agonies of death, but its struggles and its flounderings may, however, before its departure, do much mischief, and it is not less an act of justice than of humanity to endeavour, to hasten its destruction.[107]

a Preface to the 1832 edition of the *Black Book*, written while the fate of reform in parliament was still uncertain, Wade presented his work as "the Encyclopedia of English politics for the Georgian era," and claimed that it would "last as long as the abuses it exposes shall endure" (*BB*, new edn, v). As long, perhaps, but no longer: the encyclopedia of fact incorporated "the daily frauds and abuses" of the system, and would therefore share its catastrophic fate. Lurking in the margins of Wade's project was an implicit assumption that corruption would collapse only after all of its parts were identified and assembled in the form of a book. The real interest of a radical rhetoric of fact lay in the precise conditions under which information about corruption was felt to come into its own, and then catastrophically disappear. Here, where representation met "destruction," the radical movement disclosed the seditious plot that accompanied a shift from annual "kalendar" to the final "exposé." Although reformers often invoked the old puritan principle that truth was certain to prevail in a fair fight,[114] they were acutely aware that such a fight was not possible if power remained in the hands of a corrupt elite, adept at managing the public sphere through patronage and coercion. How then could facts be expected to gather their persuasive and transformative force? It may be worth returning here to the courtroom, where this chapter began, and to the role of the law in the radical conception of fact. As the debate over prosecution unfolded, "libel" came to name a discourse that was subject to competing claims about indisputability and self-evidence. For Hone, the corruptions exposed in his parodies were "as notorious as the sun at noon-day," and "universally known" to all. When he digressed in his defense into an inflammatory account of starvation in London, he expressed confidence that "similar scenes must have been witnessed by numbers of those who heard him, as well as by members of the jury." The Attorney General was equally sure that Hone's parody, which "spoke but too plainly for itself," fell under the definition of libel: "It seems impossible for me to hear it read without feeling one's-self compelled to apply to it this language."[115] These may have been conventional appeals for audience sympathy, but, under the pressure brought to bear upon "fact" and evidence by the law, they acquired an unusual intensity. The Attorney General concluded his opening remarks at Hone's first trial with an oddly redundant version of the claim for self-evidence that seemed to close upon itself:

I think it impossible that any twelve men who understand the law of England, and the precepts of Christianity, which are part and parcel of that law, can read this production of the defendant's without being decidedly of opinion that it is impossible to read it without seeing that its necessary and obvious consequence must be to bring into contempt the Liturgy of the Church of England. (*TT* 5–6)[116]

Where seventeenth-century religious reformers had waged the direct "wars of truth," early nineteenth-century political reformers waged the more circuitous wars of "necessary and obvious" fact. Libel replaced truth as the name for a discourse that carried its own conviction, and the courtroom became the leading venue for an immediate, if not entirely fair, contest between the government and its radical opponents.

The failure of the law of libel to protect or even permit truth claims made Hone's defense an offensive gesture, an extension rather than a revocation of his original case against the government. In insisting before the court that the evidence against the government was "universally known," he suggested that every verifiable statement about politics had by definition become libel. The claim was relentlessly driven home in the radical press: "When imposture is prevalent, simple truth is seditious" (*YD*, no. 1 [1818], 7); "What is commonly called sedition and blasphemy must be synonymous with truth and common sense" (*R* 4 [1820], 526); "It is TRUTH that is a *libel*!!! It is TRUTH that is sedition! It is TRUTH, that is blasphemy!" (*BD* 1 [1817], 181). This extension of the limits of sedition, from a particular utterance under court scrutiny to every authentic political statement, was also an important reversal. The radical movement succeeded in shifting attention from the truth claims of sedition to the seditious claims of truth. The *Cap of Liberty* traced this critical turn back to Lord Ellenborough's definition of a libel as a discourse calculated to bring the authorities "into hatred and contempt": "It is evident to the meanest understanding, that according to the foregoing definition of seditious libel, every plain narrative of facts – nay, the Report in the Public journals, of their own Debates, will come under that denomination, for they really hold up to our view a most contemptible idea of the speakers of either House of Parliament" (*CL* 1 [1819], 227–28).[117] Wooler invoked the same principle in court when he maintained that "it was not this paragraph or that paragraph" that had the effect "of exciting discontent against the King," but rather "a measure hateful in itself," for which "the ministers" were responsible. The radical recourse from language to the thing "in itself" was in these instances a tactical response to specific legal and political conditions, and not merely a naive and evasive consequence of reductive linguistic theories. Or, if the notion of a fact anterior to language and controversy was an evasion, it was a more knowing one than most accounts of radical discourse allow. Even when they were busy deflecting legal responsibility in this way, radical writers and editors did not altogether overlook the active role of the press. "As to bringing the present 'Administration into public hatred and contempt,'" Hunt wrote in the *Examiner*, "every journal contains a libel every day, for every journal is full of their proceedings, and it is their proceedings which bring them into hatred and contempt!" (*E*, no. 101 [December 3, 1809], 771–72). Ministerial "proceedings" produced a seditious effect only through the intervention of a public sphere ready to bring those proceedings forward for public scrutiny.

The contentious pattern of legal prosecution and defense went a long way towards energizing fact, but "the thing" in itself achieved its full power to transform the world only through the radical principle of crisis. The law assisted a process that economic retribution would complete. Even William Hazlitt, by no means as materially reductive as Cobbett nor as statistically inclined as Wade, treated "the case on the part of the people" as a zero-sum game:

There is but a limited earth and a limited fertility to supply the demands both of Government and people; and what the one gains in the division of the spoil, beyond its average proportion, the other must needs go without . . . If the Government take a fourth of the produce of the poor man's labour, they will be rich, and he will be in want. If they can contrive to take one half of it by legal means, or by a stretch of arbitrary power, they will be just twice as rich, twice as insolent and tyrannical, and he will be twice as poor, twice as miserable and oppressed, in a mathematical ratio to the end of the chapter, that is, till the one can extort and the other endure no more. (*CWH* 7: 263–64)

Political misrepresentation and financial speculation might postpone the shock, but the hard kernel of fact would prove unforgiving. Confronted with "the end of the chapter," Wooler abandoned his satirical flexibility, and wrote "without circumlocution": "The rapacious demands of the state are too heavy for the absolute resources of the country." Just as misgovernment encouraged seditious libel, so fiscal corruption spawned its own opposition:

The laws of nature avenge themselves upon those who dare to outrage their beneficent equality. "The slave may perish, but the tyrant shall not live," is written on the dust and ashes of every fallen state; and will ere long be written on the wrecked memorials of the country's greatness. The system of misrule can only be completed in its self-destruction. Despotism always ends in its own suicide, after the parracidal murder of a nation's rights. No tyranny forced upon states that have been free, has ever reached to an old age . . . The effort to destroy rebounds upon the destroyer. (*BD* 3 [1819], 841–42)

In joining post-war economic pressure with country-party eschatology, radical writers invested the world with their own habits of tactical reversal ("self-destruction," "rebounds"), and included the tactics of counter-system in "the laws of nature."

These critical pressures endowed radical facts with their transformative and prophetic energy. In defending himself in court as "an historian," Wooler also proposed to jurors that "the article before you is retrospective as well as prospective; it relates to the past, the present, and the future" (*VR* 59). The slavishly referential catalogue of corruption became a prophetic text. Wade's 1832 edition of the *Black Book*, "greatly enlarged and corrected to the present time," was according to its title page a "precis" of events "Past, Present, and to Come." An advertisement for the volume cited a favorable review in which the "Encyclopedia of English Politics" became "a Revelation from the Divinity of Truth": "A day of judgment shall wait on the offenders in this book, as certain as that man is mortal, and truth eternal" (*CEP*, no. 1 [January 29, 1820]). If apocalyptic vision disclosed the fierce argument at the core of a dispassionate rhetoric of fact, it also brought the ambiguities of the radical project to a head, by posing the paradox inherent in all prophecy. If "despotism always ends in its own suicide," what was the business of the reform movement? Was it possible, as Hone seemed to suggest in a satirical versification of the *Red Book*, to reduce the entire radical program to a hedonistic prescription to "eat and drink well to-day, for to-morrow they die"?[118] In a letter to *Sherwin's Political Register* recommending a cheap edition of the *Red Book*, the Painite poet Clio Rickman struggled to articulate the vexed relationship between a rhetoric of fact and political transformation:

It has ever been with me an irrefragable truth, when States are arrived at a certain pitch of depravity and crimes, that corruption must be left to destroy itself: and that, to enlighten the People in the mean time, by the distribution of proper books, and by education and information, that they may act judiciously, mildly and firmly, when the day of revolution shall come, is the only wise and beneficial line of conduct for the real lovers of liberty, and the true friends of mankind to pursue. (*SPR* 3 [1818], 60)

Left unresolved here was the crucial link between print politics ("distribution of proper books," "education and information") and "the day of revolution," the latter curiously equated with a determination to leave corruption "to destroy itself." There were, of course, practical reasons for this obscurity. Conservative constructions of a radical rhetoric of fact inevitably authorized severe repression. To the author of *The Loyal Man in the Moon*, the radical catalogue of corruption was nothing less than the hit list of a revolutionary conspiracy: "In a 'Black Book' a thousand names were written, / Marked in the day of vengeance to be smitten, / With the keen edge of some rebellious sword, / Whenever the usurper gave the word."[119] In a highly charged discursive field, Wade's empirical project extended into revolution on the one side, and into the courtroom and the prison cell on the other. A prophetic voice allowed radical authors and texts to obscure the dangerous question of political responsibility, while sustaining a commitment to radical reform. If nothing else, the ambiguity of prophecy confirmed that the radical project could never be confined to print. If a "system of misrule" could "only be completed in its self-destruction," so radical discourse, by virtue of its investment in an embodied public and worldly facts, could only be completed through an engagement with the wider political, legal, and economic conditions that would yield reform.

CHAPTER FOUR

Reading Cobbett's contradictions

> Wherever power is, there he is against it: he naturally butts at all
> obstacles, as unicorns are attracted to oak-trees, and feels his own
> strength only by resistance to the opinions and wishes of the rest of
> the world. To sail with the stream, to agree with the company, is not
> his humour . . . I do not think this is vanity or fickleness so much as a
> pugnacious disposition, that must have an antagonist power to
> contend with, and only finds itself at ease in systematic opposition
> . . . His principle is repulsion, his nature contradiction: he is made
> up of mere antipathies.
>
> (Hazlitt, "Character of Cobbett," 1821)[1]

"THE SYSTEM"

The taxing, funding and paper-money system has always, with me, been an
object of hatred. From the moment I understood it, I detested it. It was in 1803
that I began to examine into it. In that very year I predicted that, unless it were
put a stop to in time, it would make this the most miserable, enslaved, and
contemptible nation in the world. From that day to this, I have been at war
against this all-corrupting and all-degrading system. And, I have lived to see the
system pushed along to its utmost extent, and to see the consequences in a
greater mass of ruin and of human wretchedness than was ever before witnessed . . . All the grounds, all the causes, all effects, all the various workings of
the thing; all the whole history and mystery of this grand delusion; all its
branches and twigs; have been so fully and so frequently subjects of my pen, that
I have really very often been disgusted at the thought of saying any thing more
about the matter. Yet, it is necessary to persevere. (Cobbett, "On the Workings
of the Taxing and the Paper-System," 1820)[2]

Given Cobbett's extraordinarily single-minded obsession with "the
whole history and mystery" of what he called "the system," it is curious
that some of his most impressive critics agree on nothing more than that
he was not a systematic writer. E. P. Thompson maintains that
"Cobbett's thought was not a system but a *relationship*" with his audience;
Raymond Williams suggests that "to analyze his work . . . is not to

articulate a system but to consider certain dominant themes"; and Gertrude Himmelfarb agrees that "Cobbett's writing reminds us how untidy, unstructured, unfocused his world was."[3] While Cobbett's own sense of system no doubt differs from that of these critics – allowing, as it does, for the contradiction and "outrageous inconsistency" (*CWH* 7: 57) that have troubled commentators since Hazlitt – his work needs to be understood as a serious and systematic response to an increasingly systematic world. "Unstructured," "thematic" approaches, and impressionistic readings of "relationship," risk overlooking the logic and cunning that run through Cobbett's prose, and his related practices of publication and circulation.

For Cobbett as for his contemporary William Blake, system was a powerful and potentially oppressive means of ordering the world. The two writers conceived this ordering process in different ways, differences that correspond loosely to the definition of system as either "a set of principles" or "an organized or connected group of objects."[4] Where Blake contended with a system of mental categories, Cobbett set out here as elsewhere from "the physical means of sustaining and reproducing life."[5] His understanding of system stressed concrete institutions and practices, an order of things with important consequences for the human mind and manners. Where a Blake dictionary has entries under Golgonooza, Luvah, and Reason, a Cobbett dictionary, were one to be compiled (and it would be no less useful), would have entries under Pitt, Canning, paper money, potatoes, and turnpikes. Blake was, in addition, more thoroughly dialectical and ironic in his approach to system. He created his own system to avoid being imposed on by other systems, yet recognized that ordering the world and having it ordered for you were not mutually exclusive activities. To the Angel's complaint in *The Marriage of Heaven and Hell* that "thy phantasy has imposed upon me," the figure of the poet shrewdly responds, "we impose on one another."[6] Blake answered systematic imposition on its own terms, in order to promote the strife among contraries that would cast all systems into the consuming fires of Orc, but he did not envision an end to dialectical strife. Cobbett, by contrast, did seek to get beyond system and political dispute, in order to recover for himself and the nation a rural and domestic repose more like Blake's Beulah than like ongoing mental fight. Rather than creating his own system, Cobbett set out to describe and account for a corrupt system that already existed, in order to elicit its contradictions and encourage the popular resentment that would hasten its downfall. Although sometimes prepared to mimic the system in order to oppose it, he was unwilling to yield completely to the complex dialectics of system and countersystem; this hesitation was one of the chief sources of his inconsistency, and of the energy and tension of his prose. Part of the fascination of his career is to see how closely he shadowed the system while resisting its corrupt influences. Cobbett's aims, too, were more purely combative and exclusive than those of Blake. The imposition, as he saw it, was all on one side. System was a totalizing mode of social organization, in the service of political domination and economic exploitation; it corrupted a prior utopian order and opened an alarming chasm between starving productive laborers and idle consumers. Cobbett claimed few systems as his own, and rarely used the term in a positive sense.[7] If he conducted what Hazlitt called "systematic opposition," as in "the present *haranguing system*" of the *Rural Rides* (*CRR* 1: 118), this was a provisional attitude forced upon him by corruption, and very much a "present" contingency. His own oppositional practices were as precarious as the system, and tended to dissolve before utopian presentiments of reform. Put too systematically, the difference between Blake and Cobbett was a difference between poetry and prose, between vision and understanding, between making and remaking, and between revolution and reform.

The greatest misapprehension of Cobbett's system would be to see it as reductive and simply monolithic. The biographer John Osborne proposes that "hatred of the 'System'" is "the key to Cobbett's thought," but finds that Cobbett became "a prisoner" of his one idea: "Of course, there was no single 'System' at all. Cobbett was a perennial oversimplifier and looked instinctively for unqualified explanations . . . Though a seeker after the uncomplex when dealing with issues, Cobbett himself was a bundle of contradictions."[8] On the contrary, I would argue, Cobbett's sense of system involved a simultaneous urge towards simplicity *and* complexity; he was at once "a bundle of contradictions" and a model of absolute single-mindedness. If he insisted that oppression had a single nexus, located as Osborne observes in the "interlocking tyranny of government creditors ('fund holders') and owners of seats in the House of Commons ('boroughmongers'),"[9] he constantly revised his political analysis in the face of shifting interests and alliances within the system. Constant mutation and a proliferation of terms were part of what made systematic power difficult to detect and resist: "Thus is tyranny aggravated by its complexity" (*CPR* 19 [1811], 1060). Cobbett's own famous shift from late eighteenth-century loyalist to early nineteenth-century radical led to charges of inconsistency in his own lifetime, which he met with characteristic flexibility and aggression, first dismissing the "doctrine of *consistency*" as "the most absurd that ever was broached" (*CPR* 15 [1809], 816), and later reversing the charge by publishing accounts of the "Shocking Inconsistency" of his enemies (*CPR* 41 [1822], 626).[10]

Cobbett was acutely aware that radical reform confronted, not one, but "several systems" (*CPR* 21 [1812], 3), directed by several hands. Throughout his writing, oppressive power was disturbingly fragmented and fragmenting. It may be useful to recall some of the many systems identified and analyzed in the *Political Register*, though this risks the condescending parody into which Cobbett criticism has too often degenerated:

system of conquest	smothering system	barracks system
system of pauperdom	system of anti-Jacobinism	comforting system
system of public corruption	system of slavery	cow system
child-bed-linen system	church-going system	industry system
system of finance	military system	monkish system
Pitt system	tea-drinking system	potato system
system of banking	system of spies	system of watching
calumniating system	system of learned fraud	system of exclusion
system of beggary	Manchester system	tract system
system of influence	system of gambling	feudal system
system of paper-money	funding system	borough system

Such a list conveys the extraordinary range and specificity of Cobbett's idea of system, and suggests too the scope of his own countersystematic imagination, which could apprehend with equal seriousness and anxiety the sublime terror of Napoleon's "general system of conquest" (*CPR* 18 [1810], 636) and the quaint incursions of the philanthropist's "child-bed-linen system" (*CPR* 16 [1809], 113). What an inert list cannot communicate, however, is the sense of urgency and order that pervaded Cobbett's writing, and the complex relationships that structured these disparate elements and made them *systematic*. The system could not be reduced to a discrete set of objects (paper money, linen, potatoes), individuals (spies, priests, boroughmongers), or institutions (church, banks, parliament), but included as well the practices through which these were assembled and organized. Cobbett once glossed the term system as a "settled method of proceeding; a fixed line of conduct" (*CPR* 18 [1810], 970), and insisted that the "change of system" he sought was "not so much a change of *men*, as a change of *principles*, a change of maxims and rules of government" (*CPR* 16 [1809], 833). His own oppositional analysis exposed the implicit and often deliberately hidden "maxims and rules" of a corrupt system, and tried to disrupt their "fixed" and "settled" character.

Countersystematic analysis had to penetrate misleading surfaces to disclose an underlying structure. To this end, and with all his hostility towards industrial production, Cobbett often figured system as an instrument or *"grand machine"* (*CPR* 29 [1815], 334), operating "with steady pace" and dynamic "powers of motion" (*CPR* 25 [1814], 580).[11] This figure contained a revisionist polemic, since it placed the latest model of disruptive social change in the service of an older, more organic sense of corruption, and held the government rather than factory labor or production responsible for disorder.[12] The mechanical model revealed a good deal about Cobbett's own countersystem, as in this passage from an 1805 article on "The Budget":

The art of *financiering* consists principally in multiplying and confusing accounts, till, at last, no one has courage to undertake an examination of them. The way, therefore, to detect a financier of the Pitt school, is, to fix upon some one point, and that, too, a point as simple as possible in itself, and that will not very easily admit of being disfigured and confused. When my attention was first attracted to the subject of finance, it appeared to me, that a gross deception was played off upon the people annually; but, an annual exposition of every little wheel, peg and wire in the immense machine, would have been an endless task. I, therefore, fixed upon one single point, namely, the *surplus of the Consolidated Fund.* (*CPR* 7 [1805], 289)

From a lowly "single point," Cobbett proceeded outward by a kind of synecdoche through "every little wheel, peg and wire in the immense machine," to an overarching system of paper money and its manipulation in the Pitt system of finance. Complexity was broken down into manageable units for the purposes of analysis, but the analysis finally insisted that each unit was part of the larger system. Throughout his life Cobbett traced the mysterious threads and wires of corrupt connection with unwavering tenacity, whether his subject was a "system of paper-money" that "seems to depend for existence on war" (*CPR* 25 [1814], 9), or a system of "potatoe diet" that turned out to be "a component part of the tea-drinking system" (*CPR* 29 [1815], 167). The number of systems often multiplied to accommodate new evidence, but all were part of one "immense machine."[13] If Cobbett like Blake used the principle of connection or "ramification" (*CPR* 28 [1815], 261) to represent a world in systematic terms, it was essential to his argument that the representation was not visionary, but a prosaic and slavishly mimetic account of the only world that existed.

Where mechanical terms indicated the work done by system and countersystem, Cobbett used more conventional organic figures to trace the origin and development of corruption:

The system of managing the affairs of the nation . . . has made all flashy and false, and has put all things out of their place. Pomposity, bombast, hyperbole, redundancy, and obscurity, both in speaking and in writing; mock-delicacy in manners, mock-liberality, mock-humanity, and mock-religion. Pitt's false money, Peel's flimsy dresses, Wilberforce's potato diet, Castlereagh's and Mackintosh's oratory, Walter Scott's poems, Walter's and Stoddart's paragraphs, with all the bad taste and baseness and hypocrisy which they spread over this country; all have arisen, grown, branched out, bloomed and borne together; and we are now beginning to taste of their fruit. (*CE* 118)

The prospect of reform hinged on the claim that the life of system was a life of corruption, destined to end in blight and decay. While Cobbett resisted political quietism, warning that "the *seeds of destruction*" were like other seeds "often of very slow growth; and the plant, unfortunately, too long in ripening" (*CPR* 19 [1811], 1060), he was prepared to follow the logic of organic connection to its natural conclusion: the entire system would collapse if key components were sufficiently debilitated. "The Boroughmongers would fain shake off the fund-holders; but they *cannot*. Both must live, or die, together" (*CPR* 35 [1819–20], 303). This became a favorite argument during the heady post-war years of popular unrest and agricultural depression:

All has been sublimated, and, if the farmers come down, *all* must come down. Aye, and John Bowles and Southey and Walter Scott must find their level as well as the rest. The chariot-riding proprietor of the Times must return to the humble trade of his father; John Bowles must write last-dying-speeches and confessions; Southey must make and sing his own ballads, and Walter Scott write Christmas carroles and new histories of the Children in the Wood. (*CPR* 29 [1815], 175)

An intricate structure demonstrated that "*all* must come down together," and that the system could never be represented adequately by a list of discrete elements. Though his writing was saturated with facts and calculations, Cobbett did not enter the popular market for encyclopedias of corruption like the *Black Book*. Instead, the *Political Register* grew more discursive after the war, as Cobbett devoted his energies more and more to long essays proving that a "sublimation" of the system was imminent. Rather than allow the arbitrary order of the alphabet to disperse Pitt's paper, Wilberforce's potatoes, and Scott's poems across the printed page, Cobbett insisted on yoking everything together through his own vigorous argument and analysis.

Finance, and paper currency above all, seemed to Cobbett the weakest link in a corrupt system, and the most promising "point" of radical resistance. He frequently addressed the problem with rhetorical and political strategies of distinction, summed up in the antithetical title of his 1815 *Paper against Gold*. His letter "To the Stocking-Weavers" extended a radical boycott of taxed commodities to paper money, urging workers to keep their savings close at hand "in *metal money*": "Put it into no *funds*, no *saving banks*, no *societies*, no *common stock*; for, all these *must*, at last, rest upon the *Paper System*, than which a cobweb is not more fragile" (*CPR* 39 [1821], 125–26).[14] Yet the fragility of a corrupt system of finance could also justify intervention, in the more ironic style of radical countersystem. In 1819 he developed a plan to "*puff-out*" the system by flooding England with counterfeit currency from his privileged position in exile. The lifelong opponent of paper money reinvented himself as enthusiastic counterfeiter. Like John Wade's theory of "*virtual* controul," Cobbett's "puff-out" rested on the sense that a historical shift in oppressive power from force to fraud required a corresponding shift in political resistance. Under the new regime of paper, Cobbett complained, "a printing press, a ton or two of rags every year, and an engraver's tool" had done more harm "than all the powder, ball, cannons, swords, and musquets that Europe contains" (*CPR* 29 [1815], 334–35). Though terribly effective, this "system of rule" could not help but precipitate appropriate weapons of resistance: "They know that neither dungeons nor gags will protect them against this weapon. And, therefore, they are trying all their tricks to prevent the imitation of their paper . . . They are reduced to beg the aid of engravers, who may abandon, or betray them at pleasure . . . But what then? They can make nothing that cannot be imitated" (*CPR* 35 [1819–20], 48–50). The "*puff-out*" was an eminently dialectical strategy, a trickster's response to "all their tricks"; like Blake's "Bible of Hell," Cobbett's counterfeit money was a satirical debasement of a debased form. By answering paper not with gold but with more paper, he hoped to unleash disruptive energies embedded in corruption ("the system . . . has put all things out of their place"), which would then consume debased system and countersystem alike. Despite his own strident declarations of independence, a good deal of Cobbett's resistance to corruption can be traced back to the insight that "they can make nothing that cannot be imitated."

The struggle against the system and its modern financial instruments (commerce, banks, funds, stocks, paper) was in many ways a struggle over how people should be linked with one another in society. Under the corrupt surfaces of the world of the *Rural Rides*, Cobbett could discern traces of an ancient and less centralized agricultural society, loosely joined by market towns and traditional patterns of deference. He insisted that the "commercial system" of Pitt "*must* have a corrupting tendency" because it formed "men together into large companies, or bodies" (*CPR* 12 [1807], 900), and introduced improvements through which wealth flowed from the countryside to the city: "Talk of *roads* and *canals* and *bridges*! These are no signs of *national prosperity*. They are signs of *accumulated*, but not of *diffused* property, and this latter alone can insure *national prosperity*, which, rightly understood, is only another name for the *general happiness of the people*" (*CPR* 19 [1811], 589). Corrupt concentration could be discerned wherever the system took effect. An early *Register* campaign against the distribution of military honors through the Lloyd's Committee hinged on the fear that control over "the distribution of honours and rewards" would make the "little government at Lloyd's" into "the *centre of the whole nation*."[15] The characteristic habitations of modern life, "jails, barracks, factories," state-sponsored schools, and "populous cities," also corrupted "by their condensed numbers" (*AYM* 250–51). Cobbett famously renamed the system "the Thing" in an attempt to update the organic figure of corruption and the venerable theory of mixed government for an age of consolidated machinery, bureaucracy, and global capital:

After seeing that about three or four hundred Boroughmongers actually possess all the legislative power, divide the ecclesiastical, judicial, military, and naval departments amongst their own dependents, what a fine picture we find of that wise system of *checks* and *balances*, of which so much has been said by many great writers! What name to give such a government it is difficult to say. It is like nothing that ever was heard of before. It is neither a monarchy, an aristocracy, nor a democracy; it is a band of great nobles, who, by sham elections, and by the means of all sorts of bribery and corruption, have obtained an absolute sway in the country . . . Such is the government of England; such is the *thing* which has been able to bribe one half of Europe to oppress the other half. (*CPR* 33 [1818], 377–78)

If Cobbett frequently answered this terrifying concentration with a program of diffusion that recalled country-party politics,[16] he did not necessarily repudiate structure nor even central authority. In his early rebuke to the Lloyd's Committee, he insisted that military rewards "should pass through the hands of His Majesty" (*CPR* 8 [1805], 853). As he lost faith in the crown and his position radicalized, this central role was taken over by a reformed parliament, and by the massive figure of "Great Cobbett" himself. An effective countersystem had to meet the system on its own terms. Since corrupt parliamentary elections were "the very foundation upon which the system stands" (*CPR* 38 [1821], 181), radical resistance should apply itself to a single point: "all these evils would be cured by . . . a *Reform of Parliament*" (*CPR* 31 [1816], 533). For strategic purposes, the issue between Cobbett and his enemies was less centralization than the choice of centers.

Cobbett's willingness to reproduce the central posture of the Lloyd's Committee was among the most striking instances of radical egotism. Even as he struggled to sustain the popular character of reform, Cobbett found himself caught up in the ebb and flow of power from a systematic center. His "History of the Last Hundred Days of English Freedom," a series of letters written in 1817 to justify his flight from England after the suspension of Habeas Corpus, endorsed the scattered energies of popular resistance. The demand for "*Universal Suffrage*" issued from "the People": "They had taken the thing into their *own hands*. They no longer looked up to Palace Yard, nor to the Guildhall of London. They had met all over the kingdom; and, they had shown, that they wanted *no leaders*" (*CPR* 32 [1817], 558–59). At the same time, Cobbett organized the movement around parliamentary reform, and took personal credit for the fact that the system's old "*divide and subjugate*" strategy no longer succeeded in dissipating political resentment through futile "bickerings and divisions":

My writings tended to sweep away for ever this source of influence; they tended to withdraw the attention of the people from these petty disputes; they tended to make them one firm and united body in the cause of Reform. From all quarters and corners I called them to listen to me. I raised the standard of plain common sense, of sound reasoning, intelligible language, and the whole people gathered around it. (615–16)

Political struggle was personalized on both sides, for Cobbett went on to justify his exile through the construction of a mutually constitutive radical martyrology and demonology.[17] "Stewart of the Courier, Walter of the Times, William Gifford and Southey of the Quarterly Review, and hundreds of others; but, these four men in particular," had called "for *new laws*, to protect the Constitution against the 'Two-penny *Trash*'" (616). The powerful myth of his persecution at the hands of a few demonic individuals shifted attention from "the whole people" to his own larger than life figure, and to the central "standard" he raised. To reach democratic organization, repressive legislation had to pass through William Cobbett, the source of "the *poison* that was *weekly* going forth to the people in 'Two-Penny *Trash* publications'" (616). Whether he was fighting gangs hired to intimidate supporters at a Coventry election, or riding undeterred through weeks of rain in the *Rural Rides*, Cobbett offered his own vigorous body as the medium through which a people would again become "one firm and united body." This said, it is important to keep in mind the contingency and mobility of Cobbett's own figure in opposition. The failure of his early bids for a seat in parliament, the eccentric itinerary of the *Rural Rides*, and the composition of the "Last Hundred Days of English Freedom" in exile, all confirmed that the central standard-bearer of reform was himself radically decentered and displaced, an itinerant sign of the system's ravaging effects on its victims.

The translation of system and countersystem into demonology and martyrology raises the vexed problem of agency, and of Cobbett's reputation as a crude conspiracy theorist.[18] While he was prepared to treat injustice and exploitation as structural features of a specific form of social organization, Cobbett ultimately insisted on holding individuals, and above all politicians, to account. The idea of "the Government vortex" (*CPR* 23 [1813], 741) as a feature of corruption was useful to him, rhetorically and analytically, because it generated causal explanations. He spent a lifetime sorting through newspapers, parliamentary papers, legislation, legal proceedings, and crop reports for evidence of the obscure causal relationships that linked subordinate systems first to each other – "the *real* cause of the increase of the paper-money" was "*the increase of the Debt*" (*CPR* 18 [1810], 488), "the real cause of the war with France" was "the *dread of a Parliamentary Reform in England*" (*CPR* 21 [1812], 558) – and then to the final cause or "source," parliamentary corruption. "Look well at the evils we endure, and that we apprehend. Trace them back to their cause; and you will find them meeting at this one point: the House of Commons elected as it now is" (*CPR* 13 [1808], 863). The *Political Register* was unapologetically didactic, a relentless and sometimes violent initiation into the arcane causal mysteries of the system. "I teach them how to know the cause of all the misery they see amongst the poor," Cobbett once wrote of his readers, "I point out to them those who are the real cause of it, and, then I beat at their breasts 'till I force out loud indignation and bitter curses against the guilty party" (*CPR* 21 [1812], 168).

Whether so complex a system could be managed by any one "guilty party" remained obscure. When Cobbett refused "to ascribe" the Pitt system "to *contrivance*," on the grounds that this "would be to give to Pitt and his followers too much credit for profundity" (*CRR* 1: 87), he may simply have wanted to deny his enemies even a bad eminence. There was, however, a more important point at stake here too, one that went to the heart of the idea of system. As the set of "maxims and rules" that governed social life, system appeared to mark the limit of human agency and intention. In his attacks on party, Cobbett extended the "measures not men" tradition of political opposition by replacing personal influence with terms like "thing," "instrument," and "machine."[19] This mechanistic language informed his self-destructive understanding of corruption, and made the "change of system" he often demanded seem a matter of political necessity. The whigs, he insisted in 1809, would only find themselves in power if they were "called in . . . not by the voice of the people, or by the good opinion of the king, but by the *necessities of the system*": "It is the *system* that is in fault much more than the men; and, therefore, those are fools, who look to any set of men, without a change of that system" (*CPR* 16 [1809], 376, 428). Despite this instrumental analysis, Cobbett was nothing if not a vindictive writer, always ready to substitute the term "author" for the more abstract "cause." His prose worked at every level to lend corruption an intentional structure, from its saturation with capitalized and italicized proper names, to its formal organization in public letters to ministers and other prominent individuals. The system was an instrument, but it was "advised and carried on" by "*those persons*" in positions of responsibility: "The set of men that now rule are pursuing, without any deviation at all, without any patching or botching, the system of [Pitt]; and, if that system, or *any part* of it, is to be still pursued, my sincere wish is, that it may remain in their hands" (*CPR* 18 [1810], 1083, 1136–37). If Cobbett sometimes drew on the sense of impersonal determination that was emerging in economic and sociological analysis, he was ruthlessly critical of any effort to use the disappearance of agency as an excuse for existing conditions, or, worse yet, as a pretext for transcendental explanation. Nothing infuriated him more than the mystifications of politicians and preachers who resorted "to a supernatural agency," and held "that it is *Providence who has been the cause of our misfortunes*" (*CPR* 22 [1812], 613). This capitulation of responsibility was itself part of the deceptive logic of system. Cobbett responded by uncovering a mass of "calculations" and "evident intentions," and by insisting that political and economic decline could "never have taken place" without a human cause: "There must have been something, and something done *by man* too, to produce this change, this disgraceful, this distressing, this horrible change. God has not afflicted the country with pestilence or with famine . . . To *man*, therefore, must we look for *an account* for these evils" (*CPR* 36 [1820], 5–6).

Personal agency governed countersystem no less than system. As Cobbett initiated his readers into the intentional mysteries of the system, he insisted on the counter-intentions that resistance would require. The radical translation of independence from property (as alienated labor) to labor and mind restored the sense of personal control that an appeal to *"Providence"* tried to deny. Political strategies like the boycott of excised commodities encouraged a sense of popular sovereignty in the face of parliamentary corruption and a restricted franchise. *Cottage Economy* brought increasingly complex and global economic relationships back to the confines of the family and the cottage yard. Cobbett's linguistic theories were, as Peter Manning has observed, grounded in a "simple intentionalism" that encouraged readers, writers, and speakers to seize control of their words: "Grammar, perfectly understood, enables us, not only to express our meaning fully and clearly, but so to express it as to enable us to defy the ingenuity of man to give to our words any other meaning than that which we ourselves intend them to express" (*GEL* 7–8).[20] The *Rural Rides*, too, were governed by an extensive vocabulary of purpose – "object," "intention," "determined," "plan," "project," "search," "resolved"[21] – and their intentional structure converged in the two principal activities of the hero, writing and riding: "I intended to go from UPHUSBAND to STONEHENGE, thence to OLD SARUM, and thence, through the New Forest, to Southampton and Botley, and thence across into Sussex, to see Up-Park and Cowday House . . . I must adhere to a certain *route* as strictly as a regiment on a march. I had *written* the route" (*CRR* 1: 321). Yet the text of the *Rides* displayed Cobbett's political and economic dispossession as fully as it exercised his remarkable self-possession. Disciplined "intention" and "route" were often frustrated by the dispersal of systematic effects across the countryside. If the *Rides* were a military march, they were also the negation or demonic parody of a religious pilgrimage, with Cobbett the "Plaintive Pilgrim" tracing his own "PROGRESS" as he went "to pray for Justice at the Shrine of the GREAT UNPAID" (*CRR* 1: 250). Even the term "PROGRESS," which might satirically describe a single ride, was too optimistic and consecutive a term for the project as a whole. The Rider proceeded with horrified fascination on an eccentric and endlessly repetitive series of tours, and passed again and again from "rotten-borough" and "villanous place" to "infernal WEN" and "ACCURSED HILL."[22] Deprived of his farm at Botley and of a secure place in rural society, this "Pilgrim" was without a home and without a destination. His intentions remained as complex and manifold as the effects of corruption.

Like his "march" in the *Rides*, Cobbett's campaign to analyze the system was constantly subverted by the irrational structure of corruption, which seemed always to escape the limits of representation. I have already discussed the way his account of a "chain of dependence running through the whole nation" trailed off in a gesture of infinite regression, indicating the failure rather than the completion of encyclopedic analysis: "Army, navy, church, the law, sinecures, pensions, tax offices, war and navy offices, Whitehall, India-house, Bank, contract, job, &c. &c." Structural and explanatory categories (connection and dependence, center and periphery, cause and effect) were often overwhelmed by an atmosphere of dominance that threatened to bring the entire nation under its control. For Cobbett as for most radical critics, the most alarming evidence of a new expansion of "Old Corruption" was to be found in the wartime growth of patronage and taxation, and in a consequent set of domestic encroachments that were more sinister than any foreign empire.[23] "There is scarcely a family above the rank of day-labourers," he complained, "who is not, in some way or other, interested in the continuation of war" (*CPR* 24 [1813], 615). As the defeat of Napoleon came to seem inevitable, and British corruption prepared to extend its dominance across the Continent, Cobbett's outlook grew more desperate. America, "the *last remaining republic*" (*CPR* 28 [1815], 1), became the one global space left free of corruption, while England succumbed to a militant social order that "rendered the views, the feelings, the customs, nay the very fashions, of the people, completely warlike":

Every thing receives its tone from the events of the war; the influence of its occurrences, is not merely exemplified in our public amusements, but it determines our modes of dress; it regulates our domestic habits. It is not confined to the Exchange, to the coffee-house, to the tavern, or to the beer-house, but it forms the topic of conversation at all our meals, and is peculiarly the theme of the chit-chat of the tea-table . . . Nothing will satisfy, nothing please, nothing gratify, this enterprizing and commercial nation, but perpetual, desolating, barbarous war. (*CPR* 25 [1814], 449–50)

The density of absolute terms ("every thing," "not confined," "nothing," "perpetual") was typical of Cobbett's prose in this period, as was the focus on "domestic habits" as an arena of political struggle. Very early in the war, taxation had become a particular grievance with Cobbett, since it allowed the system to multiply "the pretexts of tax-gatherers for intruding into private houses" (*CPR* 9 [1806], 865), and to develop a "mode of collection" that opened private spaces to government inspection: "It authorises a set of officers to call you before them; to keep you

from day to day dancing attendance upon them; to treat you as a creature at their command" (*CPR* 7 [1805], 300–1).[24] Against the *Courier's*
claim that England had become "the last asylum of persecuted liberty,"
he offered instances of "the *vexations* of the taxing system, as imprinted
upon my mind by actual experience, in my own concerns, during the last
eight or nine months." By drawing these examples from his career as an
editor as well as a farmer, he extended the process by which radical
reformers made "country" idioms of protest available to urban constituencies.[25] As the owner of a farm, Cobbett faced taxes for hiring a
day-laborer, for making a cart to send to market, and for keeping a pony
for his son; as editor of the *Register*, he required a stamp to draw money
upon his publisher, and, when the publisher moved his shop, both men
were called to the Stamp Office to sign a bond. A system that could enter
the private sphere in this way also invaded the interior life of the subject,
and became an "evil genius" that followed "one at all times and in all
places" (*CPR* 10 [1806], 900–03). If this nightmare of corrupt influence
seemed to complete the hegemony of system, it also replaced a national
"chain of dependence" with immediate, local, and personal terms, offer-
ing Cobbett a way out. Returning through his own "actual experience"
to the synecdochic analysis of a "single point" of oppression, Cobbett
was again able to deploy autobiography as a means of political resistance.[26] Political independence was like corruption located "in the
mind," and in personal habits and domestic life.

WRITING AS SYSTEM AND COUNTERSYSTEM

The idea of system as an "evil genius" haunting the mind, and influ-
encing everything from "public amusements" and "modes of dress" to
"domestic habits" and "the chit-chat of the tea-table," suggests one
reason why language was central to Cobbett's understanding of system
and countersystem. In language and in human communication, structures of thought and feeling were acquired and transmitted, and power
relations negotiated and sustained. In a public letter to Lord Liverpool,
written towards the end of the war with France, as he gradually abandoned his longstanding anti-Americanism, Cobbett produced a telling
vignette of how suspicion of "the American Republic" had been cultivated among young farm laborers like himself:

It has always been the misfortune of England, that her rulers and her people
have spoken and have thought *contemptuously* of the Americans. Your Lordship
and I were boys, and, indeed, not born, or, at least, I was not, when our King

first was involved in a quarrel with the Americans. But almost as long as I can remember any thing, I can remember, that this contempt was expressed in the songs and sayings of the clod-hoppers, amongst whom I was born and bred; in doing which we conducted down to the earth that we delved the very sentiments of the "Squires and Lords". (*CPR* 26 [1814], 759)

Cobbett's preoccupation with the material world is normally taken to prove his ignorance about the more elevated spheres of culture, but in this remarkable account of how dominant attitudes were cultivated and transmitted in a pre-literate environment, we find instead a salutary reminder of the material dimension of cultural processes. As the "clod-hoppers" worked the soil, the "sentiments of the 'Squires and Lords'" were worked into their own "songs and sayings," and the whole mass of prejudice was turned into the earth they inhabited. The scene effectively linked active and passive processes, material and the immaterial conditions, reminding us once again that the idea of corruption cannot be reduced to a blunt conspiracy theory. The young Cobbett and his fellow rural laborers cultivated and were cultivated by a language that was not entirely their own.

Cobbett later undertook to instruct these "clod-hoppers" in his *Grammar of the English Language* (1818), in part to insure that different sentiments were "conducted down to the earth." The project of the *Grammar* forced him to revise his attitude towards popular education. He had long believed that literacy and formal instruction were unnecessary "to those who labour with their limbs" (*CPR* 12 [1807], 331), and he tended to dismiss contemporary educational schemes as crude instruments of social control.[27] Whether directed by the state, the church, or by individual philanthropists, schooling for the poor offered "nothing . . . but the rudiments of servility, pauperism, and slavery" (*CE* 7). It was only when the expansion of formal literacy began to seem inevitable that Cobbett produced his grammar of resistance. A literate population provided with appropriate reading material would become "so completely capable of detecting and exposing the tricks and contrivances of their oppressors, that the power of doing mischief will die a natural death in the hands of those oppressors" (*CPR* 32 [1817], 1083). An illustration of "the Time" of verbs in the *Grammar* suggests how the contest between system and countersystem came to be played out on the field of language: "'Sidmouth *writes* a Circular Letter; Sidmouth *wrote* a Circular Letter; Sidmouth *will write* a Circular Letter.' Again: 'the Queen *defies* the tyrants; the Queen *defied* the tyrants; the Queen *will defy* the tyrants'" (*GEL* 35).[28] The struggle between tyranny and opposition was registered in the verbal extension of an act through past, present, and future. Conceived as the first in a series of popular tracts on language, law, church history, and finance, the *Grammar* was itself one term in a more extensive syntax of resistance. In a public letter to William Benbow, Cobbett suggested how the tetralogy would feature in a radical countersystem: "These four works . . . will be four books independent of each other; yet, all tending to the same good end; namely, the rendering of great numbers of the people a match, at least, in point of book-learning, to more than the average of 'Noble Lords' and 'Honourable Gentlemen' . . . We shall see, in spite of all the efforts of our enemies, a *public* more than a match for *legitimacy*" (*CPR* 32 [1817], 1090–91). Cobbett's writing and the popular resentment it encouraged were, like the verbal conjugation of the queen's defiance, "a match" for corrupt power and its supporters, the equal but opposite image of system.

Cobbett's rhetorical understanding of system and countersystem extended from language to the institutions of public discourse. I have already considered, in an earlier chapter, his analysis of the two branches of state interference in the press ("the means by *Corruption*" and "the means by *Persecution*"), and his role in developing a radical ethos of editorial independence that would prevent corruption, if not persecution. The fear that the government would succeed in bringing all of print culture under its control generated some of Cobbett's most harrowing visions of systematic hegemony. In two 1813 public letters "On the subject of teaching the Children of the Poor to read," written in the period before his *Grammar*, Cobbett attacked the Lancaster school model and defended his own conviction that, "under the present circumstances of this country," popular literacy would "produce *evil* rather than *good*." He did this by sketching "the real state" of the press in England, a state of absolute subjection to official influence, and then following "one of these poor boys in his progress of reading, after he has been taught, at your Lancaster school, to read in the Bible." At every stage, corrupt power had its way: children's books rose "above the non-sensical" only "to inculcate *abject submission*"; "MOORE'S ALMANACK, that universal companion of the farmers and labourers of England," was full of "*songs* and *wonders* and *prophecies*" that served "to keep a people in a state of profound ignorance," and "to make them superstitious and slavish"; daily newspapers led if possible to "an increase of ignorance," as did magazines and reviews, "the productions, for the most part, of men actually in a state of the most mercenary and servile dependence." Popular education turned out to be a more complex and systematic version of what

Cobbett had experienced as a boy, with his fellow laborers in the fields of Surrey: "teaching the poor to read and to believe what others choose they should read and believe, and nothing more" (*CPR* 24 [1813], 747–52, 778–79).

Faced with "so extensive an empire" of corrupt writing, Cobbett was often driven to despair: "truth . . . becomes fiction; vice, virtue; defeat, victory; and victory, defeat." His only comfort was then "the satisfaction of having at least *endeavoured* to stem the torrent of general corruption, and of having entered upon record my solemn protest" (*CPR* 25 [1814], 208–09). He continued to write and publish in opposition, though, and his ongoing participation in a struggle over the nation's discursive resources provided some of the most striking evidence of his effort to distinguish himself from the system even as he engaged it on its own terms. For Cobbett as for Paine, "*truth* in *clear language*" (*CPR* 18 [1810], 20) was the only way to combat the rapid fictionalization of public life.[29] Since corruption dealt in misrepresentations and partial representations, he insisted that the reform movement undertake a complete and accurate account of existing conditions: "To make . . . a true and full representation, to put such a representation upon record, to promulgate it so that it should be familiar to the mind of every man in the country is, in my opinion, absolutely necessary . . . This representation should be a fair one; it should tell, not only the truth, but the whole truth" (*CPR* 9 [1806], 165). The encyclopedic effort to "match" the "extensive . . . empire" of print corruption was evident throughout Cobbett's career, from his early promise to gather "*all* the authentic documents" in the *Political Register*,[30] through ongoing archival projects like *Cobbett's Complete Collection of State Trials*, to the compulsive itinerary of the *Rural Rides*. His writing became a prosaic manifestation of what Kenneth Burke has called "the chart," a "realistic sizing-up of situations that is sometimes explicit, sometimes implicit, in poetic strategies." As Burke observes, even the most dispassionate chart contains "magical" elements of "verbal coercion," leaving us with a choice not "between magic and no magic, but between magics that vary in their degree of approximation to the truth": "The ideal magic is that in which our assertions (or verbal decrees) as to the nature of the situation come closest to a correct gauging of that situation as it actually is. Any *approximate* chart is a 'decree.' Only a *completely accurate chart* would dissolve magic, by making the structure of names identical with the structure named."[31] Cobbett's struggle with the system was a struggle over the authority to issue the verbal decrees that would divide truth from fiction, vice from virtue, defeat from victory. The corrosive principle of *"clear"* expression "stripped statement and reasoning of the foppery of affectation" (*CPR* 18 [1810], 20), and left in its aftermath the extensive rhetoric of corruption that filled the pages of the *Political Register*: "circumlocutions" and "double meanings," the deceptive meta-phors of "all the tribe [who] deal in tropes and figures," an "artful *selec-tion of terms*" meant to "bewilder and mislead the public," the "frothy" and "insubstantial" oratory of Pitt and Canning, and the "Learned Languages," a specialized discourse of power (Sinecure, Habeas Corpus, Ex Officio) meant to baffle and exclude the uninitiated.[32] With these by-products of a radical rhetoric of stripping cleared away, the *Register* could return to the promise of a completely accurate chart. "The mass of mankind are worked upon by the power of *words*," Cobbett complained, "They are very apt to take a thing to be, and to let it pass for, *what it is called*" (*CPR* 17 [1810], 484). The *Political Register* was instead firmly under the spell of things, and struggled to bring language back into its original and perfect correspondence with the world.

In a world that was fashioned in large part by corruption and corrupt writing, a counter-magical chart could not help but accrue magical and even apocalyptic powers. The *Rural Rides* were a revealing case in point. An endless barrage of observations, surveys, evidence, tests, inquiries, descriptions, and calculations, the project generated "real knowledge" (*CRR* 1: 288) about everything from soil and wages to parliamentary representation and the best way to treat a cold. "I know all about the matter," was a typical narrative pronouncement (*CRR* 2: 399). If Cobbett aimed at simple reference, the verbal compression of fact he achieved could also yield apocalyptic pressure: "What a misery is all this! What a mass of materials for producing that general and *dreadful convul-sion* that must, first or last, come and blow this funding and enslaving and starving system to atoms!" (*CRR* 1: 279). Gather a sufficient "mass of materials" in print, Cobbett seemed to suggest, and prophetic visions of a catastrophic outcome would follow. An advertisement for his *Paper Against Gold* reinforced the suggestion: "The work . . . does, in short, *leave nothing unknown*, appertaining to that dreadful system of Taxation, Loans and Paper-Money, which has finally brought this country to ruin and misery, which ruin and misery are not only *foretold* in this work, but the reasons are given and the proof produced why such a result ought to be expected" (*CPR* 32 [1817], 1). The ideal printed work was for Cobbett one that drew the coercive powers of prophecy and social change from a complete and accurate chart of the world.

Though he often employed the prophetic and apocalyptic idiom of the Bible,[33] Cobbett drew his prophetic authority not from divine revelation, but from his role as a periodical journalist whose painstaking record of daily events uncovered systematic patterns that extended from the past into the future. His Preface to volume eight of the *Political Register* was an important professional manifesto that insisted upon "the utility of this work, as a Register" of national and international affairs, to correct a "great source of error as to transactions of past times": "One of the principle objects of the undertaking, was, to insure to my readers the possession of *all* the authentic documents, which should, during the continuance of the work, appear in print, relative to transactions between nation and nation; and, so unremitted has been my attention thereunto, that, I think I may safely assert, that no document of that description has been omitted" (Preface, *CPR* 8 [1805], n. pag.). Like his political economy, Cobbett's textual economy was a strictly closed system in which nothing was gained or lost. As his disaffection intensified and the pressures of corruption seemed to mount, this closed system became more volatile, and the impact of an exhaustive register of events spilled over from present and "past times" into the future. The first number of the next volume of the *Register* opened with a provocative Old Testament epigraph – "Will ye NOW hear, O foolish people, which have eyes, and see not; which have ears, and hear not?" – followed by a stunning Jeremiad, under the conventional newspaper heading, "Summary of Politics":

Will nothing, oh, people of England, short of destruction itself, convince you that you are on the road to destruction? Will you, in spite of the awful admonition of events, in spite of experimental conviction, in spite of truths that you acknowledge, still listen to the falsehoods of your deceivers? When we look back upon the year that has just past over our heads . . . is it possible for us not to be impressed with the most serious apprehensions for the future? (*CPR* 9 [1806], 1)

Through its accumulation of fact and "experimental conviction," the weekly newspaper became the empirical conscience of a nation, and prophetically spanned past, present, and future. Cobbett later appended the subtitle "Notices for History" to his weekly "Summary of Politics" (*CPR* 28 [1815], 211), encouraging readers to grasp the broad dimensions of their own experience.[34] History for Cobbett was never a thing of the past, nor was prophecy entirely a thing of the future: both came together in the vivid present tense of the *Political Register*.

Cobbett's compulsive attention to present reality lent his realistic charts their magical power. He has often been praised for the transparency of his descriptive prose: Hazlitt observed that the editor of the

Register "places us in the same situation with himself, and makes us see all that he does" (*CWH* 8: 53), and E. P. Thompson agreed that the reader "is asked to look, not *at* Cobbett, but *with* him."[35] Yet even where Cobbett did seem to content himself with providing a deictic marker or a window on the world, it is not hard to discover a verbal coercion too easily elided by a phrase like "asked to look." The indexical markers that saturated the *Political Register*, above all the claim that "reform is the object which alone is worthy of our anxious attention" (*CPR* 17 [1810], 608), were never presented in isolation. Instead, they competed in a bewildering landscape of manipulative verbal gestures. The corrupt effort "to draw our attention from what we ought to attend to" was so important to Cobbett that he felt compelled to give it a name, the "*Lo here*! and *Lo there*!" The *Register*'s catalogue of corrupt tropes and figures included an extensive rhetoric of distraction: jubilee celebrations, foreign enemies, party catch-phrases, "the cry about Jacobinism," and "the hypocritical cry of '*no popery*'" were all introduced "for the purposes of turning the attention of the people" from the "real grounds" of their distress.[36] The violent discursive struggle between Cobbett and his enemies over control of public attention rescues his prose from the crude, sub-literary mimesis to which it has too often been consigned, while his fascination with the immediate and the material prevents him from falling into the other extreme of mere invective or harangue. The real interest and complexity of his prose can be found in an emphatic and provoking "*this*," and in the dynamic relationship it proposed between situations outside language ("real grounds," "real cause") and language about those situations (a relationship curiously obscured by the interpretive idiom of text and context that has assisted his disappearance from literary history). Far from abandoning the highest powers of language to transform the world, Cobbett's radical prose operated as if those powers inhered reciprocally in language and in the conditions to be transformed. Specific situations dictated specific discursive modes of empowerment or defeat.

Just as a politics of distracting indexes finally required its own index ("Lo here"), so the empire of corrupt signs brought language itself within the scope of real and material conditions. Petitions for reform, parliamentary debates, transcripts of trials, Burdettite graffiti, and cries of Jacobinism were, for Cobbett, agents and things as well as signs. The strongest evidence that he took language seriously as an element of the "real grounds" of "things" was to be found in his willingness to include printed texts in a privileged radical sphere of fact. When in 1809 he reprinted a parliamentary debate about corruption in the *Political*

Register, he presented it as a "naked fact" or "bare record": "Nor shall I
. . . offer any *comment,* or *opinion* . . . The thing will speak for itself. It is
plain matter of fact, unencumbered with any thing that can give rise to a
difference to be settled by reasoning." Linguistic structure, so often for
Cobbett a structure of interference that divided people from the world,
became in this case a structure of authenticity and verification: "I shall
take it, word for word, and letter for letter, as I find it reported." The
printed "thing" came into its own as a concrete and potentially active
element of the world, less an index of something else than an object of
attention in its own right. "This Debate . . . should be printed in all
shapes and sizes," Cobbett wrote of a House of Commons debate on
corruption, "It should be framed and glazed; and hung up in Inns,
Town-Halls, Courts of Justice, Market-Places, and, in short, the eye of
every human creature should be, if possible, constantly fixed upon it"
(*CPR* 15 [1809], 738–39). If the radical notion of "fact" meant to stabilize
the world in language, printed texts turned out, ironically, to be an ideal
incarnation of fact, since they were derived *"from the best possible source"*
and attended with markers of *"times* and *places* and other particulars"
(*CPR* 16 [1809], 34, 44). Towards the end of the war, when Cobbett
wanted to prove beyond doubt that American commerce was thriving,
he found, in the most debased of print forms, the commercial advertisement, "evidence of that sort, which is impossible to fail of producing
conviction." Normally averse to commercial influence, he enthusiastically reprinted fourteen columns of advertising from American newspapers in the *Register:* "That I have *fabricated* these advertisements is not
to be believed. I could not have invented so many names, dates, and circumstances . . . The advertisements must be genuine; and they form one
of masses of presumptive evidence, which is preferable to any positive
proof upon oath" (*CPR* 28 [1815], 240–54). Even when transported
across the Atlantic, the documentary fact was so compelling that
Cobbett's normally privileged sphere of oral communication (the oath)
seemed dubious and unstable by comparison.

Cobbett's search for communication without "difference" sometimes
extended beyond language and documentary facts to the direct
exchange of material elements of the world. In the Eighth Part of *Cottage
Economy,* "Selecting, Cutting and Bleaching the Plants of English Grass
and Grain, for the purpose of making Hats and Bonnets," he promoted
his scheme for a cottage industry that would shield the rural household
from commercial and industrial encroachment by providing women and
children with work at home:

Here all is not only performed by hand, but by hand singly, without any combination of hands. Here there is no power of machinery or of chemistry wanted. All is performed out in the open fields, or sitting in the cottage. There want no coal mines and no rivers to assist, no waterpowers nor powers of fire. No part of the kingdom is unfit for the business. Everywhere there are grass, water, sun, and women and children's fingers; and these are all that are wanted. (*CE* 173)

Much of the text was devoted to correspondence associated with an elaborate series of "experiments" Cobbett had conducted to prove that domestic grass was suitable for the project. A letter to the Secretary of the Society of Arts in London contained, in its original form, samples of "the necessary materials" (154):

With this letter I send you sixteen specimens of plat, and also eight parcels of straw, in order to show the sorts that the plat is made out of. The numbers of the plat correspond with those of the straw . . . These parcels of straw are sent in order that you may know the kind of straw, or rather of grass, from which the several pieces of plat have been made. This is very material; because it is by those parcels of straw that the kinds of grass are to be known. (*CE* 160)

This effort to make a point using "materials" rather than language or reason was the culmination of Cobbett's search for an incontrovertible defense of radical reform and its many subsidiary agendas. To be sure, the parcels of straw were here related second-hand, a derivative representation of the primary presentation, but Cobbett elsewhere sought to make a concrete medium available to wider audiences. One of the many aims of the *Rural Rides* was "to ascertain the state of the crops" (*CRR* 1: 201), and in the face of agricultural depression and commodity speculation, Cobbett did not expect to be taken at his word:

In order to enable others to judge, as well as myself, I took samples from the fields as I went along. I took them very fairly, and as often as I thought that there was any material change in the soil or other circumstances. During the ride I took sixteen samples. These are now at the Office of the Register, in Fleet-street, where they may be seen by any gentleman who thinks the information likely to be useful to him. The samples are numbered, and there is a reference pointing out the place where each sample was taken. (*CRR* 1: 241)

This quasi-scientific sampling brought Cobbett's language down to the "material" level of the crops with which he was concerned, and reduced representation to the concrete synecdoche that supervened the *Rides* at every level, from specific "samples" to a more sweeping view "of what has long been going on all over the country" (*CRR* 1: 276).

Yet just as the search for a document that carried its own "conviction"

could lead finally to newspaper advertising, so these "samples" of the
world made no sense until they were transformed into "specimens" by
an elaborate grammar of numbers and references. Their implication in
language and print was reinforced when Cobbett decided to offer them
to readers through "the Office of the Register, in Fleet-street." The very
idea of distributing "material" was substantially rhetorical: it was
unlikely, and unnecessary, that readers would flock to Fleet-street; the
promise was enough, and the samples took effect on the printed page. If
the *Rides* were a massive synecdoche, they were not always "very
material," and the system of references that threatened to obscure the
crop samples indicated how discursive procedures and immediate experience competed for Cobbett's allegiance. He delighted in the life of the
land, but was frustrated when his rural travels found him "absent from
my books and papers" (*CPR* 22 [1812], 481). The *Rides* themselves were as
fully engaged with the corrupt London press as they were with crops,
soil, and weather. The natural world was richly inscribed with legible
signs: clouds were the "language" of an oncoming storm, churches "the
traces of a great ancient population," and rushes the "sure sign of exe-
crable soil." [37] Like any true allegorical hero, the Plaintive Pilgrim was no
less committed to reading than to experiencing his world.

THE ECONOMY OF THE WORLD AND THE DISAPPEARANCE OF THE WRITER

The contradictory features of Cobbett's prose and his person were a
function of his unstable position in opposition. Political resistance
embedded him in the world of print mediation, and required the
complex tactics of system and countersystem. The problem of mediation became particularly acute during the period of his American exile,
and at one point Cobbett staged for his readers a ritual enactment of his
contradictory role. Thousands of miles from the farm at Botley that he
still considered his proper home, alienated from his fellow radicals by the
decision to flee England, yet still committed to a war against system,
Cobbett developed an extraordinary personal regimen of abstinence
and political devotion:

My hatred of the Borough villains, and my anxious desire to assist in the inflic-
tion of vengeance on them, have made me more and more rigid as to sobriety
and abstemiousness. At every stage of their oppressions I have become more
and more careful to avoid any thing that might tend to narrow my sphere of
exertion. Before they imprisoned me, I was now and then tempted to drink wine

and spirits and water. I, after the imprisonment, sometimes drank ale and porter. But, since their *dungeon Bill*, milk-and-water, or water alone, has been my drink . . . I have, lately, met with an accident *from fire*. The house, in which I lived, was burnt down. This threw me out for a month. I should have gone to New York, and remained there till the time of my departure for England. But, when I considered the *interruptions* which such a removal would occasion, and when I thought of the injury that these and the air of a city might be to my literary labours; I resolved on making a sort of *thatched tent*, in which I might enjoy tranquility and in which I might labour without intermission. From this tent, made of poles, thatch, and *English news-papers*, I now have the honour to address you. Happiness never depends upon mere *place*. It depends little more on food or raiment. My diet all comes from my own fields, and my cow is my vintner and brewer. I am asleep on my straw by nine o'clock, and I am in my orchard before four o'clock. Yet, who can be happier? My *mind* is, for the far greater part of my time, *in England*. And I have the infinite satisfaction to see, that I have, from this distance, stricken blows which have made the tyrants half distracted. (*CPR* 35 [1819–20], 11–13)

As he traced his strict personal habits to conditions imposed by corruption ("oppressions," "imprisonment," exile), it became clear that the system had produced Great Cobbett. If he renounced corrupting drink, he literally inhabited a corrupt English press: "The walls" of the tent "were made of Chronicles and Couriers" (*CPR* 36 [1820], 689). These newspapers alone secured his mental residence "*in England*," and from them he fashioned his ongoing print campaign against corruption. That he still felt up to "registering" English social and political life from thousands of miles away was a testament to the fact that print culture, and above all *corrupt* print culture, formed the limit of his political experience. At the same time, this (dislocated) Grub Street rant was firmly embedded in a rustic idyl. "Fields," "cow," and "orchard" extended outward from the newspaper tent, keeping away "the air of a city," and marking the agricultural order that Cobbett worked so assiduously to restore. The thatched roof that arched over the newspaper walls seemed to bear a sacred significance. When Cobbett received word of new economic difficulties back home, he turned from his printed walls to this roof, and uttered an oral prayer of thanksgiving: "I put my hands together, lifted up my eyes towards the straw roof of my tent . . . and exclaimed: 'God be praised! The end of delusion is at hand'" (*CPR* 36 [1820], 689).

The thatched roof marked a further limit of Cobbett's world, the rural horizons that hovered over system and countersystem alike, and allowed him to imagine "the end of delusion" and the end of his own precarious role as exiled writer in opposition. Variously marked in his prose in class, ethnic, and national terms, this boundary was finally economic, imposed by "the *natural economy* of a country" (*CRR* 1: 220). Like other leading radicals, Cobbett held commerce in contempt, and tended to treat agriculture "in physiocratic terms as the only truly productive activity."[38] Agriculture and the land were from the outset of his career "the only *source* of national wealth" (*CPR* 12 [1807], 870), and, when his position radicalized, he added "*labour*" as a second source of "the real strength and all the resources of a country" (*CPR* 31 [1816], 545). Corruption's elaborate machinery of paper money, debt, stocks, and banks could do little more than redistribute the wealth produced by agricultural labor:

Though paper-money could CREATE nothing of value, it was able to TRANSFER every thing of value; able to strip a little gentry; able to dilapidate even parsonage houses; able to rob gentlemen of their estates, and labourers of their Sunday-coats and their barrels of beer; able to snatch the dinner from the board of the reaper or the mower, and to convey it to the barrack-table, of the Hessian or Hanoverian grenadier; able to take away the wool, that ought to give warmth to the bodies of those who rear the sheep, and put it on the backs of those who carry arms to keep the poor, half-famished shepherds in order! (*CRR* 2: 373–74)

So thorough was Cobbett's commitment to economics as a zero-sum game that he found the most basic assumptions of political economy incomprehensible, and dismissed "'*free trade*' and '*mutual gain*'" as "a humbug": "It is a stupid idea, that *all nations are to gain*, by any thing. Whatever is the gain of one, must, in some way or other, be a loss to another" (*CRR* 1: 316). The conventional starting-point for economic argument ("suppose an island," "suppose a community") was in Cobbett's prose a first principle rather than a rhetorical device, and led with astonishing speed to an inevitable conclusion about limited resources. Whole volumes of political economy could be revised and refuted in a few sentences: "Suppose a nation of a hundred men, and their families, to inhabit a little island. Suppose a despotic ruler, residing on another island, to make them give up *all* their produce, under the name of tax. They must all starve. Suppose him to take away a great part. Many must suffer" (*CPR* 35 [1819], 284–85). The principle of the economic boundary applied at every level, from individual and household through village and parish to nation and world, and seemed to Cobbett so fundamental that he was annoyed when others invoked it as a particular condition or insight. A passing reference in the *Times* to the limited means of a military commander seemed to him to carry no "great signification," and drew a derisive response: "Where is the commander; where is the human being; where is the nation, whose means have not *some limits?*" (*CPR* 22 [1812], 676).

The Rural Ride "Down the Valley of the Avon in Wiltshire" was among the most impressive of Cobbett's literary expositions of the economic limit. Prefaced by a simple map identifying churches and former manor houses, the Ride proceeded to trace a pattern of abandonment and decay: "Nothing can more clearly show, than this, that all, as far as buildings and population are concerned, has been long upon the decline and decay . . . The *land* remains; and the crops and the sheep come as abundantly as ever; but they are now *sent almost wholly away*, instead of remaining as formerly, to be, in great part, consumed in these twentynine parishes" (*CRR* 2: 372). Cobbett spent a good deal of time attacking the parasites and profiteers who drew "crops and sheep" to the cities through a modern infrastructure of toll-roads and canals,[39] but he was also interested in glossing the claim that "the *land* remains." Probing beneath the superimpositions of "this wretched and most infamous system" (368), he discovered "the traces of a great ancient population" (372), and the remains of a stable rural community of reapers, mowers, shepherds, and landlords. The structure of this Ride was from the outset distinctly mythic and utopian, a journey through "my land of promise; or at least, of great expectation," in "search of the source of the AVON RIVER" (359). Fleeting glimpses of a fertile countryside realized his expectations:

Here the farmer has always an *abundance of straw*. His farmyard is never without it. Cattle and horses are bedded up to their eyes. The yards are put close under the shelter of a hill, or are protected by lofty and thick-set trees. Every animal seems comfortably situated; and, in the dreariest days of winter, these are, perhaps, the happiest scenes in the world; or, rather, they would be such, if those, whose labour makes it all, trees, corn, sheep, and every thing, had but *their fair share* of the produce of that labour. (365)

Reassuring features of containment and closure ("close under," "protected by") were an ideal setting for productive agricultural labor, and a constant reminder of the limits within which that labor transpired. Selfregulating mechanisms – "the sheep principally manure the land" (363) – guaranteed a stability and internal sufficiency that corruption and commerce systematically violated. The governing feature of "the Valley" hovered at the edge of the entire Ride, providing an insistent register of closure: "The *shelter*, in these valleys, and particularly where the downs are *steep* and *lofty* on the sides, is very complete" (365).

In the end, however, this most utopian of Rides was subject to the oppositional imperatives that governed the text as a whole. Cobbett travelled out of the valley, through attacks on such enemies of the limit as "the Scotch *feelosofers*" and the "EMIGRATION COMMITTEE" (375, 377), until he reached a final, ironic prospect from the rotten borough of Old Sarum, an "ACCURSED HILL": "It was impossible to stand on this accursed spot, without swelling with indignation against the base and plundering and murderous sons of corruption" (380). The "shelter" provided by the valley was not enough to insulate this "land of promise" from its demonic antithesis. Cobbett's *Rides* were as eccentric in their narrative as in their itinerary, and veered endlessly back and forth between description and argument, country and city, utopia and corruption. This dizzying narrative was authorized by an associative logic that emerged as systematic expansion met countersystematic closure.[40] Pressure in one place was sure to be felt elsewhere, and no feature of the landscape could be treated in isolation: the brick and stone that went into defenses at Dover denied "a neat new cottage" to "every labouring man in the counties of Kent and of Sussex" (*CRR* 1: 228), and paper money created "*new and fine houses in London*" only because it "destroyed forty mansion houses in this Vale of Avon" (*CRR* 2: 373).

Rigid and impermeable as they were, the economic borders of Cobbett's world gave way to the tactical imperatives of countersystem. His horizons widened as he devoted himself to opposition. Though he protested that he would "never *advise* any person to go to America" (*CPR* 28 [1815], 397), he joined the controversy over emigration and eventually composed an *Emigrant's Guide* (1829), in part because the pressure to leave England seemed to him indisputable evidence that the system created inhospitable conditions. His disdain for foreign trade, and for any commerce beyond that of the traditional market town, softened dramatically in the early 1810s when he discovered that the war with Napoleonic France was a war of ideological containment. "What they wanted," the Rural Rider announced, as he surveyed the ruinous wartime defenses at Dover, "was to prevent the landing, not of Frenchmen, but of French principles" (*CRR* 1: 228). Writing under the ministry's wartime "system of commercial monopoly," Cobbett discovered the "reciprocal advantages" of free trade (*CPR* 22 [1812], 616–17), and learned to speak and write the language of commercial humanism:

Men have had their eyes shut for a long while; but, peace will make them look about them. They will, like birds, whose cage door is open, all of a sudden, lift their heads, stare about them, and begin to try their wings. — Since the people of this island were shut in by war, wonderful changes have taken place in the world. Manufactures have been changing their place; money has been changing its value; the capability of living at ease has been changing its site . . . Why should we not trade and live in social intercourse with France? Why should the French not have our hardware and our cloth, and give us their wine and oil in exchange? Why should we be penned up in this island all our lives, when, at a few leagues distance, we could see so many things to delight the eye and inform the mind? (*CPR* 25 [1814], 10–11)

His conversion to commercial "intercourse" was tactical and political rather than economic. Against his deepest instincts, Cobbett was willing to encourage the free circulation of goods and ideas across national borders in order to frustrate ministerial efforts to quarantine England from alternative models of political organization.

As the war wound to an end, America replaced France as the "glorious example" of a "*really free Government*" (*CPR* 27 [1815], 48–49). New impediments were put in place to shield England from republican contagion, and Cobbett found a packet of newspapers sent to him from America loaded down "with *Forty Five Dollars of Postage*" (*CPR* 29 [1815], 347). His own narrow island mentality suddenly became a systematic imposition: "Talk of the Wall of China! It must be a fool of a thing compared to the fence that surrounds us. 'Oh! 'tis a nice little, *tight* little island'" (*CPR* 29 [1815], 347). The result of this reversal was his 1815 "PLAN, for the Publishing of TRUTH, and for Keeping Up a Literary Intercourse with America, which Intercourse Shall Tend to Assist the Cause of Freedom." The centerpiece of the "PLAN" was a literary agent in New York who "would not only cause to be printed and promulgated any original writings sent to him from England; but . . . would be able to send from America to England such American Publications as he might think likely to be useful here" (*CPR* 29 [1815], 289, 291). The ironies of the project were difficult to conceal – Cobbett undertook to circulate texts across national borders in order to protect those borders from a system of political corruption and military and imperial expansion – but he did try to distinguish his own commerce in letters from the base transactions of "Commercial Men" (292–93). The international scope of his operations could be narrowed and closure reaffirmed through figures of personal interchange: "Is it not . . . of vast importance, that the two nations should *know one another?*" (293). A letter "from a gentleman at *Nashville* in the state of TENASSEE," who wanted "to obtain the Register *regularly* in the future," condensed the entire project into a single, personal transaction: "Mine is a scheme for making people talk to each other across the Atlantic" (*CPR* 30 [1816], 101). Like all of Cobbett's economies, the economy of periodical dialogue was reassuringly circular. When he trusted his prose to the American press, he could expect not only a reply, but the return of the original utterance. Works reprinted abroad "quickly come back to me, in another print, after having been read on the banks of the Ohio and those of the Mississippi" (*CPR* 27 [1815], 643).

Cobbett's grand strategy of circulating printed texts in the face of systematic obstruction had a rhetorical counterpart in the embarrassing national comparison. This device flourished in the radical press of the 1810s, in part as a response to the stark comparisons between England and France that had been drawn by reactionary propagandists in the 1790s.[41] Where Alan Liu has recently discerned a homology between Napoleon's dialectical battlefield tactics and "the politics of opposition" in print,[42] I would link the comparison across national borders even more directly, if negatively, with the tactics of economic warfare under the guise of the French Continental System and the British Orders in Council. Cobbett himself indicated how rhetorical border crossings gathered their transgressive force when "the people of England" realized that the French Revolution "would compel the conceding of . . . reform in the parliament": "Those in power saw it too. All communication was, by war, cut off between the two countries; reform did not take place; our system of government was new steeled instead of being softened" (*CPR* 28 [1815], 380). In the framework of militant patriotism and an embargo on ideas, pointed comparisons across national boundaries served to reopen broken lines of communication, and to threaten the hegemony of "those in power" by presenting them with ideological material they could not easily assimilate or recuperate. The *Rural Rides* ostentatiously displayed Cobbett's freedom to pursue national comparisons in the aftermath of the war. The deliberate "route" and strict intentional structure of the text suddenly broke down when Cobbett arrived at Dover, and mocked his enemies with the license of an uncertain itinerary: "I am, in real truth, undecided, as yet, whether I shall go on to France, or back to the *Wen*. I think I shall, when I go out of this Inn, toss the bridle upon my horse's neck, and *let him decide for me*" (*CRR* 1: 224). Two days later he was still wandering around Dover, surrounded by the ruins of an expensive government campaign to prevent the landing of French ideas. From this position, a defiant political comparison exposing the effects of the tithing system required little effort beyond a simple gesture of the head: "Looking down from this very anti-jacobin hill, this day, I saw the parsons' shocks of wheat and barley, left in the field after the farmer had taken his away. Turning my head, and looking across the Channel, 'There,' said I, pointing to France, 'there the spirited and sensible people have ridded themselves of this burden, of which our farmers so bitterly complain'" (228–29). The close horizons of the Valley of Avon were now nowhere in evidence. The Rider violated his own economic principle of containment, and extended his purview beyond the shores of England, in order to expose the domestic effects of corruption.

The tension between Cobbett's respect for and transgression of boundaries only eased when a *"natural economy"* itself assumed the functions of political resistance. The *Political Register* was the most influential exponent of the radical principle that an expansive system created unsustainable pressures as it met and then exceeded the inflexible limits of the world. "Sooner or later," Cobbett maintained, "these issues of paper-money must, if continued without interruption, produce what all such issues, in all countries, have, at last, produced; namely, the total blowing up of the whole system, and, perhaps, of the government along with it" (*CPR* 29 [1815], 324).[43] The peculiar rhythms of Cobbett's life in opposition (the ascetic discipline of the Long Island tent, the restless itinerary of the *Rural Rides*) were a result of his struggle to contribute actively to an inevitable outcome – or simply to pass the time in the waning days before the apocalypse. He was only half joking when he wrote to Henry Hunt that there was little more for them to do than preserve their health: "Take care of that, and leave Corruption to nod and totter for a little longer. Every thing now existing, or in prospect, tends to her destruction" (*CPR* 33 [1818], 439).

As the *Rural Rides* mapped a corrupt system onto the English countryside, and translated demonology into demonography, they struggled to *realize* the figure of corruption in order to manifest its effects and accelerate its downfall. When Cobbett reached Cheltenham, "a place, to which East India plunderers, West India floggers, English taxgorgers, together with gluttons, drunkards, and debauchees of all descriptions, *female* as well as male, resort," he was seized by an impulse "to squeeze up my nose with my fingers": "It is nonsense, to be sure; but I conceit that every two-legged creature, that I see coming near me, is about to cover me with the poisonous proceeds of its impurities" (*CRR* 2: 446). The figural distension that so often disturbed radical representations of corruption threatened here to erupt across the boundary between the figural and the actual. This alarming realization of a political metaphor was no longer "nonsense" when Cobbett moved on from this "Wen" to a rural landscape of wartime industry and post-war depression, which had been emptied out to satisfy monstrous urban appetites. In these hollow places, the antithesis of agricultural pleni-tude, the *negative* excess that was corruption made its presence felt in the rhetorical extravagance of the writer's own apocalyptic critique. At Dover, Cobbett discovered "a hill containing probably a couple of square miles or more, hollowed like a honey-comb" (*CRR* 1: 227), the deteriorating remains of wartime fortifications:

All along the coast there are works of some sort or other; incessant sinks of money; walls of immense dimensions; masses of stone brought and put into piles. Then you see some of the walls and buildings falling down; some that have never been finished. The whole thing, all taken together, looks as if a spell had been, all of a sudden, set upon the workmen; or, in the words of the Scripture, here is the "*desolation of abomination, standing in high places.*" However, all is right. These things were made with the hearty good will of those who are now coming to ruin in consequence of the Debt, contracted for the purpose of making these things! This is all *just*. The load will come, at last, upon the right shoulders. (*CRR* 1: 223)

This landscape gathered its apocalyptic force not only from the language of the Bible, but from a specific sense of economic retribution suggested in the final lines. The "*just*" processes that shifted the weight of the national debt from the people to their masters also enabled the scene at Dover to "look" and tell a story very different from the one that its reac-tionary designers intended. The "things" Cobbett discovered at Dover were hyperbolic signs, capable of reaching back from the world into lan-guage and telling apocalyptic tales because they were subject to the explosive circular logic of corruption. "These things were made with the hearty good will of those who are now coming to ruin in consequence of the Debt, contracted for the purpose of making these things!" Radical writers tended to prefer "these things," transparent words, and deictic gestures to elaborate figures because they were convinced that, as "the load" returned to "the right shoulders," things themselves gathered the meaning and force normally reserved for words. The "marks" and "signs" scattered through the allegorical world of the *Rides* registered the nearly unbearable significance of a world in crisis.

Cobbett's faith in the self-destruction of system was instrumental to his own version of a political rhetoric of fact, in which the force of argu-ment was displaced from writer and writing to world. Though notori-ously egotistical, he was capable of tactical gestures of self-effacement. The achievement of the unstamped press was a case in point. Cobbett was eager to take credit for the influence of the cheap *Register*, but quickly abdicated responsibility when he found himself charged with inciting "popular hatred" of the government:

Two penny trash has nothing to do with the matter. It is the Seat Selling, the Sinecure and Pension List, the Standing Army in time of Peace, the Dungeon, the Gag, the Spies and Informers, and the vindictive prosecutions for libel. These are the things, which have had this effect upon the people, and not the poor Two Penny Trash, which has only helped to explain the nature of these horrid means of oppression. (*CPR* 33 [1818], 621)

The capitalized nouns in this litany of repression embodied in prose the force of oppressive "things," allowing Cobbett to retreat behind a screen of "explanation," a circumspect gesture in a period of renewed prosecution. Far from being inert objects, however, the "things" Cobbett indexed were the institutions and methods of a corrupt regime, considered in terms of their "effect upon the people." By including the government's reaction to the radical press among its resources and activities ("the Gag," "the vindictive prosecutions for libel"), Cobbett's list incorporated what it professed to exclude, the impact of his writing. Despite his protests, "Two-Penny Trash" had something "to do with the matter"; its prodigious impact and "very material" language were among the conditions of a political crisis.

Cobbett's tactical retreat before the energies of the world continued as the thing itself became an articulate sign, what he called a "trumpet-tongued fact" or "*speaking fact*." The search for a natural, transparent, and unmediated language culminated as word and thing coalesced in a fact that was "all eloquence."[44] The *Rural Rides* were an extensive search for such evidence. Elements of the English countryside gathered political force because they were embedded in a process of systematic self-destruction. The dialectical relationship between argument and fact hinted at in the full title of the 1830 edition of the *Rural Rides* ("With Economical and Political Observations relative to matters applicable to, and illustrated by, the State of those Counties") was fully realized when Cobbett encountered the fortifications at Dover, and allowed them to speak for themselves:

Let any man of good plain understanding, go and look at the works that have here been performed, and that are now all tumbling into ruin. Let him ask what this cavern was for; what that ditch was for; what this tank was for; and why all these horrible holes and hiding-places at an expense of millions upon millions? Let this scene be brought and placed under the eyes of the people of England, and let them be told that Pitt and Dundas and Perceval had these things done to prevent the country from being conquered; with voice unanimous the nation would instantly exclaim: Let the French or let the devil take us, rather than let us resort to means of defence like these. (*CRR* 1: 227–28)

Through Cobbett's "genius for making a sign tell something other than what its maker intended," the "anti-jacobin hill" became a jacobin hill.[45] The use of anaphora ("Let . . . ") conveyed the unexpected passivity of an interventionist prose that would transform a nation by indexing a "scene" – and again, not just any scene, but "this scene," grasped as a function of corrupt government. Polemical egotism seemed redundant. Cobbett still had to "survey" or "name" such places, and bring them before "the eyes of the people," but he was no longer the gigantic hero of popular resistance. The result was a *tour de force* of self-conviction and persuasion. While it is impossible to mark the end of a project as restless and circuitous as the *Rural Rides*, moments like this carried with them a palpable sense of completion. Cobbett's aims were at last realized: rider, writer, and writing faded from view as an outraged nation and a regenerative world came into their own.

The eclipse of the Rider by a polemical landscape was one more instance of the recurrent pressure in Cobbett's writing *against* writing, and against nearly all his own functions as a professional editor and journalist. In his hands, popular education, agricultural surveys, emigrant's guides, periodical commerce, and political organization all aimed to restore a world in which they had no place. Countersystem therefore recapitulated the self-destructive energy of system: to imagine the consummation of reform was to imagine the disappearance of print opposition. When Cobbett learned that the *Courier* had again "*called upon the government* to spread *cheap tracts* about the country," he proposed "a better way of *silencing* these cheap publications; and that is, by *removing all grounds of public complaint* by granting a reform of the Parliament . . . All our statements, all our eloquence, all our exhibitions of sinecures, &c. would lose their interest at once" (*CPR* 31 [1816], 613). Parliamentary reform would return popular politics from a counterpublic sphere to its appropriate place in the House of Commons. Cobbett elaborated this claim in the second of his three 1818 letters "To the Freemen of the City of Coventry," in which he offered himself "as a Member for that City." Prominently dated "Lancaster, State of Pennsylvania, North America," the letter posed with burning resentment the fundamental question of his career – "*Why* am I now in *exile*?" – and went on to discover the origin and the end of his alienation in the House of Commons:

If there had been a man in parliament to utter, *in speeches*, what I uttered in pamphlets, I need not have written. His speeches would have reached every corner of the country; they would have been read every where; it would have been impossible to *silence him* by means of *hatched plots*; and of course, an end must have been put to the freedom of speaking even in parliament, or, a Reform must have taken place. In short, if there had been a man to *speak* my pamphlets, England would, at this day, have been free and happy. (*CPR* 33 [1818], 453)

The whole radical counterpublic sphere became a function of the supposed exclusion of radical leaders like himself from the House of Commons: "Why were there so many *public meetings?* Why such flocks of *petitions?* Why such strings of political *Clubs and Associations? . . .* Because all these means of uttering our sentiments were resorted to in *consequence* of there being *no one to utter our sentiments in parliament*" (453–54). Print, and especially the "pamphlets" and "*Cheap* Publications" (455) that drove Cobbett into exile, gave way to oral forms of political communication ("to utter, *in speeches*"), as the nation was delivered from "the fangs of Corruption" (454). As I suggested earlier, however, elements of print mediation survived this utopian vision of a "free and happy" nation. "If I had been in parliament," or if Henry Hunt or Major Cartwright had been in parliament, "we should have rendered '*Cheap* Publications,' and all publications, except a publication of the *Debates of Parliament* wholly unnecessary" (455). The exception conceded significant ground to radical counterpublicity, and to the pivotal role of the press in ensuring that parliamentary debates were widely available. It was only through print that Cobbett's imagined "speeches" penetrated "every corner of the country."

A seat in parliament was only one half of the permanent place Cobbett assigned to himself in the aftermath of reform. The rural horizons that hovered at the edge of his prose – "the straw roof," "the *shelter*, in these valleys," the "end" to his imprisonment among "the inhabitants of a village" – registered his desire to return to the life of a farmer and landlord. Here again there was a distinct pressure against print culture. Out of a heady mix of childhood memory and historical fantasy, Cobbett reconstructed an order of agricultural production and stable social hierarchies that was emphatically pre-textual, and, in these early reflections from *The Life and Adventures of Peter Porcupine* (1796), pre-political as well:

As to politics, we were like the rest of the country people in England: that is to say, we neither knew nor thought anything about the matter. The shouts of victory or the murmurs at a defeat, would now-and-then break in upon our tranquility for a moment; but I do not remember ever having seen a news-paper in the house; and most certainly that privation did not render us less industrious, happy, or free.[46]

Cobbett's subsequent commitment to universal manhood suffrage mitigated his suspicion of politics, but the resistance to print and paper remained, especially where he confronted the empire of corrupt signs. Attacks on the prose of his enemies consistently returned to the material world of land and labor: "Can anyone pretend to say that a spade or shovel would not become the hands of this blunderheaded editor of *Bell's Messenger* better than a pen?" (*CRR* 1: 202); "A couple of flitches of bacon are worth fifty thousand Methodist sermons and religious tracts" (*CE* 103).[47]

The *Rural Rides*, with their consistent pattern of return (to a birth-place, a former home, a mortgaged farm), offered the fullest account of the dynamic that would end Cobbett's exile and restore his fixed position in a world without print resistance. Rural prospects aroused his desires as a farmer, and triggered extravagant visions of productive labor and agri-cultural revival, alongside troubling reminders of present limitations. Near Winchester, Cobbett came upon a once "beautiful down" that had deteriorated into "a district of thistles and other weeds," and described the elaborate process of planting, sowing, rotation, and feeding that would restore its value: "If I had such land as this I would soon make it down again . . . (that is to say if I had the money)" (*CRR* 1: 106). At Botley he came upon land that had in fact been his own, until it was appropri-ated by a parasitic system: "I had to ride, for something better than half a mile of my way, along between fields and coppices that were mine until they came into the hands of the mortgagee, and by the side of cottages of my own building. The only matter of much interest with me was the state of the inhabitants of those cottages. I stopped at two or three places, and made some little enquiries" (*CRR* 1: 173–74). The *Rides* allowed Cobbett to maintain a stake or "interest" in the land, and to recover some of the authority he had lost with the farm at Botley. He met and dined with farmers and landlords as his equals, and confronted rural laborers from a paternal position on horseback. Starving victims of corruption benefitted from his charity, and from political arguments they could not comprehend: "I gave him the price of a pot of beer, and on I went, leaving the poor dejected assemblage of skin and bone to wonder at my words" (*CRR* 2: 380). Yet, if the *Rides* helped Cobbett overcome a sense of exile by returning him to the land and to his readers,[48] they were also the deepest symptom of his dislocation, since they put his body as well as his prose in circulation, and forced him again and again to depart from the "land of promise" he had rediscovered. Deeply suspicious of geographical mobility, he treated his own lifelong movements as a necessary but regrettable response to the effects of system: "I could be well content never to go out of the valley, in which I live, but, the duty of a father and an Englishman, calls imperiously upon me not to stand with my arms folded and see my children and my country robbed, disgraced, and enslaved" (*CPR* 15 [1809], 550). His only comfort in the *Rides* was to discover an oppositional form of mobility, one predicated on "*labour*" rather than leisure, and committed to avoiding (or pointedly crossing) turnpikes and canals in favor of a more difficult route "amongst *bye-lanes* and *across fields*, through bridle-ways and hunting-gates" (*CRR* 1: 85).

The self-consuming energy of Cobbett's prose culminated in the *Rides* when the figure who disappeared before a polemical landscape conditionally resurfaced in a world free of corruption and mediation. Like the international dealer in radical texts, whose words seemed to "come back" to him from across the Atlantic, the Rural Rider consistently discovered himself and his prose in the regeneration of the land. "A very fine flock of *turkeys*" in Surrey turned out to be in some sense his own: "'We owe them entirely *to you*, Sir; for, we never raised one till we read your COTTAGE ECONOMY'" (*CRR* 1: 279). An encounter with a boy weaving bonnets in Kent, who similarly confessed that he learned to do so from "*a little book that had been made by Mr. Cobbett*," became the occasion for a ritual of self-disclosure and self-discovery: "I told him that I was the man" (*CRR* 1: 215). Personally satisfying though these encounters may have been, they remained imperfect, and served to confirm how thoroughly Cobbett had been fragmented and dispersed by writing in opposition, even as they foreshadowed his ultimate rehabilitation. Finding that the demands of political opposition frustrated "all my efforts to bury myself in woods and fields" (*CPR* 16 [1809], 110), Cobbett could only preserve his identity as a farmer and landlord by disseminating elements of that identity throughout rural England. The influence of a personal countersystem was so pervasive that every place became his potential home. "*Here*," he wrote from Thursley, "I am quite at home in a room, where there is one of my *American Fire-places*, bought, by my host" (*CRR* 1: 288). This self-discovery was particularly unstable because it returned him to a traditional "home" in the English countryside via an improvement he had discovered during his American exile. A return of this kind could never be complete or final. The next morning,

Cobbett inevitably rose from his fireplace, and returned to circulation and to opposition. By describing a utopian process that absorbed the wandering polemicist back into the land, the *Rides* could only suggest what kind of world might exist on the other side of system and counter-system, and what kind of Cobbett might emerge there.

CHAPTER FIVE

Leigh Hunt and the end of radical opposition

"REFORM OF PERIODICAL WRITING"

The *Examiner* closes its third volume under circumstances precisely similar to those at the conclusion of the two preceding years, – an increase of readers and a Prosecution by the ATTORNEY GENERAL. These circumstances may not be equally lucrative to the Proprietors, but they are equally flattering; and alike encourage them to persevere in a line of conduct, which enables them to deserve the one and to disdain the other. ("Postscript for the Year 1810," *Examiner*, 1810)[1]

The object of our work is not political, except inasmuch as all writing now-a-days must involve something to that effect, the connexion between politics and all other subjects of interest to mankind having been discovered, never again to be done away. We wish to do our work quietly, if people will let us, – to contribute our liberalities in the shape of Poetry, Essays, Tales, Translations, and other amenities, of which kings themselves may read and profit, if they are not afraid of seeing their own faces in every species of inkstand. ("Preface," *The Liberal*, 1822)[2]

Our POLITICS will be addressed to those, who caring little for them in detail, are desirous of becoming acquainted with anything that concerns mankind at large. Politics, in this sense, are a part of humane literature . . . Meanwhile, to descend from these grand generalities, we find ourselves in a very new position – that of being ministerialists, if not absolute courtiers. ("Books, Politics, and Theatricals," *Companion*, 1828)[3]

This Publication . . . is devoted entirely to subjects of miscellaneous interest, unconnected with politics. ("Address," *Leigh Hunt's London Journal*, 1834)[4]

These four passages offer a brief summary of Leigh Hunt's career as a political writer and editor. His reckless defiance of power in the *Examiner* was first encouraged by the public notice that accompanied a series of prosecutions for libel, and then tempered after 1812 by a conviction and prison sentence.[5] By 1815 Cobbett was complaining that, after "a good thumping fine" and two years in prison, "Mr. LEIGH HUNT . . . has not only had his hostile passions cooled, but has kissed the rod with the most filial weakness" (*CPR* 28 [1815], 196).[6] Direct political confrontation and a straightforward "line of conduct" gave way to the subtler reasonings of the *Liberal* in exile. Hunt now renounced overt political designs, but protested that "all writing now-a-days must involve something to that effect"; innocent "liberalities" became an admonishing mirror for magistrates who dared to encounter their image on the printed page. This indirect theory of political effect, which recalls Shelley's anti-didactic poetics of the same period, suggested that a political editor might achieve worthwhile ends without courting prosecution. While Hunt avoided the aggression that distinguished the early *Examiner*, his editorial practice remained provocative, and the *Liberal* was a forum for Byron's "Vision of Judgment" and irreverent "Epigraphs on Lord Castlereagh," as well as Hazlitt's brilliantly demystifying essay "On the Spirit of Monarchy." Leigh Hunt was secure in Italy, but his brother John remained in England as publisher of the *Liberal*, and was prosecuted and fined for the appearance of "The Vision of Judgment" in the first number.[7] By the time of the *Companion* and the "liberal toryism" of the late 1820s, Hunt was convinced that the political reforms he had long advocated were on the immediate horizon, and seemed comfortable with his "new," less threatening, and less threatened position of "ministerialist" writer. He gave up the insistence that politics informed all public discourse, but still allowed that it might be a "part of humane literature"; in fact, the *Companion* contained little in the way of political writing. Four years later, with the political enfranchisement of the middle class an accomplished fact, the "connection between politics and all other subjects" finally disappeared as an editorial principle. Hunt drained his *London Journal* of political content in order to create a literary refuge for "pleasure" and recreation: "We wished to create one corner and field of periodical literature, in which men might be sure of hope and cheerfulness, and of the cultivation of peaceful and flowery thoughts, without the accompaniment of anything inconsistent with them" (*LJ*, no. 23 [1834], 177).

This book has insisted on the contradictory energies generated by the radical effort to remain engaged with a corrupt system while resisting its influence. Leigh Hunt's willingness to allow strenuous opposition to be assimilated to ministerialism makes him a useful closing study. Unlike the other figures I have considered, he negotiated an end to opposition, for himself and his class, and for the press and "literature" (a category narrowed by the negotiations). What follows is not a complete account of his career, even as political writer and editor. Instead, I want to see how his powerful desire to escape the rigors of opposition sheds light on the inherent tensions of that position. In considering Hunt in this way, it is important not to overstate the trajectory suggested by my four opening passages. Hunt's desire for a discourse free of anxiety and contradiction, and for a personal and transcendent (rather than public and engaged) version of independence, was evident from the outset of his career. In its first year, the "Political Examiner" proposed an Archimedean stand-point "above the common passions and interests of men" as a way out of commercial corruption (*E*, no. 46 [November 13, 1808], 721). In an 1811 poem entitled "Politics and Poetics, or, the Desperate Situation of a Journalist Unhappily Smitten with the Love of Rhyme," Hunt repre-sented himself (with the logic if not the ambition of Milton) as a poet temporarily diverted from his vocation by political necessity. Pleasure, freedom, and personal inclination competed with politics, restraint, and duty. The poet was finally drawn out of his "fairy glade" by the "dire necessity to read the papers," and to answer "the punctual fiend, that bawls for copy": "I yield, I yield. – Once more I turn to you, / Harsh pol-itics! and once more bid adieu / To the soft dreaming of the Muse's bowers, / Their sun-streaked fruits and fairy-painted flowers."[8] When he later devoted his *London Journal* to subjects "unconnected with poli-tics," Hunt tried to recover and institutionalize in print the "bowers" of "Politics and Poetics": "There are green fields in the world, as well as fields of battle; and in making a grove, or a park, or other domestic elysium, people do not contemplate the introduction in it of fight and contest and sour speeches" (*LJ*, no. 23 [1834], 177).

At the same time, it would be a mistake to demean Hunt's political commitment, particularly in the early *Examiner* years, or to draw too sharp a distinction between his position and that of more plebeian radical figures, as William Keach risks doing when he distinguishes "liberals like Hunt" from "more radical and anarchic" positions.[9] Anarchists aside, the term "liberal" was only acquiring its modern meaning in this period, and was not yet fully distinguished from radical. Hunt's fondness for it can suggest political moderation, but it also con-nects him for example with the ultra-radical *Cap of Liberty*, which addressed "a liberal and enlightened public" (*CL* 1 [1819], 80), and with the *Radical Reformer*, which promised "a liberal investigation into the nature and object of civil government" (*RR* 1 [1819], 1).[10] Similarly, Hunt's avowed political creed, "the constitution, the whole constitution, and *nothing but the constitution*" (*E*, no. 37 [September 11, 1808], 579), linked him with Cobbett, Cartwright, and Wooler even as it distinguished him from Painite and Spencean extremes. A decade later, the more plebeian *White Hat* endorsed an identical program: "The constitution, the whole constitution, and nothing but the constitution" (*WH* 1 [1819], 132). The constitutional position of the *Examiner* was radical because it did not prevent an irreverence about existing institutions. When Hunt compared the extravagance of the Prince with "the first step which led CHARLES to the scaffold" (*E*, no. 34 [August 21, 1808], 529), and when he suggested that Napoleon was "no more the usurper" in France "than the Princes of BRUNSWICK have been the usurpers of the throne of Great Britain" (*E*, no. 144 [September 30, 1810], 609), he joined other radical editors in a dangerous and disruptive form of guerrilla journalism.

Radicalism was in this period, as E. P. Thompson has suggested, a "generalised libertarian rhetoric" that included figures as diverse as Cobbett, Wooler, Hone, and Carlile, and "stretched in the immediate post-war years" from "sophisticated representatives" like "Henry White's *Independent Whig* and John and Leigh Hunt's *Examiner*" to "ultra-Radical periodicals like the *Medusa* and *The Cap of Liberty*."[11] Hunt was fully conversant with this broad rhetoric, especially in his contempt for the government, the whig party, and political corruption. The *Quarterly Review* did not hesitate to number him with Wooler and Cobbett among "the white-hatted party" (*QR* 22 [1820], 554), and Carlile read the *Examiner* during the period of his radicalization.[12] Hunt was, furthermore, not bound by those elements of popular radical discourse that were most easily assimilated to the interests of a moderately reformist urban middle class. Confident that England could survive a continental embargo on the strength of its agriculture, he became as vigorous a radical agrarian as Cobbett: "Commerce is but the vigour of the extremities, and not of the trunk of the body politic: We might as well put on woollen gloves in cold weather and take off our shirt, as cultivate commerce at the expense of agriculture" (*E*, no. 4 [January 24, 1808], 51). If a generalized radical rhetoric acquired a "belletristic and somewhat urbane" turn in his hands,[13] this was no more eccentric than its rural inflection in the *Political Register*, or its materialist inflection in the *Republican*. Politeness and respectability competed with more plebeian values throughout early nineteenth-century radical culture, and to expose these qualities in Hunt does not by itself exclude him from participation.[14]

In the *Examiner*'s version of a flexible and opportunistic discourse of resistance, widespread radical anxieties about political position and popular affiliation were reinforced by Hunt's belletristic sensibility. Again, this was not a unique situation; Wooler, for example, was also concerned to make the *Black Dwarf* a journal of "modern literature" and "the Drama" as well as politics.[15] But Hunt more than anyone else wrote along the widening faultline within radical culture that was increasingly defined in class terms. His acute sensitivity about issues of rank and refinement was further compounded by attacks on himself as a man of "ignorance and vulgarity" and "low birth and low habits," the leader of a debased "Cockney School" of poetry (*BM* 2 [1817], 39).[16] Under these conditions, self-identification became an increasingly uncertain and contradictory procedure. Hunt disavowed acquaintance with radical leaders like Cobbett, and the mere mention of Henry Hunt prompted the defensive parenthetical, "no relation of ours" (*HA* 175).[17] At the same time, he was prepared to describe his own two-penny *Indicator* as "an accomplished specimen . . . of the *Twopenny Trash*" (*HC* 1: 149), simultaneously identifying it with, and distinguishing it from, Cobbett's cheap *Register*. The search for an effective prose style for his proposed "reform of periodical writing" (*RF* 1 [1810–1811], iii) became a particularly acute register of Hunt's self-divisions. Several months after proposing that reformers should ignore "the Revived Cry of Jacobinism" and "leave this style to our opponents" (*E*, no. 58 [February 5, 1809], 81–82), Hunt satirically reproduced every detail of the partisan style, including attacks on "Jacobinical" reformers, in "A Week's Speculation, in Humble Imitation of the Style and Sentiments of the Morning Post" (*E*, no. 88 [September 3, 1809], 562). A decade later the *Examiner* still vowed "to renounce every species of cant, and speak a language as different as possible from what is common to the insincere" (*E*, no. 637 [March 12, 1820], 161), but the *Liberal* was then launched with a promise that "the force of our answers will always be proportioned to the want of liberality in the assailant" (*L* 1 [1822], xii).

Edward Said has proposed that a "worldly" criticism, one that is "a part of its actual social world" rather than "an escape" from it, requires the "cooperation between filiation and affiliation that is located at the heart of critical consciousness."[18] Hunt's struggle to organize his discursive practice in a way that was both worldly and critical, "different" from yet "proportioned to" an antagonist, involved a complex set of filiations and affiliations. His *Autobiography* (1850) included a chapter on "The Author's Progenitors," and claimed that the "zeal for the public good" displayed by the *Examiner* "was a family inheritance" (*HA* 176). By working closely with his brother John, a printer and publisher, and by bringing in another brother, Robert, as fine arts critic, he was able to negotiate alienating professional and commercial relations through familial intimacy. Leigh Hunt's own multiple function in the *Examiner* (he was "Political Examiner," "Theatrical Examiner," and "Literary and Philosophical Examiner") translated the scattered commitments of "public writing" into the reassuring terms of domestic relationship: "I regard the various departments of this paper as children of the same family, and therefore though of different professions they all have the same surname" (*E*, no. 2 [January 10, 1808], 26). Cultural affiliation made available an even wider field of supportive relationships. While Hunt shared the radical fear of corrupt influence, he tended more than others to look to the past to discover a secure position from which to write. The native political history of letters became especially important to him when a renewed "Cry of Jacobinism" made parliamentary reform seem alien and even treasonous. The Preface to the *Liberal* invoked an extensive literary genealogy, running from "the JOHN O'GAUNTS, the WICKLIFFES, and the CHAUCERS" through "ye MILTONS and ye MARVELLS, ye HOADLEYS, ADDISONS, and STEELES, ye SOMERSES, DORSETS, and PRIORS" (*L* 1 [1822], viii). Out of this long history, Hunt laid a special claim to the legacy of the early eighteenth-century period-ical essayists, and above all to the example of Swift – adopted "god-father" of the *Examiner* (*HA* 173) – and Addison and Steele, who seemed to him the ideal of an engaged yet principled literary practice, and the model for any "reform of periodical writing."[19]

Hunt's ambitious affiliations were not untroubled. From the outset, the sense of nostalgia that haunted the *Examiner* was a source of frustra-tion as well as inspiration. Affiliative procedures were meant to create a wider discursive community and alleviate the isolation of the inde-pendent public writer, but they wound up reproducing the tension between autonomy and engagement, and generating a rhetoric of hesitation and false starts. "The age of periodical philosophy is perhaps gone by," Hunt conceded in an *Examiner* essay "On Periodical Essays," "but Wisdom is an everlasting beauty, and I have the advantage of all the lessons in philosophic gallantry which my predecessors have left behind them. Perhaps I may avoid some of the inelegancies, though I may be hopeless of attaining the general charm of these celebrated men." After surveying the achievements of Addison, Goldsmith, Johnson, and others, Hunt was still left "hopeless" and somewhat paralyzed by his own belated position. "If I can persuade the public to hear me after these celebrated men, I shall think myself extremely fortunate . . . It will be my endeavour to avoid those subjects which have been already handled in periodical works, or at any rate if I should be tempted to use them, I will exert myself to give them a new air and recommendation" (*E*, no. 2 [January 10, 1808], 26). Years later, the Preface to the *Liberal* proceeded with the same anxiety, scavenging history for the names of "progressive" rather than "retrograde" writers, but unable to escape the long shadow they cast: "If we have no pretensions to your genius, we at least claim the merit of loving and admiring it, and of longing to further its example" (*L* 1 [1822], viii).

This hesitation before a monumental past became something more than conventional modesty when Hunt mobilized history on behalf of a contemporary critique. In the 1809 *Examiner* series, "Newspaper Principle," affiliative procedures were obstructed by a painful sense of historical discontinuity:

A hundred years ago, when STEELE, ADDISON, and SWIFT wrote in the cause of party, political dispute exhibited a much more estimable character than at present. I do not say, that there was no misrepresentation, or abuse, or even rancour . . . but the periodical politics of these illustrious men exhibited a strain of virtue and *a reference to dignified principle* scarcely discernible in the present times: the interests of philosophy, of good morals, and of good letters, and the consistencies of public and private character were seldom forgotten; whereas the majority of our politicians are at variance with common sense and honesty, and the best of them content themselves with questions of political right and wrong, or in other words, of expediency. (*E*, no. 84 [August 6, 1809], 497)

If the link between political virtue and "good letters" was peculiar to Hunt, the sense that political corruption involved a fundamental break in the history of political discourse was not. Hunt echoed the *Black Dwarf*'s "Cross-Readings," and Carlile's practice of reversing hostile political opinions, when he applied a hermeneutic of resistance or reversal to the corrupt prose of his enemies: "You may read the politics of the day without end, and rise up from the perusal without the smallest additional incitement to virtue, except what . . . the subject [may] have displayed in *reverse*" (497). He did not recover from the traumatic sense of history that went along with a theory of corruption until he abandoned opposition for ministerialism, and reclaimed an uninterrupted political inheritance. The *Autobiography* claimed with remarkable confidence that the principles of radical reform were in fact those of the "newer and more thorough-going Whigs, which were known by the name of Radicals, and have since been called Whig Radicals, and Liberals." This paradoxical revisionism was brought up to the present in the only way it could be, with the proposition that the same principles "have since swayed the destinies of the country, in the persons of Queen Victoria and her ministers" (*HA* 211). The syntax that joined radical, whig, liberal, ministry, and queen may have been convoluted, but it allowed Hunt to construct for himself a continuous past and stable present position. His progressive faith was no longer undermined by a painful sense that he was cut off from the achievements of his ancestors.

A degeneration in "the cause of party" was for Hunt a primary differ- ence between early nineteenth-century political writing and that of "a hundred years ago." The motto of the *Examiner*, "Party is the madness of many for the gain of a few," announced the paper's endorsement of a radical resistance to party along country-party lines.[20] After the death of Fox and Pitt, Hunt complained, the differences between whig and tory came to rest on "relative instead of positive opinion" (*E*, no. 37 [September 11, 1808], 578), and the two parties existed, if they existed at all, "like a shadow, merely from the opposition of some body" (*E*, no. 1 [January 3, 1808], 7). Firm principle became the stable reference point for political opposition in the *Examiner*. In an 1809 article on parlia- mentary debate over the Spanish campaign against Napoleon, Hunt blamed the unprincipled whigs for the "futility" of "party opposition" and "mere Antiministerialism":

The Opposition . . . told a good deal of truth to the Ministers, but they exhib- ited, as usual, too much of the old party system; and reasonable men always have a sickening recollection, that these mere opposers have shewn, and would shew again, the same narrow excuses and principles as their antagonists. Pittite and Foxite now-a-days differ, like their names, merely in the first sound of the thing; they are both the same in the end. (*E*, no. 56 [January 22, 1809], 51)

Hunt went on to join a radical critique of "the hunters of place and pension, whether Ministerial or Anti-ministerial" (51), but he was deeply interested in the structure of party ideas as well as party interests, and traced the instincts of the "mere opposers" to a failure of imagination, an inability to see beyond a set of habitual "excuses and principles." Here lay the critical value and nearly insuperable challenge of the poli- tics of eighteenth-century letters. To the contemporary literary mind, Steele's voluntary resignation of a government post opened up a night- marish prospect:

Now I wonder what the BOWLESES, and the DIXONS, and the WHARTONS, can pos- sibly think of such conduct; or rather, have they any idea of it? Can they represent to themselves any such writer or placeman as a being of this world? To declare his sentiments when the other party was in the zenith of its power, to set bribery and flattery at nought, to go out of office when, as the phrase is, there was *no occasion for it*, and to talk to a Prime Minister as if he had no places to bestow, – what are these, but so many praeternatural actions, that only serve to strike boys with wonder, and create a sort of night-mare in consciences that cannot wake! (*E*, no. 84 [August 6, 1809], 498)

One of the most important functions of the independent writer and editor was to "represent" in his own person the example of Swift, and to develop a political vocabulary that ran beyond the "two monosyllables" shared by "the herd of *Aye* and *No* men in the House of Commons" (*E*, no. 132 [July 8, 1810], 417). The radical position was for Hunt an epistemelogical as well as a political intervention, an effort to realize something that "people cannot imagine" (*E*, no. 37 [September 11, 1808], 578).

Despite this idealist (even romantic) tendency to shift a public political issue to the sphere of mind and conscience, Hunt was prepared to blame the decline of party principle on the commercial organization of the press, and on the "system of money-making" that was "the great *lay* superstition of modern times."[21] The "Newspaper Principle" series blamed market forces for the historical fissure that divided him from his progenitors:

The cause of this deterioration is obvious: it arises entirely from the mercantile spirit . . . which is the sole principle of the publications. In the times of Whig and Tory, most of the leading writers on both sides were independent of Government, and at all events independent of the printer, the bookseller, and the whole tribe of literary hucksters: they delivered therefore their own opinions, and in endeavouring to guide the town, endeavoured to procure as much respect as possible for themselves as individual writers . . . Our former periodical politicians, then, wrote to establish their own opinions and to acquire reputation; our present, simply to get money. (*E*, no. 84 [August 6, 1809], 497–98)

This critique of the literary marketplace could lead back to the mind, through an account of the way the senses were "distempered" by "the beauties of commerce," but Hunt also joined Cobbett and other editors in a practical analysis of the way the press had been assimilated to a linked system of wartime corruption and commerce: "The trading part of this country have had a considerable voice in public matters ever since we had the misfortune to fight with money and with subsidies: they are the principal possessors of those organs of the public voice, the newspapers, and these are the men, who, whenever our commerce receives the slightest check, identify their own interest with that of the country" (*E*, no. 46 [November 13, 1808], 721). By taking possession of the press, this "trading part" compromised the political and commercial independence that Hunt's "reform of periodical writing" was concerned to reclaim:

When people fancy they are reading the real opinions, and gaining by the experience, of the periodical writers, they little imagine that the writers have nothing to do with the matter, and that it is the profits only, and not the opinions, which belong to the proprietor and his hirelings; and that the men who are the constant praise of the writers, are in point of fact, the writers of the praise. (*E*, no. 83 [July 30, 1809], 481)

Hunt's visceral fear that writers might wind up having "nothing to do with the matter" was important, since it put a professional identity at the core of his understanding of independence. Even where he held economic and material conditions responsible for the decline of political opposition, Hunt was less concerned with the broad impact of corruption and commerce than with their tendency to divide writers from their own "opinions," and from a public with whom they were once "personally acquainted."

The intimate tone and unusually discursive contents of the *Examiner* collaborated to produce a formal and stylistic protest against the commercial organization of the press. The "periodical essayist" could, according to Hunt, claim "a peculiar intimacy with the public," in part because humble periodical forms were less intimidating than "the majesty of a quarto" or "the gaiety of a beau duodecimo, smooth and well dressed" (*E*, no. 2 [January 10, 1808], 26). Anything that interfered with this intimacy was a symptom of the decline of periodical culture, and there was no more grievous sin against print etiquette than the "page of Advertisements" and the "page of Markets" that opened and closed most newspapers (*E*, no. 1 [January 3, 1808], 8). Again, discursive control seemed to slip away from writers and editors, as the "Money-lenders" and "those who 'Want Places'" became the "first causes" and prime movers of the public sphere:

People read this positive disputation, they hear of the great circulation of the papers, and imagine that it is owing to the mere force of the politics: this is a great mistake: the curiosity of the quidnuncs does much for a daily paper, but advertisements do a great deal more, and the display of politics is nothing but an advantage taken of the sale of these advertisements . . . It is the eloquence, not of the politician, but of the perruquier, the *Money-lender*, and the *Quack-doctor*, which keeps their patriotic energies in motion; and the indiscriminate eagerness with which such advertisers are welcomed is of itself a sufficient proof of the insufficiency and profligacy of these national politicians. (*E*, no. 83 [July 30, 1809], 481)

The Prospectus to the weekly *Examiner* stated unequivocally its resistance to the commercial spirit: "NO ADVERTISEMENTS WILL BE ADMITTED" (*E*, no. 1 [January 3, 1808], 8).[22] This policy accorded with a radical tendency to make political independence a matter of choice, and, given the *Examiner*'s middle-class appeal, Hunt was among the few radical editors for whom accepting advertisements was a real alternative. At the same time, Hunt's obsession with print corruption encouraged the view that the capacity to make such a choice was not evenly distributed. If independence no longer required landed property, it might still be facilitated by professional status, or by what Hunt himself termed "property" in a periodical enterprise (*HC* 1: 149). Indeed, the refusal of advertising in the *Examiner* disclosed what it tried to suppress, a professional implication in the literary marketplace. Hunt's Prospectus conceded that he and his brother were "engaged in the publication of books" that wanted the kind of promotion the *Examiner* would not allow (*E*, no. 1 [January 3, 1808], 8), and it assimilated a political rhetoric of independence to a commercial rhetoric of "puffing." The new paper was recommended to potential subscribers on the grounds that it resisted commercial influence.

Like other radical editors, Hunt ranged widely in his search for ways to reform the economic organization of the press and reimagine his own market relations. In collaborating with his brothers, and in treating the "various departments" of the *Examiner* as "children of the same family," he aligned himself with the radical effort to resist specialization in periodical discourse, and recuperate a utopian sphere of unalienated labor.[23] Dissatisfied with the way contemporary magazines tended to dismiss politics "in crude and impatient sketches," and concerned that a polite middle class was "very apt to turn away from politics as from a barren and fearful ground," Hunt promised to reintroduce the subject into his quarterly *Reflector*, on eminently radical grounds: "Politics, in times like these, should naturally take the lead in periodical discussion" (*RF* 1 [1810], iv). Emerging tenets of professional autonomy and periodical specialization were further undermined by the persistence of dependence and patronage, as Hunt turned to affluent friends for financial support. In an 1821 letter to Shelley, the impoverished Hunt conceded that the project for the *Liberal* gave Byron the power "to set . . . myself and family in our finances again" (*HC* 1: 172). The patronized editor of the *Liberal*, an avant-garde project that recapitulated older models of coterie publication, cultivated a distinctly mixed discursive practice, pitching his qualifications in the latest terms of industrial production: "I have had a good deal of experience in periodical writing, and know what the getting up of the *machine* requires" (172). A few years later, he promoted his "Wishing-Cap" essay series as the model of commercial efficiency: "All my present energy goes to the manufacture of *Wishing Caps*, and to the endeavour to raise the sale of the *Examiner* all I can. So publish everywhere that I am an infinite writer, infinitely regular. My brother has a lump of them in advance, and I manufacture daily – not one of them at a *time*, but the manufacture is always going on" (*HC* 1: 214).

The inconsistencies in Hunt's attitude towards literary commerce were only resolved when he was later able to negotiate an uneasy truce with the market by historicizing its influence. Just as his suspicion of party politics dissolved when progress, in the form of "a succession of calmly progressing ministries" (*HA* 265), replaced opposition as the dynamic of history, so his resistance to the market was blunted by a providential narrative that recuperated commercial corruption as a necessary phase in the history of an independent press. The "sordid and merely plodding morals" contained in the children's books of his own youth were "necessary perhaps for a certain stage in the progress of commerce and for its greatest ultimate purposes (undreamt of by itself)" (*HA* 50). Hunt offered a fuller account of the way trade achieved its "undreamt" purposes in an 1831 *Tatler* article, "Success of Periodicals." Just as the *Autobiography* derived a complacent Victorian liberalism from an embattled Regency radicalism, so the *Tatler*, poised on the brink of moderate reform, discovered continuity between "liberal opinion" and an "illiberal" age:

The present commercial state of the press, as far as it still exists, (for we look upon it as having received a great blow, in common with many other abuses that little suspect it, from the extraordinary events in the political world), has not been an unnatural, but a natural state; and, as far as it promises a condition of things very different, not an undesirable one; for it simply originates in the diffusion of knowledge, and the thirst for it excited among all classes.[24]

No longer evidence of the corruption and degeneration of the public sphere with respect to the past, the "commercial state of the press" became a cause for optimism about the future, the necessary consequence of a "diffusion of knowledge" that would soon liberate readers and writers from the marketplace. As in so much of his later prose, Hunt was ready to imagine reform as "natural" progress, rather than the result of disruptive opposition to an unnatural system.

THE ANTINOMIES OF INDEPENDENT OPPOSITION:EGOTISM AND COMMUNITY

A disdain for party politics encouraged the *Examiner* to join other radical periodicals in situating political agency outside parliament, "the misrepresentation that ruins the country" (*E*, no. 109 [January 28, 1810], 52). In "Reform Without Party," Hunt indicated that independent "periodical writers," who had "nothing to expect from any quarter of the state," were the true "organs of the people," or at least of those "thinking people" who constituted genuine public opinion (*E*, no. 68 [April 16, 1809], 241). As late as 1818, in a rousing series of *Examiner* essays "On the Intellectual Inferiority of Parliament to the Demands of the Age," Hunt preferred "the community" and "the newspapers" to a "corruptly chosen" House of Commons (*E*, no. 528 [February 18, 1818], 81). This was a hesitant gesture throughout radical discourse, and particularly so for Hunt. Wary of allowing the *Examiner* to be drawn into the factionalism of reform politics, and reluctant to get involved in popular radical organization and assembly, he often experienced his professional autonomy as an acute form of isolation. In an early *Examiner* essay "On Party Spirit," Hunt suggested how an editor who professed "no particular admiration" for the available political leadership was "driven to and fro from party to party, like a shuttlecock," and treated as an alien creature: "What, Sir, neither Pittite nor Foxite, nor Windhamite, nor Wilberforcite, nor Burdettite? Bless my soul, Sir, then what are you? *Who are your friends, or what are your prospects?* Were you born in England?" (*E*, no. 3 [January 17, 1808], 34). In a world where every engagement assumed the threatening aspect of party spirit and political corruption, the radical declaration of independence, originally an engaged response to a collective problem, became a form of exile and isolation.[25] "I denied myself political as well as theatrical acquaintances," Hunt recalled of the *Examiner* years, regardless of whether these involved enemies or potential allies:

> In the course of its warfare with the Tories, the *Examiner* was charged with Bonapartism, with republicanism, with disaffection to Church and State, with conspiracy at the tables of Burdett, and Cobbett, and Henry Hunt. Now, Sir Francis, though he was for a long time our hero, we never exchanged a word with; and Cobbett and Henry Hunt (no relation of ours) we never beheld; – never so much as saw their faces. I was never even at a public dinner; nor do I believe my brother was. We had absolutely no views whatsoever but those of a decent competence and of the public good. (*HA* 175)

This renunciation of public "acquaintance" (which managed to preserve the familial and editorial "we" even as it constructed a personal
"I") was not by itself a rebuke to popular radical sociability. William
Sherwin had, for example, similarly established his freedom from "influence" by disclaiming "connexion or acquaintance with any other political writer, or political man" (*SPR* 1 [1817], 63). Yet Hunt's acute
apprehensiveness about collective action did undermine the character of
his political commitment, and threaten his ability to participate in what
he (paradoxically) termed "spirited and independent discussion" (*E*, no.
115 [March 11, 1810], 145). His Prospectus to the *Examiner* suggested how
the force of social and political criticism might be vitiated by a rhetorical
attitude of retreat:

> A crowd is no place for steady observation. The EXAMINER has escaped from the
> throng and bustle, but he will seat himself by the way-side and contemplate the
> moving multitude as they wrangle and wrestle along. He does not mean to be as
> noisy as the objects of his contemplation, or to abuse them for a bustle which
> resistance merely encreases, or even to take any notice of those mischievous
> wags who might kick the mud towards him as they drive along: but the more
> rational part of the multitude will be obliged to him, when he warns them of an
> approaching shower, or invites them to sit down with him and rest themselves,
> or advises them to take care of their pockets. (*E*, no. 1 [January 3, 1808], 7)

A high-minded disdain for the "throng and bustle" of the "crowd"
undermined the commitment to "resistance," and engagement *with* the
world gave way to a detached perspective *on* it. To be fair, Hunt's practice
as political editor of the *Examiner* often belied the studied detachment of
this Prospectus. In the difficult summer of 1819, for example, he could be
found writing in support of "Reform Meetings in Various Parts of the
Country," and defending Richard Carlile against prosecution for blasphemous libel.[26] But this early account of his critical position did crystal-
ize an important weakness in Hunt's program of periodical reform, by
suggesting that the archaic idiom and attitudes of the eighteenth-
century periodical essayist might provide sufficient leverage against the
early nineteenth-century legitimate state. Misled by the escapist appeal
of his own "way-side" metaphor, Hunt allowed his ideal of "spirited and
independent discussion" to degenerate into idle chatter about the
weather, directed exclusively towards "the more rational part" of the
people.

Often charged with vanity and egotism by his adversaries, Hunt
was willing to concede that there was "a little egotism" in his personal
habit of impartial criticism.[27] Like other radical editors, he risked further

isolation when he tried to make individual integrity the foundation of his political independence. Under attack by mere "hirelings" who had sacrificed their personal autonomy to party leaders, Hunt took refuge in his own "conscience," and made the boundaries of his own "distinct character" a defense against similar influence (*E*, no. 82 [July 23, 1809], 465). He answered the partisan interrogation I quoted above – "Bless my soul, Sir, then what are you?" – with a bold collective designation that gave way immediately to an independent party of one: "Sir, I am an Englishman who chuse to think for myself" (*E*, no. 3 [January 17, 1808], 34). Where the autonomous self gathered wider significance in his prose, it tended to do so through affiliative procedures that linked the writer with ancestors rather than contemporaries – Swift was a literary "godfather," but Henry Hunt was "no relation." The designation "Englishman" could lead so quickly to "myself" because it stood for a national tradition of self-sufficiency:

In England, where individual character is in every respect better than the aggregate, individual men do every thing, and corporate bodies worse than nothing. The latter shift their consciences from member to member, till they are worn out; and responsibility comes to nothing . . . Individuals are every thing in such a country. They deteriorate in proportion as they identify themselves with bodies and opinions in fashion; and are at their best and highest when they are pursuing some enthusiastic point of good at which the sullen common-placemen laugh. If it had not been for such unwearied though solitary opponents to a court as MILTON and ANDREW MARVELL, the Puritans who turned corrupt when a body, would have done as little as the cavaliers for the public good; and Popery and Absolute Monarchy would now have played still more "fantastic tricks" with us, than the Boroughmongers do. The growth of public opinion, it is true, settles these matters at last; but opinion only grows from new seeds; and how few are there to set them! (*E*, no. 648 [May 28, 1820], 337)

Even aggregate terms like "public opinion" led back, through the dissenting language of conscience, responsibility, and enthusiasm, to the "few" past heroes who encouraged its growth. Collective identity was the debased sphere of "common-placemen," and political resistance grew instead out of the heroic efforts of "solitary opponents."

Hunt offered his fullest account of the threat that individual virtue posed to collective action and social reconciliation when he treated it as a problem of style, through what he called his "egotism of the letter" (*E*, no. 854 [1824], 369). Critical histories of the English essay have long charted his role in the process by which the *Spectator* tradition was supplanted by the familiar essay, with its prominent "I" and confessional manner.[28] (I would only add here that his "peculiar intimacy with the public," and the problems it raised, linked him as fully with radicals like Carlile, Cobbett, and Henry Hunt as with the romantic poets and the familiar essayists.) A solipsistic ideal of literary production and an intimate prose style, engaging though they may have been, finally threatened to undermine communication and community. Hunt was himself prepared to admit that his confessional habits risked estranging him from readers who were in no position to reciprocate the gesture. His *Wishing-Cap* essays, composed after he had given up his role as political editor of the *Examiner*, were filled with personal recollections later incorporated into his *Autobiography*. The eighth entry, entitled "I and We," disclosed his mounting anxiety about the implications of a familiar style. The same political and commercial forces that had undermined the sociability of the eighteenth-century coffeehouse now seemed to him to have compromised periodical communication, by precipitating a stylistic shift from a fictitious "I" or disingenuous "We" to a frankly personal "I":

I am very much hampered with this *I* of mine. If I value myself upon anything, it is upon being social; which is a thing essentially *we*. On the other hand, it is difficult to be plural, when talking of things singular: and the melody of one's prose, as I said before, is injured. *We were, – We once,* and *We were once,* are vile sounds. It is the biographical gossip into which I have been led in this paper, which made me adopt the first person singular. Vivid personal recollections, especially in solitude, produce a strong sense of one's individuality. (*E*, no. 854 [June 13, 1824], 369)

If he sounds here like a romantic essayist losing his nerve before the vast interior expanses of the egotistical sublime, Hunt kept the achievements of the eighteenth century clearly in view, and tried to justify his departure from earlier practices on the grounds of compensatory truth:

I said in the first number of the WISHING-CAP, that it was impossible for me to sustain a fictitious character, like that of Bickerstaff and others. This was said unadvisedly: for though it is impossible for a man to keep himself unknown, if he has been known at all (as Steele found it) he may take a fictitious signature, and so be as egotistical as he pleases without the charge of it. But I have a sense of truth, that haunts me in the most literal shape . . . A man does not say at table, "We once got a bruise on our knee;" or, "When we walk out, we always put a book in our pocket." I have been accustomed to chat with the readers of the *Examiner* so long and so familiarly, that I feel present, as of old, at their breakfasts and firesides. (369–70)

The precise location of these familiar relationships ("table," "breakfasts and firesides") was important, for the domestic often figured in the *Examiner* as a collective space free of threatening political engagements, and it was this imagined domestic sphere, a negotiable version of the public and collective, that triumphed in Hunt's later prose. He continued to wrestle with the anxieties that informed a "way-side" retreat and a partisan interrogation, but the terms of the struggle shifted from independent critical perspective to "egotistical" content. Having withdrawn to "solitude" and "individuality," and chosen "things singular" over things "plural," the writer found a personal voice that was no longer suspended between corruption and community. This voice remained hesitant, but was no longer energized by the tensions and contradictions that motivated polemical egotism in the radical press.

Hunt's tendency to construe political independence as personal retreat left compelling engagements to be worked out negatively, through a sense of conflict with the system rather than through radical solidarity. Interestingly, he made the establishment of the *Liberal* in 1822 an opportunity to reclaim his commitment to radical opposition. The title of the project worried him, since it suggested a flexibility and open-mindedness that might deteriorate into compromise, equivocation, or indifference. Raymond Williams has traced the modern English sense of the term "liberal" to the "strong general sense of *Liberty*" in the mid-seventeenth century, and has noted that, by the time it was "proudly and even defiantly announced in . . . *The Liberal*," it had acquired strong negative connotations, as a foreign nickname (*liberales, liberaux*) for unorthodox political positions.[29] Though Hunt credited Byron with the title, the term had an important history in his own prose.[30] In an early attempt to recover a new collective identity from factional politics, the *Examiner* appealed to "the liberal of all parties" (*E*, no. 166 [March 3, 1811], 129), substituting the real distinction between liberal and illiberal for the outmoded one between whig and tory. Hunt's correspondence with the Shelleys in the period immediately before he arrived in Italy, to collaborate on the (as yet unnamed) *Liberal*, suggested that the post-war situation had made liberalism a radical position: he related Hazlitt's complaint that Shelley went "to a *pernicious* extreme on the liberal side," and enthusiastically described a group of Plymouth schoolmasters who were "liberal to an extreme and esoterical degree" (*HC* 1: 166, 179). This paradox of liberal extremism became the central claim of his Preface to the *Liberal*, an impressive if finally imperfect effort to join the popular radical hostility of the 1810s, with its catastrophic social divisions, to an emerging, proto-Arnoldian sense of liberalism as a provocative call for social reconciliation. Writing collectively for the founders of the project, Hunt insisted that the title should "be taken in its largest acceptation, old as well as new," but he also proposed a corporate definition of liberalism that moved towards a partial and partisan identity: "All that we mean is, that we are advocates of every species of liberal knowledge, and that, by a natural consequence in these times, we go to the full length in matters of opinion with large bodies of men who are called Liberals" (*L* I [1822], viii-ix). By going "to the full length," and promising not to shrink from the "most liberal extreme," Hunt distinguished himself from "Illiberals" and from "certain pretended Liberals" who wanted nothing more than to preserve the status quo (ix).

In order to articulate the challenge of a position that could seem merely relative and accommodating, Hunt again staged an imaginary debate with the party men he pretended to avoid. He allowed his Preface to be interrupted by one of the "pretended Liberals," an "old club-house Gentleman" who was intrigued that a notorious radical was now preaching flexibility:

Now you talk sense. Extremes meet. *Verbum sat.* I am a Liberal myself, if you come to that, and devilish liberal I am. I gave for instance five guineas out of the receipts of my sinecure to the Irish sufferers; but that is between ourselves. You mean, that there are good hearty fellows in all parties, and that the great business is to balance them properly; – to let the people talk, provided they do no harm, and to let Governments go on as they do, have done, and will do for ever. Good, – good. I'll take in your journal myself; – here's to the success of it; – only don't make it too violent, you rogues; – don't spoil the balance. (ix)

Carried away by his own enthusiasm, this cynical advocate of "balance" went on to defend the "soldier-like" Wellington ("he prosecutes"), unwittingly disclosing the brutal foundations of legitimate government. Hunt vigorously rejected this distortion of his project, and all the meanings it implied:

We beg the reader's pardon in behalf of our worthy interrupter. Whatever may be his right estimation of his friends, we need not say that he misinterprets our notions of liberality, which certainly do not consist either in making the sort of confusion, or keeping the sort of peace, which he speaks of. There are, if he pleases, very silly fellows to be found in most parties, and these may be good enough to be made tools of by the clever ones; but to confound all parties themselves with one another, which is the real end of these pretended liberalities, and assume that none of them are a jot better or worse than the other, and may contain just as good and generous people, – this is to confound liberality with illiberality, narrow views with large. (x)

Insisting that it was "too late in the day to be taken in with this kind of cant, even by the jolliest of placemen," Hunt went on to condemn the present government in radical terms. Wellington "confounded the rights of nations with those of a manor," and treated "public meetings with contempt." Castlereagh was "one of the most illiberal and vindictive of statesmen": "Look at his famous Six Acts! Look at his treatment of BONAPARTE, his patronage of such infamous journals as the *Beacon*, his fondness for imprisoning, and for what his weak obstinacy calls his other strong measures" (x-xi). Hunt's vigorous contest with his "interrupter" over present definitions and alliances belied the nostalgia he often expressed for the shared meanings and consensual patterns of an eighteenth-century public sphere. Political debate in the Preface to the *Liberal* was verbal warfare rather than rational dialogue, supervened by a sense of crisis ("it is too late in the day") that hovered suggestively between apocalyptic and progressive expectations. A discussion that began with an interruption ended with a combative rejection of the legitimate state.

If Hunt was emboldened by his position in exile, he was also assisted in fashioning this liberal iconoclasm by the hostile English response that anticipated his collaboration with Byron and Shelley:

> We are forced to be prefatory, whether we would or no: for others, it seems, have been so anxious to furnish us with something of this sort, that they have blown the trumpet for us; and done us the honor of announcing, that nothing less is to ensue than a dilapidation of all the outworks of civilized society. Such at least, they say, is our intention; and such would be the consequences, if they, the trumpeters, did not take care by counterblasts, to puff the said outworks up again . . . They say that we are to cut up religion, morals, and everything that is legitimate; – a pretty carving. (v)[31]

Hunt was willing to agree with this perception that the *Liberal* threatened "everything that is legitimate," but only after he had extended the contest over language by reversing the hypocritical terms of his enemies. "Their religion . . . means the most ridiculous and untenable notions of the DIVINE BEING"; "their morals consist for the most part in a secret and practical contempt of their own professions"; "their 'legitimacy,' as they call it, is the most unlawful of all lawless and impudent things" (vi). Resolved "to oppose," Hunt turned eagerly to the critical "carving" set before him: "We are willing to accept the title of enemies to religion, morals, and legitimacy, and hope to do our duty with all becoming pro-faneness accordingly. God defend us from . . . the morality of slaves and turncoats, and from the legitimacy of half a dozen lawless old gentle-men, to whom, it seems, human nature is an estate in fee" (vi–vii). The strenuous rhythms of this Preface, so different from the polite idiom of the Prospectus to the *Examiner*, confirmed that Hunt's movement from radicalism to ministerialism was, despite his own later account of his career, not a straightforward progressive development. He was as often invigorated as he was chastened by a decade of intense literary and political warfare.

The strict distinction Hunt drew between his own discourse and English "cant" intimated one of his peculiar redactions of the reform movement's polarization of social forces. He frequently extended a radical determinism about print technology from print and from the press to more elusive categories like knowledge, intellect, style, and literature. "In these latter times," he wrote in the *Companion* in 1828, "the press has become a mighty power, which has taken its stand openly in the face of old assumptions, and is contesting the government of the world. That it will succeed is not to be doubted, if for this reason only, – that it is the interest of intellectual power to leave no part of a dispute untouched, whereas authority and assumption dare not appeal to a thousand points of knowledge."[32] This identification of "the press" with "intellectual power" and "knowledge" informed the cultural politics of the *Liberal*, and was first articulated in the pages of the *Examiner*. In an article published the year before he left England to join Shelley and Byron in Italy, Hunt vented his outrage at recent proposals for a Royal Academy of Literature in England, and insisted that the alliance between literature and the state was as impossible as it was unnatural:

It is too late in the day for such a thing as royal inspiration. It is too late in England; and it is too late all over Europe . . . There is an instinct all over the world, that Legitimacy and Literature have nothing in common; and if kings would have a little wisdom put into them, they would see, that whether literary men appear to make common cause with them or not, the inevitable progress of knowledge is counter to their pretensions. In fact, the whole secret lies here; – things of real, and things of false importance, cannot in the long run go together. That literature should have its merits acknowledged by kings, may appear flattering enough to some understandings, or even desirable to a mistaken patriotism: but as the pretensions of kings are essentially legitimate, and do not proceed on grounds of merit, so, if no other epithet will do, we must say, that the pretensions of literature are essentially levelling and jacobinical, and can acknowledge no other superiority than merit. (*E*, no. 709 [August 5, 1821], 481–82)[33]

The fear that "legitimate" government might try to appropriate "literature" and "knowledge" infused Hunt's prose with all the "jacobinical" energy of radical opposition. Again, his suggestive phrase "too late in the day" conjured expectations of progressive change and apocalyptic reversal. The "counter" energy of a republic of letters was channelled into "the inevitable progress of knowledge," but, instead of retreating here (as he so often did) to the polite idiom of the early eighteenth century, Hunt pursued a more explosive Painite distinction between royal "pretensions" to "superiority" and the "levelling" claims of literary merit.

Impressive as Hunt's formulations were, one is inclined to suspect, "this late in the day," that he protested too much. If "Legitimacy and Literature" had "nothing in common," why resist the futile effort to join them? The claim that "royal inspiration" was an oxymoron proved to be an extreme and inherently unstable statement of the case, its premise undermined by the fact that the argument had to be made at all. Like other radical editors, Hunt was more often willing to recognize that "things of real, and things of false importance" were hopelessly intertwined. Whatever their inherent character, print representations in particular, and (what we have learned to call) "cultural" matters generally, were compromised by the same system of influence and corruption that made the House of Commons a ruinous "misrepresentation." Hunt often used the "Political Examiner" to explore the intersection of culture and politics, and in an important pair of 1811 essays, "Application to Parliament for a Third London Theatre" and "Chancellorship of the University of Cambridge," he suggested the difficulty of establishing just what that intersection was or should be. The first essay opened with a bold defense of his editorial campaign against periodical specialization:

The reader will be startled perhaps at seeing this subject under the head of politics; but matters of taste and literature are more connected with the political character of the times than most people imagine or than the Pittites and their friends can allow; and the stage, in particular, is of importance to it, and felt to be so. It is for this reason that the Chamberlain of the Household, though an officer of very doubtful authority in this respect, has always taken care to keep his eyes upon the drama, ever since chance threw it in their way. (*E*, no. 168 [March 17, 1811], 161)

Conceding that government censorship of the theater was not presently exercised "to any very obnoxious degree," Hunt based his demand for a theater "responsible to the laws" rather than to "his Majesty's servants" on a fear of the more subtle corruptions of "public taste" that accompanied a courtly preference for "shew and spectacle in preference to the higher drama" (161). In the next issue of the *Examiner*, he turned from the London theater to Cambridge University, and proposed a very different link between culture and the state. An attack on the unwanted attention paid to the theater by "his Majesty's servants" gave way to a lament for the end of royal patronage, symptomatic perhaps of Hunt's own uncertain historical position between patronage and the market:

The connection between politics and literature may well be doubted by those who are accustomed to regard the former in their common-place light of news and party-struggles, and who for more than thirty years have witnessed the utter neglect with which English Ministers have treated the latter. But no doubt was ever entertained on the subject by men of enlarged minds; and no such neglect was ever entertained on the subject by intelligent rulers, whatever may have been their designs or opinions with regard to government in general. AUGUSTUS and ALFRED, two men whom in point of principle it is almost a profanation of the latter to name together, equally understood the advantages of cultivating learning, the one patronizing it for ambition's sake, the other to render his people wise. (*E*, no. 169 [March 24, 1811], 177)

If this nostalgia for Alfred's benevolent patronage was unexpected, Hunt immediately qualified the point by suggesting that the apparent contemporary "neglect" of literature was motivated by a secret hostility that in the end yielded interference and "controul":

But even these departures from what is wise and liberal betray an unconscious knowledge of the importance of what they avoid, – a sort of instinct which leads them to turn away from what is foreign to their natures and inimical to their designs. Thus power, however bigoted, has always been fond of meddling with the concerns of literature; for where its fears of self-detection have induced it to evince a contempt for learning, its jealousy of others has still been strong enough to make it interfere with it in some way, and endeavour to pollute the republic of letters by introducing into it the influence of courts. (177)

Legitimacy and literature were perhaps "inimical," but, like liberality and illiberality, they met on the field of political warfare. Despite the attractions of a necessitarian or techno-determinist argument to the contrary, radical opposition could not ignore the corruption of print culture, theatrical representation, and university education by the state. Against his own poetic aspirations and belletristic inclinations, Hunt was willing to serve as political editor of the *Examiner*, and discuss literature under a political heading, because legitimate power had put the political press on the front lines of the struggle for reform. His account of the government's repressive instincts helped explain his own career at the *Examiner*: "The Newspaper Press, which is constantly before the eyes of Ministers, and forms an obstacle which they can neither overlook nor despise, attracts the honour of their attention in preference to the more delicate and retired exercises of authorship" (177).

THE LANGUAGE OF CLASS IN A PROGRESSIVE PUBLIC SPHERE

Oppositional engagement ("enemies to religion, morals, and legitimacy") was by no means Hunt's final word on the role of the political press, nor on the relationship between the "periodical politician" and the political community. His faith in the "inevitable progress of knowledge," and in the imminent reversal of fortune that would bring down the legitimate state, suggested that an independent press contained something other than destructive energy: it could also call into being a political and discursive community with its own positive dimensions. Writers and editors completed their escape from corrupt influence when they discovered the principled positions that existed beyond negative or "relative . . . opinion." Here again, style was a central register of the contradictions involved in Hunt's discursive program. Legitimate power was clearly responsible for "all the contented and contenting sophistry, the nonsense, solemn or smiling, the round-about stuff, bad grammar, and mincing parliamentary cant" that dominated public debate, but radical opposition could not simply escape from "all that is canting and rotten." An effective campaign for periodical reform would require negative engagement as well as autonomy: "Plain, unaffected, honest language, and a contradiction of the pretensions of the stupid 'legitimate,' – these are what society want" (*E*, no. 637 [March 12, 1820], 161). Hunt assisted Cobbett in establishing the pattern by which the independent radical weekly fed off and refashioned the discourse of the more respectable daily press, and in doing so, he often derived his own "plain" style from legitimate "pretensions." The death of Queen Charlotte in 1818 triggered an "etiquette sort of eulogy" from the *Courier*, an "epitome of the cant common on these occasions," which Hunt then "translated into the language of truth and common sense": "'Eminently virtuous' means that she was not notoriously vicious; – 'unblemished and irreproachable' mean that she was chaste; 'all those points that constitute female excellence' – (what talking, to be sure!) amount to about the same thing." Having corrected legitimate circumlocution, Hunt could substitute his own demystifying plain speech: "She was chaste; but so are many vicious as well as virtuous persons. She was decorous; but so may the greatest hypocrite be. She was prudent, but so may be the greatest miser and the most cunning intriguer upon earth . . . The absence of certain vices, does not prove the possession of any virtue" (*E*, no. 569 [November 22, 1818], 737–38). The antithetical style and the moral bias of Hunt's translation indicate how the positive or reconstructive phase of his periodical reform recalled eighteenth-century models. Inspired by Swift's "wit and fine writing" rather than his tory politics (*HA* 173), the *Examiner* was guided by a properly Augustan sense of style:

It becomes a public writer . . . to shew the company his intellect keeps, and to attempt a language worthy of the sentiments he feels, and the country for which he writes. If a true style consists of "proper words in proper places," the definition is indisputable in political discussion, which ought to be the vehicle of the clearest and purest ideas. What concerns every body should be universally intelligible, though at the same time it should be written with a care for ornament, and it is for these reasons that while I have avoided as much as possible the quotation of languages in politics, in order that every body might be able to read me, I have not hesitated to employ what little pleasantry I could, in order that every body might wish to read me. (Preface, *E* [1808], n. pag.)

This high-minded defense of the "universally intelligible" exposed the exclusions upon which Hunt's version of periodical reform foundered. If he drew the line at "the quotation of languages," this "public writer" was nevertheless willing to limit his public through a commitment to "ornament," social distinction ("the company his intellect keeps"), and literary allusion. Furthermore, a sense of style as superficial "pleasantry" undermined Hunt's own radical commitment to "plain, unaffected, honest language." His complaint in the Prospectus to the *Reflector* that magazines did little more than make "*a shew of employing the Arts*" (*RF* 1 [1811], iv) can be turned against his own prose, which sometimes applied a superficial veneer of "ornament" to attract respectable readers and fend off the vulgar mob.

If "Henry Hunt (no relation of ours)" was an index of Hunt's recoil from degrading political acquaintance, William Cobbett turned out to be a nearer and more troubling cousin. His prose achieved the plain manner and universal intelligibility to which Hunt aspired: "He speaks as he writes, a good clear idiomatic style" (*E*, no. 637 [March 12, 1820], 162). If the *Indicator* was "an accomplished specimen . . . of the *Twopenny Trash*," Hunt was himself an accomplished specimen of the poor man's friend, and he shadowed Cobbett from above for much of his career. This meant keeping better company and transcending the naive verbal clarity of the *Political Register*. In an 1817 *Examiner* article on the public quarrel between Cobbett and Burdett, Hunt recorded the litany of Cobbett's transgressions against middle-class accomplishment: his tendency "to abuse the learned languages," "to ask what there was in SHAKESPEARE," "to wonder how MILTON could be endured," "to

denounce all piano-forte playing and dancing, as things vicious and friv-
olous." If there was "a good deal of egotism, and a great deal more
ignorance" in these sins, there was above all vulgarity. In the final analysis, what Cobbett failed to achieve was Hunt's own proto-Arnoldian will
to universalize the perspective of his own class: "He has no perception of
the beautiful or useful out of the ordinary pale . . . no imagination, or the
power which carries a man out of the sphere of his own grosser experience; – nothing of what the schools call humanity, or a general
apprehensiveness and appreciation of things common to his nature, as
distinguished from his class or particular likings" (*E*, no. 510 [October 5,
1817], 625–26). The ornaments of manner and style that were supposed
to attract readers, and facilitate universal communication, became for
Hunt the instruments of class exclusion. Ironically, he had been astute
enough a decade earlier to attack the class bias of Cobbett's enemies.
The series on "Newspaper Principle" dismissed the complaint that "Mr.
COBBETT swears, and is otherwise vulgar," and insisted instead on the
essential purity of his manners: "He neither games, nor drinks, nor
passes his leisure in the vilest company, like many of his brother
Proprietors and editors" (*E*, no. 83 [July 30, 1809], 482). Again, it would
be a mistake to distinguish too sharply the Hunt of 1809 from the Hunt
of 1817, since he was always anxious about matters of rank and respectability. Yet his anxious response to Cobbett was symptomatic of class
divisions within the reform movement that intensified over the course of
his career. There was far more at stake in his critique of Cobbett's failure
to transcend "his class," or the class with which he had become associated, than the pleasures of "piano-forte playing and dancing" and the
reputations of Shakespeare and Milton. Faced with the Spa Fields riots
in 1816, Hunt turned again to "taste and reputation" in order to distinguish the "leaders most acceptable to the people" from those (like
Henry Hunt, "no connexion") responsible for "the excesses of riots and
other public disturbances" (*E*, no. 467 [December 8, 1816], 769).

It would be difficult to exaggerate Hunt's investment in style and taste
as a means of redeeming radical protest from its own increasingly vulgar
constituency. His insistence on linking "CONSTITUTIONAL REFORM" with
"the cause of Literature, or Good Manners" (*E*, no. 101 [December 3,
1809], 772) often appeared superficial, but it did not want ambition. In a
coda to his 1818 series "On the Intellectual Inferiority of Parliament to
the Demands of the Age," he issued four "memorandums" to guide the
reform movement through the heady era of the radical mass platform.
The first confirmed his commitment to the radical principle that "it is

hopeless to expect a Reform from *within* the House," while the second raised the specter of *"a vengeance from without."* Where the mass platform exploited the ambiguity between violent and peaceable reform, Hunt looked for a mode of leadership that would "avert if possible" the threat of *"vengeance."* The third of his memorandums complained that "the upper classes of the democracy" and their "traffickers" in parliament had lost the vigor they displayed through earlier phases of social change: "They have no enthusiasm for any thing great, good, and unselfish; – none for natural and rural habits as in ELIZABETH's time; none for popular liberty as in that of the CHARLESES; none for elegant taste and sociality as in Queen ANNE's." On the ruins of these earlier leading classes, Hunt's fourth memorandum constructed a new progressive elite, whose refinement would guarantee reform without violence:

That the hopes of Reform and of all our influence upon mankind are in the hands of the younger part of the community; that you will do well to encourage them as much as you can, to get as many as possible into Parliament; and in a word, assist by every means in your power, the new growth of taste, liberality, popular feeling, and a love of nature and justice, as at once the only weapons, and the very best rewards, of your approaching victories over the dull and the sordid. (*E*, no. 531 [March 1, 1818], 130)

Earlier in the essay, Hunt linked this "new generation" with the "new and better school of letters" (129) he often championed. It was no accident that the same number of the *Examiner* praised Shelley, in a review of *The Revolt of Islam*, as a poet "destined to be one of the leading spirits of his age" (141), and that later in the same year the paper defended Keats, the "young man of genius," against the attacks of the *Quarterly Review* (*E*, no. 563 [October 11, 1818], 648). Just as Hunt's utopian desire for a "fusion" of literature and politics deteriorated into a political prose garnished with literary allusion, so his effort to provide common standards for the reform movement culminated in a bizarre apocalypse of uncommon taste ("your approaching victories over the dull and sordid"). Explicitly pitched against reactionary dominance of the public sphere (represented in the Shelley review by the Lake School and in the Keats article by the Quarterly Reviewers), the appeal to a "new growth of taste" also extended Hunt's campaign against vulgar leaders like Cobbett and Henry Hunt. Carl Woodring has somewhat mischievously remarked that the political ideal of the *Examiner* "would have been a legislature of London tradesmen familiar with Italian poetry."[34] It was to this hegemony of the petty bourgeoisie, as much as to "leading spirits" like Shelley and Keats, that Hunt's four "memorandums" pointed.

The *Examiner* aspired to a political discourse that was as reasonable as
it was tasteful. Philosophy, truth, and common sense joined style and
taste as key terms with which to reconstruct the "elegant . . . sociability"
of the early eighteenth century. If Hunt's tendency to discover common
sense in the distant past confirmed his elitist recoil from immediate political acquaintance,[35] his definition of the term "philosophy" in the
Preface to the *Examiner* was not without an inclusive and even levelling
potential:

Let us regard it in its original and etymological sense, as a love of wisdom, and
not its acquired and ornamental, as an attainment of it. The essence of philosophy is the cultivation of common reason, and as common things are in their
nature most useful, though subject to disesteem, and in their perfection most
delightful and admirable, so reason is in this respect like the most common of all
things, the air, which is liable to so much corruption when shut up and hindered
from circulation, but when suffered to extend abroad, encompasses the whole
earth, and is at once the medium of light, and the mover of power. And a
freedom from party-spirit supposes in some degree this necessary enlargement
of reason. (Preface, *E* [1808], n. pag.)

As he pursued his campaign for periodical reform, the same threat of
influence that reduced independence to elite seclusion made "common
reason" a mark of social distinction. "There never was a less portion of
philosophy in our political writers than at present," Hunt complained,
"They look upon the circumstances and changes of the world with so
partial an eye, that they account for every event upon the most petty
causes of party . . . These are the politicians, who unable to look or to
move out of their little sphere, are so tenacious of the prejudices of their
circle" (*E*, no. 37 [September 11, 1808], 577). Paradoxically, he could only
guarantee his access to common and collective reason by transcending
the immediate political sphere. Where refined style was the appropriate
language of independent journalism, a lofty perspective was the fitting
position from which to write:

It is absolutely necessary, in order to be sound politicians, to get out of this idiot's
sphere of judging merely from things about us, to abstract our minds from petty,
from selfish and from local feelings; and to look down upon the world from some
eminence that shall give us a collected view of mankind rather than jostle about
in a noisy and busy crowd where we can see but a few yards before us. "Give
me," said ARCHIMEDES, "a place whereon to stand, and I will move the world." It
is precisely the same in politics, and those wise men who have placed themselves
above the common passions and interests of men, have found the desideratum
of the philosopher, and have moved the whole earth. (*E*, no. 46 [November 13,
1808], 721)

This shift from philosophy as "the most common of all things" to philosophy as exalted perspective was a shift from speaking with others in the world, to speaking at them from above. Again, Hunt was driven to this position equally by his independent distaste for the trivial "little sphere" of party men, and by his middle-class fear of Cobbett's failure to rise above "the sphere of his own grosser experience." The perspective of Archimedes was, by definition, not widely shared. Most people had to remain behind in the "idiot's sphere," where they were open to manipulation precisely because they were so far removed from the philosophical critic.

What qualified someone like Hunt to rise above "common passions and interests" and achieve some leverage on the world? Given his acute middle-class consciousness, it was hardly surprising that the center rose to the top. The political "reveries" that were scattered through the *Examiner*, in which a reflective essayist imaginatively projected himself into a position of authority, were motivated by a sense that the middle class was ready for this kind of elevation. In Hunt's 1814 essay, "European Congress," the armchair politician became "the arbitrator of contending nations," and found the "disinterestedness and reason" wanted in Vienna among the English middle class: "A person taken suddenly for such a purpose from the middle ranks of society would have leaped at once over all that tends to spoil a prince for good government" (*E*, no. 356 [October 23, 1814], 673). As Hunt appropriated "common" reason for himself and his class, it became clear that his definition of philosophy as a universal "love of wisdom" served class interests. When the *Examiner* called for a disinterested assessment of Napoleon's reputation, it anticipated by a decade James Mill's celebrated argument for the political wisdom of the middle class:

There is no publication more desirable than a summary of BONAPARTE's actions and character, written by some well-informed and temperate person, who could abstract himself from the influence of the times, and regard his subject as a curiosity . . . Such a production is by no means impossible, but it is hardly to be expected for two very simple reasons; first, because the persons most likely to have an unprejudiced judgment on the occasion are of a middle, plain thinking class, not likely to become authors; and second, because the whole remaining mass of society is at present too much interested in the subject. (*E*, no. 144 [September 30, 1810], 609)[36]

The attributes that endowed this "middle, plain thinking class" with its disinterestedness became clear as Hunt went on to celebrate domestic life. The capacity to regard "present times . . . as nothing but a portion of future history" could be found "in calm domestic circles only, where taste and virtue are the chief objects of study" (609). As if to prove his own mediocre fitness to the task, Hunt soon published his essay on "Bonaparte, – His Present Aspect and Character," which tried to wrest Napoleon's reputation from the control of two class extremes: the aristocratic "denouncers of low birth" on the one hand, and vulgar and "common minds" on the other, who "in their ignorance and weakness, are struck with a consciousness of their own inferiority in proportion as the superiority of a fellow creature is manifested to their senses" (*E*, no. 192 [September 1, 1811], 555).

As Hunt rotated his critical position from a vertical to a horizontal axis, the philosopher's perspective descended from Archimedean heights: "Truth lies as usual in the middle" (555). Far from being like air "the most common of all things," reason and common sense retreated to the private sphere of the London middle class. A commitment to vigorous opposition, and to extremes even in liberalism, dissolved under the influence of this same moderation: "Wherever there have been violent political disputes, they have proved that the truth has nothing to do with extremes: its force is truly centripetal . . . Whatever is stable and accordant with the true harmony of things tends directly to a centre" (*E*, no. 37 [September 11, 1808], 577). Like refined taste, the wisdom of the middle could be mobilized against the vulgar as well as the elite. Hunt responded to the Luddite violence of 1812 with a defense of state violence:

A recourse to arms becomes necessary to save that very Constitution which . . . violence infringes. Some people think that when a King is concerned, no such recourse is allowable; and others again seem to imagine, that a mob is to be privileged from the controul; but common sense is against both; and though we may pity both King and mob, we must suffer neither to run riot, and lay waste our property and peace. (*E*, no. 241 [August 9, 1812], 497)

Where the rhetorical violence and frank extremism of the Preface to the *Liberal* distinguished Hunt from Arnold and other subsequent liberal haters of hatred, the "common sense" and rhetorical moderation of this defense of the well-constituted state anticipated Arnold's response to the Hyde Park riots in *Culture and Anarchy*.

Hunt's willingness to associate peaceful reform with the rhetorical and cognitive style of the middle class became his point of departure from popular radical opposition. This crucial transition in his career required a shift away from a radical rhetoric of fact, produced under critical conditions, towards a less straightforward rhetoric of progressive accommodation. Hunt was able to achieve limited sympathy with popular unrest when he reduced every political issue to "a pure question of fact and universal comprehension" (*E*, no. 68 [April 16, 1809], 242). His sympathetic account of the victims of Peterloo – "a body of military dashed through them sword in hand, trampled down opposition, bruised and wounded many, and bore off the flags and the speakers to the county jail" – rebuked a corrupt misrepresentation in the *Courier*, which "would have us overlook all these matters to dwell with shuddering sympathy on the wounds of constables and soldiers": "We write this article to tell them that their eternal beggings of the question, always *against* the poor and the Reformers, in *favour* of the rich and the corrupt, form nothing but a provoking and disgusting contrast with the warrantable demands and most unwarrantable sufferings of those calumniated poor" (*E*, no. 608 [August 22, 1819], 529–30). A critical process of exposure and a stark grammar of opposition ("*against*," "in *favour* of") encouraged broad sympathies that extended across class lines, and joined "the poor and the Reformers" in a united front against "the rich and the corrupt." This outlook authorized a fairly straightforward account of public opinion: support for reform was genuine, while resistance to it could be traced to corrupt influence. Matters became more complicated when the interests of the middle class intervened between popular and ministerial extremes. Hunt then abandoned a simple factual correspondence between writing and the world, between press and opinion – what Jon Klancher has called the radical "squaring of signs with things and writers with the readers they represent"[37] – and proposed instead a progressive narrative according to which a narrow stratum of opinion extended its benevolent influence. Departures from fact became something more than deceptive misrepresentation. As Terry Eagleton has observed, "committed though he believed himself to be to the disinterested pursuit of philosophic truth," Hunt "uneasily acknowledged the need to write with something less than complete candour," and to imagine for himself "a partially benighted readership" that "demanded a certain diplomatic delicacy."[38]

Cobbett again served as an important foil. In an 1820 *Examiner* article, "Mr. Cobbett, and What Is Wanted in Parliament," Hunt was enthusiastic about Cobbett's political claims, which he associated with simple descriptive representation: "There are things in Mr. COBBETT which are not to our 'fastidious' taste, but we should like much to see him in parliament," as a "representative" or "specimen" of "the popular intellect." In rhetorical terms, the relationship between the "clear idiomatic style" of the *Register* and its working-class readers entailed the same straightforward correspondence, the expressive version of descriptive representation: Cobbett had "risen, not merely from the people, but from their very poorest ranks," and could "come forward and state plainly . . . the very same arguments and feelings which occupy the enlightened part of the poorer orders" (*E*, no. 637 [March 12, 1820], 162). For himself, Hunt aspired to the higher-order relationship appropriate to a progressive intellectual and a leading class. The imperfect correspondence between writer and reader (expression) and between writing and world (description) was most explicit in his 1831 *Tatler* essay, "The Public Press," composed in the period immediately preceding the moderate reforms that Hunt came to see as the fulfillment of his political expectations and literary labors. If, as Woodring and others have suggested, the *Tatler* found Hunt resurgent as a political writer, he had returned with a new theory of political discourse.[39] The point of departure for the essay was another journalist's defense of an expressive theory of periodical representation: "'Journalism' is nothing but the expression of public opinion." Hunt saw "a good deal of truth" in this remark, but insisted that "the whole truth" had to exceed expression: "If journals had never been in advance of public opinion, public opinion would not have been so advanced as it is . . . A writer, anxious for the public good, and advanced by his studies beyond the common run of opinion, will do everything he can . . . to bring society up to him." When Hunt tried to distinguish this "full duty of a journalist" from the coercive role of the absolute monarch or legitimate minister, the awkwardness of his syntax suggested how far he had come from the plain style of radical representation: "What we meant to say was, that although the Press, for the most part, does not 'dictate' to the public, yet the whole of it may be said, more or less, to insinuate a kind of dictation; that is to say, it at once accompanies and leads the opinion of the public."

The essay was clearly a revisionist account of Hunt's own career, which shifted the dynamic of social change from crisis to progress, from inflexible opposition to consensual negotiation. He summed up his case by applying it to the *Examiner*, a paper he no longer edited: "The *Examiner* has always advocated the cause of reform. For many years it advocated it to a comparatively small circle . . . But are we to suppose that this circle was not enlarged by the advocacy? and that the Editors . . . have not a right to be proud of having assisted to lead as well as to accompany opinion?"[40] The independent political essayist now struggled with doomed residual opinion rather than intransigent state power.

By substituting a fully liberal vision of progressive accretion for a radical one of combative bifurcation, Hunt finally resolved the tension between his inclusive and exclusive impulses. The "comparatively small circle" with which he communicated at any one time was not an exclusive clique, but a prophetic anticipation of what the entire community would someday become. By enlarging its "small circle" of readers, the *Examiner* forged a political language that was by 1832 on everyone's lips. Beyond its inherent limitations, the weakness of this theory of anticipatory representation as an account of Hunt's career was that it was formulated *retrospectively*, as a ratification of what was about to become the status quo, rather than a provocative incitement to further change. The intervention of the press seemed redundant when the government itself contained progressive energies: "It is wonderful in how short a time honest discussion may be advanced by a court at once correct and unbigoted, and by a succession of calmly progressing ministries" (*HA* 265). By the 1830s, Hunt was fully prepared to abandon print intervention in the public sphere, and leave politics to the politicians. With the establishment of *Leigh Hunt's London Journal* in 1834, the ambitions with which he launched his career had become a frank discursive fantasy rather than a practical program for social change: "The *London Journal* is a sort of park for rich and poor, for the reflecting and the well intentioned of all sorts; where every one can be alone, or in company, as he thinks fit, and see, with his mind's eye, a succession of Elysian sights" (*LJ*, no. 23 [1834], 177).

Afterword: William Hazlitt – a radical critique of radical opposition?

William Hazlitt has appeared sporadically in this book, as an instance of a radical politics in print, and as an astute commentator on such radical cruxes as independence, opposition, contradiction, and personality. This treatment may trouble some readers, either because it accords him a less central presence than a canonical figure in romantic studies would seem to deserve, or because it too easily assimilates his complex political outlook to radical reform. To begin with the second point, accounts of Hazlitt's politics have tended to stress his liberal or moderate reformist commitments, and situate him outside the radical movement. John Kinnaird, for example, maintains that he "had become by 1807, if not long before, a 'constitutional Whig' in his practical politics."[1] On the contrary, constitutionalism was one feature of both radical and conservative discourse that Hazlitt wanted to refuse. Reformers like Cartwright and Burdett seemed to him to have been led astray in "wanting to go back to the early times of our Constitution and history in search of the principles of law and liberty" (*CWH* 11: 141). On other issues, he was more willing to assume a radical posture, preferring "a hatred of tyranny, and a contempt for its tools" to party identification, endorsing the radical agrarian principle that "there is but a limited earth and a limited fertility to supply the demands both of Government and people," seconding Cobbett's view that distress was the result of "the war and taxes," advocating "the principle of universal suffrage" against the representation of property, maintaining that "combinations among labourers for the rise of wages are always just and lawful," and defending Napoleon well past the bitter end.[2] Faced with ideological labels, he was cautious but not conciliatory. He once protested that "I have nowhere in any thing I may have written declared myself to be a Republican," and went on to find an even more threatening name for his belief "that there is a power in the people to change its government and its governors": "I am a Revolutionist: For otherwise, I must allow that mankind are but a

227

herd of slaves, the property of thrones, that no tyranny or insult can law-fully goad them to a resistance to a particular family" (*CWH* 14: 236–37). And, contrary to one recent biography, Hazlitt was neither unread nor entirely "misunderstood" in plebeian radical circles.[3] He was cited approvingly in the *Black Dwarf*, the *Medusa*, and in John Wade's *Political Dictionary*, and was particularly influential as an exponent of the post-war radical critique of "Legitimacy" as a "new-vamped" version of "the old doctrine of Divine Right" (*CWH* 7: 260).[4]

Why not, then, accord Hazlitt a more central role in this book? To begin with, while his principles overlapped significantly with figures like Wade, Wooler, and Cobbett, he tended to exercise those principles in a very different manner. Hazlitt avoided appealing directly to a popular reading audience, never edited or published a periodical, was not directly involved in radical organization, and neither courted nor experi-enced political prosecution for what he wrote. The tensions and contra-dictions I have associated with radical opposition were there in Hazlitt's prose, but they were sublimated, and almost entirely translated to the printed page. This shift from circulation and organization to language involved a corresponding shift, with respect to the mainstream of popular radical reform, from politics to literature, culture, and meta-physics.[5] His claim in the essay "On Court-Influence" that Edmund Burke's submission to court influence was motivated by vanity rather than self-interest, by "the circumstance of the king's having his 'Reflections on the French Revolution' bound in morocco . . . and giving it to all his particular friends," rather than the "mere grant of money" (*CWH* 7: 231), seems to me typical of his turn of mind. Brilliant, provoca-tive, and paradoxical, the remark abruptly shifted a radical critique of corruption from material and institutional concerns to a more rarified and potentially disorienting account of human nature and courtly manners.[6] Attention to the physical evidence of the book was distinctly ironic here, meant to embarrass a court culture that benefited from the influence of the *Reflections* but did not share Hazlitt's appreciation of its brilliant prose. For Hazlitt as for Hunt, a cultural construction of the political field involved distinct class prejudices: his social criticism turned out to be meritocratic rather than levelling, and distinctly anxious about vulgar influence. This was not by itself a rejection of plebeian radical culture, which also endorsed terms like merit and talent. Indeed, Wade's *Political Dictionary* cited Hazlitt when it defined the mob as an "incorrigi-ble mass of knaves and fools . . . who never think at all."[7] And Hazlitt sec-onded Carlile's paradoxical endorsement of "lofty ideas as to equality" when he claimed to be "proud up to the point of equality – every thing above or below *that* appears to me arrant impertinence or abject meanness" (*CWH* 20: 123). What was more unique to Hazlitt's prose was the way an anxiety about merit was channelled from politics into culture, resulting in a split social vision. As John Barrell has observed, "while the political republic may properly be, for Hazlitt, democratic," the "republic of taste" was "governed by an aristocracy of genius."[8]

At the same time, Hazlitt was too profoundly disenchanted and combative to share Hunt's belletristic endorsement of "the new growth of taste, liberality, popular feeling, and a love of nature" as a political program, and never succeeded in converting his "hatred of tyranny" into a faith in historical progress. He grew more skeptical towards the end of his life, but the basic outlook was established as early as his *Reply to Malthus* (1807):

Perhaps if the truth were known, I am as little sanguine in my expectations of any great improvement to be made in the condition of human life either by the visions of philosophy, or by downright, practical, parliamentary projects, as Mr. Malthus himself can be. But the matter appears to me thus. It requires some exertion and some freedom of will to keep even where we are. If we tie up our hands, shut our eyes to the partial advantages we possess, and cease to exert ourselves in that direction in which we can do it with the most effect, we shall very soon "go deep in the negative series." (*CWH* 1: 214)

Faced with the leading contemporary antagonist of Godwinian perfectibility, Hazlitt could do nothing more than make the remnants of his progressive faith a critical weapon against retrograde developments. Where he did endorse enlightenment values, these were derived from the traditions of rational dissent, and deployed retrospectively: "The Reformation . . . gave a mighty impulse and increased activity to thought and inquiry, and agitated the inert mass of accumulated prejudices throughout Europe" (*CWH* 6: 181–82). If a dissenting heritage provided Hazlitt with a more disruptive set of affiliations than Hunt found in the coffee-houses of the early eighteenth century, he was less confident than Hunt about the current viability of past practices. The dissenting sects were the most effective "checks and barriers against the insidious or avowed encroachments of arbitrary power," but they were nearly "worn . . . out," and Hazlitt wrote about them in an elegiac tone: "Their creed . . . glimmers with the last feeble eyesight, smiles in the faded cheek like infancy, and lights a path before them to the grave!" (*CWH* 7: 239–42).[9]

The potential affiliation with dissent was further complicated by the fact that sectarian religion represented centrifugal principles of "antipa-

thy" and "opposition" that seemed to Hazlitt to undermine social intercourse. His own refusal to coalesce with organized political opposition
was a legacy of the critical restlessness and "right of contradiction" that
he associated with rational dissent (*CWH* 4: 48). He managed to deploy
the radical principle of contradiction in a manner that distinguished him
from other radicals. Where Cobbett, Carlile, Wooler, and others traced
their own inconsistencies to the structure of a corrupt system, and
believed that contradiction and opposition would pass away with
reform, Hazlitt treated contradiction as an inveterate feature of human
nature. The repeal of the Test and Corporation Acts, a measure that
would have delighted his father but seemed by 1828 little more than "a
boon to indifference," drew from him this bitter apostrophe:

Spirit of contradiction! When wilt thou cease to rule over sublunary affairs, as
the moon governs the tides? Not till the unexpected stroke of a comet throws up
a new breed of men and animals from the bowels of the earth; nor then neither,
since it is included in the very idea of all life, power, and motion. *For* and *against*
are inseparable terms. (*CWH* 19: 303)

The same sense of inconsistency as an absolute rather than relative or
negative condition informed his skepticism about human progress. "All
things move, not in progress, but in a ceaseless round," he complained,
"our strength lies in our weakness; our virtues are built on our vices"
(*CWH* 4: 119). While it would be a mistake to privilege Hazlitt's
philosophical or aesthetic interests at the expense of his political convic-
tions,[10] it is true that the metaphysical aspirations with which he
launched his career remained with him throughout his life, and that his
prose tended to play out in the sphere of mind or art a set of issues (independence, opposition, contradiction, egotism, hatred, self-interest) that
popular radicalism wanted to treat as resolutely social and political. His
political despair was often underwritten by an analysis of the "spirit of
contradiction" and a related "spirit of malevolence" as inveterate features of the mind and world. The famous essay "On the Pleasure of
Hating" set out from the insight that "nature seems (the more we look
into it) made up of antipathies," and then proceeded through a hearty
disgust with his own political principles to a "universal application" of
the principle of hostility. The writer was finally engulfed in his own sple-
netic world view: "Seeing all this as I do . . . have I not reason to hate and
to despise myself? Indeed I do; and chiefly for not having hated and
despised the world enough" (*CWH* 12: 128–36).

Though not always this disabling, Hazlitt's meditations on contradiction and animosity were uniformly restless and anxious. He insisted

upon subjecting his own principles, and those of his potential allies, to the same scrupulous criticism he applied to his enemies. The 1819 Preface to the *Political Essays*, perhaps his most deliberate political manifesto, set out from a typically radical set of antagonisms: "I deny that liberty and slavery are convertible terms, that right and wrong, truth and falsehood, plenty and famine, the comforts or wretchedness of a people, are matters of perfect indifference" (*CWH* 7: 7). As the essay went on to probe the disturbing reality of post-Napoleonic Europe, these binary formulations tended to unravel, and were replaced by a more complex and transgressive critique that included the reform movement within its scope. "To this pass have we been brought by the joint endeavours of Tories, Whigs, and Reformers," Hazlitt complained, and there was no reason to exempt the reformers from responsibility: "It is, perhaps, a delicate point, but it is of no inconsiderable importance, that the friends of Freedom should know the strength of their enemies, and their own weakness as well" (13). The "delicate" project of a radical critique of radical reform discovered that the movement shared the sectarian "spirit of contradiction": "A Reformer is not a gregarious animal. Speculative opinion leads men different ways, each according to his particular fancy: – it is prejudice or interest that drives before it the herd of mankind. That *which is*, with all its confirmed abuses and 'tickling commodities,' is alone solid and certain: that *which may be* or *ought to be*, has a thousand shapes and colours" (13). The bifurcated structure of popular radical discourse remained ("speculative opinion" against "confirmed abuses," "that *which is*" against "that *which may be*"), but the value and association of antithetical terms shifted wildly in the hands of a paradoxical critic who was no more at ease with his friends than with his enemies. Robert Owen's *New View of Society* turned out to be "as old as society itself" (*CWH* 7: 98), and Shelley's "bending, flexible form" was tested and found wanting against "rooted prejudices" that Hazlitt himself often despised (*CWH* 8: 148–49). Above all, Edmund Burke became the focus of these ambivalent energies.[11] Hazlitt divided himself from fellow radicals by making it a test of the "candour of any one belonging to the opposite party, whether he allowed Burke to be a great man" (*CWH* 7: 305), and then divided the great man in a desperate attempt to manage his own divided political loyalties: "Mr. Burke, the opponent of the American war, and Mr. Burke, the opponent of the French Revolution, are not the same person, but opposite persons – not opposite persons only, but deadly enemies" (*CWH* 7: 226).

Through these and countless other paradoxical formulations,

Hazlitt's prose turned the negative energy of radical reform upon itself, and transformed the contradictions of opposition into a complex rhetorical problem to be worked out endlessly on the printed page. It is not easy to decide whether the result was a radical critique of radical opposition, or merely a virtuoso display of the writer's own celebrated flexibility of mind, what David Bromwich terms his "faculty of holding two opposed ideas in his mind at the same time."[12] Certainly figures like Carlile and Wooler managed to combine something of Hazlitt's rhetorical mobility and corrosive energy, if not his brilliance of conception and style, with more immediate political engagements. Yet there are reasons not to dismiss Hazlitt too hastily as a self-indulgent critic. To begin with, his disenchantment prevented him from sharing the illusions of a writer like Leigh Hunt. The critique of radicalism was fully a self-critique, and any faults we might find with his prose – captiousness, animosity, detachment, egotism, isolation – were fully analyzed in that prose. Critical and rhetorical mobility were not, furthermore, absolutes for Hazlitt. He set strict political limits to the exercise of his own critical faculties, although he often found it hard to imagine that such limits had much force in a post-Napoleonic world. Again, the figure of Burke was instructive. Though Hazlitt struggled to redeem the power of Burke's style and conception from the "vulgar democratical mind" (*CWH* 17: 111), he was not misled about their impact: "I should not differ from any one who may be disposed to contend that the consequences of his writings as instruments of political power have been tremendous, fatal, such as no exertion of wit or knowledge or genius can ever counteract or atone for" (*CWH* 7: 308–9). In this case, at least, a political judgment took priority over the free play of aesthetic and metaphysical intelligence.

Even Hazlitt's most desperate assessments of the viability of reform were predicated on a full sense of its virtues. If radical opposition did not promise a utopian future, it sustained principles of "freedom" and "exertion" that blunted the crippling impact of a prophet of despair like Malthus. Towards the end of his "Common Places" (1823), Hazlitt took a reading of Scott's *Heart of Midlothian* as the point of departure for a penetrating analysis of the politics of resistance:

When Effie Deans becomes a fine lady, do we not look back with regret to the time when she was the poor faded lily of St. Leonards, the outcast and condemned prisoner? So, should the cause of liberty and mankind ever become triumphant, instead of militant, may we not heave a sigh of regret over the past, and think that poor suffering human nature, with all its wrongs and insults, trodden down into the earth like a vile weed, was a more interesting topic for reflection? We need not be much alarmed for the event, even if this should be so; for the way to Utopia is not the "primrose path of dalliance"; and at the rate we have hitherto gone on, it must be many thousand years off! (*CWH* 20: 138)

The forestalling of "Utopia" in the last sentence clinched an ironic tone, but there was an underlying seriousness too, and Hazlitt's political terminology provided a clue as to what was at stake. In an 1816 *Examiner* review of *The Lay of the Laureate*, he responded to what he considered Southey's careless orientalism with a similar distinction between a "militant" and "triumphant" cause, applied here to the consummation of "divine right" authority in the East:

Legitimacy is not there militant, but triumphant . . . It is long since the people had any thing to do with the laws but to obey them, or any laws to obey but the will of their task-masters. This is the necessary end of legitimacy . . . Things there are perfectly settled, in the state in which they should be, – still as death, and likely to remain so. (*CWH* 7: 92)

If "the cause of liberty" seemed foolish from the perspective of a utopian future that would always lie "many thousand years off," it became a more serious and perhaps even heroic matter when set against the "necessary end" of legitimacy. Hazlitt's meditation on Effie Deans took on a darker tone in his later "Aphorisms on Man" (1830–31), where he proposed that "it is essential to the triumph of reform that it should never succeed":

If reform were to gain the day, reform would become as vulgar as cant of any other kind. We only shew a spirit of independence and resistance to power, as long as power is against us. As soon as the cause of opposition prevails, its essence and character are gone out of it; and the most flagrant *radicalism* degenerates into the tamest servility . . . This may point out the little chance there is of any great improvement in the affairs of the world. Virtue ceases with difficulty; honesty is *militant*. (*CWH* 20: 333–34)

The paradoxical claim that reform had to fail to succeed, that key radical virtues ("independence," "resistance," "opposition") required their oppressive opposite, exposed the connection between Hazlitt's political skepticism and his will to opposition, but it also showed how he could derive inspiration even from despair, once the triumph of legitimacy seemed to leave him little else. Disenchantment did not preclude an ironic mode of political commitment. If Hazlitt's critical practice situates him outside the scope of this book, the insights he provided into the structure of radical opposition have informed its method and its development.

Notes

INTRODUCTION: LOCATING A PLEBEIAN COUNTERPUBLIC SPHERE

1 See for example Kenneth Neill Cameron, *The Young Shelley: Genesis of a Radical* (New York: Macmillan, 1950), David V. Erdman, *Blake: Prophet Against Empire* (Princeton University Press, 1954), Michael Scrivener, *Radical Shelley: The Philosophical Anarchism and Utopian Thought of Percy Bysshe Shelley* (Princeton University Press, 1982), and Nicholas Roe, *Wordsworth and Coleridge: The Radical Years* (Oxford: Clarendon Press, 1988).

2 The distinction is made by Jerome J. McGann in his Introduction to *The New Oxford Book of Romantic Period Verse* (Oxford University Press, 1993), pp. xix–xx.

3 For useful surveys of the new historicism in romantic studies, see Alan Liu, review of *Wordsworth's Historical Imagination: The Poetry of Displacement*, by David Simpson, in *The Wordsworth Circle* 19 (1988), 172–73, 180–81, and Jon Klancher, "English Romanticism and Cultural Production," in *The New Historicism*, ed. H. Aram Veeser (New York: Routledge, 1989), pp. 77–88.

4 Anne Janowitz, review of *Radical Culture: Discourse, Resistance, and Surveillance, 1790–1820*, by David Worrall, and *Dangerous Enthusiasm: William Blake and the Culture of Radicalism in the 1790s*, by Jon Mee, in *Studies in Romanticism* 32 (1993), 297–303. Janowitz's own forthcoming study of Chartist poetry promises to be an important contribution to plebeian romantic studies.

5 Jon Mee, *Dangerous Enthusiasm: William Blake and the Culture of Radicalism in the 1790s* (Oxford: Clarendon Press, 1992), David Worrall, *Radical Culture: Discourse, Resistance, and Surveillance, 1790–1820* (Detroit: Wayne State University Press, 1992), Jon Klancher, *The Making of English Reading Audiences, 1790–1832* (Madison, Wisconsin: University of Wisconsin Press, 1987), Michael Scrivener (ed.), *Poetry and Reform: Periodical Verse from the English Democratic Press, 1792–1824* (Detroit: Wayne State University Press, 1992), Marcus Wood, *Radical Satire and Print Culture, 1790–1822* (Oxford: Clarendon Press, 1994), Paul Thomas Murphy, *Toward a Working-Class Canon: Literary Criticism in British Working-Class Periodicals, 1816–1858* (Columbus, Ohio: Ohio State University Press, 1994), and Leonora Nattrass, *William Cobbett: The Politics of Style* (Cambridge University Press, 1995). For the influence of Thompson and Williams on "the way we read

literature in history," see Marilyn Butler, "Thompson's Second Front," *History Workshop Journal* 39 (1995), 72.

6 Iain McCalman's *Radical Underworld: Prophets, Revolutionaries and Pornographers in London, 1795–1840* (Cambridge University Press, 1988) has been particularly influential, and Mee also cites an unpublished paper by McCalman delivered at the 1990 Historicizing Blake Conference (*Dangerous Enthusiasm*, p. 4). Other historians interested in radical language include Gareth Stedman Jones, "Rethinking Chartism," in *Languages of Class: Studies in English Working Class History, 1832–1982* (Cambridge University Press, 1983), pp. 90–178; James Vernon, *Politics and the People: A Study in English Political Culture, c. 1815–1867* (Cambridge University Press, 1993); James Epstein, *Radical Expression: Political Language, Ritual, and Symbol in England, 1790–1850* (New York: Oxford University Press, 1994); and Jonathan Fulcher, "Contests over Constitutionalism: The Faltering of Reform in England, 1816–1824" (Ph.D. dissertation, University of Cambridge, 1992).

7 Mee, *Dangerous Enthusiasm*, pp. 3–4, 8.

8 Nattrass, *William Cobbett*, pp. 9, 98, 108.

9 Worrall, *Radical Culture*, pp. 12, 27.

10 Jürgen Habermas, *The Structural Transformation of the Public Sphere: An Inquiry into a Category of Bourgeois Society*, trans. Thomas Burger and Frederick Lawrence (Cambridge, Massachusetts: MIT Press, 1989), p. xviii.

11 See Peter Dahlgren, Introduction, in *Communication and Citizenship: Journalism and the Public Sphere in the New Media Age*, ed. Peter Dahlgren and Colin Sparks (London: Routledge, 1991), pp. 3–4.

12 Bruce Robbins, "Introduction: The Public As Phantom," in *The Phantom Public Sphere*, ed. Bruce Robbins (Minneapolis: University of Minnesota Press, 1993), p. xvii. See also Craig Calhoun, "Introduction: Habermas and the Public Sphere," in *Habermas and the Public Sphere*, ed. Craig Calhoun (Cambridge, Massachusetts: MIT Press, 1992), p. 37, and Dahlgren, Introduction, *Communication and Citizenship*, p. 6. The formative work of Negt and Kluge has appeared in English as *Public Sphere and Experience: Toward an Analysis of the Bourgeois and Proletarian Public Sphere* (Minneapolis: University of Minnesota Press, 1993).

13 Geoff Eley, "Nations, Publics, and Political Cultures: Placing Habermas in the Nineteenth Century," in *Habermas and the Public Sphere*, ed. Craig Calhoun, p. 306.

14 *The Complete Poetry and Prose of William Blake*, ed. David V. Erdman (Garden City, New York: Anchor Books, 1982), p. 95.

15 *Prompter*, no. 1 (1830), 8, and *Prompter*, no. 42 (1831), 752. For the Rotunda, see Epstein, *Radical Expression*, pp. 136–46.

16 Terry Eagleton, *The Function of Criticism, from the Spectator to Post-Structuralism* (London: Verso, 1984), p. 36.

17 Klancher, *Making of English Reading Audiences*, p. 24.

18 The phrase is from E. P. Thompson, *The Making of the English Working Class* (New York: Vintage Books, 1966), p. 603.

19 Robbins, "Introduction: The Public As Phantom," p. xiii.

20 For the theory of virtual representation, see J. R. Pole, *Political Representation in England and the Origins of the American Republic* (London: Macmillan, 1960), pp. 452–55; John Cannon, *Parliamentary Reform, 1640–1832* (Cambridge University Press, 1973), pp. 31–33; and John Phillip Reid, *The Concept of Representation in the Age of the American Revolution* (University of Chicago Press, 1987), pp. 50–62.

21 For descriptive representation, see Catherine Gallagher, *The Industrial Reformation of English Fiction* (University of Chicago Press, 1985), pp. 222–24, and Hanna Fenichel Pitkin, *The Concept of Representation* (Berkeley: University of California Press, 1972), pp. 60–91.

22 For Cobbett's appearance as "William Cobbett, of Botley, in the County of Hants, now residing at North Hampstead, in the State of New York," see *CPR* 33 (1818), 161, and 539, 635.

23 Eagleton, *Function of Criticism*, p. 37. Compare Fredric Jameson's remarks in "On Negt and Kluge," in *The Phantom Public Sphere*, ed. Robbins, p. 50.

24 Epstein, *Radical Expression*, p. 150.

25 Curran, "Rethinking the Media as Public Sphere," in *Communication and Citizenship*, pp. 29–30.

26 See Pole, *Political Representation in England*, pp. 441–42, 479–80.

27 For an excellent account of Carlile and free discussion, see Epstein, *Radical Expression*, pp. 100–46.

28 For the radical desire for unity, see Craig Calhoun, *The Question of Class Struggle: Social Foundations of Popular Radicalism during the Industrial Revolution* (University of Chicago Press, 1982), pp. 87–89.

29 *Reformists' Register*, no. 8 (1811), 125.

30 The poem is reprinted and attributed to Davenport by Scrivener in *Poetry and Reform*, pp. 205–06.

31 See Eagleton, *Function of Criticism*, pp. 38–39. Hunt's attitude was by no means eccentric, and more plebeian writers like Wooler, Hone, and Cobbett also signalled their debt to eighteenth-century practices.

32 Eley, "Nations, Publics, and Political Cultures," p. 306.

33 Thompson, *Making of the English Working Class*, p. 15. For the revisionist view, see for example Jones, *Languages of Class*, pp. 104–07; Iorwerth Prothero, *Artisans and Politics in Early Nineteenth-Century London: John Gast and his Times* (Baton Rouge, Louisiana: Louisiana State University Press, 1979), pp. 83–87; and Iorwerth Prothero, "William Benbow and the Concept of the 'General Strike,'" *Past and Present* 63 (1974), 141–47, 156–62.

34 Jones, *Languages of Class*, pp. 8, 104.

35 Jones, *Languages of Class*, p. 22.

36 John C. Belchem, "Radical Language and Ideology in Early Nineteenth-Century England: The Challenge of the Platform," *Albion* 20 (1988), 251.

37 See Asa Briggs, "Middle-Class Consciousness in English Politics, 1780–1846," *Past and Present* 9 (1956), 69–71; James Curran, "Capitalism and Control of the Press, 1800–1975," in *Mass Communication and Society*, ed.

James Curran, Michael Gurevitch, and Janet Woollacott (London: Edward Arnold, 1977), pp. 210–11; and Jones, *Languages of Class*, pp. 104–05. For radical remarks on a class alliance, see *R* 1 (1819), 61–62; *R* 3 (1820), 148–50; *BD* 1 (1817), 33–38; and *G*, no. 10 (1818), 74–80.

1   A RHETORIC OF RADICAL OPPOSITION

1 See William Thomas, "Radical Westminster," in *The Philosophic Radicals: Nine Studies in Theory and Practice, 1817–1841* (Oxford: Clarendon Press, 1979), p. 57.

2 Steven N. Zwicker, "Lines of Authority: Politics and Literary Culture in the Restoration," in *Politics of Discourse: The Literature and History of Seventeenth-Century England*, ed. Kevin Sharpe and Steven N. Zwicker (Berkeley: University of California Press, 1987), pp. 230–31.

3 Pierre Bourdieu, *Outline of a Theory of Practice* (Cambridge University Press, 1977), pp. 167–69.

4 Similar gestures can be found in *HR* 1 (1817), 33, and *WH* 1 (1819), 4, 7. For this generation of radicals, the turn against both parties can be dated to 1806–07, and the perceived failure of the "Ministry of All the Talents" to distinguish itself from previous tory ministries. See Asa Briggs, *The Making of Modern England, 1783–1867: The Age of Improvement* (New York: Harper and Row, 1965), p. 180; J. Anne Hone, *For the Cause of Truth: Radicalism in London, 1796–1821* (Oxford: Clarendon Press, 1982), pp. 149–59; Clive Emsley, *British Society and the French Wars, 1793–1815* (London: Macmillan, 1979), p. 129; and Frank O'Gorman, *The Emergence of the British Two-Party System, 1760–1832* (London: Edward Arnold, 1982), pp. 36–38.

5 Arthur Aspinall, *Politics and the Press, c. 1780–1850* (London: Home and Van Thal, 1949), pp. 270–349.

6 Leonora Nattrass makes a similar point when she suggests that writers like Cobbett and Hone posited both the fact of national division and the necessity of national unity; see *William Cobbett: The Politics of Style* (Cambridge University Press, 1995), pp. 210–11, 216.

7 John Brewer, *Party Ideology and Popular Politics at the Accession of George III* (Cambridge University Press, 1976), p. 15. For the role of Burke and the Rockingham whigs in the development of British theories of party, see also Archibald S. Foord, *His Majesty's Opposition, 1714–1830* (Oxford: Clarendon Press, 1964), pp. 316–18; Frank O'Gorman, *The Rise of Party in England: The Rockingham Whigs, 1760–1840* (London: George Allen and Unwin, 1975), pp. 258–71; and H. T. Dickinson, *Liberty and Property: Political Ideology in Eighteenth-Century Britain* (London: Methuen, 1979), pp. 208–09.

8 *The Works of Lord Bolingbroke*, 4 vols. (Philadelphia: Carey and Hart, 1841), 2: 168. For Bolingbroke and the country attitude to party, see Brewer, *Party Ideology and Popular Politics*, pp. 45–46, and Isaac Kramnick, *Bolingbroke and His Circle: The Politics of Nostalgia in the Age of Walpole* (Cambridge, Massachusetts: Harvard University Press, 1968), pp. 24–30, 155–56. For the

links between country-party opposition and nineteenth-century radical opposition, see Gareth Stedman Jones, *Languages of Class: Studies in English Working Class History, 1832–1982* (Cambridge University Press, 1983), pp. 102–03, 121; Brewer, *Party Ideology and Popular Politics*, pp. 253–57; and Dickinson, *Liberty and Property*, pp. 195–97.

9 For tory concerns that radicalism would dissolve a two-party system, see Southey, "On the Rise and Progress of Popular Disaffection," in *EMP* 2: 95–96.

10 The phrase is John Belchem's, in "Republicanism, Popular Constitutionalism and the Radical Platform in Early Nineteenth-Century England," *Social History* 6 (1981), 4. For the unprecedented domestic impact of the wars with France, particularly after 1803, see Clive Emsley, *British Society and the French Wars*, pp. 2–3, 115–16, and "The Social Impact of the French Wars," in *Britain and the French Revolution, 1789–1815*, ed. H. T. Dickinson (London: Macmillan, 1989), p. 211.

11 O'Gorman, *The Emergence of the British Two-Party System*, pp. 81, 83; compare John Derry, "Governing Temperament under Pitt and Liverpool," in *The Whig Ascendancy: Colloquies on Hanoverian England*, ed. John Cannon (London: Edward Arnold, 1981), pp. 143–44. For party consensus in the *Edinburgh* and *Quarterly Review*, see Marilyn Butler, *Romantics, Rebels, and Reactionaries* (Oxford University Press, 1981), p. 116.

12 Jon Klancher, *The Making of English Reading Audiences, 1790–1832* (Madison, Wisconsin: University of Wisconsin Press, 1987), p. 119.

13 Gareth Stedman Jones, *Languages of Class: Studies in English Working Class History, 1832–1982* (Cambridge University Press, 1983), p. 121. See also W. D. Rubinstein, "The End of 'Old Corruption' in Britain, 1780–1860," *Past and Present* 101 (1983), 55, 59–64; J. R. Dinwiddy, "The 'Influence of the Crown' in the Early Nineteenth Century: A Note on the Opposition Case," *Parliamentary History* 4 (1985), 189–92; and Iain McCalman, *Radical Underworld: Prophets, Revolutionaries and Pornographers in London, 1795–1840* (Cambridge University Press, 1988), p. 39.

14 Rubinstein, "End of 'Old Corruption' in Britain," p. 68.

15 Compare Hazlitt's desperate account of the "dungeon of Legitimacy" as "the very tomb of freedom," in *CWH*, 7: 10.

16 Rubinstein, "End of 'Old Corruption' in Britain," p. 71.

17 E. P. Thompson, *The Making of the English Working Class* (New York: Vintage Books, 1966), p. 770.

18 Compare the treatment of "radical" and "opposition" as "convertible terms" in the tory *John Bull*, no. 55 (1821), 436.

19 For an account of this campaign, see Thomas, "Radical Westminster," pp. 66–89.

20 *A Dialogue on the Approaching Trial of Mr. Carlile, for Publishing the Age of Reason* (London: T. J. Wooler, 1819); the text appeared in *WBG* 1 (1819), 121–23.

21 For the radical culture of public meetings and debating societies, see McCalman, *Radical Underworld*, pp. 113–51; James Epstein, *Radical*

Expression: Political Language, Ritual, and Symbol in England, 1790–1850 (New York: Oxford University Press, 1994), pp. 147–65; and David Worrall, *Radical Culture: Discourse, Resistance, and Surveillance, 1790–1820* (Detroit: Wayne State University Press, 1992), pp. 35–41, 89–96, 165–86.

22 *TT*, pp. 200, 203, 209, 222.

23 For the distinction between "respectable" and "unrespectable" or "rough" radicalism, see McCalman, *Radical Underworld*, pp. 26–49, 130–32, 181–203, and Nattrass, *William Cobbett*, pp. 27–29.

24 For radicalism and violence, see Thompson, *Making of the English Working Class*, pp. 624–25.

25 *BD* 2 (1818), 417.

26 See H. T. Dickinson, "Popular Conservatism and Militant Loyalism, 1789–1815," in *Britain and the French Revolution*, pp. 103–25; Linda Colley, "Whose Nation? Class and National Consciousness in Britain, 1750–1830," *Past and Present* 113 (1986), 109–10, 117; and Linda Colley, "The Apotheosis of George III: Loyalty, Royalty, and the British Nation, 1760–1820," *Past and Present* 102 (1984), 96–99, 111–29.

27 V. G. Kiernan, "Labour and the Literate in Nineteenth-Century Britain," in *Poets, Politics and the People* (London and New York: Verso, 1989), pp. 159–60.

28 François Furet, *Interpreting the French Revolution* (Cambridge University Press, 1981), p. 51.

29 See Furet, *Interpreting the French Revolution*, pp. 48–49.

30 Thomas Laqueur, "Toward a Cultural Ecology of Literacy in England, 1600–1850," in *Literacy in Historical Perspective*, ed. Daniel P. Resnick (Washington: Library of Congress, 1983), p. 44.

31 Michael Warner, *The Letters of the Republic: Publication and the Public Sphere in Eighteenth-Century America* (Cambridge, Massachusetts: Harvard University Press, 1990), pp. 5–9.

32 Lord Mansfield, quoted in Francis Ludlow Holt, *The Law of Libel* (London: W. Reed, 1812), p. 75.

33 For the use of the press by conservatives in this period, see Dickinson, "Popular Conservatism and Militant Loyalism," in *Britain and the French Revolution*, pp. 104–13; Colley, "Apotheosis of George III," p. 98; and J. A. W. Gunn, *Beyond Liberty and Property* (Montreal: McGill-Queen's University Press, 1983), pp. 301–06.

34 Brewer, *Party Ideology and Popular Politics*, p. 220. A related distinction between "direct" and "indirect" controls can be found in Fred S. Siebert, "The Authoritarian Theory of the Press," in *Four Theories of the Press*, ed. Fred S. Siebert, Theodore Peterson, and Wilbur Schramm (Urbana, Illinois: University of Illinois Press, 1956), pp. 19–27.

35 *OED*, 1971 edn, s.v. "estate." For a related use of the phrase in Hazlitt, see *CWH*, 11: 278–79.

36 George Boyce, "The Fourth Estate: The Reappraisal of a Concept," in *Newspaper History from the Seventeenth Century to the Present Day*, ed. George

Boyce, James Curran, and Pauline Wingate (London: Constable, 1978), pp. 20–21. For the low reputation of journalists, see Arthur Aspinall, "The Social Status of Journalists at the Beginning of the Nineteenth Century," *Review of English Studies* 21 (1945), 216–32.

37 See J. R. Pole, *Political Representation in England and the Origins of the American Republic* (London: Macmillan, 1960), pp. 402–04, 486–91; A. Aspinall, "The Reporting and Publishing of the House of Commons' Debates, 1771–1834," in *Essays Presented to Sir Lewis Namier*, ed. Richard Pares and A. J. P. Taylor (London: Macmillan, 1956), pp. 227–57; Fredrick Seaton Siebert, *Freedom of the Press in England, 1476–1776* (Urbana, Illinois: University of Illinois Press, 1965), pp. 202–18, 279–88, 346–63; and Dror Wahrman, "Virtual Representation: Parliamentary Reporting and the Languages of Class in the 1790s," *Past and Present*, no. 136 (1992), 86–91.

38 Wahrman, "Virtual Representation," p. 90.

39 See for example *BM* 8 (1821), 492, and *EMP*, 1: 12–13, 414. For the defense of corruption in this period, see J. R. Pole, *Political Representation in England and the Origins of the American Republic* (London: Macmillan, 1960), pp. 457–61, and J. A. W. Gunn, "Influence, Parties and the Constitution: Changing Attitudes, 1783–1832," *Historical Journal* 17 (1974), 306–11, 317–24.

40 *DPR* 1 (1819), 1–2. See Wahrman, "Virtual Representation," pp. 85–86, 108–11, for the argument that all parliamentary reporting in this period involved "*virtual representations*" that were "manipulated to serve the public's own concerns."

41 For the letters of parliamentary candidates, see Frank O'Gorman, *Voters, Patrons, and Parties: The Unreformed Electoral System of Hanoverian England, 1734–1832* (Oxford: Clarendon Press, 1989), p. 129.

42 *RB*, v, and *RB*, 4th edn, v.

43 For the "legislational attorney" scheme, see Thompson, *Making of the English Working Class*, pp. 682–83; Epstein, *Radical Expression*, pp. 66–67; T. M. Parssinen, "Association, Convention and Anti-Parliament in British Radical Politics, 1771–1848," *English Historical Review* 88 (1973), 516–17; and John Belchem, *"Orator" Hunt: Henry Hunt and English Working-Class Radicalism* (Oxford: Clarendon Press, 1985), pp. 101–02.

44 For the "mass platform," see Belchem, "Republicanism, Popular Constitutionalism and the Radical Platform," and *"Orator" Hunt*, pp. 3–7.

45 The phrase is from David Jones, quoted in Geoff Eley, "Re-Thinking the Political: Social History and Political Culture in 18th and 19th Century Britain," *Archiv für Sozialgeschichte* 21 (1981), 449. "Weak organization" had tactical advantages during periods of repression, since the press was a flexible yet open public forum. Carlile argued that a "system of Espionage" dictated "open and undisguised" communication: "Our several and united efforts are best to be made by communications with each other through the press" (*R* 1 [1819], 50–51). See Thompson, *Making of the English Working Class*, pp. 494–95, 498.

46 Brewer, *Party Ideology and Popular Politics*, pp. 15–17, 158–60.
47 Raymond Williams, "The Press and Popular Culture: An Historical Perspective," in *Newspaper History*, eds. George Boyce *et al.*, p. 47.
48 For the national circulation of the early nineteenth-century radical press, see James Curran, "Press History," in James Curran and Jane Seaton, *Power without Responsibility: The Press and Broadcasting in Britain* (London: Methuen, 1985), p. 21; for the role of the press in nationalizing politics over the course of the eighteenth century, see O'Gorman, *Voters, Patrons, and Parties*, pp. 285–89.
49 "New Series of the Black Dwarf," *BD* 11 (1823), n. pag.
50 See *BD* 1 (1817), 39–43, 99–100; *BD* 2 (1818), 241; *R* 2 (1820), 193–95; *R* 11 (1825), 737–38, 749; and *CPR* 36 (1820), 81–152.
51 Catherine Gallagher, *The Industrial Reformation of English Fiction* (University of Chicago Press, 1985), p. 222.
52 Radical theories of language have recently received a good deal of attention, most of it focused on the "Revolution Controversy." See Olivia Smith, *The Politics of Language, 1791–1819* (Oxford: Clarendon Press, 1984); Tom Furniss, "Rhetoric and Revolution: The Role of Language in Paine's Critique of Burke," in *Revolution and English Romanticism: Politics and Rhetoric*, ed. Keith Hanley and Raman Selden (New York: St. Martin's Press, 1990), pp. 23–48; Tom Furniss, *Edmund Burke's Aesthetic Ideology: Language, Gender, and Political Economy in Revolution* (Cambridge University Press, 1993); Stephen Prickett, "Radicalism and Linguistic Theory: Horne Tooke on Samuel Pegge," *Yearbook of English Studies* 19 (1989), 1–17; and John Turner, "Burke, Paine, and the Nature of Language," *Yearbook of English Studies* 19 (1989), 36–53.
53 Henry Hunt, *The Green Bag Plot* (London: T. Davison, 1819), p. 5.
54 Pierre Bourdieu, "The Corporatism of the Universal: The Role of Intellectuals in the Modern World," *Telos* 81 (1989), 101. Compare Daniel Cottam, *Social Figures: George Eliot, Social History, and Literary Representation* (Minneapolis: University of Minnesota Press, 1987), p. 22, on the "framework of opposition and alliance" that guided liberal intellectuals.
55 For independence in the history of the press, see Boyce, "Fourth Estate," pp. 19–23; Ian Christie, "British Newspapers in the Later Georgian Age," in *Myth and Reality in Late-Eighteenth Century British Politics* (Berkeley: University of California Press, 1970), pp. 328–30; and Alan Liu, *Wordsworth: The Sense of History* (Stanford University Press, 1989), pp. 413–16. For independence in parliamentary politics, see O'Gorman, *Voters, Patrons, and Parties*, pp. 259–85, 300–303, and D. E. D. Beales, "Parliamentary Parties and the 'Independent' Member, 1810–1860," in *Ideas and Institutions of Victorian Britain: Essays in Honour of George Kitson Clark*, ed. Robert Robson (London: G. Bell and Sons, 1967), pp. 1–19.
56 For the political history of property, see J. G. A. Pocock, *Virtue, Commerce, and History* (Cambridge University Press, 1985), pp. 48–50, 103–23; J. G. A. Pocock, *The Machiavellian Moment: Florentine Political Thought and the Atlantic*

Republican Tradition (Princeton University Press, 1975), pp. 406–09, 462–67, 486–87; Dickinson, *Liberty and Property*, pp. 279–85, 310–12; and John Phillip Reid, *The Concept of Representation in the Age of the American Revolution* (University of Chicago Press, 1987), pp. 31–42.

57 Eley, "Re-Thinking the Political," p. 442.

58 For Locke's role in English radicalism in this period, see Jones, *Languages of Class*, p. 138, n. 116.

59 For Cobbett's theory of property, see Malcolm Chase, *"The People's Farm": English Radical Agrarianism, 1775–1840* (Oxford: Clarendon Press, 1988), pp. 181–83.

60 John Brewer, "English Radicalism in the Age of George III," in *Three British Revolutions: 1641, 1688, 1776*, ed. J. G. A. Pocock (Princeton University Press, 1980), p. 345.

61 See Pocock, *Machiavellian Moment*, pp. 464–66, and Pocock, *Virtue, Commerce, and History*, pp. 103–04, 108–12.

62 Warner, *Letters of the Republic*, pp. 42–49; compare Cottam, *Social Figures*, pp. 6–10.

63 For the politics of personality in Britain, see *Politics and Personality, 1760–1827*, ed. M. J. Barnes (Edinburgh: Oliver and Boyd, 1967); James Vernon, *Politics and the People: A Study in English Political Culture, c. 1815–1867* (Cambridge University Press, 1993), pp. 251–91; Thomas W. Laqueur, "The Queen Caroline Affair: Politics as Art in the Reign of George IV," *Journal of Modern History* 54 (1982), 455–57; and Colley, "Whose Nation?," p. 105. For an astute discussion of autobiography as a polemical strategy in Cobbett's prose, see Nattrass, *William Cobbett*, pp. 90–96, 119–32, 201–04.

64 Carlile elsewhere endorsed anonymity, in a critical discussion of the American republic (*R* 8 [1823], 14). For Carlile on anonymity, see Epstein, *Radical Expression*, p. 118; for an important discussion of related issues of anonymity and "impersonation" in *Blackwood's*, see Peter T. Murphy, "Impersonation and Authorship in Romantic Britain," *ELH* 59 (1992), 625–49.

65 See Anne Janowitz's argument that we should learn to read literary forms for "conflicts of *intervention* rather than of *representation*," in "Class and Literature: The Case of Romantic Chartism," in *Rethinking Class: Literary Studies and Social Formations*, ed. Wai Chee Dimock and Michael Gilmore (New York: Columbia University Press, 1994), p. 241.

66 Hazlitt posed the same contradiction in the form of a literary common-place: "I am proud to the point of equality – every thing above or below *that* appears to me arrant impertinence or abject meanness" (*CWH* 20: 123).

67 David Vincent, *Literacy and Popular Culture: England, 1750–1914* (Cambridge University Press, 1989), pp. 243–44. For a good discussion of the vernacular rhythms of Cobbett's prose, see Nattrass, *William Cobbett*, pp. 135–56.

68 Craig Calhoun, *The Question of Class Struggle: Social Foundations of Popular Radicalism during the Industrial Revolution* (University of Chicago Press, 1982), pp. 101–02.

69 *G*, no. 9 (1818), 69, and *The Triumphal Entry of Henry Hunt, Esq. into London* (London: Hay and Turner, [1819]), p. 3.

70 Calhoun, *Question of Class Struggle*, p. 101.

71 Constitutional Association for Opposing the Progress of Disloyal and Seditious Principles, "Address," reprinted in Richard Mence, *The Law of Libel*, 2 vols. (London: W. Pople, 1824), 1: 188. Compare Southey in *EMP*, 1: 125–30, 135, 415–20.

72 See also *BD* 3 (1819), 703, and *HR* 2 (1817), 256, 287–88.

73 Donald Thomas, *A Long Time Burning: The History of Literary Censorship in England* (New York: Frederick A. Praeger, 1969), p. 146.

74 Thomas, *Long Time Burning*, p. 147. For versions of Ellenborough's statement, see *CPR* 5 (1804), 854, and "Trial of William Cobbett," in volume 29 (1804–1806) of *A Complete Collection of State Trials*, ed. Thomas Jones Howell (London: T. C. Hansard, 1821), p. 49.

75 See Thompson, *Making of the English Working Class*, p. 604.

76 See *YD*, no. 3 (1818), 19; *BD* 1 (1817), 135, 250; John George, *A Treatise on the Offence of Libel* (London: Taylor and Hessey, 1812), p. 287; Holt, *The Law of Libel*, pp. 118–20; *The Prince of Wales v. the Examiner. A Full Report of the Trial of John and Leigh Hunt* (London: John Hunt, [1813]), pp. 25–28; *VR*, pp. 39–42, 80; and James Mill, "Liberty of the Press," in *Essays on Government, Jurisprudence, Liberty of the Press, and Law of Nations* (New York: Augustus M. Kelley, 1967), pp. 21–22.

77 Compare *Mr. Cobbett's Taking Leave of His Countrymen* (London: W. Molineux, 1817), pp. 9–10.

78 See Epstein, *Radical Expression*, pp. 43–46.

79 For anti-professionalism in the *Political Register*, see *CPR* 13 (1808), 518; *CPR* 22 (1812), 8–9; and *CPR* 28 (1815), 398.

80 Klancher, *Making of English Reading Audiences*, p. 48.

81 Richard Carlile, *The Life of Thomas Paine* (London: M. A. Carlile, 1820), p. xvi. This is not to say that the production of radical discourse was free of the hierarchies found elsewhere in the public sphere; see McCalman, *Radical Underworld*, pp. 153–62, for a brilliant reconstruction of the complex and often perilous relations of patronage and clientage in a plebeian "republic of letters."

82 For merit and talent in the dissenting tradition, see Isaac Kramnick, "Religion and Radicalism: English Political Theory in the Age of Revolution," *Political Theory* 5 (1977), 515–20. For professionalism and the professional classes in the nineteenth century, see Harold Perkin, *The Origins of Modern English Society* (London: Routledge, 1969), pp. 252–70, 319–26.

83 Anti-aristocratic appeals to merit and talent can be found in *CL* 1 (1819), 89–90, and *R* 10 (1824), 289–302.

84 For a skeptical account of radical respectability, see Trygve R. Tholfsen, "The Intellectual Origins of Mid-Victorian Stability," *Political Science Quarterly* 86 (1971), 57–91.

85 G. A. Cranfield, *The Press and Society, From Caxton to Northcliffe* (London: Longman, 1978), p. 84. See also Christie, "British Newspapers in the Later Georgian Age," pp. 319–21, 328–29; Leonore O'Boyle, "The Image of the Journalist in France, Germany, and England, 1815–1848," *Comparative Studies in Society and History* 10 (1968), 313–14; and Ivon Asquith, "The Structure, Ownership and Control of the Press, 1780–1855," in *Newspaper History*, pp. 108–11.

86 For radical distrust of advertising, see Marcus Wood, *Radical Satire and Print Culture, 1790–1822* (Oxford: Clarendon Press, 1994), pp. 159–61.

87 See his "Capitalism and Control of the Press," pp. 195–98, 208; "The Press as an Agency of Social Control: An Historical Perspective," in *Newspaper History*, pp. 51–53; "Communications, Power and Social Order," in *Culture, Society and the Media*, ed. Michael Gurevitch, Tony Bennett, James Curran, and Janet Woollacott (London: Methuen, 1982), pp. 223–24; and "Press History," in James Curran and Jane Seaton, *Power without Responsibility: The Press and Broadcasting in Britain* (London: Methuen, 1985), pp. 7–9, 11–12, 20–21.

88 Curran, "Press History," p. 16; see also Raymond Williams, "The Press and Popular Culture," pp. 46–47.

89 Raymond Williams, "The Writer: Commitment and Alignment," in *Resources of Hope: Culture, Democracy, Socialism*, ed. Robin Gable (London: Verso, 1989), p. 82.

90 "Trial of Jeremiah Brandreth," in volume 32 (1817) of *A Complete Collection of State Trials*, ed. Thomas Jones Howell (London: Longman, 1824), p. 875; Constitutional Association, "Address," in Mence, *Law of Libel*, 1: 194; and *QR* 22 (1820), 554. See also *BM* 4 (1818–1819), 355, and Southey, *EMP*, 2: 85.

91 See Epstein, *Radical Expression*, p. 203, n. 50.

92 The "Joint Stock Book Company" was a costly failure for Carlile; see Joel Wiener, *Radicalism and Freethought in Nineteenth-Century Britain: The Life of Richard Carlile* (Westport, Connecticut: Greenwood Press, 1983), p. 123.

93 Edmund Burke, *Reflections on the Revolution in France*, ed. J. G. A. Pocock (Indianapolis: Hackett Publishing Company, 1987), pp. 96–99.

94 For the politics of mobility, see Pocock, *Virtue, Commerce, and History*, pp. 107–23, 261–62. For Cobbett's financial embarrasments, see George Spater, *William Cobbett: The Poor Man's Friend*, 2 vols. (Cambridge University Press, 1982), 1: 168–74, 2: 358, 398, 519–21, and for similar difficulties among other radical leaders, see Thompson, *Making of the English Working Class*, p. 626.

95 See the title page of *BD* 1 (1817), and *E*, no. 46 (November 13, 1808), 721.

96 See Thompson, *Making of the English Working Class*, pp. 608–10, and Naomi Miller, "John Cartwright and Radical Parliamentary Reform, 1808–1819," *English Historical Review* 83 (1968), 719–21.

97 *PD* 41 (1819–1820), 390; compare Liverpool's remarks to Grenville, quoted in Belchem, *"Orator" Hunt*, p. 118.

98 For the relevant text of the Bill, see *PD* 41 (1819–20), 1655–60.

 99 *Works of Lord Bolingbroke*, 2: 369–70.
100 *R* 7 (1823), 179; see also 278, 301.
101 Bourdieu, "Corporatism of the Universal," p. 101.
102 V. G. Kiernan, "Patterns of Protest in English History," in *Poets, Politics, and the People* (London: Verso, 1989), p. 28.
103 For the radical boycott, see Iorwerth Prothero, "William Benbow and the Concept of the 'General Strike,'" *Past and Present* 63 (1974), 153–54.
104 For a more explicit version of this common radical pun, see Wooler's article, "Virtual Acquittal of Mr. Hunt and his Associates," in *WBG* 2 (1820), 105.
105 Liu, *Wordsworth*, p. 411. Compare Walter Ong, "The Barbarian Within: Outsiders Inside Society Today," in *The Barbarian Within and Other Fugitive Essays and Studies* (New York: Macmillan, 1962), p. 283.
106 For the Great Northern Union, see Belchem, *"Orator" Hunt*, pp. 143–57.
107 For Carlile's similar concerns about satire as a political mode, see *R* 4 (1820), 615; *R* 6 (1822), 432; and Epstein, *Radical Expression*, p. 117.
108 See *R* 1 (1819), 1; *R* 4 (1820), 181–91; *R* 7 (1823), 1; *R* 9 (1824), iii; and *R* 11 (1825), 327–29. For Carlile's "deistic sectarianism," see McCalman, *Radical Underworld*, pp. 187–89, and Epstein, *Radical Expression*, pp. 100–46.
109 Thompson, *Making of the English Working Class*, pp. 80, 88.
110 Belchem, "Republicanism, Popular Constitutionalism and the Radical Platform," p. 9; Belchem, "Radical Language and Ideology in Early Nineteenth-Century England: The Challenge of the Platform," *Albion* 20 (1988), 256; and Epstein, *Radical Expression*, pp. 76–77. See also Jonathan Fulcher, "Contests over Constitutionalism: The Faltering of Reform in England, 1816–1824" (Ph.D. dissertation, University of Cambridge, 1992). For a more critical account of the limitations of a challenge in traditional languages, see Eley, "Re-Thinking the Political," p. 438, and Curran, "Press as an Agency of Social Control," p. 65.
111 Holt, *Law of Libel*, pp. 76–78. See *VR*, p. 87, for the invocation of Holt in court.
112 J. G. A. Pocock, "Radical Criticisms of the Whig Order in the Age Between the Revolutions," in *Origins of Anglo-American Radicalism*, ed. Margaret Jacob and James Jacob (London: George Allen and Unwin, 1984), p. 51. For Paine and Bentham as discursive breaks, see Christopher Hill, "The Norman Yoke," in *Puritanism and Revolution* (New York: Schocken Books, 1964), p. 102; Thompson, *Making of the English Working Class*, pp. 84, 86–7, 168–69; and Pocock, *Virtue, Commerce, and History*, pp. 276–77. For popular radicalism as a mixed discourse, see Jones, *Languages of Class*, pp. 125–26; Epstein, *Radical Expression*, pp. 75–77; Belchem, *"Orator" Hunt*, p. 87; Mark Philp, "The Fragmented Ideology of Reform," in *The French Revolution and British Popular Politics*, ed. Mark Philp (Cambridge University Press, 1991), pp. 74–76; and Jon Mee, *Dangerous Enthusiasm: William Blake and the Culture of Radicalism in the 1790s* (Oxford: Clarendon Press, 1992), pp. 1–19.
113 Epstein, *Radical Expression*, p. 10.

114 *R* 7 (1823), 179–80, 277–78. For radical toasting, see Epstein, *Radical Expression*, pp. 147–65, and James Vernon, *Politics and the People: A Study in English Political Culture, c. 1815–1867* (Cambridge University Press, 1993), pp. 306–07.

115 Title page, *BD* 1 (1817).

116 See also *CWH*, 7: 260–61.

117 Foord, *His Majesty's Opposition*, p. 150; see also Brewer, *Party Ideology*, p. 66.

118 J. E. Cookson, "Political Arithmetic and War in Britain, 1793–1815," *War and Society* 1 (1983), 37–42, 53.

119 Noel Thompson, *The People's Science: The Popular Political Economy of Exploitation and Crisis, 1816–34* (Cambridge University Press, 1984), pp. 191–93, 217.

120 *CPR* 21 (1812), 168; *WBG* 3 (1821), 33; *CWH*, 7: 108, 264. Carlile extended the figure from mathematics to chemistry: "The political hemisphere increases its lower: the gases of misery and oppression are dangerously predominant in its atmosphere; and unless the electric fluid be carefully separated, and withdrawn by some skilful conductor, an explosion becomes inevitable" (*R* 3 [1820], 145). For the contest between capitalist expansion and a radical closed system as a "zero-sum game," see Calhoun, *Question of Class Struggle*, p. 97.

121 For corruption as exploitative mediation, see Pocock, *Virtue, Commerce, and History*, pp. 121–22.

2 RADICAL PRINT CULTURE IN PERIODICAL FORM

1 *CPR* 31 (1816), 613.

2 *PD* 41 (1819–20), 344.

3 For Cobbett on political clubs, see E. P. Thompson, *The Making of the English Working Class* (New York: Vintage Books, 1966), p. 638.

4 Thompson, *Making of the English Working Class*, p. 720.

5 Jürgen Habermas, *The Structural Transformation of the Public Sphere: An Inquiry into a Category of Bourgeois Society* (Cambridge, Massachusetts: MIT Press, 1989), pp. 183–84.

6 Thompson, *Making of the English Working Class*, pp. 467, 603.

7 Constitutional Association for Opposing the Progress of Disloyal and Seditious Principles, "Address," reprinted in Richard Mence, *The Law of Libel*, 2 vols. (London: W. Pope, 1824), 1: 186–88.

8 James Vernon, *Politics and the People: A Study in English Political Culture, c. 1815–1867* (Cambridge University Press, 1993), pp. 105–06, 131, 142–43, 147. For speech as a more threatening form of communication, see Iain McCalman, *Radical Underworld: Prophets, Revolutionaries and Pornographers in London, 1795–1840* (Cambridge University Press, 1988), p. 152, and David Worrall, *Radical Culture: Discourse, Resistance, and Surveillance, 1790–1820* (Detroit: Wayne State University Press, 1992), pp. 19, 77–78, 89.

9 *CPR* 22 (1812), 110, and *R* 8 (1822), 352.

10 Thomas Laqueur, "Toward a Cultural Ecology of Literacy in England, 1600–1850," in *Literacy in Historical Perspective*, ed. Daniel P. Resnick (Washington: Library of Congress, 1983), p. 44.

11 "The Loyal Man in the Moon," in *Radical Squibs and Loyal Ripostes: Satirical Pamphlets of the Regency Period, 1819–1821* (Bath, Somerset: Adams and Dart, 1971), p. 132.

12 Michael Warner, *The Letters of the Republic: Publication and the Public Sphere in Eighteenth-Century America* (Cambridge, Massachusetts: Harvard University Press, 1990), pp. 73–74.

13 William Hone, *The Political Showman – at Home!*, in *Facetiae and Miscellanies* (London: William Hone, 1827), n. pag. For the anthropomorphic press in Cruikshank's work, see Robert L. Patten, *George Cruikshank's Life, Times, and Art, Volume One: 1792–1835* (New Brunswick, New Jersey: Rutgers University Press, 1992), pp. 162, and 444, n. 34. For something more like Franklin's epitaph, see Leigh Hunt, "The Critic's Farewell to His Readers," reprinted in *Prefaces by Leigh Hunt, Mainly to His Periodicals*, ed. R. Brimley Johnson (Port Washington, New York: Kennikat Press, 1967), p. 25.

14 This image appears towards the end of *The Political Showman – at Home* as the "EYE" of the Showman, and then represents "PUBLICATION" in *The Queen's Matrimonial Ladder.*

15 See *The Prince of Wales v. The Examiner* (London: John Hunt, [1813]), pp. 10–11.

16 *Mr. Cobbett's Taking Leave of His Countrymen* (London: W. Molineux, 1817), p. 25.

17 Iorwerth Prothero, *Artisans and Politics in Early Nineteenth-Century London: John Gast and His Times* (Baton Rouge, Louisiana: Louisiana State University Press, 1979), p. 94.

18 *Trial of Thos. Jonathan Wooller [sic], Publisher of a Paper called the Black Dwarf, for two libels against the government generally, and against Mr. Canning and Lord Castlereagh* (Glasgow: E. Miller, 1817), pp. 6–7. Versions of the remark can also be found in *VR*, p. 17, and *A Correct Report of the Trials of Thomas Jonathan Wooler* (London: W. N. Jones, 1817), p. 35. I have not found contemporary evidence of this method of composition, but it is confirmed in the notice of Wooler's death in the *Gentlemen's Magazine* 40 (1853), 647–48, and in *Notes and Queries*, 3rd Series, 8 (1865), 359. The *DNB* entry for Wooler picks up the *Gentleman's Magazine* suggestion that Wooler was acquitted on the grounds that he set the offensive material in type, but never actually wrote it. Contemporary accounts of the trial do not support this claim, and it fails, in any case, to accord with a law of libel, which targeted publication rather than authorship.

19 *Correct Report of the Trials of Thomas Jonathan Wooler*, p. 35.

20 William Wickwar, *The Struggle for the Freedom of the Press, 1819–1832* (London: George Allen and Unwin, 1928), pp. 51–52.

21 See *CPR* 31 (1816), 520, 737, and Arthur Aspinall, *Politics and the Press, c. 1780–1850* (London: Home and Van Thal, 1949), p. 57.

22 The story of the phenomenal impact of the cheap *Register* has been told many times, usually following Cobbett's own detailed account in the *Register*. See George Spater, *William Cobbett: The Poor Man's Friend*, 2 vols. (Cambridge University Press, 1982), 2: 347–49; G. D. H. Cole, *The Life of William Cobbett* (London: Home and Van Thal, 1947), pp. 206–10; Richard Altick, *The English Common Reader: A Social History of the Mass Reading Public, 1800–1900* (University of Chicago Press, 1957), pp. 324–28; G. A. Cranfield, *The Press and Society, From Caxton to Northcliffe* (London: Longman, 1978), pp. 92–108; Joel H. Wiener, *The War of the Unstamped: The Movement to Repeal the British Newspaper Tax, 1830–1836* (Ithaca: Cornell University Press, 1969), pp. 3–6; Aspinall, *Politics and the Press*, pp. 29–32, 57–60; and Wickwar, *Struggle for the Freedom of the Press*, pp. 49–55.

23 See *SPR* 1 (1817), 326, and *SPR* 2 (1817–1818), 4, 106. Serial portions of the *Rights of Man* have been removed from the British Library copy of Sherwin's *Register*, but they can be found intact, separately paginated, in the Nuffield Library copy.

24 *Anti-Cobbett* 1 (1817), 95–96.

25 Cranfield, *Press and Society*, pp. 90–91.

26 See Wickwar, *Struggle for the Freedom of the Press*, p. 51.

27 See R. K. Webb, *The British Working Class Reader* (London: George Allen and Unwin, 1955), pp. 49–50. Cobbett's account confirms Marcus Wood's suggestion, in *Radical Satire and Print Culture, 1790–1822* (Oxford: Clarendon Press, 1994), p. 57, that "radical propaganda in this period was shaped by loyalist forms of publication."

28 The policy came with two conditions – reprints must contain "the *whole* of any article," and "retain both *date and the name*" – meant to frustrate Cobbett's enemies, who often reprinted extracts from his early loyalist writings in order to discredit him and confuse his readers. By January 1817, the persistence of this practice forced him to secure the copyright and rescind his offer of unlimited republication. See *CPR* 31 (1816), 520, 523, and *CPR* 32 (1817), 33, 65.

29 For the origin of the phrase, see Spater, *William Cobbett*, 2: 348, and n. 115; see also Cobbett's later *Two-Penny Trash* 1 (1830), 5.

30 Thompson, *Making of the English Working Class*, pp. 459, 466. For the re-emergence of Painite rationalism in Carlile's "Zetetic Culture" of the 1820s, see James Epstein, *Radical Expression: Political Language, Ritual, and Symbol in England* (New York: Oxford University Press, 1994), pp. 100–01.

31 Mark Philp, "The Fragmented Ideology of Reform," in *The French Revolution and British Popular Politics*, ed. Mark Philp (Cambridge University Press, 1991), pp. 56, 58–59, 66.

32 See Wood, *Radical Satire and Print Culture*, pp. 88–89; Wood compares the periodicals of the 1790s with the "Black Neb" feature of the *Black Dwarf*, in which Wooler indiscriminately gathered political extracts from earlier writers.

33 See Mary Thale's Preface to *Selections from the Papers of the London*

Corresponding Society, 1792–1799, ed. Mary Thale (Cambridge University Press, 1983), p. xviii.

34 For publications like *The Correspondence of the London Corresponding Society*, see Thale, *Papers of the London Corresponding Society*, p. viii.

35 For the later Chartist use of the newspaper as a way around the Corresponding Societies Act of 1799, see Eileen Yeo, "Some Practices and Problems of Chartist Democracy," in *The Chartist Experience: Studies in Working-Class Radicalism and Culture, 1830–1860*, ed. James Epstein and Dorothy Thompson (London: Macmillan, 1982), pp. 360–62.

36 Epstein, *Radical Expression*, p. 101.

37 Carlile came to prefer atheism and materialism to the deism of his master. He rejected as "sheer nonsense" not only the Koran and the Old Testament and New Testament, but also Paine's injunction to "read the Book of Nature" for "the full proof of a religion revealed by God" (*R* 8 [1823], 133).

38 See Wiener, *War of the Unstamped*, p. 5.

39 Thompson, *Making of the English Working Class*, p. 674.

40 Carlile traced his work to this kind of improvisation: "The starting of 'The Republican' was the work of a moment" (*R* 11 [1825], 103).

41 Compare Worrall, *Radical Culture*, p. 12, on the way an earlier generation of Spenceans sought "to occupy representational niches which circumvented the law or stayed one step ahead of it."

42 Title page, *BD* 1 (1817).

43 *LA*, no. 1 (1819), 1; *WH* 1 (1819), 1; and *B*, no. 1 (1819), 2. See also *Gracchus*, no. 1 (1818), 1; *RR*, 1 (1819), 1; and *DR*, no. 1 (1819), 1.

44 For Carlile's epic legal struggles, see Wickwar, *The Struggle for the Freedom of the Press*, pp. 67–75, 82–102, 124–28, 205–45, and Joel Wiener, *Radicalism and Freethought in Nineteenth-Century Britain: The Life of Richard Carlile* (Westport, Connecticut: Greenwood Press, 1988), pp. 33–100.

45 Carlile's bizarre stratagem for protecting his shopkeepers from identification and arrest seemed a ritual performance of the temporal structure of periodical production and distribution: "In the new Temple of Reason my publications are sold by CLOCK WORK!! In the shop is the dial on which is written every publication for sale: the purchaser enters and turns the hand of the dial to the publication he wants, when, on depositing his money, the publication drops down before him" (*R* 5 [1822], 481–82).

46 Warner, *Letters of the Republic*, pp. 65–66. For regular appearance in newspaper form, see Jeremy Popkin, *News and Politics in the Age of Revolution* (Ithaca: Cornell University Press, 1989), pp. 6–7.

47 Popkin, *News and Politics*, p. 7. See also Lennard Davis, *Factual Fictions: The Origins of the English Novel* (New York: Columbia University Press, 1983), pp. 73–74.

48 Warner, *Letters of the Republic*, p. 65.

49 "Postscript for the Year 1810," *E* (1810), n. pag.

50 See for example Hone's two-penny, single-sheet accounts of "The Meeting

in Spa Fields" and "The Riots in London" (London: William Hone, [1816]).

51 See Wickwar, *Struggle for the Freedom of the Press*, p. 212. Carlile seems to have discovered his ideal of timely and flexible production in the work of Paine; see his *Life of Thomas Paine* (London: M. A. Carlile, 1820), pp. viii, xi.

52 For regular readership and periodical production, see Margaret Beetham, "Towards a Theory of the Periodical as a Publishing Genre," in *Investigating Victorian Journalism*, ed. Laurel Brake, Aled Jones, and Lionel Madden (New York: St. Martin's Press, 1990), p. 28. For radical readership as organization, see Thompson, *Making of the English Working Class*, p. 494; Raymond Williams, *Cobbett* (Oxford University Press, 1963), p. 16; and Geoff Eley, "Re-Thinking the Political: Social History and Political Culture in 18th and 19th Century Britain," *Archiv für Sozialgeschichte* 21 (1981), 449.

53 See also *PD* 41 (1819–1820), 460–61, 1591.

54 For a more recent account of the ideological effects of regular newspaper consumption, see Richard Terdiman, *Discourse / Counter-Discourse: The Theory and Practice of Symbolic Resistance in Nineteenth-Century France* (Ithaca: Cornell University Press, 1985), pp. 117–35.

55 Cranfield, *Press and Society*, pp. 141–42; see also Patricia Hollis, *The Pauper Press: A Study in Working-Class Radicalism of the 1830s* (Oxford University Press, 1970), pp. 136–40.

56 *PD* 41 (1819–1820), 539–42, 1538–41, 1546.

57 For the central role of the daily newspaper, see Stephen Koss, *The Rise and Fall of the Political Press in Britain, Volume One: The Nineteenth Century* (London: Hamish Hamilton, 1981), p. 49. For a radical response to parliamentary claims about the respectable daily press, see *BB*, pp. 333–35.

58 Terdiman, *Discourse / Counter-Discourse*, p. 121.

59 When Cobbett tried to revive the defunct *Evening Post* in 1821 and 1822, he once again sought to track a dense political scene; see *CPR* 40 (1821), 1533–36, 1598–1600, and *CPR* 41 (1822), 635–38.

60 Jeremy Black, "The Eighteenth Century British Press," in *Encyclopedia of the British Press*, ed. Dennis Griffiths (London: Macmillan, 1992), p. 15.

61 Wood, *Radical Satire and Print Culture*, p. 187.

62 For the shifting commercial conditions of the newspaper press in the late eighteenth and early nineteenth centuries, see Black, "The Eighteenth Century British Press," pp. 13–15; Ian Christie, "British Newspapers in the Later Georgian Age," in *Myth and Reality in Late-Eighteenth Century British Politics* (Berkeley: University of California Press, 1970), pp. 319–23; Raymond Williams, "The Press and Popular Culture: An Historical Perspective," in *Newspaper History from the Seventeenth Century to the Present Day*, ed. George Boyce, James Curran, and Pauline Wingate (London: Constable, 1978), pp. 46–48; Ivon Asquith, "The Structure, Ownership and Control of the Press, 1780–1855," in *Newspaper History*, pp. 108–11; James Curran, "Press History," in James Curran and Jane Seaton, *Power without Responsibility: The Press and Broadcasting in Britain* (London: Methuen,

1985), pp. 7–9, 11–12; James Curran, "Capitalism and Control of the Press, 1800–1975," in *Mass Communication and Society*, ed. James Curran, Michael Gurevitch, and Janet Woollacott (London: Edward Arnold, 1977), pp. 206–11; and Lenore O'Boyle, "The Image of the Journalist in France, Germany, and England, 1815–1848," *Comparative Studies in Society and History* 10 (1968), 313–16.

63 In *Victorian News and Newspapers* (Oxford: Clarendon Press, 1985), p. 16, Lucy Brown has estimated that by the Victorian period a newspaper was financially secure if half of its space was devoted to advertising.

64 Cranfield, *Press and Society*, p. 109.

65 For Carlile's imprisonment, see Wiener, *Radicalism and Freethought*, pp. 65–68.

66 My argument here qualifies the sweeping judgment of Hollis, in *The Pauper Press*, pp. 99–100, that Carlile's writings "were almost independent of time, place, and politics"; this was more true after the Queen Caroline affair, but until then he shared the radical sense of imminent crisis.

67 Popkin, *News and Politics*, p. xi.

68 *The British Parliament* (London: Thomas Dolby, 1819), p. 1.

69 *DPR* 1 (1819), 17, 80, 191, 1058.

70 *R* 4 (1820), 615.

71 Terdiman, *Discourse / Counter-Discourse*, pp. 117–18, 122.

72 See Stanley Morison, *The English Newspaper* (Cambridge University Press, 1932), pp. 184–85.

73 Terdiman, *Discourse / Counter-Discourse*, pp. 120, 127.

74 In *News and Politics in the Age of Revolution*, p. 100, Jeremy Popkin observes that, while "authors of books in the eighteenth century could afford to remain relatively ignorant of the mechanics of printing," journalists "were continually reminded of the constraints technology imposed."

75 Jerome McGann, *"Don Juan" in Context* (University of Chicago Press, 1976), pp. 103, 107–09, 115–17.

76 Morison, *English Newspaper*, pp. 185, 206; see also Wood, *Radical Satire and Print Culture*, pp. 186–87.

77 For the production of the magazine, see Wiener, *Radicalism and Freethought*, pp. 91–92.

78 Benedict Anderson, *Imagined Communities: Reflections on the Origin and Spread of Nationalism* (London: Verso, 1983), p. 37.

79 Anderson, *Imagined Communities*, p. 31. For a related temporal distinction, see Simon During, "Lines of Communication: Some Notes on the Relation between Periodical Writing and Modernity," in *Outside the Book: Contemporary Essays on Literary Periodicals*, ed. David Carter (Sydney: Local Consumption Publications, 1991), p. 34.

80 *R* 3 (1820), 546, 547, 560, 591; *R* 4 (1820), 111; *BD* 1 (1817), 24; *BD* 2 (1818), 33; *CPR* 32 (1817), 1–2; *CPR* 38 (1821), 426; *CPR* 40 (1821), 588–89; *CL* 1 (1819), 180; and *WH* 1 (1819), 133.

81 For the provision in the Newspaper Stamp Duties Act requiring the appearance of the date, see *PD* 41 (1819–1820), 1679–82.

82 *R* 6 (1822), 605, 737, 751, 769, 772, 801, and *R* 7 (1823), 225, 251, 321.
    Compare Henry Hunt's *To the Radical Reformers, Male and Female, of England,*
    Scotland, and Ireland (London: T. Dolby, 1820–1822), a series of public letters
    dated from the "year of the MANCHESTER MASSACRE, without retribution or
    inquiry."

83 James Epstein, *Radical Expression*, pp. 119–23.

84 See Wiener, *Radicalism and Freethought*, pp. 82–86.

85 See *BD* 1 (1817), 225–26, 240. For the prison as school in radical culture, see
    McCalman, *Radical Underworld*, p. 191; Epstein, *Radical Expression*,
    pp. 129–30; and Wiener, *Radicalism and Freethought*, pp. 61–65. For the law
    requiring formal identification of the printer and publisher, see Wickwar,
    Struggle for the Freedom of the Press, pp. 30–31.

86 For newspaper parody, see Marcus Wood, *Radical Satire and Print Culture*,
    pp. 186–214. For Wooler as satirist, see Craig Calhoun, *The Question of Class*
    Struggle: The Social Foundations of Popular Radicalism during the Industrial
    Revolution (University of Chicago Press, 1982), p. 113; Richard Hendrix,
    "Popular Humor and 'The Black Dwarf,'" *Journal of British Studies* 16
    (1976), 109–28; Jon Klancher, *The Making of English Reading Audiences,*
    1790–1832 (Madison, Wisconsin: The University of Wisconsin Press, 1987),
    pp. 113–19; and Steven Jones, "*The Black Dwarf* and Satiric Performance; or
    The Instabilities of the 'Public Square,'" paper delivered at the 1995
    conference of the North American Society for the Study of Romanticism.
    Klancher is especially good on the diversity of radical modes, contrasting
    "Wooler's extravagant language" with the "opposite" and "deliberately
    muted" style of Wade's *Gorgon*. Though tempting, it would be a mistake to
    treat popular radical discourse as uniformly festive and destabilizing, since
    the fear of corrupt power often carried with it a desire for rhetorical stabil-
    ity that dictated against irony and satire.

87 *BD* 1 (1817), 109–12, 703–7, 735–36.

88 *BD* 1 (1817), 416; *BD* 2 (1818), 93; and *BD* 3 (1819), 287. A similar pattern of
    satirical resentment can be found in Carlile's habit of dedicating successive
    volumes of the *Republican* to those responsible for damaging fines and
    confiscations, rather than to wealthy patrons.

89 Cranfield, *Press and Society*, p. 84.

90 See *CPR* 39 (1821), 130–44, 213–16, 358–60. In the following year Cobbett
    introduced a regular list of market prices, but insisted that it serve his bias
    against commerce: he listed agricultural commodities, and treated the
    information in "a political point of view," with critical commentary on the
    damaging effects of speculation. See *CPR* 43 (1822), 703; *CPR* 46 (1823),
    764–66; and *CPR* 47 (1823), 187–90.

91 Wood, *Radical Satire and Print Culture*, pp. 4, 40.

92 *BD* 1 (1817), 361–62, 416, 588, 746. The first set of "Cross Readings" was
    signed "J. H. G.," but later examples were not attributed.

93 See for example *R* 2 (1820), 223, and *E*, no. 84 (August 6, 1809), 497.

94 Davis, *Factual Fictions*, pp. 95–97.

95 The phrase is from *HR* 1 (1817), 367; see Cranfield, *Press and Society*, pp. 103–04, and Arthur Aspinall, "The Circulation of Newspapers in the Early Nineteenth Century," *Review of English Studies* 22 (1946), 38–39.

96 See *PD* 41 (1819–1820), 1678–80.

97 For the illegal revival of the unstamped press in the 1830s, see Wiener, *War of the Unstamped*, and Hollis, *The Pauper Press*.

98 For related announcements, see *M* 1 (1819), 359, 369–71.

99 *PD* 41 (1819–1820), 396, 577–78, 1505, 1545.

100 *PD* 41 (1819–1820), 1677–78. This passage suggests that those in power shared the radical commitment to timely intervention in an immediate crisis; see also *Parliamentary Debates* 41 (1819–1820), 90, 379, 463, 601, 1177.

101 *Speech of the Right Hon. George Canning, to his Constituents at Liverpool, On Saturday, March 18th, 1820, at the Celebration of His Fourth Election* (London: John Murray, 1820), p. 10.

102 *G*, no. 1 (1818), 1.

103 *PD* 41 (1819–1820), 1591.

104 Prothero, *Artisans and Politics*, pp. 93–94.

105 For a good general discussion of radical reading audiences and popular literacy in this period, see Olivia Smith, *The Politics of Language, 1791–1819* (Oxford: Clarendon Press, 1984), pp. 155–65. For the purpose of the stamp taxes, see A. P. Wadsworth, "Newspaper Circulations, 1800–1954," *Transactions of the Manchester Statistical Society* (1954–1955), pp. 3–4; John Brewer, *Party Ideology and Popular Politics at the Accession of George III* (Cambridge University Press, 1976), p. 219; and Asquith, "Structure, Ownership and Control," pp. 111–12.

106 See also *PD* 38 (1818), 1110, and *TT*, p. 133.

107 For Cobbett on the conditions of 1816, see Spater, *William Cobbett*, 2: 343–46.

108 Sidmouth's notorious circular letter of 1817 allowed Justices of the Peace to issue warrants for the arrest of hawkers based on the oath of an informer, effectively providing for punishment without trial; see Wickwar, *Struggle for the Freedom of the Press*, pp. 39–40, and Hollis, *The Pauper Press*, p. 38. For Cobbett's account of the harassment of his hawkers, see *CPR* 31 (1816), 770–71, and *CPR* 32 (1817) 94, 97–98, 129.

109 Mary Poovey, *Uneven Developments: The Ideological Work of Gender in Mid-Victorian England* (University of Chicago Press, 1988), p. 106. See Martha Woodmansee, "On the Author Effect: Recovering Collectivity," in *The Construction of Authorship: Textual Appropriation in Law and Literature*, ed. Martha Woodmansee and Peter Jaszi (Durham: Duke University Press, 1994), pp. 15–17, for a similar distinction between pre-romantic conceptions of "the numerous craftsmen involved in the production of a book" and the romantic idea that "the writer is a special participant in the production process – the only one worthy of attention."

110 For the "communications circuit," see Robert Darnton, "What Is the

History of Books?" in *Reading in America: Literature and Social History* (Baltimore: Johns Hopkins University Press, 1989), p. 30.

111 See, for example, Hone's notices "To Readers" in *HR* 1 (1817), 288, 384, 415–16, 609; for the distribution of unstamped papers, see Hollis, *Pauper Press*, pp. 95–97.

112 Roger Chartier, "Texts, Printing, Readings," in *The New Cultural History*, ed. Lynn Hunt (Berkeley: University of California Press, 1989), pp. 158–59. Chartier has also written on this subject in "Leisure and Sociability: Reading Aloud in Early Modern Europe," in *Urban Life in the Renaissance*, ed. Susan Zimmerman and Ronald F. E. Weissman (Newark: University of Delaware Press, 1989), pp. 104–20; "The Practical Impact of Writing," in *Passions of the Renaissance*, ed. Roger Chartier, volume 3 of *A History of Private Life* (Cambridge, Massachusetts: Belknap Press, 1989), pp. 147–57; and *The Order of Books: Readers, Authors, and Libraries in Europe between the Fourteenth and Eighteenth Centuries* (Stanford University Press, 1994), pp. 8–9, 17–20.

113 David Vincent, *Literacy and Popular Culture: England, 1750–1914* (Cambridge University Press, 1989), pp. 12–13, and "The Decline of the Oral Tradition in Popular Culture," in *Popular Culture and Custom in Nineteenth-Century England*, ed. Robert Storch (New York: St. Martin's Press, 1982), pp. 27–28.

114 For popular reading habits, see Aspinall, *Politics and the Press*, pp. 24–32; Thompson, *Making of the English Working Class*, pp. 717–19; Webb, *Working Class Reader*, pp. 32–35; and Asquith, "Structure, Ownership and Control," pp. 100–01. For the term "bridging," see R. S. Schofield, "The Measurement of Literacy in Pre-Industrial England," in *Literacy in Traditional Society*, ed. Jack Goody (Cambridge University Press, 1968), pp. 312–13.

115 See Aspinall, *Politics and the Press*, p. 29; Webb, *Working Class Reader*, pp. 49–50; and Hollis, *The Pauper Press*, pp. 38–39. See the *Morning Chronicle*, no. 15,717 (September 14, 1819), for a report of a "Warning to Publicans" about the suspension of their licenses if they received seditious publications.

116 Wickwar, *Struggle for the Freedom of the Press*, pp. 61–62; for the "Political Protestants," see Thompson, *Making of the English Working Class*, pp. 674–75, and Calhoun, *Class Struggle*, pp. 86–87.

117 *BD* 3 (1819), 840; *R* 1 (1819), xvi; *CPR* 36 (1820), 78; and *M* 1 (1819), 362.

118 Walter Benjamin, *Charles Baudelaire: A Lyric Poet in the Era of High Capitalism* (London: Verso, 1983), p. 112, and Terdiman, *Discourse / Counter-Discourse*, p. 125.

119 Anderson, *Imagined Communities*, p. 39; for the privatization of reading habits, see Chartier, "The Practical Impact of Writing," pp. 124–44, and Elizabeth Eisenstein, *The Printing Revolution in Early Modern Europe* (Cambridge University Press, 1983), p. 94.

120 Vincent, *Literacy and Popular Culture*, p. 243.

121 Radical leaders inclined towards temperance often preferred the political club or private home to the tavern, while those wary of repression warned about the conspiratorial associations of formal clubs. For radical suspicion

of taverns as the appropriate theater for reading, see *CPR* 31 (1816), 611–12, and *G*, no. 15 (1818), 116; for radical sobriety, see Thompson, *Making of the English Working Class*, pp. 58–59, 740–44.

122 Wooler responds to Cobbett here, but for evidence that Cobbett's suspicion of political clubs did not extend to collective reading, see *CPR* 31(1816), 610–12, and *CPR* 32 (1817), 356–61.

123 Throughout this period, government spies and other hostile observers gathered evidence about the public consumption of radical print discourse; for a Home Office report detailing the way the *Political Register* and *Examiner* were read aloud at political meetings, see Worrall, *Radical Culture*, p. 95.

124 *The Periodical Press of Great Britain and Ireland: Or an Inquiry into the State of the Public Journals, Chiefly as Regards Their Moral and Political Influence* (London: Hurst, Robinson, and Co., 1824), pp. 53–54.

125 Vincent, *Literacy and Popular Culture*, p. 235.

126 See Terdiman, *Discourse / Counter-Discourse*, p. 120.

127 Thompson, *Making of the English Working Class*, p. 674.

128 Hollis, *The Pauper Press*, p. 258. The short-lived *London Alfred* was devoted entirely to reports of radical meetings; see *LA*, no. 1 (1819), 1.

129 Epstein, *Radical Expression*, p. 114.

130 See for example *LA*, no. 2 (1819), 9, and *LA*, no. 3 (1819), 20. For readers as reporters in a later phase of the radical press, see Curran, "Capitalism and Control," pp. 207–08.

131 *CPR* 40 (1821), 764–66, 828, 1020–22, and *CPR* 41 (1822), 638.

132 See *G*, no. 19 (1818), 148–51; *G*, no. 20 (1818), 153–60; *G*, no. 22 (1818), 169–74; and *G*, no. 28 (1818), 217–23.

133 See Calhoun, *Question of Class Struggle*, p. 130.

134 Curran, "Press History," p. 23.

135 See Calhoun's remarks in *Question of Class Struggle*, p. 76. For "Radical Breakfast Powder" and Hunt's commercial enterprises in the 1820s, see Thompson, *Making of the English Working Class*, p. 626, and John Belchem, *"Orator" Hunt: Henry Hunt and English Working-Class Radicalism* (Oxford: Clarendon Press, 1985), pp. 139–40, 167–72. Advertisements for Hunt's beverage powder can be found in *CEP*, no. 2 (January 31, 1820); *CL* 1 (1820), 282; and *M* 1 (1819), 360.

136 Thompson, *Making of the English Working Class*, p. 758.

137 Advertisement, *CPR* 1 (1802), n. pag.

138 "New Series of the Black Dwarf," *BD* 11 (1823), n. pag.

139 See also *R* 2 (1820), 298, 400; *R* 4 (1820), 621; R 6 (1822), 321. For Carlile's efforts to negotiate religion and politics, see Epstein, *Radical Expression*, pp. 104–07, 126–27, and Robert Hole, *Pulpits, Politics and Public Order in England, 1760–1832* (Cambridge University Press, 1989), pp. 206–13.

140 The advertisement appeared in many of Cobbett's published works; I quote from the third edition of *A Year's Residence in the United States of America* (London: n.p., 1828).

141 Here, forms of assembly and forms of periodical expression coincide: radical meetings displayed the same structural ambiguity, posing a threat to social order through their military discipline and their random mob outbreaks. See Thompson, *Making of the English Working Class*, pp. 681–82.

142 For tory support of the periodical division of labor, see *BM* 16 (1824), 524–25.

3 THE TRIALS OF RADICALISM: ASSEMBLING THE EVIDENCE OF REFORM

1 *The Prince of Wales v. the Examiner. A Full Report of the Trial of John and Leigh Hunt* (London: John Hunt, [1813]), pp. 36–39, 45–46; this response first appeared in *E*, no. 260 (December 20, 1812), 802.

2 For the two campaigns against the radical press, see Donald Thomas, *A Long Time Burning: The History of Literary Censorship in England* (New York: Frederick A. Praeger, 1969), pp. 153–60, 162–64.

3 *TT*, pp. 154, 207; *E*, no. 260 (December 20, 1812), 801; and *YD*, no. 3 (1818), 19. The *Edinburgh Review* took both sides of the question: James Mill complained about the lack of definition of libel (*ER* 18 [1811], 105), but Brougham insisted that "the nature of the thing precludes all minute definition" (*ER* 27 [1816], 108).

4 Jeremy Bentham, "The Elements of the Art of Packing, as Applied to Special Juries, Particularly in Cases of Libel Law," in *The Works of Jeremy Bentham*, 11 vols. (Edinburgh: William Tait, 1843), 5: 112.

5 Francis Ludlow Holt, *The Law of Libel* (London: W. Reed, 1812), p. 35.

6 Holt, *Law of Libel*, p. 78.

7 Constitutional Association for Opposing the Progress of Disloyal and Seditious Principles, "Address," reprinted in Richard Mence, *The Law of Libel*, 2 vols. (London: W. Pople, 1824), 1: 191–92. For the definition of criminal libel in this period, see William Wickwar, *The Struggle for the Freedom of the Press, 1819–1832* (London: George Allen and Unwin, 1928), pp. 19–28.

8 David Saunders and Ian Hunter, "Lessons from the 'Literatory': How to Historicise Authorship," *Critical Inquiry* 17 (1991), 490–91. Saunders and Hunter are interested in obscenity, and I extend their case to sedition and blasphemy.

9 *A Correct Report of the Trials of Thomas Jonathan Wooler* (London: W. N. Jones, 1817), pp. 24–25; see also *WBG* 3 (1821), 33.

10 See Wickwar, *Struggle for the Freedom of the Press*, pp. 19–20, and Mence, *Law of Libel*, II: 33, 172.

11 Constitutional Association, "Address," in Mence, *Law of Libel*, 1: 188.

12 Saunders and Hunter, "Lessons from the 'Literatory,'" pp. 485–87.

13 For the "war of the shopmen," see Joel Wiener, *Radicalism and Freethought in Nineteenth-Century Britain: The Life of Richard Carlile* (Westport, Connecticut: Greenwood Press, 1988), pp. 86–96.

14 *Trial of Mr. Daniel Isaac Eaton, for Publishing the Third and Last Part of Paine's Age of Reason* (London: Daniel Isaac Eaton, 1812), p. 15.

15 *Trial of Thos. Jonathan Wooller [sic], Publisher of a Paper called the Black Dwarf, For Two Libels* (Glasgow: E. Miller, 1817), p. 6; compare *VR*, p. 46.

16 Thomas, *Long Time Burning*, p. 155.

17 *Trial of Mr. Daniel Isaac Eaton*, pp. 23–24, 29. Even where the law preserved its framing role, it did not always operate to the government's advantage: Ellenborough soon reversed himself and encouraged Eaton to read his address (p. 30), evidently out of a reluctance to be seen to interfere with the rights of free speech and trial by jury.

18 In a note dated November 21, 1840, on the back of the manuscript of the prepared "Defence" that Jane Carlile read at her 1820 trial (Huntington Library, no. RC 556–58), Richard Carlile observed: "The Attorney or Solicitor General of that day, Sir John Copley, afterward Lord Lyndhurst, observed on hearing this defence, that it was worse than the offence, which was the judgment of Richard Carlile, that all Government Prosecutions for sedition and blasphemy should be so met."

19 Alan Liu, "Wordsworth and Subversion, 1793–1804: Trying Cultural Criticism," *Yale Journal of Criticism* 2 (1989), 68. For related formulations, see James Epstein, *Radical Expression: Political Language, Ritual, and Symbol in England, 1790–1850* (New York: Oxford University Press, 1994), pp. 32–33, and David Worrall, *Radical Culture: Discourse, Resistance, and Surveillance, 1790–1820* (Detroit: Wayne State University Press, 1992), p. 67.

20 See also *R* 3 (1820), 342.

21 *Trial of Thos. Jonathan Wooller*, p. 4.

22 Wickwar, *Struggle for the Freedom of the Press*, p. 94.

23 See J. Anne Hone, *For the Cause of Truth: Radicalism in London, 1796–1821* (Oxford: Clarendon Press, 1982), pp. 331–39; James Curran, "Press History," in James Curran and Jean Seaton, *Power without Responsibility: The Press and Broadcasting in Britain* (London: Methuen, 1985), pp. 12–13; James Curran, "Capitalism and Control of the Press, 1800–1975," in *Mass Communication and Society*, ed. James Curran, Michael Gurevitch, and Janet Woollacott (London: Edward Arnold, 1977), p. 199; and Ivon Asquith, "The Structure, Ownership and Control of the Press, 1780–1855," in *Newspaper History from the Seventeenth Century to the Present Day*, ed. George Boyce, James Curran, and Pauline Wingate (London: Constable, 1978), p. 112.

24 See also *QR* 22 (1820), 545–46.

25 See Curran, "Capitalism and Control of the Press," p. 199, and Asquith, "Structure, Ownership, and Control," p. 111.

26 Olivia Smith, *The Politics of Language, 1791–1819* (Oxford: Clarendon Press, 1984), p. 177; for the trials of this period as political theater, see also Epstein, *Radical Expression*, pp. 39–54.

27 "The King against William Cobbett," in volume 2 (1823–1831) of *Report of State Trials*, New Series, ed. John MacDonell (London: Eyre and Spottiswoode, 1889), pp. 792, 828; *Suppressed Defence. The Defence of Mary-*

Anne Carlile to the Vice Society's Indictment (London: R. Carlile, 1821), pp. 10–11; and *TT*, pp. 160–61.

28 *Prince of Wales v. the Examiner*, p. 39; *TT*, p. 134; and *VR*, p. 69.

29 See for example *Bridge-Street Bandatti, versus the Press* (London: R. Carlile, 1821), p. 52; *Correct Report of the Trials of Thomas Jonathan Wooler*, pp. 31–34; and *VR*, pp. 87–90.

30 For the public framework of radical trials, see Epstein, *Radical Expression*, pp. 33–35.

31 *Correct Report of the Trials of Thomas Jonathan Wooler*, p. vii.

32 See, for example, *VR*, p. 32, and "The King against William Cobbett," pp. 789–90.

33 Thomas W. Laqueur reads the Queen Caroline affair in this way, in "The Queen Caroline Affair: Politics as Art in the Reign of George IV," *Journal of Modern History* 54 (1982), 417–66. Anna Clark has effectively refuted Laqueur's approach in "Queen Caroline and the Sexual Politics of Popular Culture in London, 1820," *Representations* 31 (1990), 47–68.

34 *Trial of Thos. Jonathan Wooler*, p. 7. Compare Wooler's own account of the occasion: "the audience . . . entered fully into the feelings of the Editor" (*BD* 1 [1817], 307).

35 For Wooler's early career, see Epstein, *Radical Expression*, pp. 36–37.

36 Mary Jacobus, "The Art of Managing Books: Romantic Prose and the Writing of the Past," in *Romanticism and Language*, ed. Arden Reed (Ithaca: Cornell University Press, 1984), p. 217. See also David Simpson, *Romanticism, Nationalism, and the Revolt against Theory* (University of Chicago Press, 1993), pp. 135–36, where "the Romantic proclivity for the oral" is contrasted with "the belief of the radicals of the 1790s in the powers of print."

37 Craig Calhoun, *The Question of Class Struggle: Social Foundations of Popular Radicalism during the Industrial Revolution* (University of Chicago Press, 1982), p. 8.

38 *The Triumphal Entry of Henry Hunt, Esq. into London* (London: Hay and Turner, [1819]), pp. 3–5. (Page three of the pamphlet is incorrectly numbered page four, and I have corrected this in my citations.) This text is similar to the accounts that appeared in *S*, no. 4246 (September 14, 1819), and in the *Morning Chronicle*, no. 15,717 (September 14, 1819).

39 James Vernon, *Politics and the People: A Study in English Political Culture, c. 1815–1867* (Cambridge University Press, 1993), pp. 106–07.

40 Mona Ozouf, *Festivals and the French Revolution* (Cambridge, Massachusetts: Harvard University Press, 1988), pp. 206–09.

41 The term is from E. P. Thompson, "Patrician Society, Plebeian Culture," *Journal of Social History* 7 (1974), 396: "There is a sense in which rulers and crowd needed each other, watched each other, performed theater and countertheater to each other's auditorium." See also Clark, "Queen Caroline and the Sexual Politics of Popular Culture," p. 50.

42 Vernon, *Politics and the People*, pp. 93–95.

43 See *CL* 1 (1819), 18–19, and *S*, no. 4246 (September 14, 1819).

44 See, for example, John Wade, *A Political Dictionary; or, Pocket Companion* (London: T. Dolby, 1821); *BD* 2 (1818), 241, 499–500; *CPR* 26 (1814), 611; and *CWH*, 7: 235–36, 268, 272, 17: 316, and 19: 264.

45 Compare *WBG* 1 (1819), 306.

46 Ozouf, *Festivals and the French Revolution*, pp. 126–52. Compare David Cannadine's remarks on London's appropriateness for royal ceremonies in "The Context, Performance and Meaning of Ritual: The British Monarchy and the 'Invention of Tradition,' c. 1820–1977," in *The Invention of Tradition*, ed. Eric Hobsbawm and Terence Ranger (Cambridge University Press, 1983), pp. 113–14.

47 Inexpressibility was a standard topos in radical descriptions of crowd events; see for example *CL* 1 (1819), 21, and *TT*, p. 134.

48 Carlile's eyewitness account of Peterloo situated a rhetoric of inexpressibility at the intersection of radical antipathy and desire: if the assembly of reformers in St. Peter's Field "exceed[ed] the power of description," it was also "impossible to find words to express the horror" of the massacre that followed (*SPR* 5 [1819], 237, 240).

49 See, for example, Linda Colley, "The Apotheosis of George III: Loyalty, Royalty and the British Nation, 1760–1820," *Past and Present* 102 (1984), 120; Frank O'Gorman, "Campaign Rituals and Ceremonies: The Social Meaning of Elections in England, 1780–1860," *Past and Present* 135 (1992), pp. 80–81; and Mark Harrison, *Crowds and History: Mass Phenomena in English Towns, 1790–1835* (Cambridge University Press, 1988), p. 170.

50 Harrison, *Crowds and History*, p. 234.

51 *CPR* 16 (1809), 396, 515, 648; see also *E*, no. 96 (October 29, 1809), 689–90.

52 Compare *CPR* 16 (1809), 653.

53 Compare *CL* 1 (1819), 20, and *BD* 3 (1819), 601.

54 For contemporary examples of the printed account of a coronation procession, see T. C. Banks, *An Historical and Critical Enquiry into the Nature of the Kingly Office* (London: Sherwood, Neely, and Jones, 1814), pp. 28–30, and *A Faithful Account of the Processions and Ceremonies Observed in the Coronation of the Kings and Queens of England*, ed. Richard Thompson (London: John Major, 1820), pp. 4–8.

55 For conflict and ambiguity in radical discourse and symbolic display, see Epstein, *Radical Expression*, p. 164.

56 *PD* 41 (1819–1820), 45, 346, 1665–66; see also *QR* 22 (1820), 499–500, 521.

57 Compare the definitions of "Coronation" and "Pageant" in Wade, *Political Dictionary*, pp. 19, 69; see also *E*, no. 707 (July 22, 1821), 450, and *WBG* 1(1819), p. 105.

58 See, for example, *A Faithful Account of the Processions and Ceremonies*, pp. 40–45.

59 For agency in symbolic display, see Vernon, *Politics and the People*, pp. 106–09.

60 There was an element of class privilege here too, for "gentlemen" (8) were also found at the windows rather than in the street.

61 Leonore Davidoff and Catherine Hall, *Family Fortunes: Men and Women of the English Middle Class, 1780–1850* (University of Chicago Press, 1987),

pp. 447–48. For further evidence of the women's position at the window in crowd activities, see Harrison, *Crowds and History*, pp. 171, 215, 242.

62 For solidarity in political ritual and crowd activity, see Epstein, *Radical Expression*, pp. 147–65, and Harrison, *Crowds and History*, pp. 264–66.

63 For the imperfect distinction between participant and spectator in public spectacle, see Vernon, *Politics and the People*, pp. 108–09, 115–16, and Christian Jouhaud, "Printing the Event: From La Rochelle to Paris," in *The Culture of Print: Power and Uses of Print in Early Modern Europe*, ed. Roger Chartier (Princeton University Press, 1989), p. 297.

64 Compare Mary Ryan's account of descriptive representation in the later nineteenth-century American parade, in "The American Parade: Representations of the Nineteenth-Century Social Order," in *The New Cultural History*, ed. Lynn Hunt (Berkeley: University of California Press, 1989), pp. 134, 137.

65 For "Wilkes and Liberty," see John Brewer, *Party Ideology and Popular Politics at the Accession of George III* (Cambridge University Press, 1976), pp. 169–71.

66 Calhoun, *Question of Class Struggle*, pp. 100–01.

67 Compare Wooler's claim that an incomplete crowd qualified the impact of George IV's coronation, in *BD* 6 (1821), 87.

68 In *Crowds and History*, pp. 155–57, Harrison suggests that the retreat indoors involved an upward shift in rank and privilege.

69 John Belchem, *"Orator" Hunt: Henry Hunt and English Working-Class Radicalism* (Oxford: Clarendon Press, 1985), pp. 54–56, 71, 77, 104–5, 109, 121–27; I am indebted to Belchem's account throughout this paragraph. See also Iain McCalman, *Radical Underworld: Prophets, Revolutionaries and Pornographers in London, 1795–1840* (Cambridge University Press, 1988), p. 135.

70 Holt, *Law of Libel*, pp. 145, 287–88.

71 *VR*, pp. 34, 36, 45.

72 For Spence, see Worrall, *Radical Culture*, pp. 47–48.

73 See Epstein, *Radical Expression*, pp. 108–09, and Wickwar, *Struggle for the Freedom of the Press*, p. 95.

74 *Suppressed Defence*, pp. 10–11.

75 Liu, "Wordsworth and Subversion," pp. 68–69.

76 *Mr. Cobbett's Taking Leave of His Countrymen* (London: W. Molineux, 1817), p. 25.

77 For libel trials and the jury system, see Epstein, *Radical Expression*, pp. 46–69.

78 "The King against Richard Carlile," in volume 2 (1823–1831) of *Report of State Trials*, New Series, p. 461.

79 Liu, "Wordsworth and Subversion," p. 68.

80 *TT*, p. 206, and *WBG* 1 (1819), 257.

81 See *BD* 3 (1819), 827–30; *CPR* 34 (1818–1819), 505–32; and *Substance of the Speeches of John Gale Jones, Delivered at the British Forum* (London: R. Carlile, 1819), p. 20.

82 *Prince of Wales v. The Examiner*, pp. 39–60.

83 Wiener, *Radicalism and Freethought*, pp. 84–85, and n. 31.
84 See *BD* 2 (1818), 465–72, and *Another Ministerial Defeat! The Trial of The Dog, for Biting the Noble Lord; with the Whole of the Evidence at Length* (London: W. Hone, 1817). For Hone and trial parody, see Marcus Wood, *Radical Satire and Print Culture, 1790–1822* (Oxford: Clarendon Press, 1994), pp. 144–54.
85 See Hone, *For the Cause of Truth*, pp. 330–39, and Epstein, *Radical Expression*, pp. 39–69.
86 Holt, *Law of Libel*, pp. 280–81.
87 *BD* 5 (1820), 759.
88 The term is from Edward Said, *The World, the Text, and the Critic* (Cambridge, Massachusetts: Harvard University Press, 1983), pp. 151–52.
89 See J. R. Spencer, "The Press and the Reform of Criminal Libel," in *Reshaping the Criminal Law: Essays in Honour of Glanville Williams*, ed. P. R. Glazebrook (London: Stevens, 1978), pp. 271–74; Arthur Aspinall, *Politics and the Press, c. 1780–1850* (London: Home and Van Thal, 1949), pp. 37, 384; Lennard Davis, *Factual Fictions: The Origins of the English Novel* (New York: Columbia University Press, 1983), pp. 87–94; and Thomas, *Long Time Burning*, pp. 61, 145. For contemporary accounts, see Holt, *Law of Libel*, pp. 76–78, 277–82; John Jones, *De Libellis Famosis; or, the Law of Libels* (London: R. Rousseau, 1812), pp. 46–47; and Thomas Starkie, *A Treatise on the Law of Slander, Libel, Scandalum Magnatum, and False Rumours* (New York: George Lamson, 1826), pp. 498–501. Mence, *Law of Libel*, I: 124, 135–38; II: 180, disputes the doctrine through an extensive critique of Holt; see also John George, *A Treatise on the Offence of Libel* (London: Taylor and Hessey, 1812), pp. 16–17, 265–66, 287–90.
90 Jones, *De Libellis Famosis*, pp. 46–47. See also George, *Offence of Libel*, p. 16; Mence, *Law of Libel*, 2: 183; and Wickwar, *Struggle for the Freedom of the Press*, p. 24.
91 Epstein, *Radical Expression*, pp. 53–54.
92 *VR*, pp. 109, 114, 116, 119.
93 See Aspinall, *Politics and the Press*, p. 37.
94 Wickwar, *Struggle for the Freedom of the Press*, p. 51.
95 *E*, no. 226 (April 26, 1812), 257, and *E*, no. 260 (December 20, 1812), 802.
96 Jon Klancher, *The Making of English Reading Audiences, 1790–1832* (Madison, Wisconsin: University of Wisconsin Press, 1987), p. 110.
97 W. D. Rubinstein, "British Radicalism and the 'Dark Side' of Populism," in *Elites and the Wealthy in Modern British History: Essays in Social and Economic History* (Sussex: Harvester, 1987), p. 358.
98 McCalman, *Radical Underworld*, p. 172, citing an unpublished version of Rubinstein's "British Radicalism and the 'Dark Side' of Populism."
99 P. F. M'Callum, *Le Livre Rouge; or, A New and Extraordinary Red Book* (London: J. Blacklock, 1810), p. v.
100 See *The Court and City Register; or, Gentleman's Complete Annual Kalendar for the Year 1771* (London: J. Jolliffe, 1771), and *The Royal Kalendar; or, Complete and Correct Annual Register* (London: J. Debrett, 1792).
101 *Links of the Lower House* (London, 1821), p. 1.

102 *The Englishman's Mirror; or, Corruption & Taxation Unmasked* (London: J. Johnston, 1820), title page, and *RB*, p. iii.

103 *Links of the Lower House* (London, 1821), p. 1.

104 These works continue to prompt remarks about their accuracy. See for example E. P. Thompson, *The Making of the English Working Class* (New York: Vintage Books, 1966), p. 770; W. D. Rubinstein, "The End of 'Old Corruption' in Britain, 1780–1860," *Past and Present* 101 (1983), 62–63; and Linda Colley, *Britons: Forging the Nation, 1707–1837* (New Haven: Yale University Press, 1992), pp. 152–53.

105 See, for example, *PD* 37 (1818), 568, and *PD* 38 (1818), Appendix.

106 See Thompson, *Making of the English Working Class*, pp. 769–74.

107 *A Peep at the Commons* (London: T. Dolby, 1820), p. 2.

108 In his Preface to *Le Livre Rouge*, P. F. M'Callum indicates that "this work is intended to be an annual publication," like the *Court Kalendar* it would supplement.

109 See for example Wade's *Supplement to the Black Book; or Corruption Unmasked!*, volume 2 (London: John Fairburn, 1823).

110 Conversely, Cobbett's early ambition to make the *Political Register* a repository for "*all* the documents" relating to public affairs discloses an encyclopedic impulse in the development of the radical weekly; see the Preface to *PR* 8 (1805), n. pag.

111 For Wade's facts, see Thompson, *Making of the English Working Class*, pp. 770–74.

112 For the serial production of the *Black Book*, see the Prospectus bound in the British Library's copy of the 1820 edition of the *Black Book*.

113 *A Peep at the Commons*, pp. 1–2; see also McCalman, *Radical Underworld*, pp. 172–73.

114 Hone, *Cause of Truth*, p. 237; for instances of this, see *CL* 1 (1819), 275–76, and *A Dialogue On the Approaching Trial of Mr. Carlile* (London: T. J. Wooler, 1819), p. 14.

115 *TT*, pp. 2, 66, 120–23.

116 See also *Prince of Wales v. the Examiner*, p. 4.

117 In *Factual Fictions*, p. 71, Lennard Davis suggests that the subversive potential of fact was evident in the earliest legal efforts to distinguish news from less dangerous fictional narratives.

118 *The Political "A, Apple-Pie;" or, The "Extraordinary Red Book" Versified*, reprinted in *Radical Squibs and Loyal Ripostes*, ed. Edgell Rickword (Bath: Adams and Dart, 1971), p. 143.

119 *Radical Squibs*, ed. Rickword, p. 132.

4 READING COBBETT'S CONTRADICTIONS

1 *CWH*, 8: 54–55.

2 *CPR* 36 (1820), 684–86.

3 E. P. Thompson, *The Making of the English Working Class* (New York: Vintage Books, 1966), p. 758; Raymond Williams, *Cobbett* (Oxford University Press,

1983), p. 28; and Gertrude Himmelfarb, *The Idea of Poverty: England in the Early Industrial Age* (New York: Alfred A. Knopf, 1984), p. 229. For an important discussion of the literary and political history of "system" and "method," see David Simpson, *Romanticism, Nationalism, and the Revolt against Theory* (University of Chicago Press, 1993).

4 *OED*, 1971 edn, s.v. "system."

5 Williams, *Cobbett*, p. 38.

6 *The Complete Poetry and Prose of William Blake*, ed. David V. Erdman (Garden City, New York: Anchor Books, 1982), p. 42.

7 There were exceptions, as when he praised "the republican system" in America (*CPR* 27 [1815], 170) and "the Napoleon system" that put "personal merit and well-known services" above "the Aristocracy and the Church" (*CPR* 23 [1813], 772), and when he recommended for Ireland a "system of emancipation by teaching rational truths" (*CPR* 29 [1815], 71). It is worth noting that these positive systems were located far from home: burdened with the Pitt system of finance and its attendant political and social practices, English society had little need of more systematic organization.

8 John W. Osborne, *William Cobbett: His Thought and His Times* (New Brunswick, New Jersey: Rutgers University Press, 1966), pp. 16, 35, 56.

9 Osborne, *William Cobbett*, p. 16.

10 Cobbett's radicalization is normally dated to the period 1806–1808, though in *William Cobbett and Rural Popular Culture* (Cambridge University Press, 1992), pp. 23–33, Ian Dyck has argued that the "agrarian base of his radicalism was taking a distinct shape" as early as 1804; see also Leonora Nattrass, *William Cobbett: The Politics of Style* (Cambridge University Press, 1995), pp. 89–118.

11 Here as elsewhere Cobbett worked from Paine's description of "the funding system" as a "modern complicated machine"; see "The Decline and Fall of the English System of Finance," in *The Writings of Thomas Paine*, 4 vols., ed. Moncure Daniel Conway (New York: AMS Press, 1967), III: 309.

12 See Thompson, *Making of the English Working Class*, pp. 189–91, for the machine as a "symbol of social energies which were destroying the very 'course of nature.'"

13 Although Williams identified the link between "the ruling-class State and the financial system" as Cobbett's most important and enduring insight (*Cobbett*, p. 73), it was an insight derived from Paine's "Decline and Fall of the English System of Finance," which exposed "a mysterious, suspicious connection, between the minister and the directors of the bank" (*Writings of Thomas Paine*, III: 307).

14 For a related scheme to pay laborers on his own farm in kind, see Daniel Green, *Great Cobbett* (Oxford University Press, 1985), p. 270.

15 *CPR* 8 (1805), 851, 903, and *CPR* 11 (1807), 102.

16 See J. G. A. Pocock, *The Machiavellian Moment* (Princeton University Press, 1975), pp. 437–38.

17 Thompson, *Making of the English Working Class*, p. 604.

18 See for example Green, *Great Cobbett*, p. 167.

19 For "measures not men," see John Brewer, *Party Ideology and Popular Politics at the Accession of George III* (Cambridge University Press, 1976), pp. 68–69.

20 Peter Manning, "William Cobbett: The Writer as Rider," unpublished paper, p. 10.

21 See, for example, *CRR*, 1: 85, 144, 171, 198; 2: 359.

22 *CRR*, 1: 231, 356; 2: 368, 379. The "Wen" was Cobbett's term for London, or sometimes for cities generally.

23 For Cobbett's role in the critique of an "unholy alliance" of "the ruling oligarchy and the war establishment," see H. T. Dickinson, *British Radicalism and the French Revolution* (Oxford: Basil Blackwell, 1985), pp. 64–65, 70–71.

24 For this kind of opposition to "the powers of entry, search, and seizure" as much as "to the tax *per se*," see John Brewer, "English Radicalism in the Age of George III," in *Three British Revolutions: 1641, 1688, 1776*, ed. J. G. A. Pocock (Princeton University Press, 1980), p. 339.

25 For the paradox of urban enthusiasm for country ideology, see Brewer, "English Radicalism in the Age of George III," pp. 330–36.

26 For Cobbett's "method of arguing through autobiography," see Nattrass, *William Cobbett*, pp. 90–96.

27 See G. D. H. Cole, *The Life of William Cobbett* (Westport, Connecticut: Greenwood Press, 1971), pp. 433–34, and George Spater, *William Cobbett: The Poor Man's Friend*, 2 vols. (Cambridge University Press, 1982), II: 539–41.

28 In "Writer as Rider," p. 8, Manning observes that the first illustration "marks the unchanging oppression of the administration."

29 See Olivia Smith's account of Cobbett's linguistic ideal in *The Politics of Language, 1791–1819* (Oxford: Clarendon Press, 1984), p. 247.

30 Preface, *CPR* 8 (1805), n. pag.

31 Kenneth Burke, *The Philosophy of Literary Form: Studies in Symbolic Action*, 3rd edn (Berkeley: University of California Press, 1973), pp. 3–7.

32 *CPR* 9 (1806), 133; *CPR* 25 (1814), 160; *CPR* 22 (1812), 580; *CPR* 15 (1809), 393; *CPR* 19 (1811), 1121; *CPR* 11 (1807), 36; *CPR* 12 (1807), 225–27; and *CPR* 22 (1812), 67–68.

33 For apocalyptic language in the *Political Register*, see Nattrass, *William Cobbett*, pp. 104–07.

34 Cobbett's proposal in his *Advice to Young Men* (1830) that the usual "dozen pages about Edward the Third dancing at a ball" be replaced by information about "a labourer's wages" and "the prices of the food" (*AYM*, 260) reads like an early manifesto for social history from below. Political foresight was also (potentially) democratized in the *Register*, since "what I foresaw" was "what any other man" who attended to the facts "might have foreseen as well" (*CPR* 25 [1814], 319–20).

35 Thompson, *Making of the English Working Class*, pp. 751–52.

36 *CPR* 11 (1807), 816, 873, 968; *CPR* 16 (1809), 426–28; *CPR* 18 (1810), 488, 625–26; and *CPR* 26 (1814), 161–62.

37 *CRR*, 1: 117, 165, and 2: 372, 395.

38 Noel Thompson, *The People's Science: The Popular Political Economy of Exploitation and Crisis, 1816–34* (Cambridge University Press, 1984), p. 113; see also Green, *Great Cobbett*, pp. 247–48.

39 This resistance to modern avenues of mobility distinguished Cobbett from the Board of Agriculture surveyors, who were, according to John Barrell, "anxious to open out the countryside, by making it more accessible to the traveller, and by making individual villages more obviously part of a national economy"; see *The Idea of Landscape and the Sense of Place, 1730–1840* (Cambridge University Press, 1972), pp. 87–88.

40 For the associative logic and antithetical structure of the *Rides*, see Manning, "Writer as Rider," p. 11, and George Woodcock, Introduction to *Rural Rides* (Harmondsworth, England: Penguin, 1967), p. 7.

41 For comparison in the 1790s, see Gerald Newman, "Anti-French Propaganda and British Liberal Nationalism in the Early Nineteenth Century: Suggestions towards a General Interpretation," *Victorian Studies* 18 (1975), 388–89, 392–95, and H. T. Dickinson, "Popular Conservatism and Militant Loyalism, 1789–1815," in *Britain and the French Revolution, 1789–1815*, ed. H. T. Dickinson (London: Macmillan, 1989), pp. 104–9.

42 Alan Liu, *Wordsworth: The Sense of History* (Stanford University Press, 1989), pp. 401–26.

43 This idea was derived from Paine, who argued that the funding and paper system was self-destructive: "In the first part of its movements it gives great power into the hands of government, and in the last part it takes them completely away" (*Writings of Thomas Paine*, III: 309). Cobbett cited the passage in *CPR* 32 (1817), 366, and *CPR* 35 (1819–1820), 169.

44 *CPR* 17 (1810), 193, 561, and *CPR* 18 (1810), 21.

45 Manning, "Writer as Rider," p. 13.

46 William Cobbett, *The Life and Adventures of Peter Porcupine* (Philadelphia: William Cobbett, 1796), p. 14.

47 To project the end of paper money was to return to the pastoral world of his youth: "The corn and the grass and the trees will grow without paper-money; the Banks may all break in a day, and the sun will rise the next day, and the lambs will gambol and the birds will sing and the carters and country girls will grin at each other and all will go on just as if nothing had happened" (*CPR* 20 [1811], 131–32).

48 See Manning, "Writer as Rider," p. 18.

5 LEIGH HUNT AND THE END OF RADICAL OPPOSITION

1 "Postscript for the Year 1810," *E* (1810), n. pag.

2 *L* 1 (1822), vii.

3 *Companion* 1 (1828), 6–7.

4 *LJ*, no. 1 (1834), 1.

5 For details of Hunt's trial and imprisonment, see Donald Thomas, "Leigh Hunt's *Examiner*," *Censorship* 2 (1966), 38–42, and Carl Woodring, "The

Hunt Trials: Informations and Manœuvres," *Keats–Shelley Memorial Bulletin* 10 (1959), 10–13.

6 See also Edmund Blunden, *Leigh Hunt: A Biography* (London: Cobden-Sanderson, 1930), p. 112, and Carl Woodring, "Leigh Hunt as Political Essayist," introduction to *Leigh Hunt's Political and Occasional Essays*, ed. Lawrence Huston Houtchens and Carolyn Washburn Houtchens (New York: Columbia University Press, 1962), pp. 26–27.

7 William H. Marshall, *Byron, Shelley, Hunt and "The Liberal"* (Philadelphia: University of Pennsylvania Press, 1960), pp. 126–31, 205–09.

8 *The Poetical Works of Leigh Hunt*, ed. H. S. Milford (London: Oxford University Press, 1923), pp. 143–44; compare *HA*, p. 175. For Hunt's "escapist tendency," and his treatment of practical duty as a form of restraint, see Greg Kucich, "Leigh Hunt and Romantic Spenserianism," *Keats–Shelley Journal* 37 (1988), 112–14.

9 William Keach, "Cockney Couplets: Keats and the Politics of Style," *Studies in Romanticism* 25 (1986), 190.

10 Richard Carlile was also fond of the term; see, for example, *R* 2 (1820), 78, 150.

11 E. P. Thompson, *The Making of the English Working Class* (New York: Vintage Books, 1966), p. 604.

12 Carlile soon decided that the paper "did not go far enough," but he extended the same reservation to Cobbett's *Political Register* and Hone's *Reformists' Register* (*R* 11 [1825], 101).

13 Woodring, "Leigh Hunt as Political Essayist," p. 6.

14 For the tensions within radicalism over respectability, see Iain McCalman, *Radical Underworld: Prophets, Revolutionaries and Pornographers in London, 1795–1840* (Cambridge University Press, 1988), pp. 26–49, 130–32, 181–203.

15 "New Series of the Black Dwarf," *BD* 11 (1823), n. pag.

16 For class in the "Cockney School," see Jerome McGann, "Keats and the Historical Method in Literary Criticism," in *The Beauty of Inflections* (Oxford University Press, 1985), pp. 29–31; Marjorie Levinson, *Keats's Life of Allegory: The Origins of a Style* (Oxford: Basil Blackwell, 1988), pp. 3–5; Gareth Stedman Jones, "The 'Cockney' and the Nation, 1780–1988," in *Metropolis London: Histories and Representations Since 1800*, ed. David Feldman and Gareth Stedman Jones (London: Routledge, 1989), pp. 282–83; and Kim Wheatley, "The *Blackwood's* Attacks on Leigh Hunt," *Nineteenth-Century Literature* 47 (1992), pp. 2–11.

17 See also *E*, no. 467 (December 8, 1816), 769.

18 Edward Said, *The World, the Text, and the Critic* (Cambridge, Massachusetts: Harvard University Press, 1983), pp. 15–16.

19 See Louis Landré, *Leigh Hunt (1784–1859): Contribution à l'Histoire du Romantisme Anglais*, 2 vols. (Paris: Société d'Édition "Les Belles-Lettres," 1935–1936), II: 61, and Terry Eagleton, *The Function of Criticism, From the Spectator to Post-Structuralism* (London: Verso, 1984), pp. 37–39.

20 The attribution was corrected, from Swift to Pope, in 1815; see *E*, no. 378 (1815), 193.

21 Leigh Hunt, *Lord Byron and Some of His Contemporaries*, 2nd edn, 2 vols. (London: Henry Colburn, 1828), ii: 190.

22 The policy remained in place until 1820, when declining circulation forced the introduction of advertising in the *Examiner*.

23 The family organization of these enterprises may have given them a middle-class inflection; see Leonore Davidoff and Catherine Hall, *Family Fortunes: Men and Women of the English Middle Class, 1780–1850* (University of Chicago Press, 1987), pp. 32, 215–19.

24 *The Tatler*, no. 195 (1831), 777.

25 For the way that "oppositional participation" in society can deteriorate into "a shrill withdrawal from it," see Edward Said, "Opponents, Audiences, Constituencies, and Community," *Critical Inquiry* 9 (1982), 6.

26 See *E*, no. 595 (May 23, 1819), 322–23; *E*, no. 596 (May 30, 1819), 337–38; *E*, no. 600 (June 27, 1819), 401–3; and *E*, no. 604 (July 25, 1819), 465–66.

27 "The Critic's Farewell to his Readers," reprinted in *Prefaces by Leigh Hunt, Mainly to his Periodicals*, ed. R. Brimley Johnson (Port Washington, New York: Kennikat Press, 1967), p. 24. For attacks on Hunt's egotism, see the reviews of his work in the *Satirist, or Monthly Meteor* 2 (1808), 76, and the *Eclectic Review* 10 (1818), 485; see also Woodring, "Leigh Hunt as Political Essayist," p. 36.

28 Marie Hamilton Law, *The English Familiar Essay in the Early Nineteenth Century* (Philadelphia: n.p., 1934), pp. 55–56, 207–19; Melvin R. Watson, "The *Spectator* Tradition and the Development of the Familiar Essay," *ELH* 13 (1946), 199–205; and Kenneth E. Kendall, *Leigh Hunt's "Reflector"* (The Hague: Mouton, 1971), pp. 53, 56–58, 163.

29 Raymond Williams, *Keywords: A Vocabulary of Culture and Society*, rev. edn (New York: Oxford University Press, 1983), pp. 179–81.

30 For the attribution to Byron, see Hunt, *Lord Byron and Some of His Contemporaries*, 1: 80; Edmund Blunden, *Shelley: A Life Story* (New York: Viking, 1947), pp. 351–52; and Peter L. Thorslev, "Post-Waterloo Liberalism: The Second Generation," *Studies in Romanticism* 28 (1989), 444–46.

31 For the early response to the Pisan collaboration, see Marshall, *Byron, Shelley, Hunt, and "The Liberal,"* pp. 444–45.

32 *Companion* 1 (1828), 6.

33 For similar objections to the poet laureateship, "the office of Rhyming Flatterer to the King," see *E*, no. 108 (January 21, 1810), 33–34.

34 Woodring, "Leigh Hunt as Political Essayist," p. 38.

35 See, for example, *E*, no. 84 (August 6, 1809), 498.

36 For Mill's argument in his *Encyclopaedia Britannica* essay on "Government," see John Dinwiddy, *From Luddism to the First Reform Bill* (London: Basil Blackwell, 1986), pp. 15–16; the passage in question can be found in *Utilitarian Logic and Politics*, ed. Jack Lively and John Rees (Oxford: Clarendon Press, 1978), pp. 93–94.

37 Jon Klancher, *The Making of English Reading Audiences, 1790–1832* (Madison, Wisconsin: University of Wisconsin Press, 1987), p. 110.

38 Terry Eagleton, *The Function of Criticism, from the Spectator to Post-Structuralism* (London: Verso, 1984), p. 39.

39 Woodring, "Leigh Hunt as Political Essayist," p. 29.

40 *The Tatler*, no. 191 (1831), 761–62.

AFTERWORD: WILLIAM HAZLITT – A RADICAL CRITIQUE OF RADICAL OPPOSITION?

1 John Kinnaird, *William Hazlitt: Critic of Power* (New York: Columbia University Press, 1978), pp. 107–08.

2 See *CWH*, 7: 7, 263, 276, and 19: 308–09.

3 Stanley Jones, *Hazlitt: A Life, from Winterslow to Frith Street* (Oxford University Press, 1991), pp. 241–42.

4 See *BD* 4 (1820), 88; *M* 1 (1819), 215; and John Wade, *A Political Dictionary; or, Pocket Companion* (London: T. Dolby, 1821), pp. 51, 61. For popular radical attacks on legitimacy in the manner of Hazlitt, see *CPR* 33 (1818), 407; *BD* 1 (1817), 147; *G*, no.1 (1818), 3; *B* 1 (1818), 63–64; *SPR* 2 (1817–18), 12; and *SPR* 3 (1818), 65.

5 See for example Hazlitt's dispute with Coleridge over whether Caliban was "a prototype of modern Jacobinism" or "the legitimate sovereign of the island" (*CWH*, 19: 207), and his comparison of Edmund Kean the "radical actor" with Charles Mayne Young the "courtly and loyal" actor (*CWH*, 19: 257).

6 For Burke's appearance as pensioner in the radical catalogue of corruption, see *BB*, p. 23.

7 Wade, *Political Dictionary*, p. 61.

8 John Barrell, *The Political Theory of Painting from Reynolds to Hazlitt* (New Haven: Yale University Press, 1986), p. 337.

9 For the role of dissent in Hazlitt's prose, see Kinnaird, *Hazlitt: Critic of Power*, pp. 10–21, and Herschel Baker, *William Hazlitt* (Cambridge, Massachusetts: The Belknap Press, 1962), pp. 3–36; for the ambiguity of Hazlitt's attitude to dissent, see David Bromwich, *Hazlitt: The Mind of a Critic* (New York and Oxford: Oxford University Press, 1983), pp. 59–60.

10 See, for example, Kinnaird, *Hazlitt: Critic of Power*, pp. 33–34, and Roy Park, *Hazlitt and the Spirit of the Age: Abstraction and Critical Theory* (Oxford: Clarendon Press, 1971), p. 6.

11 See John Whale, "Hazlitt on Burke: The Ambivalent Position of a Radical Essayist," *Studies in Romanticism* 25 (1986), 465–81.

12 Bromwich, *Hazlitt*, p. 22.

Index

Cambridge Studies in Romanticism

GENERAL EDITORS
MARILYN BUTLER, *University of Oxford*
JAMES CHANDLER, *University of Chicago*